THE CAMBRIDGE
EROTIC LIT

The Cambridge Companion To Erotic Lit
debates in the study of erotic literature from
one of the longest standing controversies ̣_ ̣ ̣oundary
between acceptable and unacceptable treatn ̣ ̣ ̣ ̣an sexuality. Whether
scurrilous Roman satire, irreverent Restoration drama, or bold Modernist
novel, erotic literature pushes the boundaries of the acceptable and challenges
the conventions of more mainstream literatures. In fifteen chapters that range
from ancient Greece and Rome to twentieth-century American, English, French,
and Dutch literature, experts in the field confront a variety of related topics,
such as the definition and scope of erotic literature, the nature of textual
pleasure, historical shifts in the understanding of the normal and the perverse,
the relationship between gender and genre, sexual violence, homosexuality,
sadomasochism, necrophilia, satire, pornography, etc. Students new to the
scholarship are provided a clear and useful introduction; those already familiar
with the field are given an exciting glimpse into the most recent work.

Bradford K. Mudge is the author of *Sara Coleridge* (1989) and *The Whore's
Story: Women, Pornography, and the British Novel* (2000); and the editor
of *British Romantic Novelists* (1992) and *When Flesh Becomes Word: An
Anthology of Libertine Literature* (2004). In addition, he has published
numerous essays on eighteenth-century English art and literature.

A complete list of books in the series is at the back of this book.

THE CAMBRIDGE
COMPANION TO
EROTIC
LITERATURE

EDITED BY
BRADFORD K. MUDGE

CAMBRIDGE
UNIVERSITY PRESS

CAMBRIDGE
UNIVERSITY PRESS

University Printing House, Cambridge CB2 8BS, United Kingdom

One Liberty Plaza, 20th Floor, New York, NY 10006, USA

477 Williamstown Road, Port Melbourne, VIC 3207, Australia

4843/24, 2nd Floor, Ansari Road, Daryaganj, Delhi – 110002, India

79 Anson Road, #06-04/06, Singapore 079906

Cambridge University Press is part of the University of Cambridge.

It furthers the University's mission by disseminating knowledge in the pursuit of education, learning, and research at the highest international levels of excellence.

www.cambridge.org

Information on this title: www.cambridge.org/9781107184077

DOI: 10.1017/9781316875117

First published 2017

Printed in the United Kingdom by Clays, St Ives plc

A catalogue record for this publication is available from the British Library.

ISBN 978-1-107-18407-7 Hardback
ISBN 978-1-316-63533-9 Paperback

When I'd got so far, presto, he opened his quiver, selected
    An arrow to lay me low,
Then bent the springy bow in crescent against his knee, and
      Let fly. 'Hey, poet!' he called, 'you want a theme? Take *that*!'

                    – Ovid, *The Amores*

CONTENTS

CONTENTS

FIGURES

CONTRIBUTORS

COLETTE COLLIGAN, Simon Fraser University

DAVID GREVEN, University of South Carolina

GERT HEKMA, University of Amsterdam

DEBORAH LUTZ, University of Louisville

IAN FREDERICK MOULTON, Arizona State University

BRADFORD K. MUDGE, University of Colorado Denver

MARIANNE NOBLE, American University

DANIEL ORRELLS, King's College London

ELIZABETH ROBERTSON, University of Glasgow

SARAH SALIH, King's College London

RICHARD C. SHA, American University

SARAH TOULALAN, University of Exeter

JAMES GRANTHAM TURNER, University of California, Berkeley

AMY S. WYNGAARD, Syracuse University

PREFACE

Not too terribly long ago, scholarship that concerned itself either directly or indirectly with erotic literature was generally assumed to partake of the prurience attributed to its subject. This was the case because that scholarship was recognized – quite rightly – as having descended in part from a small group of amateur book collectors, bibliographers, and historians who were passionate about 'curious books'. That phrase, 'curious books,' often just meant books that were 'rare' or 'interesting,' but it also meant books that were especially rare or especially interesting because they were in some fashion erotic, obscene, or pornographic. Attracted as they were to things that were more rather than less difficult to collect, nineteenth-century English book collectors, for example, recognized that erotic books provided a significant challenge for even the most seasoned of bibliomaniacs. Not only did these 'curiosities' comprise a small and difficult-to-acquire portion of the market, but they were also prone to deception: they routinely faked publisher, date, or place of publication, in addition to author or title. They often pretended to be translations from nonexistent originals, and they had no reason to disclose when they were pirated or borrowed piecemeal from another source. Occasionally, too, they offered themselves as works of science or medicine or history when in fact their allegiances were quite different. Often, for example, they began as biography or travelogue or trial proceeding, only to fantasize their way into sensational fiction. As a group, then, they were rather devious; they disrespected generic boundaries, infiltrated fine, upstanding disciplines, and moved easily from language to language across time periods and over national borders. Collectible they most certainly were, and, as a result, they were afforded respect by both bookseller and auctioneer. But there was no disguising the fact that the collectors themselves – no matter how well educated, wealthy, or scholarly – were able to enjoy this material sexually as well as aesthetically.

The case in point here is Henry Spencer Ashbee. He was a wealthy London textile trader who devoted himself to collecting and documenting

erotic literature. He published three substantial bibliographies in the 1870s
and 1880s and bequeathed his book collection after his death in 1900 to the
British Museum. He also continues to be a prime candidate for the authorship of *My Secret Life* (1888–1895), an anonymous eleven-volume sexual
autobiography that makes Casanova look like an amateur. Ashbee's claims
to respectability – socially, culturally, and scholarly – were undermined from
the outset by the suspicion that his achievements were tainted by perversion.
His gift to the British Museum, for example, was accepted only because
officials there wanted his collection of Cervantes, and Ashbee had been
smart enough to make them take the erotica as well. Famously, the latter
collection became the 'Private Case,' for decades and decades completely
invisible in the Museum's catalogue and even today subject to bizarre, now
comical, restrictions. Ashbee's legacy, in other words, was one that perpetu-
ated the idea that any scholarly attention shown to erotica must be to some
degree unseemly. That changed in 1966, when Stephen Marcus published
his groundbreaking study *The Other Victorians*. Marcus was a scholar, not
a collector, and he was interested in what erotica and pornography actually
signified about the nineteenth-century cultural imagination. He considered
Ashbee and *My Secret Life* and concluded that literary history was best
served by inclusive inquiry – by thinking about 'literature' as potentially all-
encompassing – rather than by exclusionary presuppositions.

The world does not change overnight, least of all the scholarly world,
but after Marcus's efforts Ashbee proved much less powerful a specter.
Gone was everyone's creepy uncle, and in his place there seemed a new
and genuine curiosity about the role of sex and sexuality in literary culture.
According to a logic all their own, scholars of different periods and different nations began asking similar questions about gender and genre, pleasure
and aesthetics, desire and decadence.

When, ten years after Marcus, Michel Foucault published the first volume
of his *Histoire de la sexualité* and feminist scholars in Britain, France, and
the United States offered their significant and far-reaching challenges to status quo scholarship, the way was finally clear to understand the connections
between somatic and textual pleasure within the context of different disci-
plinary mandates. In literary studies, for example, feminist pressure on the
canon and canon-making made it much easier to understand the historicity
of the idea of the 'literary' and the degree to which critical practice continued to be driven by Victorian assumptions about the sanctity of art. Aided
by pioneering work in history and philosophy – Thomas Laqueur, Robert
Darnton, Lynn Hunt, Walter Kendrick, and Judith Butler come immediately
to mind – literary scholars moved forward into more versatile ideas about

sex, gender, and performance and into cultural contexts that were no longer exclusively Eurocentric. Ashbee's ghost now appears rather quaint in the cultural scheme of things, although looking at one of his books at the British Library still requires that you sit at a special desk under the watchful eyes of the librarians.

Contributors to this volume have expertise in a variety of literatures – Greek and Roman, American, English, French, Italian, and Dutch – and range predictably over a variety of time periods – including ancient, medieval, Renaissance, eighteenth-century, Romantic, Victorian, and modern. Even so, the volume itself could never claim to do anything more than gesture towards inclusivity. Given the scope of the subject matter (where, after all, doesn't eros flourish?) and the many authors and nations and periods that it cannot directly examine, this volume can only be considered an introduction to the wealth of materials that exist beyond its boundaries. In the chapters that follow, the experts take up a variety of topics and pursue a variety of approaches. Some consider questions of influence (Daniel Orrells, James Grantham Turner), while others explore the archives (Ian Frederick Moulton, Colette Colligan), and still others contemplate alternative sexualities (Amy S. Wyngaard, Deborah Lutz, David Greven) or alternative discursive influences (Sarah Salih, Sarah Toulalan). Some chapters focus on close readings of key texts (Elizabeth Robertson, Marianne Noble), while others range more widely over genre or period (Bradford K. Mudge, Richard C. Sha, Gert Hekma). Some of the topics discussed include textual pleasure; venereal disease; religious ecstasy; sadomasochism; necrophilia; reproduction; rape; homosexuality; bibliomania; obscenity; satire; and pornography, among others. Regardless, however, of their widely different interests and varying approaches, the contributors are in agreement about the centrality of eros to literary studies and the importance of continuing a free and frank discussion. To that discussion, all interested parties are welcome.

CHRONOLOGY

*c.*570 BCE	d. Sappho
458 BCE	Aeschylus, *Oresteia*
442BCE	Sophocles, *Antigone*
411 BCE	Aristophanes, *Lysistrata*
*c.*365 BCE	Plato, *Phaedrus*
*c.*340 BCE	Philaenis, *Sex Manual fragments*
*c.*56 BCE	Lucretius, *De Rerum Natura*
29–19 BCE	Virgil, *Aeneid*
*c.*15 BCE	Ovid, *Amores*
*c.*1 BCE	Ovid, *Ars Amatoria*
*c.*40 BCE–15 CE	*Priapeia*
90 CE	Martial, *Epigrams*
95–127 CE	Juvenal, *Satires*
400 CE	Saint Augustine, *Confessions*
426 CE	Saint Augustine, *City of God*
*c.*1130	Chretien de Troyes, *Le Chevalier de la Charette*
*c.*1170	Marie de France, *Lais*
1190	Capellanus, *De Amore*
*c.*1225–1250	Wooing Group Prayers

c.1308–1320	Dante Alighieri, *Divina Commedia*
c.1340	Richard Rolle, *Incendium amoris*
c.1353	Giovanni Boccaccio, *Decameron*
c.1383	Geoffrey Chaucer, *Troilus and Criseyde*
1386	Geoffrey Chaucer, *The Miller's Tale*
c.1438	Margery Kempe, *The Book of Margery Kempe*
1470	Thomas Malory, *Le Morte d'Arthur*
c.1524–1527	*I Modi*, engravings by Marcantonio Raimondi with sonnets by Pietro Aretino
1534–1536	Pietro Aretino, *Ragionamenti*
1593	William Shakespeare, "Venus and Adonis"
1594	William Shakespeare, "The Rape of Lucrece"
c.1595	William Shakespeare, *Romeo and Juliet*
1604–1611	*King James Bible*
1609	William Shakespeare, *Sonnets*
1633	John Donne, *Songs and Sonnets*, posthumous
1654	John Donne, *Elegy XIX: To His Mistress Going to Bed*, posthumous
1655 (?)	Michel Millot, *L'Ecole des filles*
c.1668	Nicolas Chorier, *Satyra sotadica*
1673	John Wilmot, Earl of Rochester, *Signior Dildo*, attributed
1675	William Wycherly, *The Country Wife*
1677	Aphra Behn, *The Rover*
1680	Michel Millot *The School of Vénus* John Wilmot, Earl of Rochester, *Poems*, posthumous
1683	Jean Barrin, *Vénus dans le cloître*
1684	Charles Cotton, *Erotopolis: The Present State of Bettyland*

1890	Oscar Wilde, *The Picture of Dorian Gray*
1895	Oscar Wilde convicted of 'gross indecency'
1897	John Addington Symonds and Henry Havelock Ellis, *Sexual Inversion* Oscar Wilde, *De Profundis*
1899	Sigmund Freud, *The Interpretation of Dreams*
1904	Marquis de Sade, *The 120 Days of Sodom* published in Paris
1905	Sigmund Freud, *Three Essays on the Theory of Sexuality*
c.1919	Edith Wharton, 'Beatrice Palmato'
1920	D. H. Lawrence, *Women in Love*
1922	James Joyce, *Ulysses*
1928	Georges Bataille, *Histoire de l'œil* Radclyffe Hall, *The Well of Loneliness* D. H. Lawrence, *Lady Chatterley's Lover*
1934	Henry Miller, *Tropic of Cancer*
1954	Pauline Réage, *The Story of O*
1955	Vladimir Nabokov, *Lolita*
1957	George Bataille, *L'Erotisme*
1960	Giacomo Girolamo Casanova, *Histoire de ma vie*, 12 vols., posthumous
1977	Anaïs Nin, *Delta of Venus,* posthumous
1979	Anaïs Nin, *Little Birds,* posthumous
1994	"Pauline Réage," author of *The Story of O,* is identified as Dominique Aury

I

BRADFORD K. MUDGE

Eros and Literature

I

The relationship between eros and literature begins with pleasure: pleasure of the body, pleasure of the text, pleasure of wondering how each affects the other. Common sense (never fully to be trusted) tells us to start with the pleasure of the body, that stable ground from which all else derives, whose needs – food, sleep, sex – are written deep within our corporeal selves. "Eros," then, would figure those desires common to the sexual and/ or romantic body, those desires we generally think of first, before "storge" ("familial love"), before "philia" ("friendship"), also before "agape" ("spiritual love").[1] The pleasures of eros track the beauty of the beloved in all of its myriad forms, and – comfortable in each of the five senses – they attend a variety of events: discovery, courtship, consummation, commitment, etc. If the word "love" expands routinely into affections of an all-inclusive sort (applicable in English equally to spouse, favorite color, and family pet), then the word "erotic" denotes pleasures of a specifically or potentially sexual nature. As inflexible as chromosomes, as self-evident as genitalia, as relentless as hunger, those pleasures tempt us with an idea of "human nature" as unequivocal as the flesh of which it is composed. Who are we to argue, so the reasoning goes, if the body simply wants what it wants? In fact, however, the pleasures of the erotic body have never *not* been regulated by cultural forces both large and small: by religion, by law, by science, by gender, of course; but also by etiquette, by propriety, and by a variety of seemingly innocuous social conventions. Christianity used the doctrine of original sin to condemn and control sexual pleasure; codes of law, ancient as well as modern, prohibited rape, incest, and polygamy; medical science, particularly since the late seventeenth century, labored to define the normal and diagnose the perverse; while ideas of gender – masculinities and femininities from a variety of diverse cultural moments – struggled to maintain an understandable and stable difference between the sexes. At the same time, codes of propriety and decorum have regulated social interactions generally and courtship and mating rituals in particular. We are all aware that much depends on who holds the door for whom, who is allowed to wear what when, and which topics are broached and how. The erotic body, as a result, however much it may tempt us to think otherwise, never appears outside the social, political, and cultural contexts within which it is defined. Nor are its so-called "natural" pleasures ever fully separate from the historical moment that seeks to regulate them. On the contrary, bodies of flesh, bodies of words, and bodies of knowledge are unavoidably, inextricably interdependent.[2]

In Genesis, for example, the bodies of Adam and Eve serve that interdependence precisely. Mortality, hunger, fatigue, pain in childbirth, and sexual desire are all encoded upon textual bodies in such a way that actual flesh and blood gets rewritten in their likeness for the next three thousand years. An originary myth that begins by asking, "Where did we come from?" and "Why do we die?" imagines humanity's own prequel so powerfully that Saint Augustine could use it to transform the pleasures of sex into the pains of sin.[3] Subsequently, shame, guilt, and self-loathing attended procreation, and key details about whose rib was taken from whom, who was created first, and who was allowed or not allowed to speak directly to God confirmed a gender hierarchy so self-evident that it reappeared indelibly thereafter in body height, weight, and muscle mass. Thus, the acts of recognition required to feel shame or acknowledge female inferiority began with erudition and over generations became common sense. No less prone to warfare than bodies of flesh, bodies of knowledge adapted themselves to cultures and geographies and, just like their more political counterparts, sought dominance. That dominance achieves itself most perfectly when the three bodies align: flesh, word, and knowledge all in perfect reciprocity. At those moments, cultural context and historical specificity fade away and the body *au naturel* stands before us in all its seemingly simple splendour, its nakedness a reminder that ideology's triumph is never more successful than when it disappears entirely from view.

Unsurprisingly, the erotic body and its pleasures are not fond of submission. Serve a variety of masters, they most certainly do, but the relationships are fraught. Consider an example from Plato, an author not generally appreciated for his eroticism. In his dialogue the *Phaedrus*, a treatment of love and lust well known for its devious complexities, the body of the eponymous interlocutor is erotically charged from beginning to end, even after Socrates explains himself out of the temptations of physical pleasure and into the higher truths of philosophy.[4] In fact, Plato foregrounds the body of the beloved as a significant philosophical problem that requires a full explanation of the nature of the soul, the rules of reincarnation, and the structure of the cosmos. This is the case because the beauty of the body and its ongoing invitations to carnal pleasure constitute a nexus that, when poorly navigated, can result in errors no less profound than those of Genesis. Whereas Genesis laid the groundwork for subsequent ideas about the inherent sinfulness of the body, the *Phaedrus* warns that carnal pleasures distract us from the higher truth, much in the same way that shadows on the wall of a cave can impede our desire to walk in the light of the sun.

Plato's dialogue establishes a love triangle in which Socrates, smitten by the physical beauty of Phaedrus, must compete with the rhetorician Lysias for the affections of the boy. Socrates flirts and allows himself to be agreeable initially by making no objection to a speech by Lysias that Phaedrus recites. The speech warns of the destructive passions of love and encourages the youth to submit to non-lovers rather than lovers because it will be ultimately more efficacious and less messy. Socrates plays along until he no longer can, and then makes a speech of his own in which he defends the divine madness of love. His speech then closes with a prayer to Eros:

> Thus, dear Love, I have made and paid my recantation as well and as fairly as I could: the poetical figures I was forced to use, for Phaedrus would have them. Please forgive my former speech; grant this one your favor. Be kind and merciful to me. Do not blind me in anger. Grant me to be even more esteemed than I am now by the beautiful. If in our former speech Phaedrus or I said anything harsh against you, blame Lysias, the begetter of that discourse. Make him cease from such speeches and turn him to philosophy, just as his brother Polemarchus has been turned; so that his lover here may no longer waver as he does now, but may wholeheartedly live for love, together with philosophy.[5]

Anticipating the prayer that will end the dialogue – "grant me to be beautiful within" – Socrates pleads for divine guidance in his pursuit of Truth and Beauty, at the same time asking for forgiveness for his former untruths.[6] Pointedly, he also asks forgiveness for his "poetical figures," referring not just to those of the charioteer and the two horses but also to those of the tumescent wings, which "sprout," "grow," and "swell" every time the soul is excited by the beloved. These figures, which Socrates uses only because Phaedrus likes them, pull the textual body and the somatic body into exact correspondence, acknowledging an excitement that pleasures both flesh and word. Like Lysias, in other words, Socrates is aroused by beauty; but unlike Lysias, he moves past carnal pleasure – and its erotically suggestive language – to an appreciation of transcendent Truth.

For Ovid, on the other hand, writing in imperial Rome nearly four hundred years after Plato, the beauty of the body metamorphoses in less predictable directions. A reflection in a pool causes Narcissus to become enamored of himself; an overheard prayer transforms Pygmalion's cold statue into a warm wife and mother; the music from the lyre of Orpheus brings Eurydice back from the dead. Unlike Plato – famously intolerant of the representations of art and literature, suspicious even of writing itself as a technology that leads away from the immediacy of thought – Ovid accepts not only the inevitability of chaos and change but also the inevitability (and power) of love's imaginative guises. Why shouldn't Jupiter take Danae as a shower of gold? Why shouldn't the boundaries between the human and the divine, porous as they are, give way again before the relentless and creative passions of eros? Above all, why shouldn't literature and art honor those passions and exercise their ability to animate and reanimate both the human and the divine?

In the *Amores*, for example, his first published poem, Ovid chooses love over war, and with it the power of language to enact, as well as describe, human passion. In the midst of contemplating his own "regular epic" with its formal march of hexameters, he tells us of being interrupted by Cupid, who first shouts: "Hey, poet! … you want a theme? Take *that*!" and then lets loose with one of his arrows.[7] Struck by desire, literally and figuratively, Ovid is forced to relinquish hexameters for elegiacs and to proceed with a poem that now takes eros as it subject. This "anatomy of desire," as he describes it, depends for its success on its clever, irreverent, occasionally hapless narrator, who satirizes the pretensions of epic poetry while entertaining the reader with the ongoing comedy of love: he outwits drunken husbands at dinner parties, entertains married women in the afternoon, and seduces his mistress's maid, all the while proclaiming his innocence and good intentions. An anti-hero of the first order, he gets locked out, lied to, and cheated on. In fact, the *Amores* ends with Ovid's narrator losing his mistress to a rival, a loss that he attributes ironically to the success of his verses:

> That's it: *she* was prostituted by *my* art,
> And serve me right for trumpeting her beauty abroad! If my darling's
> On the market, it's all my fault –
> I've pimped her charms.[8]

So "charm[ing]" was his body of words that the body of flesh was able to find a more desirable lover, a turn of events that underscores the reciprocity between aesthetic and sexual pleasure. Thanks to Cupid's arrow, in other words, Ovid the lover and Ovid the poet conflate: the beauty pursued by the one subsumed nicely into that composed by the other.

However much, therefore, we might want to stabilize our understanding of eros with the solid truths of the body – the body male or female, young or old, beautiful or not so much – Ovid is there to remind us that that body always seems to arrive as part of someone else's story. It comes, like the very God it serves, as a figure in a narrative whose historical specificity can indeed be chased down and better understood, but whose purported identity can never fully escape the conditions imposed by the language that represents it. For Plato, what we see, feel, and do (erotically) is always already a reminder of a divine Truth from which we have fallen but to which we would like to return. Philosophy, not art or literature, provides the only reliable way back, and the Socratic method, reworked as Platonic dialogue, stands as vastly superior to both the sophistry of rhetoricians and the make-believe of poets. For Plato, in other words, the erotic body in life and the erotic body in language have analogous dangers, and we must pray to the gods for the strength to resist the temptations proffered by each. For Ovid, on the other hand, those same human experiences – erotic seeings, feelings, and doings – are a source of pleasure; inseparable as they are from the myriad stories of which they are a part, they are equally delightful in flesh and in word. As a result, poetry provides the perfect opportunity to enact, not simply reflect, the pleasures of the body.

II

Consideration of the relationship between eros and literature requires, in addition to an ongoing preoccupation with the body, close attention to the pleasures specific to language. Those pleasures might arise from diction, syntax, or narrative; or they might attend character, setting, or plot. They might be tied directly to the erotic body they purport to describe, or they may have an erotic charge specific to language but at significant remove from the sexual and/ or romantic body to which they eventually return. Thematically, they might serve Plato's fears about human beauty, or they might tilt towards Ovid and his obvious delight in the transformative powers of love. Either way, they also move comfortably from genre to genre. They happily attend plays, poems, and novels; short stories, essays, and non-fiction of various kinds. In late seventeenth- and early eighteenth-century England, for example, a reader might have enjoyed the ribald wit of Aphra Behn's comedy, the full-frontal obscenity of the Earl of Rochester's poems, or the titillating voyeurism of Delarivier Manley's scandal fiction. For the more adventurous, there were also bawdy ballads, obscene travelogues, salacious medical manuals, whore dialogues, and scandalous trial reports.[9] Although we may be tempted to build our own monolithic "eroticism" from canonical love stories – from, say, Sappho and Shakespeare, Boccaccio and Petrarch, Donne and Richardson, or Byron and

Browning – literary history suggests a far more complicated affair. Literary history suggests that the "erotic" was always a diverse and overwhelming menu of possibilities; that genres high and low, elite and popular, literary and not, all made use of romantic and/or sexual content, often for very different purposes; and that the languages of eroticism were as numerous and as varied as the bodies and the desires they describe.

Canonically speaking, there is in English no more famous a meditation on language and the lover's body than that spoken by Juliet on the balcony:

> JULIET   O Romeo, Romeo! Wherefore art thou Romeo?
> Deny thy father and refuse thy name;
> Or, if thou wilt not, be but sworn my love,
> And I'll no longer be a Capulet.
> ROMEO   *(aside)* Shall I hear more, or shall I speak at this?
> JULIET   'Tis but thy name that is my enemy.
> Thou art thyself, though not a Montague.
> What's Montague? It is nor hand, nor foot,
> Nor arm, nor face, nor any other part
> Belonging to a man. O, be some other name!
> What's in a name? That which we call a rose
> By any other word would smell as sweet.
> So Romeo would, were he not Romeo called,
> Retain that dear perfection which he owes
> Without that title. Romeo, doff thy name,
> And for that name; which is no part of thee
> Take all myself.[10]

Juliet's plea, of course, is that Romeo unclothe himself of name, that he "doff" his linguistic identity, his "title," and be a body naked of familial and social connection. For that "dear perfection," she offers herself "all" in exchange. To take "off" is to be revealed "as," the less of social affiliation becoming the more of revealed essence, which, like the scent of the rose or the body of the beloved, can be experienced directly. That this consummation can only occur through the very language Juliet wishes to do without is precisely the point, as Romeo makes clear:

> I take thee at thy word.
> Call me but love, and I'll be new baptized;
> Henceforth I never will be Romeo.[11]

To "take" here is first to "understand," second to "trust," and third to "have," with the last an erotically appropriate response to Juliet's "Take all myself." Obviously, too, the word he "take[s]" from her speech is "love," which he reclaims for himself and is born again, this time naked of affiliation, untrammeled by kinship. Giving up the name of the father lays claim to a purity of self that "take[s] all" in return. Crucially, however, that union is predicated on the language of the beloved: "Call me but love" puts back on Juliet the power to remake the old "Romeo" anew. With the word "Call," Romeo is asking Juliet to reveal an inner truth – her own love for him – that will be strong enough to supplant the authority of the father and recreate the beloved in its own image.

The conventions of genre dictate that in *Romeo and Juliet* (1595) the power of eros will be undone by fate – the truth of love, like the pleasures of consummation, transient. In tragedy, death is the ultimate winner, emerging at the end to confirm the futility of individual desire and the play's own high seriousness. In comedy, however, love becomes a joke, irrational and unpredictable, absurd and humbling, always amusing. In *A Midsummer Night's Dream* (1597), for example, Shakespeare allows eros to revert to the mischievous imp, the agent of chaos and confusion with the power to turn the world upside down. Social order is defined at the outset by a hierarchy of paired lovers and by the authority of a patriarch who insists on marriage by his own design. Fleeing the authority of the father, the lovers take to the forest on a midsummer night's eve, where – thanks to the mischief of Puck and his magic potions – chaos ensues. As we might expect, Shakespeare's chaos is carefully orchestrated. His "green world" inverts conventional hierarchies and, for the space of a single night, allows for the ascendancy of nature over culture, dream over waking, imagination over reason – and, of course, eros over all else.[12]

In *A Midsummer Night's Dream,* the erotic body is everywhere and nowhere, incongruent and volatile, likely to be held hostage to vicissitudes beyond its control. Identities are mistaken and confused and shifting because the play imagines desire as the defining characteristic of the self and then creates a magic spell – derived not coincidentally from Cupid's arrow – capable of transforming the libidinal object at a moment's notice. Both the original desire and its magical replacement are equally true, and the more characters articulate what and who they want, the more the audience can enjoy making fun of an irrationality from which there is no escape. In this perfect hall of mirrors, taking someone at his word – as Romeo was eager to do – is at once an impossibility (because that someone is no longer himself) and the only correct option (because the desire is no less real for being magical). Lysander's speech to Helena in Act II provides a case in point:

> Not Hermia but Helena I love.
> Who will not change a raven for a dove?
> The will of man is by his reason swayed,
> And reason says you are the worthier maid.
> Things growing are not ripe until their season:
> So I, being young, till now ripe not to reason.

> And touching now the point of human skill,
> Reason becomes the marshal to my will
> And leads me to your eyes, where I o'erlook
> Love's stories, written in love's richest book.[13]

The deluded lover rationally defends his irrational "change" by insisting on his "skill" in a two-part interpretive process: first, he has listened attentively to what his own internal "reason" has had to "say," and then he has read correctly the "stories" inscribed externally upon the body of the beloved. His failure at both is evident from the wonderful "o'erlook," a contronym that means at once "to look at" (look over) and "to look past" (over look). Capturing the logical impossibility of explaining desire, "o'erlook" uses the traditional relationship between sight and insight, perception and knowledge, to highlight the comedy of arbitrary, "changeful" passion. Helena, being of right mind, can only assume that Lysander's appeal is comedic mockery.

Although Shakespeare will resolve this erotic chaos at the play's end into the stable order of proper marriage, Puck famously gets the last word, reminding the audience that if "offended" they should consider the comedy itself "but a dream" easily "mend[ed]."[14] The epilogue confirms the primacy of the magic spell, aligns fairy trickster and playwright, and to the ongoing problem of changeful passion offers as a solution only additional change: "amend[ation]." If the erotic body of tragedy stands on the balcony congruent and absolute – inviting us both to love it at first sight and take it at its word – then its comedic counterpart sits, like Bottom with the head of an ass, polymorphous and perverse, promising only to confuse and mislead. The former follows in the tradition of Plato and is respectful of a love true and unchanging; the latter descends from Ovid, irreverent and promiscuous.

Of course, eros flourished offstage as well. Textual bodies were – like their flesh-and-blood counterparts – eager to transgress and just as eager to do so in low venues as high venues. During the Restoration, for example, while audiences were delighting in the drama of Wycherley, Behn, and Congreve, obscene satire circulated at the Court of Charles II, bawdy street ballads flooded London pubs and coffeehouses, and "curious" books became increasingly lucrative for booksellers. The languages of eroticism were many and varied. John Wilmot, Earl of Rochester, passed manuscript copies of his poems to friends at court, who no doubt appreciated how effective sexual obscenity could be when mocking the high and mighty: "Signior Dildo" personifies the artificial penis as a visiting Italian nobleman; "The Imperfect Enjoyment" muses on the ignominy of impotence; and "Against Constancy" offers tribute to polyamory.[15] "Cunts" and "pricks" proliferate throughout, a choice of diction that violates social and literary protocols as it enlists the sexual body as a weapon against hypocrisy and pretension.

This kind of "libertine literature" circulated behind the scenes and was fashionable among the dissipated rakes with whom Rochester associated. But the word "libertine" also suggests a freedom from propriety and constraint. Elitist in origin it most certainly was, and unrepentantly misogynistic as well, but Rochester's obscene satire also served anarchical tendencies: it was so adversarial in nature, and so single-minded in pursuit of personal pleasure, that it could not but be disruptive and disordering.

Meanwhile, on the streets of London, cheap ballads like "The Pleasures of a Single Life" (1701) or "The Fifteen Comforts of Cuckoldom" (1706) would have amused those who appreciated the bawdy and those who, to partake in the fun, need not have been literate.[16] Distant relatives of Chaucer's "The Miller's Tale," these ballads treated a variety of comedic topics but preferred cuckoldry of one sort or another to all else. They might have been sung or recited in the coffee house or pub, and they help us to understand an oral tradition that thrived apart from both court and bookshop. Theirs was the world of fair and carnival; it was communal not solitary, boisterous not refined. Very different, of course, were the bookshops. There, scandalous novels and risque poetry would have competed with a whole host of "curious" books generally ignored by literary historians. These include whore dialogues like Michel Millot's *The School of Venus* (1680), prurient pseudo-medical treatises like John Marten's *Gonosologium Novum* (1709), and sensational criminal accounts like Henry Fielding's *The Female Husband* (1746). As the word "curious" suggests, eros was linked to secret or forbidden knowledge about the sexual body. *The School of Venus* made use of anti-ecclesiastical satire to share with its reader what was really going on between nuns behind closed doors; *Gonosologium Novum*, subtitled *A New System Of All the Secret Infirmities and Diseases, Natural, Accidental, and Venereal in MEN and WOMEN*, promised to share the hidden truths of sex and its diseases; and *The Female Husband* offered a fictionalized treatment of a real cross-dressing Sapphite who took advantage of unsuspecting women and was subsequently caught and tried. Whether at court, in the pub or coffee house, or on the shelves of a bookshop, the languages of eroticism proved both varied and enterprising.

The most influential of all the erotic languages being written and read during the eighteenth century was that belonging to the novel. No other genre entertained England's growing readership in the same way; no other genre adapted so beautifully to the expanding middle classes and their demand for increased leisure. Over the course of the first half of the century, the English novel outgrew its scandalous beginnings and attained something that resembled cultural legitimacy. Early-eighteenth-century novelists had followed continental models and put women, romance, and sex front and center. Some retold famous scandals, some experimented with voyeurism and the secret spaces of bedroom and garden, some used letters and letter writing for heightened intimacy. Maligned as manipulative, pleasure-seeking, and sub-literary, the novel became associated with both women writers and women readers, the result of which was that the genre's success in the marketplace was viewed as a kind of cultural prostitution.[17] When Samuel Richardson published *Pamela* in 1740, he attempted to defend both women and the novel by celebrating female virtue over female vice. His heroine, a chaste servant with a knack for letter writing, protects her honor from a lustful and scheming master until he becomes convinced of her virtue and marries her in the end. If novelists would only respect and encourage morality in the same way that good women protected their chastity – so Richardson's logic went – then prose fiction could and would inculcate Christian values among its readership.

His intervention sparked a controversy that would be continued by fits and starts for the next two hundred and fifty years, a controversy between those who believed that readers needed to be protected from immoral books and those who did not. The former held that fiction was dangerous and could do real damage in the world; the latter believed that even naive readers should be able to negotiate the various differences between bodies and books. At the time, Henry Fielding wrote *Shamela* (1741) and *Joseph Andrews* (1742) in protest, both of which depicted sex as far less dangerous than vanity, hypocrisy, and greed. His "comic epic in prose" was anchored by a faith in simple generosity and love; it ridiculed self-serving piety and sanctimonious pseudo-superiority. Soon after, John Cleland wrote *Memoirs of a Woman of Pleasure* (1748) – another "anti-Pamela," but one that treated openly and repeatedly of sex and sexual pleasure. As Fanny Hill tells us early on, her memoir is an attempt to tell "the stark, naked truth" of her physical experiences. Eschewing the "cunts" and "pricks" of Rochester, Cleland adopts throughout the language of metaphor – prodigious male "machines" batter female "ramparts," etc. – and describes carefully a variety of activities beyond simple intercourse: lesbianism, group sex, flagellation, and sodomy among them. Like Fielding, however, Cleland maintains a comic vision, never letting the reader forget that the novel is making fun of the very erotic effects it is working so hard to achieve.

Of course, poets too continued to experiment with eros and language. When, for example, John Keats decided to rewrite *Romeo and Juliet* as *The Eve of St Agnes*, he found a way of pushing the possibilities of poetic diction until the beauties of language seem indistinguishable from the aroused bodies of his lovers. At a crucial moment just before Porphoro melds into

Madeline's dream, the poet describes the food that Porphoro arranges for his sleeping lover:

> ... he from forth the closet brought a heap
> Of candied apple, quince, and plum, and gourd,
> With jellies soother than the creamy curd,
> And lucent syrops, tinct with cinnamon;
> Manna and dates, in argosy transferr'd
> From Fez; and spiced dainties, every one,
> From silken Samarcand to cedar'd Lebanon.[18]

The sweet pleasures of fruit are "heap[ed]" noun by noun and spiced with a Middle Eastern exoticism calculated to draw attention to language's ability to transform one kind of materialism into another: organic molecules shapeshift into consonants and vowels, but their sweetness is no less palpable. Like Ovid, Keats celebrates the power of poetry to facilitate such transformations. He positions Porphoro "in a closet, of such privacy / That he might see her beauty unespy'd," allowing the lover first to watch his beloved undress, get into bed, and fall asleep, before permitting him to arrange his "heap / Of candied apple, quince, and plum, and gourd" at her bedside and before orchestrating his singing of the ballad, "*La belle dame sans merci.*"[19] It is only then – after the pleasures of sight, taste, and sound have been dutifully represented by the poet's words – that Madeline awakens from her dream to physical consummation, a "solution sweet" that prioritizes both the sense of touch, body to body, and the ability of language to communicate that most prized of pleasures. Appropriately enough, years later, the young Tennyson would run afoul of critics for his following of Keats's linguistic experiments.[20] The overt sensuality of the diction was considered dangerous and "effeminate."

Keats expects his readers to appreciate that Porphoro's love, Madeline's dream, and the poem in which they appear are all of a piece, that the poet uses his imagination to create a space – his own "solution sweet" – where the lover's pursuit of the beloved, the dreamer's prophetic fantasies, and poetry's desire to represent ideal beauty can all occur simultaneously. In a now famous passage in a letter to his friend Benjamin Bailey, Keats likens the creative imagination to Adam's dream: "What the imagination seizes as Beauty must be truth – whether it existed before or not – for I have the same Idea of all our Passions as of Love: they are all, in their sublime, creative of essential Beauty ... The imagination may be compared to Adam's dream, – he awoke and found it truth ..."[21] What had begun with Keats as an appreciation for both the poetic diction of Spenser and Shakespeare and the ancient myths of Greece and Rome had evolved by 1817 into a larger theory of which both

Plato and Ovid may have approved. The lover and the poet were essentially one and the same: each pursued beauty until the pleasures of the body – whether fashioned in flesh or in word – led to a consummation with a larger and more profound truth. That truth is, of course, initially engendered as female – Adam is after all dreaming of Eve – but Keats's genius would not be satisfied with the conventional: he was fully aware of the need to reach beyond the categories of gender. As a result, a Grecian urn, a nightingale's song, a temple to Psyche, all provided opportunities for imaginative flight well beyond the erotic body proper. What had begun as comparatively simple experiments with the pleasures of poetic diction led in short order to brazen and relentless attempts to rethink the power and scope of poetry itself.

III

Ironically, Keats's ambitious rethinking of the connections between somatic and textual pleasure derived in large part from his own insecurities as an artist – and, in particular, from his lack of formal education, which sent him back to ancient myths precisely because of their centrality to the poetic tradition. He wanted above all to be a poet, and myth provided compensatory authority. He was well aware too that myth also provided a way of knowing the world. These were stories that served knowledge of various sorts – religious, scientific, sexual, sociological, cultural, etc. – and Keats, like his fellow Romantic poets, was eager to insist that poetry wielded the highest of powers. Keats's letters, Blake's *Marriage of Heaven and Hell* (1790), Wordsworth's Preface to *Lyrical Ballads* (1800), and Shelley's *Defense of Poetry* (1821) were variations on a theme, together anticipating the master argument of Matthew Arnold's *Culture and Anarchy* (1868), which, having considered the threats to religious values posed by the Industrial Revolution and the rise of science, argued for the centrality of literature and literary studies in the modern world. Arnold's real contribution was neither his famous definition of literary culture – "the best which has been thought and said" – nor his insistence that literature could civilize the barbarians and refine the philistines.[22] His real contribution was the recognition that literature was a body of knowledge that needed to be taught to student–citizens by a nation state unafraid to wield its authority. With that authority, established as it was by the "disinterestedness" of "right reason," the literary canon could defend the whole of culture from the forces of anarchy.[23]

To be sure, what Arnold feared most about anarchy was not overtly sexual: he feared a growing political instability brought about by ignorant self-interest, which he associated, by the way, with "machinery," "newspapers," and "Americans." Nevertheless, his description of the root evil – "that passion for doing as one likes" – blames selfish pleasure-seeking for the chaos that the "sweetness and light" of high culture are intended to remedy.[24] Moreover, his argument, insisting as it does on state intervention, comes just a decade after the Obscene Publications Act of 1857, the first modern attempt to control the production and distribution of pornography. If understanding the relationship between eros and literature requires finally an appreciation for the ways in which bodies of knowledge drive the uses to which both bodies of flesh and bodies of words are put, then this particular historical nexus reminds us that our own attempt to think about erotica can not but be influenced by a larger discursive conflict between "literature" and "pornography" inherited from the Victorians. As Walter Kendrick argued so compellingly in *The Secret Museum: Pornography in Modern Culture* (1987), that conflict signifies far more than the series of famous legal cases by which it is known: it is indeed an ongoing dilemma for the modern state, one that pits individual freedoms on one side against community standards on the other. At the center of the debate is sexual pleasure and its representations, with the key questions being how much of what kinds are acceptable, where, and for whom.

Common usage suggests that "eroticism" names an acceptable middle ground, a place where human desire is varied and complex, a place where – ideally at least – mystery and respect can coexist with danger and excitement.[25] Somewhere between the stolid truths of literature proper and the crass and blatant displays of pornography, the erotic works its magic. In *The Pleasure of the Text* (1975), Roland Barthes offers the following:

> Is not the most erotic portion of a body where the garment gapes? In perversion (which is the realm of textual pleasure) there are no "erogenous zones" (a foolish expression, besides); it is intermittence, as psychoanalysis has so rightly stated, which is erotic: the intermittence of skin flashing between two articles of clothing (trousers and sweater), between two edges (the open-necked shirt, the glove and the sleeve); it is this flash itself which seduces, or rather: the staging of an appearance-as-disappearance.[26]

The moment of seduction occurs in a "flash," a brief glimpse of skin between articles of clothing, along the edges that frame the visible. Seeing here is knowing, and the glimpse is of the body beneath, the truth below, exciting with the possibility that revelation and pleasure follow. Most emphatically, however, knowledge disappoints. Or, rather, it fails to satisfy. Seeing all is never seeing enough, and once seen the body of the beloved disappears instantly into the very light by which it is revealed.

Significantly, the passage concludes by enacting rhetorically the very intermittence it describes. At a moment of declarative certainty, it stops ("or rather") and begins again, replacing one flash of insight with another. Seeing the body where the garment gapes, we are reminded, becomes a perfect analogue for the way the text intermittently discloses itself to the reader. In what could be an homage to Plato, Barthes emphasizes the ongoing reciprocity between seeing and knowing, but unlike Plato he depicts a truth whose erotic essence is fragmentary and dynamic, not absolute and unchanging. This eroticism, Barthes makes clear, is indistinguishable from reading itself: in the same way that the lover's body pleasures its viewer by intermittent flashes, glimpses of skin fortuitously revealed, so too does the text offer itself up by fits and starts, flashes of meaning that are quickly confirmed, qualified, or contradicted by those that succeed it. The centrality of reading establishes a bond between the erotic body and the literary text that subordinates each to the process of interpretation by which they are to be known. Pleasure, in other words, is process not product, something that happens in the space between rather than in the possession of: "where the garment gapes." So formulated, the erotic body can never be fully known, no more than the play, the novel, or the poem, the flesh of one as elusive as the language of the other.

Intermittence, then, is less a condition of sight (as friction is to touch) than it is a condition of knowledge. Moving beneath its clothes, the body of flesh offers itself as pieces of a whole that can be perceived first by the sense of sight, then perhaps by touch, and finally by the mind. In Barthes's formulation, the body in its entirety is all that we would ever want to know, and intermittence is the name he gives to the way that body is revealed and occluded by it own unavoidable textuality, by its appearance first as a material reality and its subsequent disappearance into unknowable other. Eroticism, in turn, names the pleasure of moving between – between the seen and unseen, the known and unknown, of course, but also between the language of flesh, with its infinite vocabulary and complex narratives, and the flesh of language, with its features no less warm and palpable for being wrought from consonant and vowel. Barthes reads each in terms of the other, his own writing playful and teasing, incisive and erudite, fully aware of its own onanistic pleasures and the degree to which it was driven above all by the simple need to know. In fact, his is the perfect rewriting of Genesis: it too is an originary myth about the temptations of pleasure and knowledge – albeit without an omnipotent God and his satanic counterpart – in which language itself assumes the central role. Barthes's temptation occurs not in a single action – a mistake, a transgression, a fall – but instead as the condition of possibility for knowledge itself, knowledge that is inseparable from the human subject and the language within which that subject lives. If Genesis explains where we come from and who we are in terms of "God" – the name we give to a parental power and authority (and knowledge) beyond human experience – then *The Pleasure of the Text* explains our origins in terms of "language," that most human of technologies from whence all else derives: our pleasures, our knowledge, our selves. From this perspective, eros is not marginal to, or a small piece of, our human experience: it is instead precisely that by which we know that we are most alive.

NOTES

1 See, for example, C. S. Lewis, *The Four Loves* (New York: Harcourt Brace, 1960); and *Pornography and Representation in Greece and Rome*, ed. Amy Richlin (Oxford: Oxford University Press, 1992).

2 Historians of human sexuality are many and prolific. For those that conceive of the "body" as I am suggesting, see in particular Roland Barthes, *The Pleasure of the Text* (New York: Hill and Wang, 1975); Michel Foucault, *The History of Sexuality*, vols. 1–3 (New York: Vintage, 1990); and Thomas Laqueur, *Making Sex: Body and Gender from the Greeks to Freud* (Cambridge, MA: Harvard University Press, 1990).

3 Augustine's interpretation of sexual arousal as a recapitulation of the Fall is well known. See *The City of God* (New York: Penguin, 2003), Book XIV, 547–94. See also Elaine Pagels, *Adam, Eve, and the Serpent: Sex and Politics in Early Christianity* (New York: Vintage, 1989).

4 See Jacques Derrida, "Plato's Pharmacy," in *Dissemination* (Chicago: University of Chicago Press, 1981), 61–119.

5 *Phaedrus*, eds. W. C. Helmbold and W. G. Rabinowitiz (Indianapolis: Bobs-Merrill, 1960), 42.

6 *Phaedrus*, 75.

7 The Amores, I. 1. ll. 21–4 (*The Erotic Poems*, ed. Peter Green [New York: Penguin, 1982], 86).

8 The Amores, III. 12. ll. 8–11 (160).

9 See Bradford Mudge, *When Flesh Becomes Word: An Anthology of Early Eighteenth-Century Libertine Literature* (Oxford: Oxford University Press, 2004).

10 II. ii. 33–49. *Shakespeare: The Complete Works* (New York: Riverside, 1969), 868–9.

11 II. ii. 50–52. *Shakespeare*, 869.

12 The phrase "green world" was made famous by Northrop Frye, *The Anatomy of Criticism* (Princeton: Princeton University Press, 1957), 182–4.

13 II. ii. 112–22. *Shakespeare*, 158.

14 V. i. 412–27. *Shakespeare*, 173.

15 *The Complete Poems of John Wilmot, Earl of Rochester*, ed. David Vieth (New Haven: Yale, 1968), 54–9, 37–40, 82.

16 Mudge, *When Flesh Becomes Word*, 61–78.

17 Mudge, *The Whore's Story: Women, Pornography, and the British Novel, 1684–1830* (New York: Oxford University Press, 2000), 59–88.

18 Keats, *The Complete Poems*, ed. Miriam Allott (New York: Longman, 1975), 470–1.
19 *The Complete Poems*, 463.
20 See John Wilson Croker's famous essay in *The Quarterly Review,* April 6, 1833.
21 *The Letters of John Keats,* ed. Robert Gittings (Oxford: Oxford University Press, 1970), 37.
22 Matthew Arnold, *Culture and Anarchy* (Cambridge: Cambridge University Press, 1960), 6.
23 For Arnold's use of "authority" and his appeal to the power of the state, see *Culture and Anarchy*, chapter 2, "Doing as One Likes," and in particular, 82–3, 85, 87, 89, 90, 93, 96–7.
24 Arnold comments on "the great obvious faults of our animality" and implies a link to what he describes as "the anarchial tendency of our worship of freedom in and of itself" (55, 76).
25 If scholars of sex and sexuality are generally enthusiastic about the ways that eroticism disrupts the status quo, then the crucial exception is Catherine MacKinnon. See *Feminism Unmodified: Discourses on Life and Law* (Cambridge: Harvard University Press, 1987); and "Sexuality, Pornography, and Method: Pleasure under Patriarchy," *Ethics,* 99:2 (1989), 314–46.
26 Barthes, 10.

2

DANIEL ORRELLS

Classical Antiquity and Modern Erotic Literature

Ancient Greek and Latin were equipped with rich sexual vocabularies, which concerned and excited early-Christian, Renaissance and modern writers in equal measure. While there has been much scholarly debate about whether Greeks and Romans would have recognised the categories of 'heterosexual', 'homosexual' and 'bisexual', it is safe to say that ancient Greek and Latin possessed broad lexicons of terms to describe numerous sexual acts and pleasures.[1] The erotic possibilities of the Latin language have especially captivated the post-ancient imagination.[2] Although it is a moot point as to whether classical Latin possesses any terms to denote sexual identity or orientation, it seems to be the case that the Romans described sex in terms of phallic penetration. That is to say, there is not simply a word for 'to have sex' or 'to fuck' in Latin. Instead, there are no less than six basic terms: the verb *futuere* means 'to fuck the vagina'; *crisare*, 'to get fucked in the vagina'; *pedicare*, 'to fuck the ass'; *cevere*, 'to get fucked in the ass'; *irrumare*, 'to fuck the mouth'; *fellare*, 'to suck the penis'.[3] But it has not just been the abundant eroticism of Roman texts that has fascinated modern readers: Roman material and visual culture has also captivated the modern gaze. The excavations of Pompeii and Herculaneum in the second half of the eighteenth century uncovered erotic wall and vase paintings and unearthed numerous unusual phallic objects. Drinking cups and oil lamps were decorated with scenes of sex and seduction. Phallic pendants adorned ancient necks and hung from doorways. Statues with erect penises were used as boundary stones and signposts in ancient Greece, whereas ancient Romans seemed to have enjoyed looking at statues of satyrs, nymphs and hermaphrodites.[4]

Since the Renaissance, western erotic literature has been inspired by the pornutopia of classical antiquity, where all sorts of sexual possibilities seemed available. There is also a long history of scholarly expurgation and bowdlerisation of ancient erotic texts.[5] But how literary criticism might read and interpret the representation of desire, pleasure and sex in erotic literature has been a much more recent preoccupation of scholars. And the discourse of psychoanalysis has been central to this mode of reading. Indeed, psychoanalysis has been central to twentieth- and twenty-first-century conceptualizations of the eroticism of literature – of literature *as* erotics. Not only has the impact of psychoanalysis on the modern history of reading literature been profound and far-reaching, but the elucidation – the psychoanalysis – of literary texts was also of great importance to Sigmund Freud himself, the founder of psychoanalysis. The interpretation of Sophocles' tragedy *Oedipus Tyrannus* (429 BC) was crucial for *The Interpretation of Dreams* (1899), Freud's first published magnum opus. There would be no psychoanalysis without the remarkable Greek myth about a man who killed his father and slept with his mother. Indeed, the discourse of myth was central to Freud's theorisation of the history of an individual's desire: our adult sexualities are dependent upon fantasies about our childhoods. What we think we want and know is what we tell ourselves about our past, childhood selves. Our psyches were conceived as texts to be deciphered and read. In the twentieth century, literature came to be interpreted as (some sort of) a representation of our (the author's and the reader's) eroticism at least partly as a result of psychoanalysis. And yet the idea that there might be a scientific language, such as psychoanalysis, which could both contain and know the truth of sexuality would certainly be contested. Indeed, Freud's erotic method of interpreting literature raised ongoing questions about the relationship between sexuality and textuality: could our erotic sensibilities be encoded by texts, which could then be interpreted? Was there not something banal and reductive about the idea that erotic feelings could be captured within language? Was there not something unrepresentable about sex?[6]

Freud's eroticisation of literature, however, did not emerge out of nowhere. He would never have turned to the story of Oedipus without a long history of the reception of antiquity that preceded him.[7] This chapter offers one account of how this reception history of ancient texts made it possible for Freud and his twentieth-century literary-critical readers to view literature as erotic. It concentrates on the eighteenth- and nineteenth-century venereology and sexology that provided the context for Freud's innovations. To be more precise, this chapter examines the role ancient texts played in this history of medical reading. Freud's mythologizing was a response to an earlier, different understanding of the relationship between literature and eroticism, between texts and sexual desire. Our story begins with what is often regarded as the first modern text on venereal disease, Jean Astruc's *De morbis venereis*, which first appeared in 1736 and became the standard authority on the subject for much of the eighteenth century. Astruc was also a biblical scholar; his interest in the burgeoning science of biblical textual criticism was crucial for his argument that biblical and classical antiquity offered no evidence of syphilis, which, Astruc contended, first made its appearance on European soil subsequent to Christopher Columbus' 'discovery' of the so-called New World. Although the majority of subsequent venereological publications followed Astruc's aetiology of syphilis, the remarkable discoveries at Pompeii and Herculaneum and then the publication in 1824 of a hitherto lost manuscript of erotic Renaissance Latin epigrams renewed scholarly interest in ancient Greek and Latin erotic poetry, as we shall learn. This, in turn, encouraged Julius Rosenbaum, a physician from Halle, to argue that the origins of modern venereal disease could indeed be traced back to the ancient world. We will examine how his *Geschichte der Lustseuche im Alterthume* (*History of the Plague of Lust in Antiquity*), first published in 1839, meticulously surveyed numerous Greek and Latin texts, and Roman epigram in particular, to make his argument. This rich sexual vocabulary of epigram, collated by Rosenbaum, offered Richard von Krafft-Ebing, the Austrian psychiatrist and sexologist, a technical language to describe the 'perverse' sexual acts recorded in his 1886 work *Psychopathia Sexualis: A Clinical-Forensic Study*. The sexual cityscape of degenerate imperial Rome provided a mirror for Krafft-Ebing's depiction of a similarly decadent and debauched *fin de siècle*. As we shall see, containing knowledge of sexuality within a scientific language was to be a difficult issue for these medical writers. It was out of this context that Freud's attempt at a scientific instrumentalisation of Greek myth would then emerge.

Venereal Philology

Although Jean Astruc (1684–1766), the personal physician to Louis XV, was never a great clinician, his *De morbis venereis* became the standard account of venereal disease until the end of the eighteenth century.[8] The first book set out what became a compelling case for the arrival of syphilis after Columbus returned from his momentous voyage. Astruc argued for the non-existence of syphilis and gonorrhoea in antiquity. We should not be surprised, then, that Astruc engaged very closely with biblical and classical texts to prove his point. Indeed, Astruc was also to play a fundamental role in the modern origins of critical textual analysis of works of scripture. He was the first to attempt to demonstrate that the book of Genesis was composed from several different sources.[9] In the preface to *De morbis venereis*, he counters the assertions that 'the Leprosy, describ'd by Moses in the fourteenth chapter of Leviticus, was the same distemper with the present Venereal Disease', that 'the sore boils, wherewith Satan smote Job, by God's permission, from the sole of his foot to the crown of his head, are ... to be understood of the same distemper', that 'David himself had ... the Venereal Disease, as he seems to have given a lively description of its symptoms in some of his Psalms' and that 'the Author of the Book of Ecclesiasticus ... allude[s] to the Venereal Disease'.[10] 'Let the Criticks sweat to find out their meaning', Astruc goes on to exclaim when he turns to Greek and Roman texts: 'For of what Signification is it to contend about an Author's Meaning, if we are at Liberty to fix what Sense we please upon his Words?'[11] Nothing in the medical writers (Hippocrates, Galen), nothing in the historians (Thucydides, Tacitus and Suetonius) and nothing in the satirical poets (Horace, Juvenal and Martial) corresponds with what Astruc knew about the symptoms of syphilis and gonorrhoea. The boils, sores and ulcers mentioned by those ancient writers cannot be linked to sexually transmitted diseases, and the sexual promiscuity of the ancients did not seem to have been a factor in the emergence of these conditions. Readings of these texts that have uncovered venereal disease in antiquity are 'strange misinterpretation[s]' and 'notable conjecture[s] indeed'.[12] An engagement with textual sources, then, which attempted to adopt a professional philological procedure, was crucial to Astruc's argument about the history of venereal disease. Critical textual criticism was put into the service of venereology.

Even if Astruc's argument in favour of an 'American' aetiology for syphilis had become widely accepted, the discovery of a manuscript in the early nineteenth century would offer the opportunity to utilise classical philology to contradict Astruc's interpretation of ancient texts. The 'signification' of those ancient authors – the relationship between ancient literature and modern sexual experience – was not to be left uncontested. In 1825, the German philologist Friedrich Karl Forberg (1770–1848), Conservator of the Aulic Library at Coburg, published his edition of a manuscript of Renaissance Latin epigrams he had discovered in the library. Back in the 1420s, Antonio Beccadelli (1394–1471) had circulated two books of sexually explicit epigrams written in the style of the Roman writers of epigram, Catullus and Martial, in the hope of attracting the patronage of Cosimo de' Medici. Roman epigram was often a caustic, invective and highly sexually explicit poetic medium, which made full use of Roman sexual obscenity. These were short, sharp poems with a sting in the tail, designed to show off the poetic prowess of the writer. Beccadelli took a risk, then, in aping this often deliberately offensive form of poetry, in order to capture Cosimo's attention. Beccadelli defended his choice of language and used Catullus' famous apology for using sexual, obscene language in poetry:

> it is proper for a pious poet to be chaste
> himself, but it is not at all necessary for his little verses to be.

(Catullus, 16.5–16.6)

In this poem, Catullus says he will anally and orally fuck two readers of his poetry who have called him 'effete' for writing poetry about love. Catullus' language of penile insertion makes use of the language of Roman fucking with which we began this chapter. But Catullus' poetry was only in the process of being edited when Beccadelli was writing, and so had not yet stably entered the classical canon of Renaissance humanism. It was still an open question as to how one might respond to Catullus' phallic threat and to his defence that one can say what one likes in poetry as long as one lives an upright life.[13] Beccadelli's attempts at writing Latin epigram were, then, highly experimental. Beccadelli called his work *The Hermaphrodite* because it, in his words, contained 'at the same time cunt and cock' (1.3.3). Indeed, the book might be seen as a collection of sexual obscenity. But Beccadelli's poetic experimentation backfired: his poems provoked much controversy and he didn't get the patronage he desired.[14] Most likely, the poems were not even widely read. And although selections of Beccadelli's poems were published after their original circulation, it was only with the discovery of the manuscript at Coburg that a full, scholarly edition became possible.

Forberg appended his commentary on Beccadelli with a long essay about sex in ancient Greece and Rome, which he called 'Apophoreta: De Figuris Veneris' ('Party Gifts: On the Shapes/Figures of Speech of Love'). Forberg took his title 'Apophoreta' from a book of Martial's poetry, which consisted of epigrams describing gifts taken home after a party. Like Beccadelli's book, Forberg's essay can be seen as a collection of sexual epigrammatic experiences, culling passages from Aristophanes; Catullus; Horace; Ovid; Juvenal; Martial; the *Carmina Priapeia*, neo-Latin epigram and pornography. Following the structure of Roman sexual vocabulary, he organised his 'Apophoreta' around whether one is penetrating with or being penetrated by the penis, as can be seen from the section titles:

> *De fututione* ('On fucking the vagina with the penis')
> *De paedicando* ('On fucking the ass with the penis')
> *De irrumando* ('On fucking the mouth with the penis')
> *De masturbando* ('On masturbating')
> *De cunnilingis* ('On licking the cunt with the tongue')

De tribadibus ('On tribads')
De coitu cum brutis ('On coitus with animals')
De spintriis ('On group sex')

After exploring various modes of phallic penetration and then masturbation, Forberg discusses the penetration of the vagina with the tongue, then the penetration of the vagina with the enlarged clitoris of a 'tribad' (a woman who enjoys sexually penetrating another woman), finally concluding with penetration with animals and penetration in groups.

Forberg's edition demonstrated his philological skills; his essay is the first modern scholarly and comprehensive account about ancient sexual practices, and so might be said to have created a new area of research. His efforts reflected a broader culture of intellectual endeavour in the early nineteenth century, when classical studies were becoming institutionalised in the German university system. Forberg seems to celebrate the possibility that his book might not just be for serious scholars in search of a scholarly account of ancient sex, but might also land in the hands of more lascivious persons. He closes the 'Apophoreta' with an erotic Latin epigram of his own:

> *Haec prima est, lector cordate, et mensa secunda.*
> *Ut sileas, videor velle videre tuum.*
> *Cernere vis patrantes. Εἰκοσιμήχανον offert.*
> *Bibliopola dabit. Virgo pudica fuge.*[15]

> [That is the first and the second course, wise reader.
> Although you're silent, I seem to see what you want.
> You want to see them in action. The *Eikosimechanon* provides that.
> You can get it at the bookstore. Modest virgin, take flight.]

Forberg then concludes with an epigram advertising a booklet that contains plates illustrating the sexual positions discussed in his essay (the *Eikosimechanon*). The epigram is addressed to the male reader – indeed, the 'wise male reader' – who has enjoyed the Beccadelli and the 'Apophoreta', the first two courses. Forberg knows his wise reader wants to see the acts that have been described in the pages of his edition. But instead of being disseminated via manuscript as Beccadelli had been in the 1420s, Forberg's nineteenth-century reader, 400 years later in the 1820s, can visit the 'bookstore'. The epigram closes with a line from Beccadelli (1.4.2), in which the Renaissance writer in an opening poem had advised 'chaste virgins' to stay away from reading his lines. Beccadelli's poem continues, however, by saying that sexually voracious women like 'Ursa' ('Bear') are free to enjoy his writing. Similarly, Martial had warned women off from reading his obscene epigrams, and yet they continue to read:

> I already told and warned you before, chaste lady,
> Not to read the rude part of my book, but here you are reading it.

(3.86.1–2)

Martial then suggests the 'chaste lady' read on. Forberg also realises that women might be reading his book: he is literally and knowingly addressing such a reader – a 'modest virgin' – at the end of his tome.

Forberg's anthology emerged at a time when the study of ancient sexual pleasure was coming into focus. The archaeological excavations at Pompeii and Herculaneum in the second half of the eighteenth century unearthed a very different antiquity from that being idealised in the writings of the famous antiquarian Johann Joachim Winckelmann, whose famous description of the Apollo Belvedere sublimated the homoerotic charge of the viewer's gaze at the nude Greek form into a quasi-religious experience. Pompeii and Herculaneum offered a view into the 'everyday' lives of the ancients, seemingly warts and all.[16] Numerous bizarrely shaped phallic objects emerged from the sites: a cock's head with a phallus for a nose, winged phalli with tails and bells, and phallic doorknockers. Soon antiquarian publications about ancient 'phallic worship' began to appear. Richard Payne Knight's *An Account of the Remains of the Worship of Priapus* (1786) became a landmark work in the burgeoning scholarship on ancient phallic religions. And the seemingly abundant supply of ancient phallic artefacts that emerged from the southern Italian soil saw to it that, by 1819, Naples had established a 'secret museum' to house these special objects. Educated gentlemen, including eminent figures such as Goethe, even began to build collections of *phallica*.[17]

Ancient Roman culture appeared to offer a vision of a past that was not structured according to Christian sexual ethics, and so became an attractive vision for sexual and social radicals and anti-clericals around the year 1800. The network of *phallica* collectors was also a network of subversive countercultural intellectuals.[18] Forberg himself had published an academic article back in 1798 that defended Johann Fichte's philosophy of religion; a controversy that cost both Forberg and Fichte their jobs at the time. Forberg's edition, although scholarly, was also a rare volume to be collected just like the ancient and modern phallic artefacts circulating around Western Europe. Astruc had sought to utilise his philological skills as a textual scholar to deny that biblical and classical texts had anything to teach the modern doctor about venereal disease. Because of the excavation of Pompeii and Herculaneum, which began just twenty years after the original publication of Astruc's book, Forberg could entertain a very different – countercultural – relationship with ancient texts, which might offer the modern reader an inflaming and alluring panorama into a world of alternative desires and pleasures.[19]

Sexual Pathology and Erotic Literature

Although Forberg joked about the possibility that his book might fall into the wrong hands and be read with pleasure by a 'chaste virgin', he probably would not have anticipated that it would become a key text for Julius Rosenbaum (1807–74), a doctor and medical historian working in Halle, who published the first part of a (never to be completed) trilogy, *The Plague of Lust in Antiquity*, which was designed to prove that the origins of venereal disease could be found in the ancient world. Rosenbaum 'gladly acknowledg[ed] the no small assistance we have received' from the philologist Forberg, while also noting the importance of the phallic discoveries and classical scholarship about sexuality that had emerged since the end of the eighteenth century.[20] The bizarre sexual customs of the ancients, such as temple prostitution and phallus cults, which had received much scholarly attention since the rediscovery of Pompeii and Herculaneum, allowed Rosenbaum to argue that a general cultural framework provided a context for increased misuse of the genital organs, which must have led to venereal disease.[21] Just as Astruc the doctor took up the role of textual scholar in order to disprove the existence of syphilis and gonorrhoea in the ancient world, so Rosenbaum the doctor also played philologist to prove the exact opposite: 'Venereal disease, though not recognized and described as such by the ancient physicians, was as a matter of fact existent in antiquity'.[22]

Yet it was the lack of relevant ancient medical opinion that clearly troubled Rosenbaum: 'if only the medical writers had appended to the records of their observations in each case the words "got by infection in coition"'.[23] He repeatedly observes how evidence for venereal disease is brought out by the ancient 'layman', 'whereas the physicians say nothing about this.'[24] An interesting situation, then, emerges in Rosenbaum's book: ancient poets – the Roman epigrammatist Martial, especially – offer the most perspicacious comments on venereal disease in classical antiquity, which are best interpreted by a modern doctor-cum-philologist.[25] Again and again, Rosenbaum figures himself, the doctor, as a better philologist than professional classical scholars.[26] The modern doctor, Rosenbaum, is the best reader of ancient poetry in this book, whereas the ancient doctor could not see what the ancient poet could. Ironically, then, in the nineteenth century the doctor and the poet come to speak the same language, whereas in antiquity the discourse of the doctor and that of the poet are presented by Rosenbaum as quite different. One might have expected exactly the opposite situation, whereby modern doctors are keen to differentiate themselves from ancient non-scientific discourse – indeed, as with Astruc. Instead, for instance, Rosenbaum can read an epigram 'of great importance' by Martial (1.78), which describes a certain Festus whose 'unworthy throat' is affected by 'a corrupting disease' and over whose face 'a black contagion [*lues*] creeps'. Rosenbaum interprets the poem:

> The words *indignae fauces* (unworthy throat) obviously point to the practice of fellation, whereby he had brought on himself the *pestis tabida* and *atra lues* (corrupting disease, black contagion), and so we have here a clear statement of the cause by one *doctus venereae cupidinis* (learned in the passion of love), which cause was quite unknown to the *artifex medicus* (medical practitioner).[27]

Although it would have been clear to the book's nineteenth-century readers that *lues* was the neo-Latin term for syphilis, Rosenbaum does not argue that that is what Martial is saying in the poem. But the word would have spoken clearly to Rosenbaum's readership, and so helps him make the more general point that Martial was saying that fellation caused disease. Then when Rosenbaum says that this is a statement from someone "learned in the passion of love unknown to the medical practitioner," the Latin he uses is lifted from Apuleius' Roman novel *Metamorphoses* (10.2), where the narrator, Lucius, tells a tale about a stepmother who desires to have sex with her stepson: doctors would not able to diagnose her love fever, whilst any educated man in matters of love would, Lucius says. For Rosenbaum, then, it was ancient literature that provided evidence of ancient venereal illness, so much so that the modern medical doctor could sound like an ancient literary writer. Whereas Astruc had utilised philological methods to differentiate his modern medical Latin from ancient literary texts back in 1736, Rosenbaum would do the opposite a century later after the discovery of Pompeii and Herculaneum and impersonate the ancient literary author – even though Forberg had suggested that ancient texts might inflame the desires of the modern reader rather than aid medical diagnosis.

Rosenbaum's contention that venereal disease could be traced back to the ancient world would play its role in a debate about the origins of syphilis that would continue among venereologists into the twentieth century.[28] But it was his depiction of ancient society 'plagued by lust' that captured the imagination of the nineteenth century's most famous sexologist, Richard von Krafft-Ebing, whose best-known work *Psychopathia Sexualis* first appeared in 1886. It consisted of numerous case studies of sexual perversion and criminality. By the early twentieth century, some twelve editions had appeared, each larger than the previous, so that it seemed like an encyclopaedic anthology of sex.[29] If one were to take a look at the works consulted by Krafft-Ebing in writing *Psychopathia Sexualis* one would see that, along with other contemporary sexological and criminological writings, Krafft-Ebing's bibliography only lists Rosenbaum's *Plague of Lust* and two other nineteenth-century German works of classical scholarship on imperial Rome. This historical scholarship provided the vocabulary for Krafft-Ebing's history of civilisation more broadly.

These two other works on ancient Rome are Ludwig Friedländer's *Darstellungen aus Sittengeschichte Roms* (*Roman Life and Manners under the Early Empire*, first published in 1862) and Friedrich Wiedemeister's *Der Cäsarenwahnsinn* (or *The Madness of the Caesars*, first published in 1875). Both works examined how the height of Roman luxury and decadence were also signs of the degeneration of Roman society, thereby providing Krafft-Ebing with a detailed historical image for his own *fin de siècle*. Wiedemeister's interest in the insanity of the Caesars supplied Krafft-Ebing with the possibility of linking Roman history with theories of heredity and degeneration, as Wiedemeister argued that the key to the madness of the Julio-Claudians lay in their family history. This infamous tale of 'family degeneration', as Wiedemeister described it, offered a potent image for the family trees that Krafft-Ebing constructed of his patients.[30] Just as Rosenbaum painted a portrait of a sexually debauched antiquity in which there was sacred prostitution and phallic worship, Krafft-Ebing could not help but make comparisons between ancient Rome and modern sexual practices in the various case studies of sexual perversion that comprised his book. So in *Psychopathia Sexualis*, modern women, 'inflamed to lasciviousness', are like Roman wives who have been whipped by priests as described by the Roman satirist Juvenal (2.140–3). One young man bereft of sexual desire wishes he could 'open his veins as Seneca [the Roman philosopher] did in the bath'. Grandmothers horny for boys and women lusty for power are 'Messalinas', the lascivious Roman empress as presented by Tacitus. Sexual sadists who cut up and eat their victims claim to have learnt their trade from the tales in Suetonius' imperial biographies.[31]

Just as Rosenbaum appropriated ancient literature to construct a modern scientific discourse, so Krafft-Ebing also adopted the Roman vocabulary set out in Forberg and then in Rosenbaum as *'termini technici'*, as he calls it, 'in order that unqualified persons should not become readers'.[32] Krafft-Ebing had collated the sexual autobiographies of numerous correspondents. He turned to Forberg's Latin, which had been cited by Rosenbaum, whenever a subject came to describe their genitals, penetration or the transmission of bodily fluids. A few examples will suffice: '*membrum meum in os recepit*' ('he receives my member in the mouth'); '*linguam meam in os eius immitto*' ('I insert my tongue into his mouth'); '*magna mentula puellam futuat*' ('he fucks the girl with his big cock'); '*penem aliorum puerorum in os arrigere*' ('to erect his penis into the mouth of other boys'). And terms like 'cunnilingus', '*irrumare*' (fucking the face with the penis) and '*paedicatio*' (fucking the anus with the penis) pepper Krafft-Ebing's text. By using Latin so that only a certain portion of the general public could read his book, Krafft-Ebing sought to bolster the authority of the youthful intellectual discipline of sexology. *Psychopathia Sexualis* argued that criminalising sexual perverts was the incorrect method for dealing with such individuals because many of them suffered under their perversions due to heredity. Krafft-Ebing was attempting to arrogate the sexual pervert for the domain of psychiatry rather than criminology. His use of Latin reflected his attempts to enhance the social prestige of his discipline.[33]

Nevertheless, the tone of Krafft-Ebing's so-called technical Latin is itself quite difficult to read. Interestingly, he uses obscene words such as '*mentula*' ('cock') and '*futuat*' ('he fucks') from Roman and Renaissance epigram interchangeably with more neutral terms like 'penis' and 'membrum' and euphemisms such as '*immitto*' ('I insert') and '*recepit*' ('he receives'), which Forberg and then Rosenbaum had used to define Roman sexual vocabulary. It becomes very difficult to judge the register of Krafft-Ebing's Latin. The following example comes from a case history of a man who is classified as an '*Urning*' (a person with a woman's soul trapped inside a man's body):

> At the same time, I have a very lively fancy, and spend most of my leisure hours thinking of handsome men with strong limbs; and I would be delighted to look on when a powerful fellow, using force, *magna mentula praeditus me praesente puellam futuat; mihi persuasum est, fore ut hoc aspectu sensus mei vehementissima perturbation afficiantur et dum futuit corpus adolescentis pulchri tangam et, si liceat, ascendam in eum dum cum puella concumbit atque idem cum eo faciam et membrum meum in eius anum immittam*

> [endowed with a large cock might fuck a girl in my presence; I was convinced that with this sight my senses would be affected by the most violent passion and while he fucks, I will touch the body of the beautiful adolescent and, if allowed, I would mount him while he is lying with the girl and do the same to him and insert my member into his anus].[34]

Krafft-Ebing reverts into Latin when the subject starts using sexually explicit language ('large cock', 'fuck'), but then closes the section with 'insert my member into his anus'. The Latin segment contains what sounds like the subject's most sexually explicit confession (a fantasy of witnessing a rape), but then ends with a circumlocution, which – as we now know – can be traced back to the medical and scholarly Latin of the middle of the nineteenth century. Forberg had used the verb '*immitto*' to describe what the penis does in anal sex. Did the original words of Krafft-Ebing's correspondent also shift in register? Is that what Krafft-Ebing meant to suggest? When he turns to Latin to represent the sexual practices and fantasies expressed by his correspondents, the language of the layperson and the language of the doctor become blurred, so the question yet again arises of the relationship between the discourse of modern medical science and that of ancient erotic poetry.

If Krafft-Ebing's Latin can look like both an obscene and a scientific language, then this reflected the fact that *Psychopathia Sexualis* became one of the most public statements of a discourse that blurred the boundaries between the healthy and the pathological. Krafft-Ebing's book was filled with numerous case studies of bourgeois individuals who appeared to be respectable members of their communities but nevertheless enjoyed strange sexual activities and fantasised about unusual sexual encounters and desires.[35] His *fin-de-siècle* book depicted a seemingly high-functioning modern world, peopled by individuals of responsibility and of moral value, who simultaneously concealed uncivilised and regressive sexual identities within. It was a rich portrait of what many saw as the decadence and degeneration of late-nineteenth-century urban society, a world exquisitely sophisticated and yet also on the verge of collapse.[36]

The ambivalence of Krafft-Ebing's book – both scientific discourse and layperson's autobiographical correspondence – was encapsulated in his Latin: it was the respectable language of scientific taxonomy and classification and a sign of education and civilisation, but also an obscene language of debauchery and sexual perversion. The book was indeed controversial; rather than offering a step towards the successful management of sexual pathology, Krafft-Ebing was seen by many as a decadent voice for its proliferation. He seemed to give a sense of identity to various subjects at the turn of the century and is even mentioned as doing so in literary texts of the time.[37] In further editions, Krafft-Ebing included case studies in which correspondents described reading *Psychopathia Sexualis* while masturbating. Krafft-Ebing, it seemed, did not manage to turn the erotic Latin of Roman and Renaissance epigram into a modern scientific language for sexual pathology. Indeed, Krafft-Ebing even included autobiographical accounts that critiqued his descriptions of non-heterosexual sexualities as perverse, reflecting his increasing sympathies. This can be seen most clearly in the accounts of those correspondents who were sexually attracted to their own sex. The English author and classicist John Addington Symonds – though married – was attracted to male youths and adult men, and sent a letter to Krafft-Ebing describing 'the Iliad of their sufferings and constant excitations'.[38] The feeble and nervous disposition of

28

such men, Symonds argued from personal experience, was due not to some congenital perversion but rather the psychological pressure an intolerant modern society impressed upon the individual.

Symonds's allusion to Homer's epic was not simply rhetorical. His turn to the Greeks represented a more widespread trope in nineteenth-century writing, which looked back to more positive examples of same-sex desire.[39] This turn to the Greeks also reflected a very different way of viewing the relationship between the past and the present. When Pompeii was being excavated, Winckelmann was looking back to ancient Greece as an idealised place; an artistic culture that provided a model to subsequent Roman artists and intellectuals, but simultaneously a place that was inimitable and irre-coverable.[40] Greece hovered between a historical and an ideal place in the nineteenth-century European imagination. Symonds tried to see himself as a modern Homeric hero, and yet the possibility of bringing ancient Greek homoerotic culture back to life was also nothing but a fantasy.[41] Whereas classical and Renaissance Latin seemed to offer an accurate, literal – scientific – description of sexual experience, classical Greek supplied a language of sexual possibility and potentiality.

Freud's Greek Mythology

This is precisely where Freud enters the story. When Freud began analysing his patients' 'hysteric' symptoms, he became very interested in their pasts in a particular sort of way. While sexologists such as Henry Havelock Ellis and Krafft-Ebing listened to and closely read their patients' autobiographies, this type of narrative seemed unhelpful to Freud. In a footnote in his *Three Essays on Sexuality* (1905), he wrote:

> Havelock Ellis has published a number of autobiographical narratives. [...] These reports naturally suffer from the fact that they omit the prehistoric period of the writers' sexual lives, which is veiled by infantile amnesia and which can only be filled in by psychoanalysis in the case of an individual who has developed a neurosis.[42]

Freud was interested in the 'prehistoric period' that had been 'veiled by infantile amnesia' – that is, the things the patient could not consciously remember; things she talked about without realising it; things that might never have happened. A patient's words were a mythical text representing a deeper psychoanalytical truth that the doctor was tasked to locate and interpret correctly. The psychoanalyst was to take control of the narrative the patient told about herself. In short, the sexological autobiography was no longer reliable.[43] If Krafft-Ebing's Latin recorded the secrets of people's everyday sexual lives, then Freud pointed to an earlier and more significant period of sexuality in the individual's life, which might only be remembered in dreams and other forms of representation such as literature and visual art. In this way, then, when Freud 'discovered' the Oedipus complex he subscribed to the philhellenism of the nineteenth century – as reflected in the writings of other contemporary intellectuals such as Symonds, who viewed ancient Greece as a model for his modern life but at the same time just out of reach and irrecoverably ancient. Our Oedipal desires were buried, inaccessible, deep in our personal pasts – and yet they also constructed our 'modern', adult sexual identities.[44]

When Freud delivered his paper on 'The Aetiology of Hysteria' in 1896, he reported that it was met with silence and that Krafft-Ebing thought it 'sounded like a fairy tale' (SE 3: 189). While Krafft-Ebing was, as we have seen, very invested in the scientificity of his version of sexology, Freud thought very differently about the nature of the relationship between the literary text and psychoanalytic discourse. But he did not think that sexology inflamed its readers' desires. Even if, wrote Freud, 'simple-minded people attribute such a large share of the responsibility for the production of perverse tendencies' to the publication of Krafft-Ebing's book, 'unconscious *phantasies*', Freud continued, 'show precisely the same content as the documentarily recorded *actions* of perverts' (SE 7: 50, emphases original). Classical and Renaissance Latin would provide nineteenth-century doctors with a vocabulary to describe the actions of the 'pervert'; for Freud, on the other hand, Greek myth provided records of our unconscious infantile sexual fantasies. And whereas those nineteenth-century physicians thought that ancient literary texts and modern autobiographical accounts collated by doctors recorded actual sexual experiences, for Freud, literature was made up of symbols of sexual desires that had not entered our consciousness. For Rosenbaum, modern venereal disease could be traced back to Roman epigram, and for Krafft-Ebing, the language of Roman and Renaissance epigram offered a language that could accurately and scientifically record modern sexual experience. Roman literature and its nineteenth-century historiographical reception supplied, it was argued, a literal account of sexual activity. And so it was against this understanding of the relationship between eroticism and literature, between textuality and sexuality, that Freud constructed his own very influential psychoanalytic account of the relationship between our modern sexual selves and ancient Greek myth.

While utilising the methods of the textual critic, Astruc wrote as a doctor who sought to distinguish ancient and modern discourses on sexual desire. But after the excavations at Pompeii and Herculaneum were conducted in the generation after Astruc's death, Roman culture seemed to provide support for the argument that ancient poetry – Roman epigram in particular – offered a language for modern venereology and sexology. Freud emerges out of this intellectual history of the medical reception of classical antiquity to find a position in the middle. There would neither be no relationship between ancient literature and modern sexual medicine, nor would ancient literature straightforwardly, accurately and literally record modern sexuality. In the words of Elizabeth Wright, Freud 'draws attention to the effects of desire in language and in all forms of symbolic interaction'.[45] For Freud, literature would offer symbolic (metaphorical, metonymic) representations of sexual desire. This insight contended that all literature was erotic, thereby bringing about a history of debates about the relationship between sex and textuality – about the possibility that sexuality could be known in language. Those twentieth-century and contemporary debates about what was erotic about the literary, which trace their origins back to Freud, would not have happened without a longer history of the medical reception of classical antiquity.

NOTES

With warmest thanks to Dr Steve Taylor and his colleagues at Heartlands Hospital, Birmingham, England.

1 On this debate about the history of sexuality, see most recently: Kirk Ormand, 'Foucault's *History of Sexuality* and the Discipline of Classics' in Thomas K. Hubbard (ed.), *A Companion to Greek and Roman Sexualities* (Oxford: Wiley-Blackwell, 2014), 54–68.

2 See Alastair Blanshard, *Sex: Vice and Love from Antiquity to Modernity* (Oxford: Wiley-Blackwell, 2010) and Daniel Orrells, *Sex: Antiquity and its Legacy* (New York: Oxford University Press, 2015).

3 For more in-depth discussions of sex in Latin, see J.N. Adams, *The Latin Sexual Vocabulary* (Baltimore: Johns Hopkins University Press, 1990) and Craig Williams, *Roman Homosexuality*, second edition (Oxford: Oxford University Press, 2010). On Ancient Greek terminology, readers will enjoy the discussions in Jeffrey Henderson, *The Maculate Muse: Obscene Language in Attic Comedy* (New Haven: Yale University Press, 1991) and David Bain, 'Six Greek Verbs of Sexual Congress (βινῶ, κινῶ, πυγίζω, ληκῶ, οἴω, λαικάζω)', *The Classical Quarterly*, 41, 1 (1991), 51–77.

4 See Caroline Vout, *Sex on Show: Seeing the Erotic in Greece and Rome* (London: British Museum Press, 2013).

5 See Stephen Harrison and Christopher Stray, *Expurgating the Classics: Editing Out in Greek and Latin* (London: Bloomsbury Academic, 2014).

6 See Elizabeth Wright, *Psychoanalytic Criticism: A Reappraisal* (Cambridge: Polity, 1998) for a history of psychoanalytic literary criticism in the twentieth century.

7 See Peter Rudnytsky, *Freud and Oedipus* (New York: Columbia University Press, 1987), Richard Armstrong, *A Compulsion for Antiquity: Freud and the Ancient*

World (Ithaca, NY: Cornell University Press, 2005), Miriam Leonard, *Tragic Modernities* (Cambridge: Harvard University Press, 2015) and Orrells, *Sex*.

8 See J.D. Oriel, *The Scars of Venus: A History of Venereology* (London: Springer-Verlag, 1994), 25.

9 See John Jarick, *Sacred Conjectures: The Context and Legacy of Robert Lowth and Jean Astruc* (London: Bloomsbury, 2007) and John Rogerson, 'Jean Astruc', in Donald K. McKim (ed.), *Dictionary of Major Biblical Interpreters* (Downers Grove, IL/Nottingham, England: IVP Academic /Inter-Varsity Press, 2007), 126–28. Astruc's *Conjectures on the Original Documents that Moses Appears To Have Used in Composing the Book of Genesis* would appear anonymously in 1753.

10 Jean Astruc, *A Treatise of the Venereal Disease*, translated by William Barrowby (London: Printed for W. Innys and R. Manby, 1737), 1: v–vi. I am citing from the English translation, which appeared in 1737. For the original Latin edition, see Jean Astruc, *De Morbis Venereis Libri Sex* (London: Lutetiæ Parisiorum, 1736).

11 Astruc, *Treatise*, 1: 14, 7.

12 Astruc, *Treatise*, 1: 6–15, and see page 13.

13 See Julia Haig Gaissner, 'Catullus in the Renaissance', in Marilyn Skinner (ed.), *A Companion to Catullus* (Oxford: Blackwell, 2007), 439–60.

14 On Beccadelli and his poems, see Antonio Beccadelli, *The Hermaphrodite*, translated and edited by Holt Parker (Cambridge, MA: Harvard University Press, 2010) and Orrells, *Sex*, 21–37.

15 Antonio Beccadelli, *Hermaphroditus: primus in Germania edidit et Apophoreta adjecit Frider. Carol. Forbergius* (Coburg: Mensel, 1824), 384.

16 See Chantal Grell, *Le dix-huitième siècle et l'antiquité en France 1680–1789* (Oxford: Voltaire Foundation, 1995) and Shelley Hales and Joanna Paul (eds.), *Pompeii in the Public Imagination from its Rediscovery to Today* (Oxford: Oxford University Press, 2011).

17 See Walter Kendrick, *The Secret Museum: Pornography in Modern Culture* (Berkeley, CA: University of California Press, 1987) and Orrells, *Sex*, 68–73.

18 On these collectors, see Whitney Davis, 'Homoerotic Art Collections from 1750–1920', *Art History*, 24, 2 (2004), 247–77.

19 On Forberg, see also Günther E. Thüry, 'Der Coburger Gelehrte Friedrich Karl Forberg (1770–1848) und die Erforschung der antiken Sexualgeschichte', *Jahrbuch der Coburger Landesstiftung*, 55 (2010/2011), 71–86.

20 Julius Rosenbaum, *Geschichte der Lustseuche, erster Theil: die Lustseuche im Alterthume* (Halle: J.F. Lippert, 1839), 46, note 1; 62, note 1; 117–118, note 1 and Julius Rosenbaum, *The Plague of Lust, Being a History of Venereal Disease in Classical Antiquity*, 2 vols, trans. 'An Oxford M.A.' (Paris: Charles Carrington, 1901), 1: 12, note 1; 1: 33, note 1; 1: 110, note 1.

21 Julius Rosenbaum, *Plague of Lust*, 1: 12–132.

22 Julius Rosenbaum, *Plague of Lust*, 2: 320.

23 Julius Rosenbaum, *Plague of Lust*, 2: 315.

24 Julius Rosenbaum, *Plague of Lust*, 2: 88.

25 See Julius Rosenbaum, *Plague of Lust*, 2: 65.

26 For example, see the extended discussion at Julius Rosenbaum, *Plague of Lust*, 1: 143–256 and especially page 256.

27 Julius Rosenbaum, *Plague of Lust*, 2: 41.

28 See Oriel, *Scars*, 1–22.

29 On Krafft-Ebing's work, see Harry Oosterhuis, *Stepchildren of Nature: Krafft-Ebing, Psychiatry and the Making of Sexual Identity* (Chicago: University of Chicago Press, 2000) and Heinrich Ammerer, *Am Anfang war die Perversion: Richard von Krafft-Ebing, Psychiater und Pionier der modernen Sexualkunde* (Vienna: Styria, 2011).

30 See Richard von Krafft-Ebing, *Psychopathia Sexualis, with Especial Reference to Contrary Sexual Instinct: A Medico-Legal Study* (Philadelphia, PA: F.A. Davis, 1894), note 1, where he provides a bibliography of works he consulted.

31 Krafft-Ebing, *Psychopathia Sexualis*, 30, 45, 55, 58, 88.

32 Krafft-Ebing, *Psychopathia Sexualis*, v.

33 See Oosterhuis, *Stepchildren of Nature*.

34 Krafft-Ebing, *Psychopathia Sexualis*, 297, emphases added.

35 On Krafft-Ebing's bourgeois correspondents and readership, see Oosterhuis, *Stepchildren of Nature*, 217–18, 237–8, 244–5, 248, 254.

36 On the cultural politics of the *fin de siècle*, see Sally Ledger and Scott McCracken (eds.), *Cultural Politics at the Fin de Siècle* (Cambridge: Cambridge University Press, 1995) and Gail Marshall (ed.), *A Cambridge Companion to the Fin de Siècle* (Cambridge: Cambridge University Press, 2007).

37 See Anna Katharina Schaffner, *Modernism and Perversion: Sexual Deviance in Sexology and Literature, 1850–1930* (Basingstoke: Palgrave Macmillan, 2011).

38 Sean Brady (ed.), *John Addington Symonds (1840–1893) and Homosexuality: A Critical Edition of Sources* (Basingstoke: Palgrave Macmillan, 2012), 167, 210.

39 See Robert Aldrich, *The Seduction of the Mediterranean: Writing, Art and Homosexual Fantasy* (London: Routledge, 1993); Linda Dowling, *Hellenism and Homosexuality in Victorian Oxford* (Ithaca, NY/London: Cornell University Press, 1994); Stefano Evangelista, *British Aestheticism and Ancient Greece: Hellenism, Reception, Gods in Exile* (Basingstoke: Palgrave Macmillan, 2009); and Daniel Orrells, *Classical Culture and Modern Masculinity* (Oxford: Oxford University Press, 2011).

40 See Orrells, *Classical Culture*, for further discussion.

41 See Orrells, *Sex*, 122–3.

42 From 'Three Essays on Sexuality', in Sigmund Freud, *The Standard Edition of the Complete Psychological Works of Sigmund Freud*, 24 vols, ed. James Strachey in collaboration with Anna Freud (London: The Hogarth Press and the Institute of Psychoanalysis, 1953–74), 7, 190–1. All quotations from Freud will follow this edition (henceforth *SE* in main body of the text).

43 See Adam Philips, *Becoming Freud: The Making of Psychoanalysis* (New Haven, CT: Yale University Press, 2014).

44 See Armstrong, *Compulsion for Antiquity* and Leonard, *Tragic Modernities*.

45 Wright, *Psychoanalytic Criticism*, 1.

3

SARAH SALIH

Performances of Suffering

Secular and Devotional Eros in Late Medieval Writing

Erotic literature in medieval England was neither a genre nor a commodity. While books were not mass produced, it could not be a commodity. Although erotic content occurred, often unpredictably, in various genres, there was no category of pornography, and no kind of text that could be relied upon for erotic content. Readers might resist eroticism, or discover it in unlikely places. Medieval literary commentary, as Andrew Taylor argues, privileged desexualised readings of prestigious but ostensibly erotic texts such as the Song of Songs and the writings of Virgil and Ovid; conversely, he also finds that one reader of John Gower's *Confessio Amantis* – an analysis of the shortcomings of human eros – opportunistically found and marked up titillating narratives of sexual violence.[1] I have previously argued that in medieval visual art, erotic content and erotic affect are so divergent that they should be treated as separate categories, and the same is true of medieval erotic writing.[2] The relation between sexual content and sexual affect tends to the negative. Writing that directly and unambiguously concerns human sexual behaviour is more likely to intend to amuse or to disgust than to arouse, while sexually appealing writing is usually allusive rather than explicit and is most fully developed in relation to devotional, rather than merely human, desire. The early Middle English anchoritic texts provide examples of both points. *A Letter on Virginity* tries to persuade young women to choose a life of virginity by generating sexual horror at the responsibility of a wife to submit to 'that indecent heat of the flesh, that burning itch of physical desire before that disgusting act, that animal union, that shameless coupling, that stinking and wanton deed, full of filthiness'.[3] The life of virginity, by contrast, is an opportunity to enjoy the exquisite (but soft-focus) pleasures of devotional eros, marriage to Christ, the husband 'whose beauty the sun and moon admire, whose face the angels are never weary of gazing at'.[4]

This apparent shortage of erotic literature accords with some persistent conceptions of medieval innocence; Jean Leclercq, for example, cautions against projecting sexual concerns onto a 'less erotically-preoccupied society'.[5] The sexual content of fabliaux – short comic stories – is said to be 'bawdy' or 'earthy', terms that posit a naïve, unconsidered and not at all sexy sexuality. Recent criticism, however, argues that medieval sexuality was neither absent nor subdued, but different. Karma Lochrie argues that the modern division of heterosexuality and homosexuality was inoperative; Ruth Mazo Karras that the most important binary division was between the chaste and the sexually active.[6] The medieval sexual realm, Robert Allen Rouse and Cory James Rushton argue, was a 'preheterosexual paraphiliac culture, a world of sexual experiences and desires as potentially infinite as the number of existing individuals'.[7] Even apparently familiar organisations of sexuality, such as marriage, might on examination be very different. As Marilynn Desmond argues, 'Medieval discourse on sexuality and marriage assumes a conceptual link between eros and violence' that modern readers are likely to find disturbing.[8] Medieval sexuality, and its literature, need to be approached through a lens of defamiliarisation, and attention to the contribution of violence to eros does indeed produce a workable map.

According to one encyclopaedia of erotic literature (aiming 'to be universal in scope, both geographically and historically'), there are only three erotic texts in Middle English, all by Chaucer: *Troilus and Criseyde*, *The Miller's Tale* and *The Wife of Bath's Tale*.[9] Though this patently arbitrary list has no particular authority, it is a convenient starting point for a survey of the genres of medieval literature most receptive to erotic content. *The Miller's Tale* is a fabliau ostensibly driven by the desire of the student Nicholas for the carpenter's wife Alison. But this story and other fabliaux neither analyse erotic experience nor aim to generate erotic response. Sexual desire in these stories is the McGuffin used to get the characters in motion, but the tales are not greatly interested in the ostensible goal of their plots; the real pleasure of these narratives is in the intricacies of plotting and wordplay. Nicholas's scheme for getting the very willing Alison into bed by persuading her husband of the imminence of a second Flood is dementedly elaborate and counterproductive – as Mark Miller puts it, 'an excessively clever construction designed to crush an enemy that needs no defeating, a perverse deferral of animal pleasure' – but the plot itself is the point.[10] The consummation is briskly summarised in conventional and general terms: 'And thus lith Alison and Nicholas, / In bisynesse of myrth and of solaas', while the true climax of the story is the collision of the storylines of Nicholas, Absolon and John in the fatefully misunderstood cry of 'Help! water!'[11]

Troilus and Criseyde, meanwhile, introduces the concept of what is commonly known as 'courtly love': one of late-medieval Europe's significant contributions to erotic history, a discourse crossing from literature to life and back again. Courtly love posits a subject, usually but not always a man, who is centred on playing the lover.[12] It is a learnt and bookish eros, which, its theorist Andreas Capellanus argues, is to be differentiated from mere sex, which even 'farmers' can accomplish 'in the natural way like a horse or a mule'.[13] The courtly lover's 'consolations of love' may be restricted, for he is more invested in frustration, longing, sublimation and deferral than in satisfaction.[14] In Andreas's scheme, courtly love is a discipline of masculine self-affirmation through subjection: the lover hones his character by subjecting himself to a set of arbitrary rules and submitting his intimate life to the examination and judgement of powerful ladies.[15]

Thus, courtly love's pleasures are centrally those of masochism, as Jeffrey Jerome Cohen writes of Chrétien de Troyes's *Lancelot*: 'the paradoxical but joyous gains of contingency, subordination'.[16] Anita Phillips emphasises masochism's origins as 'lived fiction', in which 'The boundaries [of literature and life] did not just overflow into each other: they positively energised and fuelled one another in a mutual dynamic which was playful, serious, extraordinarily productive and possibly rather exhausting.'[17] Courtly love likewise entered into medieval life as a form of serious play, which added flavour or highlights to elite life. Translations and adaptations of courtly literature muted the extremes of love discourse with strands of realism. Thomas Malory's fifteenth-century English Lancelot greets the kidnapped Guinevere with an asperity that would have been quite impossible to his twelfth-century French prototype, who does not even dare to wonder why the queen should snub her rescuer.[18] The fiction conversely bled over, imperfectly and unevenly, into life. Larry D. Benson argues that 'courtly love did exist, perhaps not in the twelfth century, but certainly in the fourteenth, fifteenth, and even sixteenth centuries', and to the extent that it existed, it did because it had been learnt from romance.[19] Richard Firth Green confirms that:

> by the end of the fourteenth century the notion of a man's dying for love had become a social fiction as well as a literary one, for whilst medieval noblemen may have been in as little danger of death from unrequited passion as ourselves, they seem to have felt that they should at least appear capable of such an extreme of emotion.[20]

Noblemen vowed to prove themselves to their ladies not only in the sport of the tournament but also on some occasions in actual warfare.[21] Public readings of romances were themselves erotogenic events.[22] Hence the literature of courtly love is both an analysis of eros and – up to a point – a script for it.

But only up to a point: its reach was superficial. As C. Stephen Jaeger says, 'Ennobling love had always been primarily a way of acting and behaving, and only secondarily a way of feeling'.[23] It provided a style of elite behaviour and etiquette, but there is little evidence for its lived enactment in intimate relationships. Licit sexual intimacy between men and women was overwhelmingly understood through the paradigm of marriage – and the literature of marriage was resolutely unerotic, though the experience was no doubt more complicated. Many romances culminate in the happy ending of marriage, but such marriages typically, as Ilan Mitchell-Smith argues, mark the successful achievement of adult masculinity rather than being sites of erotic pleasure.[24] In this spirit, Marie de France's King Arthur 'apportioned lands and wives' to his knights, enabling them to function as noblemen, but there is no erotic or narrative interest in the wives, who play no part in the ensuing tale of Lanval's intensely erotic non-marital relationship with a fairy lady.[25] There was a normative expectation that marriages ought to be founded in mutual respect and affection, but such emotions were distinguished from sexual desire. Emma Lipton argues that 'sacramental' marriage, a late-medieval development, disassociated marriage from sex while defining it as love.[26] The Knight of the Tower warned his daughters that those who marry for 'playsaunce [or] for loue' are rightly scorned, for marriage is a matter of family strategy.[27] His account of one exemplary wife, the biblical Rebecca, understands marital affection to be an aspect of patriarchal authority: 'she loued and worshipped her lord aboue al thing / and shewed her to hym meke and humble'.[28] Such a wife might have a respected place as the deputy and counsellor of her husband – a component of his social self, in David Gary Shaw's phrase[29] – but her subordination made her unavailable as an object of erotic obsession or courtly fetishism.

Troilus and Criseyde, English literature's masterpiece of courtly love literature, is also an exploration of the imperfect hold of that style of eros. It is certainly an erotic text, though not at all sexually explicit, in its precise and delicate mapping of the tumultuous emotions of its protagonists. Watching from her window the wounded hero who she has just learnt loves her, Criseyde is struck with a shudder of desire: "Who yaf me drynke?' / For of hire owen thought she wex al reed'.[30] The protagonists are case studies in subtly differentiated forms of love. Troilus, a courtly lover by the book, falls in love at first sight, offers himself as Criseyde's servant and is inspired by her love to excel in battle. Criseyde considers herself a pragmatist who

rationally debates whether she should accept Troilus's love, but she too is
swayed by the discourse of courtly love when she hears it in a female voice,
as her niece sings a woman's lyric, a fictive trobaritz song of Chaucer's own
invention.[31] But the poem ends with the failure and transience of human
love. Its audience is originally interpellated as 'ye loveres', devotees of the
God of Love and expert assessors of love questions; reading or hearing the
poem constitutes them as insiders of the courtly game of love.[32] By the end,
they are urged to abandon love in favour of God:

> O yonge, fresshe folkes, he or she,
> In which that love up groweth with youre age,
> Repeyreth hom fro worldly vanyte,
> And of youre herte up casteth the visage
> To thilke God that after his ymage
> Yow made, and thynketh al nys but a faire
> This world, that passeth soone as floures faire,[33]

At the end of *Troilus*, the discourse of love has run out. The characters
fall silent: Criseyde recedes from view, Pandarus at last 'kan namoore seye',
Troilus goes wordlessly to his death, and the poem turns to God, leaving
its pagan characters behind.[34] Chaucer's Christian audience, however, has
the option of turning to other books, other writers and another discourse
of love.

For love of God has no limitations, and the most exciting and powerful medieval erotic texts are not concerned with human but devotional
love. Religious eros is late-medieval Europe's other great contribution
to erotic history; like courtly love, it fashions and tests the self, and like
courtly love, its pleasures are organised around the paradox of voluntary
subjection. 'Now wax I pale and wan / For luve of my lemman', sings
Richard Rolle, directing the courtly trope of the suffering lover to Jesus.[35]
Devotional writing explores heightened and intensified desires that test
the limits of selfhood, taking the lover of God through a process that, for
some, aims for dissolution of identity altogether, just as the river loses
itself in the sea.[36] Devotional eros produces collaborative, queering, gender-fluid counterpleasures, 'strategies of pleasure against the simple gratifi-
cations of desire', which a self-selected elite of God's lovers practised with
total commitment.[37]

Literature was just one element in devotional eroticism; writing might
stimulate devotional emotion, and also record it for the instruction of others. For Rolle, the Psalms were erotic literature, and singing them brought
about embodied multisensory rapture in which 'als wer loueynge I had
þinkand'.[38] Literature was written specifically to induce such affect. The

meditations of the Wooing Group, directed to anchoresses, were not only erotic writing but also 'erotic script[s] for the performance of feeling' that produce lived affect.[39] The end of 'The Wooing of Our Lord' emphasises the efficacy of the meditation, instructing the anchoress to perform it so that 'through his grace he will open your heart to his love, / and to pity for his pain'.[40] The anchoress, addressing her crucifix and speaking the refrain: 'Ah, Jesus, my sweet Jesus, grant that the love of you be all my pleasure', engages in performative action; she speaks her love for Jesus in order to produce that emotion.[41] Generating desire is the point of the exercise: the anchoress desires to desire, to love Him even more intensely than she does. An anchoress would have owned very few books, and so would have read and performed the same ones repeatedly, honing and improving her performance through her years of enclosure. So every occasion when the anchoress uses her book to perform her love for Christ refers to the whole sequence of such performances, building up continuities, repetitions and variations over a lifetime.

The literature of devotional eros enabled the construction of relationships between authors, readers and God, establishing a textual space in which devout men and women might share and encourage one another's emotions. Richard Misyn, translating Rolle's *Incendium Amoris* for 'Systere Margarete', explains that the purpose of the book is to generate love for God, and among its readers:

> Þerfore all redars here-of I pray, if ȝour discrecyon oȝt fynde þankeworthy, to god þerof gyf loueynge, & to þis holy man ... But parfyte lufe, what may þat be? certan, when þi god (as þe aght) for hym-self þou lufes, þi frende in god, and þin enmy þou lufes for god.[42]

The translation and dissemination of the text create an 'emotional community', in Barbara Rosenwein's phrase, united in its pursuit of the love of God.[43] Later readers would be interpellated into virtual community with Rolle, Misyn and Margaret. Texts enabled such communities to expand beyond their origins in time and space.

The fifteenth-century mystic Margery Kempe was one such disciple of Rolle at a distance. She had *Incendium Amoris* read to her, and her devotion included such distinctly Rollean features as 'ardowr of lofe' and envisioning Christ's wounded body as a 'duffehows' full of holes.[44] Membership of a textually mediated Rollean virtual emotional community gave Margery a respite from the material community of her daily life, her unsympathetic neighbours and demanding husband. In turn, her *Book* validated devotional erotic performance to its readers, such as the annotator who noted the likeness of Margery's 'ardowr' to that of the Carthusian mystic Richard Methley.[45] *The Book of Margery Kempe* offers a remarkably detailed account of the performance of devotional eros in the context of one woman's sexual history and will be the case study for the remainder of this chapter.

A highlight of the *Book*, and of Margery's life experience, was her pilgrimage to Jerusalem, where she took the standard tour, guided by Franciscan friars, around the Church of the Holy Sepulchre:

> Than the frerys lyftyd up a cros and led the pylgrimys abowte fro on place to another wher owyr Lord had sufferyd hys peynys and hys passyons, every man and woman beryng a wax candel in her hand. And the frerys alwey, as thei went abowte, teld hem what owyr Lord sufferyd in every place. And the forseyd creatur wept and sobbyd so plentyowsly as thow sche had seyn owyr Lord wyth hir bodyly ey sufferyng hys Passyon at that tyme. Befor hir in hyr sowle sche saw hym veryly be contemplacyon, and that cawsyd hir to have compassyon. And whan thei cam up on to the Mownt of Calvarye, sche fel down that sche mygth not stondyn ne knelyn, but walwyd and wrestyd wyth hir body, spredyng hir armes abrode, for in the cite of hir sowle sche saw verily and freschly how owyr Lord was crucifyed.[46]

Margery's performance of her love and grief for the suffering Christ is fed by her preparatory reading, the devotional art, drama and literature that have taught her to rehearse her emotional response to the image of the Crucifixion. The location offers a rich combination of stimuli: the material place acts as a portal to the eternal, its power no doubt intensified by the artworks lit by flickering candles. The friars' narration and participation in the procession following Christ's footsteps brings Margery a vision of Christ, which she then mirrors with her own body. Margery undergoes *com-passion*, suffering with Christ; spreading her arms to imitate the pose of crucifixion, she finds Christ within her, in the 'cite of hir sowle'. The performance generates further affects in the responses in those who view it, both at that moment and in the later repetitions. The analysis of the cryings in the text teaches its readers to recognise what a holy woman overcome by divine eros looks like, and perhaps to imitate those behaviours themselves.

These performances of love are centrally performances of pain. Margery writes that she is forced to cry out because she had 'so gret peyn to se owyr Lordys peyn' (p. 163). Lochrie argues for the prevalence of violence in devotional eros:

> Mystical sex is not just 'sex as we know it', but that more troubling field of experience that strays into the realms of violence, suffering, and torture ...

aggression, violence, masochism, and dark despair are as fundamental to the visions of some women mystics as the tropes of marriage and the languorous desire that we usually think of in connection to mystical sex.[47]

If, as Desmond argues, medieval eros is already characterised by 'erotic violence … the construction of subjectivities around gestures of dominance and submission, or the construction of desire and pleasure around violence, pain, or abuse', devotional eros might either challenge or intensify these pleasures of pain.[48] God's love might be imagined as a refuge from the violence of human sexual relationships: the *Letter on Virginity* advises women to commit to virginity rather than to suffer sexual abuse and domestic violence in marriage.[49] Yet the alternative lifestyle of the virgin has its own forms of suffering, in the asceticism of anchoritic life, in which 'My body hangs with your body, nailed on the cross, / enclosed securely within four walls'.[50] The Crucifixion was always at the centre of devotional eros, even for an often joyous mystic such as Rolle. Sharing Christ's suffering, as the anchoress does, is one facet of identification, but as sinners, devotees might also position themselves as responsible for that suffering. Elizabeth of Spalbeek's regular enactments of the Passion were exhibitions of self-harm that made her audience wonder 'how o persone maye booth smyte and soffre so many, soo swifte and heuy strokes'.[51] The rapture and self-annihilation of devotional love of God may be achieved through or experienced as violence and suffering.

Margery Kempe produces the spectacle of violent, compulsive eros when her body becomes the focal point of divine agency, and she is seen to be overwhelmed and acted upon. Margery's raptures stage her abandonment of bodily control:

> And therfor, whan sche knew that sche schulde cryen, sche kept it in for as long as sche mygth and dede al that sche cowde to withstond it er ellys to put it awey, til sche wex as blo as any leed, and evyr it chuld labowryn in hir mende mor and mor into the tyme that it broke owte. And whan the body myth ne lengar enduryn the gostly labowr, but was ovyrcome wyth the unspekabyl lofe that wrowt so fervently in the sowle, than fel sche down and cryed wondyr lowde. And the mor that sche wolde labowryn to kepe it in er to put it awey, mech the mor schulde sche cryen and the mor lowder. And thus sche dede in the Mownt of Calvarye, as it is wretyn beforn.[52]

The spectacle is of an uncannily animated puppet of greater forces; Margery is not alone in her body. The performance is the external testimony to Margery's internalisation of the crucifixion. She experiences the cryings as a struggle, which she will inevitably lose, against the unspeakable love rising within her; she gives up the boundaries of herself to this thing within her that is not her. The process is powered by mutually productive love and violence. Margery expounds on the image of Christ within that generates all this activity: 'hys precyows tendyr body – alto-rent and toryn wyth scorgys', and explains that her bodily movements are controlled by 'the fyer of lofe that brent so fervently in hir sowle'.[53] The violence done to Christ, suffered for love, prompts Margery's love, compassion and co-suffering, and is made visible in the violent motions of her body.

Margery Kempe's narratives of human and divine sexuality share patterns of compulsion and violence. Licit, marital sexuality is already understood within a framework of obligation and compulsion; the marital debt of mutual sexual obligation. While marriage might not always be experienced as such – Margery recalls the 'delectabyl thowtys, fleschly lustys, and inordinat lovys' of the early years of her marriage – marital obligation comes into play once Margery's desire to live in chastity disrupts the relationship.[54] Margery registers her sexual obligation to her husband John Kempe in horrific terms: 'sche had levar, hir thowt, etyn or drynkyn the wose, the mukke in the chanel, than to consentyn to any fleschly comownyng, saf only for obedyens … he usyd her as he had do befor, he wold not spar'.[55] The language shows visceral disgust at being subjected to the compulsions of marital sex, which is imagined as the penetration of her body's boundaries by disgusting foreign substances. Margery's love for Christ, by contrast, is marked by gentleness and mutual respect; indeed, it seems somewhat vanilla after the lurid extremes of revulsion and desire of her mundane sexual life. Confirming Margery's marriage to the Godhead, Christ says to her: 'thu mayst boldly take me in the armys of thi sowle and kyssen my mowth, myn hed and my fete as swetely as thow wylt'; the relationship could not be more different from the marital scenes of threat, humiliation and disgust that it replaces.[56] Christ returns agency to Margery, offering himself as an object at her disposal for her active desires and giving her, in contemporary terms, affirmative consent to let her desires run free.

While Christ's verbalised encounters with Margery remain affirmative and supportive, he continues to subject her to the involuntary cryings, exposing her to the 'schamys, despitys, scornys, and reprevys of the pepil' that he assures her he loves best.[57] The cryings align to a strand in the book that figures sexual compulsion as both sexy and compelling. Margery is tempted by the approaches of a neighbour who threatens that: 'he wold ly be hir and have hys lust of hys body, and sche schuld not wythstond hym, for yf he mygth not have hys wyl that tyme, he seyd, he schuld ellys have it another tyme, sche schuld not chese'.[58] Margery is not repulsed by this threatened sexual violence, but so thrilled that 'sche was labowrd wyth the other man for to syn wyth hym in-as-mech as he had spoke to hir. At the last … sche was ovyrcomyn and consentyd in hir mend'.[59] Human and divine eros work on her through very similar mechanisms. This incident describes the same psychological process as her account of resistance to the cryings of holy love, which 'labowryn in her mende', until she 'myth no lenger enduryn', 'but was ovyrcome wyth the unspekabyl lofe'.[60] In both instances, Margery is assailed by a powerful external force; her resistance to it only serves to intensify the surrender of body and will that climaxes the narrative. A later incident when Margery is assaulted with unwanted sexual visions repeats the pattern. She is already invaded, as images of men appear in the intimacy of her senses, as 'sche myth not enchewyn hem ne puttyn hem owt of hir syght, schewyng her bar membrys unto hir'; even more frightening is the prospect that she might respond to the threat of demonic compulsion by being, once more, overcome:

> Sche must nedys do hys byddyng, and yet wolde sche not a don it for alle this worlde. But yet hir thowt that it schulde be don, and hir thowt that thes horrybyl syghtys and cursyd mendys wer delectabyl to hir ageyn hir wille.[61]

In this instance, Christ, who has allowed the temptations, also protects her; the surrender never quite happens. But the pattern of desire is consistent: human, divine and demonic lovers all approach Margery with violent desires that provoke pleasures in her that she is unable to control.

Margery Kempe's account of her erotic life shows human and devotional eros to be mutually exclusive precisely because of their resemblance; both draw on compulsion and submission, but lead respectively to horror or rapture. Margery is a rare witness to the normal, but largely unarticulated, experience of married women. She mixed confidently with bishops and aristocrats, respected as 'John of Burnamys dowtyr of Lynne', but there was no trace of courtliness in her worldly relationships, which were governed by canonical and bourgeois expectations of marriage, or in her engagement with literature.[62] She is a witness who speaks powerfully of the discontents of human eros, and of the alternative possibilities that can be opened up by an attentive reader of the literature that teaches the love of God.

NOTES

1 Andrew Taylor, 'Reading the Dirty Bits', in *Desire and Discipline: Sex and Sexuality in the Premodern West*, eds. Jacqueline Murray and Konrad Eisenbichler (Toronto: University of Toronto Press, 1996), 280–95, 282, 284.

2 'Erotica', in *A Cultural History of Sexuality in the Middle Ages*, ed. Ruth Evans (Oxford: Berg, 2010), 181–212.

3 In *Medieval English Prose for Women from the Katherine Group and Ancrene Wisse*, eds. and trans. Bella Millett and Jocelyn Wogan-Browne (Oxford: Clarendon Press, 1990), 9.

4 *Medieval English Prose*, 37.
5 Jean Leclerq, *Monks and Love in Twelfth-Century France: Psychohistorical Essays* (Oxford: Clarendon Press, 1979), 100.
6 Karma Lochrie, *Heterosyncracies: Female Sexuality When Normal Wasn't* (Minneapolis: University of Minnesota Press, 2005), xiv; Ruth Mazo Karras, *Sexuality in Medieval Europe: Doing Unto Others* (New York: Routledge, 2005), 9.
7 Robert Allen Rouse and Cory James Rushton, 'Introduction', in *Sexual Culture in the Literature of Medieval Britain*, eds. Amanda Hopkins, Robert Allen Rouse and Cory James Rushton (Cambridge: D. S. Brewer, 2014), 1–12, 5.
8 Marilynn Desmond, *Ovid's Art and the Wife of Bath: The Ethics of Erotic Violence* (Ithaca, NY: Cornell University Press, 2006), 31.
9 *Encyclopaedia of Erotic Literature*, eds. Gaëtan Brulotte and John Phillips (New York: Routledge, 2006), x.
10 Mark Miller, 'Naturalism and Its Discontents in the Miller's Tale', *ELH*, 67.1 (2000): 1–44, 9.
11 'The Canterbury Tales', in *The Riverside Chaucer*, gen. ed. Larry D. Benson (Oxford: Oxford University Press, 1987), I.3653–54, I.3815.
12 The main exception being the poems of the women troubadours, the trobaritz, which may unsettle the gender positions of the tradition; Kathryn Gravdal, 'Mimicry, Metonymy, and "Women's Song": the Medieval Women Trobairitz', *Romanic Review*, 83.4 (November 1992): 411–28.
13 *Andreas Capellanus on Love*, ed. and trans. P. G. Walsh (London: Duckworth, 1982), 223.
14 *Andreas*, 117.
15 *Andreas*, 251–71, 283–85.
16 Jeffrey Jerome Cohen, 'Masoch/Lancelotism', *New Literary History*, 28 (1997): 231–60, 232.
17 Anita Phillips, *A Defence of Masochism* (London: Faber & Faber, 1998), 19.
18 Thomas Malory, *Complete Works*, ed. Eugène Vinaver (Oxford: Oxford University Press, 1971), 655; Chrétien de Troyes, *Arthurian Romances*, trans. William W. Kibler and Carleton W. Carroll (London: Penguin, 1991), 256.
19 Larry D. Benson, 'Courtly Love and Chivalry in the Later Middle Ages', in *Fifteenth-Century Studies: Recent Essays*, ed. Robert F. Yeager (Hamden: Archon Books, 1984), 239.
20 Richard Firth Green, *Poets and Princepleasers: Literature and the English Court in the Later Middle Ages* (Toronto: University of Toronto Press, 1980), 114.
21 Maurice Keen, *Chivalry* (New Haven: Yale University Press, 1984), 212–13.
22 Evelyn Birge Vitz, 'Erotic Reading in the Middle Ages: Performance and the Re-Performance of Romance', in *Performing Medieval Narrative*, eds. Nancy Freeman, Regalado Vitz and Marilyn Lawrence (Cambridge: Brewer, 2005), 73–88.
23 C. Stephen Jaeger, *Ennobling Love: In Search of a Lost Sensibility* (Philadelphia: University of Pennsylvania Press, 1999), 200.
24 Ilan Mitchell-Smith, 'The Double-Bind of Chivalric Sexuality in the Late-Medieval English Romance', in *Sexuality, Sociality and Cosmology in Medieval Literary Texts*, eds. Jennifer N. Brown and Marla Segol (New York: Palgrave Macmillan, 2013), 101–22, 104.

25 'Lanval', in *The Lais of Marie de France*, trans. Glyn S. Burgess and Keith Busby (London: Penguin, 1986), 73.

26 Emma Lipton, *Affections of the Mind: The Politics of Sacramental Marriage in Late Medieval English Literature* (Notre Dame: University of Notre Dame Press, 2007), 5.

27 *The Book of the Knight of the Tower*, trans. William Caxton, ed. M. Y. Offord, EETS ss 2 (London: Oxford University Press, 1971), 151.

28 *Knight of the Tower*, 112.

29 David Gary Shaw, *Necessary Conjunctions: The Social Self in Medieval England* (New York: Palgrave Macmillan, 2005).

30 *Troilus and Criseyde*, in *The Riverside Chaucer*, II.651–52.

31 *Troilus*, II.824–903.

32 *Troilus*, I.22.

33 *Troilus*, V.1835–41.

34 *Troilus*, V.1743.

35 Richard Rolle, 'A Song of Love for Jesus', in *Medieval English Lyrics: A Critical Anthology*, ed. R. T. Davies (London: Faber & Faber, 1963), ll. 31–32.

36 Margaret Porette, *The Mirror of Simple Souls*, trans. Edmund Colledge, J. C. Marler and Judith Grant (Notre Dame: University of Notre Dame Press, 1999), 107.

37 Karmen McKendrick, *Counterpleasures* (New York: State University of New York Press, 1999), 14.

38 Richard Rolle, *The Fire of Love*, trans. Richard Misyn, ed. Ralph Harvey, EETS os 106 (London: Kegan Paul, Trench, Trübner, 1896), 36.

39 Sarah McNamer, 'Feeling', in *Oxford Twenty-First Century Approaches to Literature: Middle English*, ed. Paul Strohm (Oxford: Oxford University Press, 2007), 241–57, 249.

40 *The Wooing of Our Lord and the Wooing Group Prayers*, ed. and trans. Catherine Innes-Parker (Ontario: Broadview, 2015), 111.

41 *Wooing of Our Lord*, 83.

42 Richard Rolle, *The Fire of Love*, 1.

43 Barbara H. Rosenwein, 'Worrying about Emotions in History', *The American Historical Review*, 107.3 (June 2002): 821–45, 842.

44 *The Book of Margery Kempe: Annotated Edition*, ed. Barry Windeatt (Cambridge: D. S. Brewer, 2004), 115, 97, 166.

45 *Margery Kempe*, 97.

46 *Margery Kempe*, 162–63.

47 Karma Lochrie, 'Mystical Acts, Queer Tendencies', in *Constructing Medieval Sexuality*, eds. Peggy McCracken, Lochrie and James A. Schultz (Minneapolis: University of Minnesota Press, 1997), 180–200, 182–83.

48 Desmond, *Ovid's Art*, 6.

49 *Medieval English Prose*, 29.

50 *Wooing of Our Lord*, 109.

51 Philip of Clairvaux, 'The Middle English Life of Elizabeth of Spalbeek', in *Three Women of Liège: A Critical Edition and Commentary on the Middle English Lives of Elizabeth of Spalbeek, Christina Mirabilis, and Marie d'Oignies*, ed. Jennifer N. Brown (Turnhout: Brepols, 2008), 37.

52 *Margery Kempe*, 165–66.

53 *Margery Kempe*, 166, 167.
54 *Margery Kempe*, 332.
55 *Margery Kempe*, 62–63.
56 *Margery Kempe*, 196.
57 *Margery Kempe*, 302.
58 *Margery Kempe*, 67–68.
59 *Margery Kempe*, 69.
60 *Margery Kempe*, 166.
61 *Margery Kempe*, 282.
62 *Margery Kempe*, 225.

4

ELIZABETH ROBERTSON

Can a Woman Rape a Man?

Rape and the Erotic in Shakespeare's 'The Rape of Lucrece' and 'Venus and Adonis'

It is generally accepted that rape is an act of violence, not of sexual desire, yet rape and sexual assault continue to be considered suitable subjects for erotica. In the 2003 legal definitions of sexual offences in Britain, rape is defined as penetration of one person by another against that person's will, and sexual assault as an event in which a person is caused to engage in sexual activity against his or her will. Absence of consent is thus foundational to the assessment of these sexual acts as crimes. Shakespeare's two long poems, 'Venus and Adonis' and 'The Rape of Lucrece' (published in 1593 and 1594, respectively), widely popular in their own time presumably because of their apparent erotic content (indeed, editor John Roe states that 'Venus and Adonis' 'has always been recognized as a leading example of the erotic narrative tradition'[1]), represent sex acts perpetrated against the will.

The poems raise the question of the degree to which erotic literature depends on the representation of an unequal distribution of power, since coercion figures prominently in both. In 'Venus and Adonis', a female goddess tries to assert her power over a young man; in 'The Rape of Lucrece', the barbarian Tarquin asserts his power over a helpless Lucrece. Both trace the progress of a wilful desire that overcomes reason. In 'Venus and Adonis' the act of sexual congress is lingered over in detail, whereas in 'The Rape of Lucrece' the violent sex act is described briefly and is devoid of pleasure for the perpetrator, the victim and even for the reader. Shakespeare's representation of rape exposes how sexuality of this kind is shaped by competition between men; furthermore, he challenges the ideology that demands that the female victim of rape commit suicide. 'Venus and Adonis', on the other hand, invites the reader to indulge in a feminised erotic desire presented as a force on a continuum with the often uncontrollable energies of a lush but capricious nature. In both poems, sexual pursuit ends in tragedy: one with the death of the male victim, who dies from the masculine ferocity of a boar; the other with the death, by her own hand, of the female victim of aggressive male desire.

In both poems, sexual excess is expressed through what some see as rhetorical excess; indeed, early critics dismissed the poems as immature technical displays that show Shakespeare learning, but not fully in control of, his craft. However, as we shall see, Shakespeare's use of form – rhyme royal in 'The Rape of Lucrece' (ababbcc) and sizains in 'Venus and Adonis' (ababcc) – as well as of rhetorical tropes – such as antithesis and apostrophe – contribute to his exploration of the relationship between uncontrollable erotic or sexual energies and the strengths and limits of the human will.

'The Rape of Lucrece'

I begin with 'The Rape of Lucrece' because the power dynamics that shape its representation of a sexual act are clearly delineated. Shakespeare's emphasis on the violence, aggression and homosocial desire that drive rape in this poem undermines its potential eroticism. Shakespeare bases his poem on Livy's *Ab Urbe Condita*, which recounts Lucrece's rape as part of the history of the founding of Rome.[2] Livy tells of the Roman Collatinus, who boasted about his wife's superior chastity to his soldiers, including Sextus Tarquinius, son of the ruling king. The men steal back to Collatium, where they observe the other wives passing the time in feasting but find Lucrece at home weaving. Inflamed by the sight of Lucrece, Tarquin returns a few days later to rape her. Overwhelmed by grief after the rape, she gathers her husband and other Romans around her and cries out for revenge before killing herself. Her suicide motivates the Romans to overthrow the barbarian Tarquins and to replace rulership by kings with a republican form of government, ruled by consuls.[3]

Shakespeare makes several significant changes to Livy's text, many of which have been seen as simply offering him opportunities to show off his budding rhetorical prowess. He infuses the poem with antitheses and expands the Livy plot to include two extended soliloquies: one in which Tarquin experiences a struggle between reason and will as he debates whether or not he should rape Lucrece, and another in which Lucrece laments her rape and then decides to kill herself.

Shakespeare's interest in showing off his skill in rhetoric is certainly evident in these additions, but his rhetorical experiments are also crucial to his investigation of the relationship between sex and power that is only partially expressed in Livy's version of the story. His elaborate rhetoric is not simply ornamental, however, but rather serves his larger themes. For example, the phrase Shakespeare uses to describe Tarquin at the moment after he rapes Lucrece – 'A captive victor who hath lost in gain' – epitomises the quintessential link between structures of sexuality and power, for Tarquin's personal victory inevitably leads to his public ruin.[4] Joel Fineman argues that antithesis in the poem is an 'expression of an eros whose contrapposto energy, the resistance to resistance, simulates the action of a rape'.[5] Antithesis does indeed create tension – and especially so in 'Venus and Adonis' – but the primary function of the antithesis throughout this poem is not to intensify the eros of approach and resistance but rather, as Heather Dubrow puts it, to act as 'a linguistic analogue to the competitiveness that ... is the primary characteristic of the world Shakespeare evokes'.[6]

Shakespeare's first change to Livy, as Coppelia Kahn and others have astutely noted, brings to the fore the link between rape and homosocial competition between men at war: whereas in Livy the sight of Lucrece motivates Tarquin to rape her, in Shakespeare it is Collatinus's report of her superior chastity that incites him.[7] Lucrece's status as an object prized by men is developed throughout the poem. Described by metaphors of jewels, wealth or treasure, she is Collatine's most valued possession:

> For he [Collatine] the night before, in Tarquin's tent,
> Unlock'd the treasure of his happy state;
> What priceless wealth the heavens had him lent
> In the possession of his beauteous mate. (15–18)

Throughout the poem, Shakespeare makes use of the rhyme royal stanzaic form to reinforce his themes; here, it is Lucrece's status as an object that serves Collatine's position in patriarchy (Collatine loans his mate to Tarquin in his 'tent'; her spousal status as a 'mate' determines his and the community's 'state'). She is 'that rich jewel he should keep unknown / from thievish ears because it is his own' (34–5). In this line, the wife's name is withheld until her status as Collatine's property is established: Tarquin 'lurks to aspire / And girdle with embracing flames the waist / Of Collatine's fair love, Lucrece the chaste' (5–7).

Even Lucrece's dead body incites rivalry between men, as we see at the end of the poem when her husband and father quarrel over who should claim her body:

> Then son and father weep with equal strife
> Who should weep most, for daughter or for wife.
>
> The one doth call her his, the other his;
> Yet neither may possess the claim they lay.
> The father says 'She's mine.' 'O, mine she is,'
> Replies her husband ...

'My daughter' and 'my wife' with clamours fill'd
The dispersed air, who, holding Lucrece' life,
Answer'd their cries, 'my daughter' and 'my wife'. (1791–7; 1804–6)

Women's bodies, far from sites of erotic desire, are – whether alive or dead – possessions to be fought over by men.

The poem devotes surprisingly little time to the rape itself. Much of the beginning focuses its attention on Tarquin's self-doubts, and the last two-thirds to Lucrece's decision-making process after the rape. The vast majority of the description of the sexual encounter focuses on Lucrece's verbal attempts to dissuade Tarquin from raping her. The sexual act occupies no more than two stanzas and penetration only a few lines; a description that might be described as erotic, if not pornographic: 'the Wolf hath seized his prey, the poor lamb cries / Till with her own white fleece her voice controlled / Entombs her outcry in her lips' sweet fold' (677–9). The passage links the lips of the mouth to the lips of the vagina, and the fold simultaneously evokes the sheepfold and labial folds.[8] The next stanza makes it clear that, in this rather obscure passage, Tarquin muffles Lucrece's cries with her nightdress. In its invitation to the reader to draw close to the most intimate part of Lucrece's body, this passage is among the very few that might be called erotic. The body here seems separated from the mind or will – a division that particularly worries Christian commentators such as Augustine and Abelard.[9] Here, as in 'Venus and Adonis', Shakespeare focuses on the lips as particularly erogenous, and the image momentarily affords the reader an opportunity for imaginative expansion. However, the proleptic metaphor of death (which anticipates Lucrece's suicide) in the verb *entomb* forecloses that imaginative possibility, despite its play on the renaissance pun for sexual climax. The erotic potential is further eclipsed by the brutal image of the wolf devouring the lamb.

Given that critics such as Fineman view resistance as an aspect of the erotic, Tarquin's stealthy approach to Lucrece might also be described as erotic. But Shakespeare so infuses the narrative of his approach with martial imagery that the erotic is subsumed in the poem's larger lesson that rape is ultimately not only a violation of a person, a household and a city, but also of the state itself.[10] The poem maps Lucrece's body onto an invaded household and then onto a city under siege: 'The locks between her chamber and his will, / Each one by him enforced, retires his ward' (301–2). Then:

His hand, that yet remains upon her breast,–
Rude ram, to batter such an ivory wall!–
May feel her heart-poor citizen!–distress'd,
Wounding itself to death, rise up and fall,

> Beating her bulk, that his hand shakes withal.
> This moves in him more rage and lesser pity,
> To make the breach and enter this sweet city. (462–8)

Lucrece herself describes her rape as a disruption of the house:

> Her house is sack'd, her quiet interrupted,
> Her mansion batter'd by the enemy;
> Her sacred temple spotted, spoil'd, corrupted. (1170–2)

And as the siege of a city:

> She says, her subjects with foul insurrection
> Have batter'd down her consecrated wall. (722–3)

The inviolability of Lucrece's body stands for the integrity of the household, the city and the state; however, state might be defined in this period.

In both Shakespeare and Livy, Lucrece's rape and suicide provide the motivation for war in which the Romans succeed in banishing the Tarquins and replacing rulership by kings with that by consuls – a republic ruled by consent. That Lucrece's suicide motivates imperialist aggression is captured in the fifteenth-century painting by Botticelli, 'The Rape of Lucrece', which marginalises the rape of Lucrece to one edge of the painting and places at centre her corpse on a bier surrounded by soldiers. Rape, then, is not an erotic act of lust but rather a political act.

Shakespeare's second major change to Livy – the addition of two apparent digressions – shows that, far from being interested in the erotic, the poem is more involved in exploring the place of men and women in patriarchal cultures dominated by male hierarchies of honour. In a long preamble to the rape that dissipates his lustful advance, Tarquin resists the destruction of his honour that will inevitably ensue. Lucrece's long lament for her rape and her failure to find a means to escape its inevitable consequence in her suicide exposes the brutality of the pagan patriarchal system in which she resides; a system in which the potential eroticism of rape – the wolf's ravenous attack on the innocent quivering lamb – depends on the subordination of her subjectivity to her role as a patriarchal wife.

Lucrece's soliloquy allows Shakespeare to explore the potential for women to escape their objectification under patriarchal culture by probing the possible freedom from that objectification afforded by Christian ideology. In the Roman pagan tradition, suicide was seen as a noble act; one that is consonant with an honour and shame culture. In a crucial passage in *The City of God* that challenges that ideology on the basis that all individuals – male or female – have inviolate souls, Augustine raises the question of whether or not women should commit suicide if they have been raped, and concludes:

> We must rather draw the inference that just as bodily chastity is lost when mental chastity has been violated, so bodily chastity is not lost even when the body has been ravished, while the mind's chastity endures. Therefore, when a woman has been ravished without her consenting, and forced by another man's sin, she has no reason to punish herself by a voluntary death.[11]

Shakespeare leaves open the possibility that in order to protect her husband's honour, Lucrece consents – though under coercion. Augustine makes clear, however, that such consent is ultimately indiscernible to anyone but God, and that only God can judge her. Lucrece's discernible guilt, from Augustine's point of view, was in violating her soul by committing suicide. On the basis that both men and women equally possess inviolate souls, Augustine's argument powerfully argues against a pagan patriarchal ideology that produces rape and requires suicide.

Shakespeare recalls this Christian Augustinian position when Lucrece expresses the war between her body and her soul:

> 'To kill myself,' quoth she, 'alack, what were it,
> But with my body my poor soul's pollution?
> They that lose half with greater patience bear it
> Than they whose whole is swallow'd in confusion.
>
> . . . .
>
> 'My body or my soul, which was the dearer,
> When the one pure, the other made divine?
> Whose love of either to myself was nearer,
> When both were kept for heaven and Collatine? (1156–9; 1163–6)

Lucrece here considers the possibility that her soul is inviolate in an Augustinian sense, but ultimately her intuition of that inviolability is bound up with her competing understanding of her self – body and soul – as ultimately belonging to Collatine.

In her three apostrophes to Night, Opportunity and Time, Lucrece explores her potential to escape the pagan patriarchal definitions that so constrain her. Failing to locate fault in the patriarchal system she herself upholds, she at first blames night, opportunity and time for her rape, before finally accusing herself. In Lucrece's lament, we witness the fact that the very act that denies her subjectivity – rape – paradoxically gives her a hitherto unknown potential as a free agent. She asserts, 'I am the mistress of my fate' (1069), and considers potential courses of action she could take other than suicide. Although the agency she demonstrates ultimately becomes self-destructive, Shakespeare momentarily presents her as a choosing subject. At the beginning of the poem, Lucrece is described as a possession, a precious jewel, a treasure; during the rape, she is presented as a passive victim of Tarquin's desire; it is only after she is raped that she is dislodged from her patriarchal identity. No longer a valued possession of her husband, she is damaged goods; yet in that state she discovers she is an agent in control of her fate and one with the potential to choose alternative identities. Within patriarchal ideology, however, there is only one solution to her newly unstable subject position, and that is for her to become an object again in death.[12]

We see Lucrece's internalisation of such self-destructive patriarchal precepts in her contemplation of a painting of Troy:

> At last she calls to mind where hangs a piece
> Of skilful painting, made for Priam's Troy:
> Before the which is drawn the power of Greece.
> For Helen's rape the city to destroy ... (1366–9)

One would think that Lucrece would identify with the woman who has been raped, Helen, but she dismisses her as a whore:

> Show me the strumpet that began this stir,
> That with my nails her beauty I may tear.
> Thy heat of lust, fond Paris, did incur
> This load of wrath that burning Troy doth bear:
> Thy eye kindled the fire that burneth here. (1471–5)

Instead, it is Hecuba – the prop of the patriarch, Priam – with whom she identifies:

> To this well-painted piece is Lucrece come,
> To find a face where all distress is stell'd.
> Many she sees where cares have carved some,
> But none where all distress and dolour dwell'd,
> Till she despairing Hecuba beheld ...
>
> . . . .
>
> In her the painter had anatomized
> Time's ruin, beauty's wreck, and grim care's reign...
>
> . . . .
>
> On this sad shadow Lucrece spends her eyes,
> And shapes her sorrow to the beldam's woes. (1443–51; 1457–8)

Subsumed by grief at the death of her husband, Hecuba – like Lucrece – embodies the ruins of an invaded city. Although Helen had been subject to competition between men, her abduction leaves open the degree to which she consented to that abduction, and it is this potential desiring agency – an agency that allows Helen to be the subject as well as the object of erotic desire – that Lucrece rejects. Lucrece condemns both Paris and Helen for pursuing private pleasures as she laments, 'Why should the private pleasure of some one / Become the public plague of many more?' (1479–80). Ultimately, Lucrece redescribes herself as a patriarchal daughter who identifies her body as having only public identity, and as a besieged city whose breach can only be healed through her suicide.

In conclusion, the erotic in 'The Rape of Lucrece' is displaced by a study of what it means to rape: what motivates it – competition between men – and what its consequences are – suicide and imperialist war. In his representation of Lucrece's attempts to find an agency outside of patriarchy, Shakespeare considers but rejects an alternative identity for Lucrece, which might have emerged had he fully embraced Augustine's argument that women have souls to protect above everything else (even above the claims of patriarchy) – a position that firmly rejects suicide as an adequate response to rape. A less self-destructive agency – one that would allow Lucrece to enact her own desires rather than those of others – might have yielded her own eros. It would take Mary Wollstonecraft to discover in the Christian idea that women, like men, have inviolate souls – a feminist ideology that would challenge patriarchy's description of women as nothing but possessions of men.[13] But given the recurring fact of female suicide after rape, we have yet to find a way to assert Augustine's powerful insight that suicide should not be the inevitable consequence of rape, or Shakespeare's insight that there is little or no eros to be found in an act of rape or its representation.

'Venus and Adonis'

Unlike 'The Rape of Lucrece', in which a violent masculine sexuality inflamed by female resistance and homosocial competition undermines the erotic aspects of the sexual encounter described in the poem, in 'Venus and Adonis' a nourishing but smothering feminine sexuality, contrasted with a destructive hypermasculine one, shapes the poem's eroticism. The erotic energies of the poem – both male and female – are bound up with (and perhaps subsumed by) those of nature, which is presented as at once lush and nutritive and rapacious and destructive. While to some extent the erotic is closely aligned with the instinctive sexual drives observable in nature, it is actually distinct from nature's drives because of the activity of the will in both the human and the divine. Although the reader is invited to relish in the eroticism associated with nature, the human and the divine, in the end the poem's representation of the dire consequences of two gendered extremes of sexuality – that of Venus and that of the boar – undermines its eroticism.

It is difficult to pin down a primary meaning of the poem. As William Keach writes in his paradigmatic essay:

> the elusive complexity of the poem's formal order defeats all our attempts to reduce the poem's meaning to complete conceptual clarity even as it guides, teases, and compels us to think coherently about the ambivalence of sexual experience ... its intricate artificiality and its disturbingly persistent wit, both clarifies and complicates the closely entwined conflicting relationship of the two main figures.[14]

Keach admires the poem's vitality and argues that its energies – divine, human and natural – in tension with one another are its subject. These conflicting energies are further enhanced by Shakespeare's exuberant rhetorical displays. Despite the fact that nature and sexuality are so intertwined in the poem, the poem asks us to tease out the relationships between gendered sexuality and power that are expressed within its natural matrix.

Shakespeare bases his poem on a short narrative in Book X of Ovid's 'Metamorphoses' that is interpolated within a more extended account of Orpheus. The fact that Adonis' story is framed by that of Orpheus – a figure who stands for the artist and who exhibits a fluid sexual identity as he moves from uxoriousness to homosexuality – may suggest that Adonis's sexuality is meant to be understood as similarly complex. Shakespeare's version of Ovid's story both expands and significantly alters the power relations between Venus and Adonis. Ovid's Venus, unlike Shakespeare's, chooses to leave her heavenly realm to haunt an earthly one and roams and hunts as an equal with Adonis. Shakespeare represents Adonis not as a man but as a boy who petulantly resists Venus' advances. As Keach points out, Shakespeare may have been influenced to represent Adonis as a reluctant lover by his sight of Titian's sixteenth-century painting (or copies of it) in which Adonis dramatically tries to tear himself away from an importuning Venus.[15] Alternatively, Shakespeare may have pieced together his image of a reluctant lover from the many examples of them presented elsewhere in Ovid.[16] Aggressive, temperamental and coercive, Shakespeare's Venus is driven by a lustful desire for union with Adonis that she cannot fulfil. Adonis is equally driven by desire, but only to hunt. In Ovid's version there is no suggestion that the two are not lovers. Whereas in Ovid nature is a backdrop for their meeting, in Shakespeare's version character is defined by and in contrast to nature.

Shakespeare uses a variety of rhetorical features – especially antithesis, hyperbole and chiasmus – to reinforce the ways in which the battle of wills between Venus and Adonis reflects, but also conflicts with, nature. The very first stanza of the poem sets such rhetorical play in motion:

> Even as the sun with purple-colour'd face
> Had ta'en his last leave of the weeping morn,
> Rose-cheek'd Adonis hied him to the chase;
> Hunting he loved, but love he laugh'd to scorn;
> Sick-thoughted Venus makes amain unto him,
> And like a bold-faced suitor 'gins to woo him.(1–6)

Shakespeare moves quickly here from a personification of the sun leaving an abject morning to a representation of Adonis, whose rosy cheeks seem to emerge directly from the sun itself; at the same time, Adonis' human desires distinguish him sharply from nature, as captured in the chiasmus that sets his desire to hunt against both nature and Venus. Throughout the poem, Shakespeare reinforces the excesses of Venus' wilful pursuit of Adonis through the use of hyperbole. She offers Adonis 'A thousand honey secrets' (16), and in this stanza (drawing from Catullus Carmen V) seeks a 'thousand kisses' (516). Furthermore, the poem is permeated with antitheses, conveyed especially through Shakespeare's use of chiasmus. Antithesis, as Roe points out, is not simply rhetorical ornamentation, for it serves to create in the poetry itself the tension between Venus and Adonis.[17] Such tensions are enhanced by the contrasts produced by the form of the stanzas themselves. The ababcc structure of the sizains allows for alternation followed by close comparison or contrast in the last couplet. Rhythm, syntax and line endings further reinforce the poem's expression of antithetical conflict.

'Venus and Adonis' thus reverses the power hierarchy between the genders that appears in *The Rape of Lucrece*. In the latter poem, the aggressive male forces himself upon the powerless female; in 'Venus and Adonis', Venus, whose feminine power is enhanced by her divinity, is the aggressor. The reversal of gender positions, however, still produces gender asymmetries. In one poem, the pursued (Lucrece) cannot repel the advances of her male aggressor, whereas in the other poem the pursued (Adonis) successfully eludes her aggressor. Despite her power, the female aggressor, Venus, is unable to bend Adonis to her will. In addition, whereas in 'The Rape of Lucrece' male aggression is linked with (or indeed originates from) male homosocial competition, Venus' power in 'Venus and Adonis' has no such support from female allies; rather, her power is both aligned with and limited by the forces of nature.

The forces of nature with which Venus is associated are, on the whole, benign. Like the fairies of A *Midsummer Night's Dream*, she is one with the flowers:

> Bid me discourse, I will enchant thine ear,
> Or, like a fairy, trip upon the green,
> Or, like a nymph, with long dishevell'd hair,
> Dance on the sands, and yet no footing seen:
> Love is a spirit all compact of fire,
> Not gross to sink, but light, and will aspire.
>
> Witness this primrose bank whereon I lie;
> These forceless flowers like sturdy trees support me;
> Two strengthless doves will draw me through the sky,
> From morn till night, even where I list to sport me. (145–54)

Venus' command of nature anticipates another Shakespearean divinity (again from A *Midsummer Night's Dream*): Titania, who also forces her desire on a mortal. Venus' moods vary like the weather as she alternates between gentle entreaty and blasts of frustrated rage. There are times, however, when her power – like nature's – becomes rapacious:

> Now quick desire hath caught the yielding prey,
> And glutton-like she feeds, yet never filleth;
> Her lips are conquerors, his lips obey,
> Paying what ransom the insulter willeth;
> Whose vulture thought doth pitch the price so high,
> That she will draw his lips' rich treasure dry. (547–52)

Venus bears down on Adonis like a vulture.

Venus' eroticism, however, seems predominantly consonant with the benign forces of nature. In perhaps the most erotic passage in the poem, she asks Adonis to behave as a deer in her park:

> 'Fondling,' she saith, 'since I have hemm'd thee here
> Within the circuit of this ivory pale,
> I'll be a park, and thou shalt be my deer;
> Feed where thou wilt, on mountain or in dale:
> Graze on my lips; and if those hills be dry,
> Stray lower, where the pleasant fountains lie.
>
> Within this limit is relief enough,
> Sweet bottom-grass and high delightful plain,
> Round rising hillocks, brakes obscure and rough,
> To shelter thee from tempest and from rain
> Then be my deer, since I am such a park;
> No dog shall rouse thee, though a thousand bark. (229–40)

Whereas 'The Rape of Lucrece' offers only a single brief moment with erotic potential (in the image of Lucrece's lips), here the poet lingers as he invites the reader to stray with Adonis from the facial lips to the labial lips. The focus on the lips recalls the many other instances of kisses in the poem that enhance the poem's eroticism, as in this passage:

> Pure lips, sweet seals in my soft lips imprinted,
> What bargains may I make, still to be sealing?
> To sell myself I can be well contented,
> So thou wilt buy and pay and use good dealing;
> Which purchase if thou make, for fear of slips
> Set thy seal-manual on my wax-red lips. (511–15)

In her invitation to Adonis to be his park, Venus offers a sexual encounter that is both expansive and nourishing in a place that offers protection and shelter. The opening and last lines qualify this expansiveness, however; Adonis is hemmed in, and the thousand dog barks ominously evoke not only the dogs with which Adonis likes to hunt (as critics have observed) but also the dogs that pull Acteon apart for similarly transgressing on a goddess' private sexuality.[18]

Unlike Venus, who seems to emerge from nature, Adonis seeks to rise above nature in wishing to control and tame it. In Shakespeare's famous description of the encounter between a mare and Adonis' stallion, Shakespeare paints a picture of sexual desire that is almost human in its lusty energy:

> But, lo, from forth a copse that neighbors by,
> A breeding jennet, lusty, young and proud,
> Adonis' trampling courser doth espy,
> And forth she rushes, snorts and neighs aloud:
> The strong-neck'd steed, being tied unto a tree,
> Breaketh his rein, and to her straight goes he. (259–64)

The horse, like Venus, is overwhelmed with sexual desire, but unlike both Venus and Adonis, his energetic desire is purely instinctual. Not yet a man, Adonis is unable to catch his horse and force him to submit to his control:

> His testy master goeth about to take him;
> When, lo, the unback'd breeder, full of fear,
> Jealous of catching, swiftly doth forsake him,
> With her the horse, and left Adonis there. (318–21)

His desire, however, is to take control of nature as a hunter. The desires of the divine and the human are ultimately governed not by instinct but by the will. Venus obsessively desires only to bend Adonis' will to her own, but Adonis wills only to hunt.

The boar overcomes Adonis' desire to conquer nature. Like Adonis' horse, the boar is described in highly sexualised terms. When Venus comes across the boar, he appears as one who has violated a virgin with a 'frothy mouth, bepainted all with red, / Like milk and blood being mingled both together' (900–2), and Adonis' death is presented as if it were a rape:

> Tis true, 'tis true; thus was Adonis slain:
> He ran upon the boar with his sharp spear,
> Who did not whet his teeth at him again,
> But by a kiss thought to persuade him there;
> And nuzzling in his flank, the loving swine
> Sheathed unaware the tusk in his soft groin. (1,111–16)

This encounter exudes homoerotic overtones, as Richard Rambuss and others have observed.[19] Adonis's rejection of Venus raises questions about his sexual inclinations, since to reject the advances of the goddess of love seems inexplicable; as the poet puts it, 'she's love, she loves, and yet she is not loved' (610). Venus views that rejection as unnatural: 'Thou wast begot, to beget is thy duty ... by law of nature thou art bound to breed, / That thine may live when thou thyself are dead' (168; 171–2). Rambuss convincingly argues that Adonis rejects Venus not because he is unnatural, but rather because his desire is relentlessly anti-heterosexual. As Rambuss points out, Adonis far prefers the company of his fellow male hunters to that of Venus; he wants nothing more than to hunt the boar, an animal who is described in erotic, hypermasculine terms. Adonis' phallic substitute, the javelin, is inadequate in comparison to that of the boar's tusk; Venus warns Adonis:

> thou know'st not what it is
> With javelin's point a churlish swine to gore,
> Whose tushes never sheathed he whetteth still,
> Like to a mortal butcher bent to kill (615–18)

Rambuss points out that Venus describes Adonis as – like the 'master-mistress of his passion' that Shakespeare praises in *Sonnet 20* – 'lovelier than a man', and remarks: 'Thou art no man though of a man's complexion' (215).

Although Adonis' death suggests a homoerotic encounter, an important aspect of Shakespeare's representation of Adonis undermines the reader's ability to identify him clearly with homosexual desires: his boyishness. Rambuss underdevelops the insight to which the title of his essay, 'What It Feels Like for a Boy', refers. However much Adonis wishes to participate in the hypermasculinised world of the boar, he is not adult enough to do so. As Venus herself admits, he has yet to reach maturity: 'the tender spring upon thy tempting lip / shows thee unripe' (126–7). He is small enough to be picked up and tucked under Venus' arm, as we see in a passage that tips the poem from Petrarchan lyricism into the realm of farce:

> desire doth lend her force
> Courageously to pluck him from his horse.
>
> Over one arm the lusty courser's rein,
> Under her other was the tender boy,
> Who blush'd and pouted in a dull disdain.(29–33)

As a boy, he accepts Venus' kisses and sometimes even returns them; however, his are not sexualised kisses but rather those of a cossetted child. Adonis himself asserts his childishness as an excuse to resist Venus' advances: '"Fair queen," quoth he, "if any love you owe me, / Measure my strangeness with my unripe years"' (523–4).

If the boar represents a hypermasculinised eroticism, it could be argued that Venus offers a hyperfeminised – if not suffocating – maternal form of eroticism. We have already seen that Venus treats Adonis as a boy and speaks to him as a child in terms such as 'fondling' (229). To Adonis, she promises to 'smother thee with kisses' (18). Her maternal instincts come to the fore when she hears the sounds of the boar hunt and rushes to Adonis: 'Like a milch doe whose swelling dugs do ache, / Hasting to feed her fawn, hid in some brake' (875–6). Although she offers him a luxuriant deer park, that invitation emerges only after she has constrained him by her milky white maternal arm. Even when she is underneath him in a sexual encounter, it is he rather than she who is overwhelmed; he complains: '"Fie, fie," he says, "you crush me; let me go; / You have no reason to withhold me so"' (611–12). Although Venus is generally associated with a luxuriant form of nature, her erotic energies can quickly become dangerous – as discussed earlier, when Adonis' kiss turns Venus from an eagle to a vulture. The potentially dangerous hyperfeminine realm into which she invites Adonis is contrasted with the hypermasculine realm of the boar. The very idea of the boar only increases Venus' desire to restrain Adonis. Yet, like the boar she can be equally violent. Venus recognises the affinity between her own sexual aggression and that of the boar: 'Had I been tooth'd like him, I must confess, / with kissing him I should have kill'd him first'(117–18).

One might view this representation of feminine sexuality – along with all the comic scenes of Venus' clumsy and outsized love – as misogynistic.[20] Yet perhaps the main fault of her love is not in its inept smothering qualities but rather in the imbalance it represents. The infinite but constrained sexuality offered by Venus in images such as that of the deer park recall the womb, and as such are a regressive and abject form of eros. Neither the phallic realm of the symbolic nor the abject realm of the semiotic in themselves offer a non-destructive form of sexuality. The poem structurally falls into two parts: the wooing and the hunt – or as Don Cameron Allen puts it, the 'soft hunt' of love and 'the hard hunt' for the boar[21] – a structure that emphasises the contrast in the poem between one kind of erotic desire that is smothering, maternal and feminine and another that is aggressive, violent and homoerotic.

However threatening this semiotic form of the erotic might be, it is as deadly as the hypermasculine sexuality of the boar or the relentless aggressive sexuality of Tarquin. Like Tarquin, Venus attempts to force Adonis into a sexual congress against his will. The boar's sexualised penetration of Adonis is contrasted with Venus' attempts to seduce Adonis, and the scenes of Venus' near success raise the question of whether or not an unwilling man can be raped by a woman. A feminised young man can be raped by a masculinized, aggressive boar, but it is not clear that Adonis can be raped by Venus. Venus forces herself on Adonis physically – but he obdurately refuses her advances until she faints, and he kisses her in order to awaken her. Shakespeare treads carefully here, suggesting that desire is awakened in Adonis but that it is short-lived; he is not physically able to consummate their love, and never consents to it:

> Hot, faint, and weary, with her hard embracing,
>
>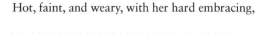
>
> He now obeys, and now no more resisteth,
> While she takes all she can, not all she listeth. (559; 563–4)

When she learns that he means to hunt the boar, she attacks him in a frenzy of passion – but even then cannot overcome his emotional and physical reluctance:

> 'The boar!' quoth she; whereat a sudden pale,
> Like lawn being spread upon the blushing rose,
> Usurps her cheek; she trembles at his tale,
> And on his neck her yoking arms she throws:
> She sinketh down, still hanging by his neck,
> He on her belly falls, she on her back.
>
> Now is she in the very lists of love,
> Her champion mounted for the hot encounter:
> All is imaginary she doth prove,

> He will not manage her, although he mount her;
> That worse than Tantalus' is her annoy,
> To clip Elysium and to lack her joy. (589–600)

She attempts to achieve her desires, but fails:

> The warm effects which she in him finds missing
> She seeks to kindle with continual kissing.

> But all in vain; good queen, it will not be:
> She hath assay'd as much as may be proved;
> Her pleading hath deserved a greater fee;
> She's Love, she loves, and yet she is not loved. (605–10)

The boar, however, succeeds where Venus fails. How are we to read these contrasting highly erotic scenes? At the very least, we can conclude that aggressive masculinised, as well as hyperfeminized, force – whether from humans, goddesses or wild nature – stands in the way of the erotic.

The two poems, then, present sexual acts against the will, and both raise the question of whether or not such force ultimately undermines the erotic potential of the representations of such acts. In 'The Rape of Lucrece', the brutality of the act and its emergence from homosocial competition subsume any potential erotic pleasure that might be evoked by its representation. In 'Venus and Adonis', sexual desire is consonant with the instinctual and the natural, but ultimately the activities of the will separate human and divine sexuality from that of animals. In both poems, however much a woman tries to force herself on a man, rape is a masculine act – that of the swine with a tusk.[22]

NOTES

1 John Roe, ed., *The Poems: 'Venus and Adonis', 'The Rape of Lucrece', 'The Phoenix and the Turtle', 'The Passionate Pilgrim', 'A Lover's Complaint'* (Cambridge: Cambridge University Press, 1992), 3, line 730.
2 Stephanie Jed argues that Lucrece's suicide leads to the foundation of both a republic and humanism; see her *Chaste Thinking: The Rape of Lucretia and the Birth of Humanism* (Bloomington, IN: Indiana University Press, 1989).
3 Titus Livius (Livy), *Ab Urbe Condita (The History of Rome)*, eds. H. E. Gould and J. L. Whiteley (London: Macmillan & Co Ltd, 1964), Book I, section 58, 90–1.
4 William Shakespeare, 'The Rape of Lucrece', in John Roe, ed., *The Poems*, (Cambridge : Cambridge University Press, 2006) line 730. All further citations from 'The Rape of Lucrece' or 'Venus and Adonis' will be taken from this edition and line numbers will be provided within parentheses in the text.
5 Cited in Coppelia Kahn, 'Publishing Shame, "The Rape of Lucrece"', in *A Companion to Shakespeare's Works: The Poems, Problem Comedies, Late Plays*, eds. Richard Dutton and Jean E. Howard (Oxford: Blackwell Publishing, 2003), 263.

6 Heather Dubrow, cited in Kahn, 'Publishing Shame', p. 263.
7 Coppelia Kahn, 'The Rape in Shakespeare's Lucrece', *Shakespeare Studies* 9 (1976), 52, but see the entire discussion 45–72.
8 As pointed out by Roe in his note to line 679, p. 176.
9 See Peter Abelard, *Ethics*, in *Ethical Writing*, trans. Paul Vincent Spade (Cambridge: Hackett Publishing, 1995), Book 1, 2–15; and Augustine, *The City of God: Concerning the City of Gods Against the Pagans,* trans. Henry Bettenson (London: Penguin Classics, 1972), Book 1, 26–32.
10 For a discussion of the anthropological history of the relationship between the body and state, see Linda Woodbridge, *Palisading the Elizabethan Body Politic, in Texas Studies in Literature and Language* 33, 3 (1991), 327–54.
11 Augustine, *City of God*, Book 1, 28.
12 I discuss this paradox more fully in my essay 'Public Bodies and Psychic Domains: Rape, Consent and Female Subjectivity in Geoffrey Chaucer's "Troilus and Criseyde"', in Elizabeth Robertson and Christine M. Rose, eds., *Representing Rape in Medieval and Early Modern Literature* (New York: Palgrave, 2001), 281–310, especially in my discussion of the Lucrece legend, 283–8. My discussion of Lucrece's contemplation of the Troy painting here closely follows the language of my previous analysis.
13 Mary Wollstonecraft, *A Vindication of the Rights of Women* (London: Penguin, 1975; rpt. 2004).
14 William Keach, 'Venus and Adonis', in his *Elizabethan Erotic Narratives: Irony and Pathos in the Ovidian Poetry of Shakespeare, Marlowe and Their Contemporaries* (Rutgers: Rutgers University Press, 1977), 52–84; 84.
15 See Keach, 55. My reading of 'Venus and Adonis' is indebted to William Keach's sensitive and illuminating chapter.
16 Keach, 56, suggests Hermaphroditus, Narcissus and Hippolytus as Ovidian examples of 'supremely beautiful young men full of self-love and self-ignorance who come to tragic ends when they refuse to acknowledge the power of sexual love'. I do not agree that Adonis refuses the power of sexual love, because in my argument he is not yet old enough to make sexual choices – whether heterosexual or homosexual.
17 See Roe, 4.
18 See Roe, note to line 240, 92.
19 Richard Rambuss, 'What it Feels like For a Boy: Shakespeare's "Venus and Adonis"', in Dutton and Howard, *A Companion*, 240–58.
20 See the discussion by Richard Halpern, '"Pining their maws": Female Readers and the Erotic Ontology of the Text in Shakespeare's "Venus and Adonis"', in P. C. Kolin, ed. '*Venus and Adonis': Critical Essays* (New York: Garland, 1997), 377–88.
21 Don Cameron Allen, 'On "Venus and Adonis"', in Herbert Davis and Helen Gardner, eds., *Elizabethan and Jacobean Studies Presented to Frank Percy Wilson* (Oxford: Oxford University Press, 1959), 100–19; cited in Keach, 56.
22 I am grateful to Karen Robertson for comments on the first part of this chapter and to Jeffrey Robinson for comments on the whole.

5

IAN FREDERICK MOULTON

The Manuscript Circulation of Erotic Poetry in Early Modern England

A mayds Embleme

Downe in a garden my sweete Rose did sport her
For grace and beauty earth had none fayrer
I went unto her and did gently court her
Hoping that shee would [be] as kind as fayre
But with a pretty grace shee smiling sayd
my mother bid me keepe my mayden head
her pretty words soe sweetly charmed me
I could not chuse but take her by thee middle
And sitting downe under a shadowy tree
Fayre love (quoth I) come you expound a ridle
    The Fayrest of Flowers the delitious Rose
    with out a Pricke it never growes;
with that a blush did dye her cheeks in graine
And streight she askt me what did meane by this
But ere I could my riddle more explaine
She seald my lips up with a silent kisse
enough (quoth she) you need noe more disclose
Be you the Pricke, and I will bee thy Rose.[1]

This bawdy anonymous poem is found on folio 54 of Ashmole MS 47 in Oxford's Bodleian Library. The manuscript is a bound octavo volume of 167 leaves. The first 130 leaves, including this poem, were 'closely written ... in a coarse hand' by an unknown compiler in the mid-seventeenth century.[2] The concluding 37 leaves of the volume were used several years later by the antiquarian Elias Ashmole to copy out a variety of poetry. The volume was donated to the Bodleian with the rest of Ashmole's library on his death in 1692. Besides this anonymous verse, the volume contains copies of poems by Richard Corbett, William Strode, Richard Brome and other well-regarded poets of the period, as well as poems misattributed to John Donne, Ben Jonson and Sir Philip Sidney.[3] While many items in the volume are lewd or humorous, it also contains such somber material as a poem attributed to King James I upon the death of his wife (f. 38r), two poems on the death of Prince Frederick, son of the Queen of Bohemia (f. 74v; f. 78v) and several epigrams on the death of children and infants (f. 38v; f. 52v). Devotional material is intermixed with secular texts. For example, William Strode's poem 'On Death and Resurrection' is found within two pages of John Taylor's bawdy verses 'On a mayds legg' (f. 43v; f. 42r).

Most surviving erotic verse from early modern England is collected in this sort of manuscript – handwritten collections of lyric poetry, compiled mostly by young men at the universities or the Inns of Court and in aristocratic families and households.[4] These collections, called 'manuscript miscellanies', offer an enormous variety of evidence for erotic expression in the period. They include crude and offensive scraps of verse as well as copies of some of the most sophisticated lyric poetry in English – the poems of John Donne; Ben Jonson; Shakespeare; Carew, Herrick and others. In terms of content, the surviving volumes are extremely heterogeneous – they contain prose as well as verse; texts both sacred and profane; epigrams; epitaphs; satire; romantic lyrics; jests; riddles; copies of petitions; political verse; gossip and much else besides. Though loose sheets of manuscript verse have in some cases survived, more common are bound collections, written by their compilers in blank books for personal use.[5] Compilers actively sought out poems worth copying from friends and relatives. In a letter of 31 July 1639, for example, Constantia Fowler of Tixall in Staffordshire wrote to her brother Herbert Aston, 'Send me some vereses for I want some good ones to put in my book'.[6] (Her book is now in the collection of the Huntington Library in California.)[7] Constantia Fowler's tastes in poetry seem to have been fairly decorous, but for many compilers, erotic or bawdy verse – however crude or urbane – was clearly 'good' enough to merit the time and energy to copy by hand. Erotic poems circulating primarily or entirely in manuscript included Thomas Nashe's scandalous 'Choice of Valentines' (a narrative poem about a young man's encounter with a prostitute),[8] John Donne's Elegy 19, 'To His Mistress Going to Bed'[9] (in which a young man encourages his lover to take off her clothes), Thomas Carew's 'The Rapture'[10] (an ironically hyperbolic celebration of heterosexual intercourse) and many others.

For the purposes of this chapter, 'erotic writing' is to be understood as a general term referring to writing that deals explicitly with what we would now call sexual practices: various forms of sexual intercourse (anal, oral, vaginal), masturbation (either solitary or mutual) or sexual arousal more generally. It includes sexual riddles, bawdy epigrams and rude jokes, as well as some satirical and political poems and much poetry dealing with love and desire. 'Erotic writing' was not a category or term that anyone in the early modern period would have used or recognized. Certain texts were characterized as being lewd, bawdy, naughty or obscene, but there was no strictly defined category of the 'erotic' as such. I use the expression as a useful analytical term to describe writing that deals more or less directly with 'eros' – sexual desires and practices, broadly conceived. 'Erotic writing' is not the same as 'pornography' (a distinct category strictly set off from other forms of cultural production), and it has little to do with the modern category of 'erotica', often used to refer to sexually explicit materials that are more socially acceptable than pornography.[11] I intend 'erotic writing' as a descriptive term, not as a moral or aesthetic one; some early modern erotic writing may appeal to modern sensibilities, other examples may be deeply offensive and disturbing. Some may seem sexy, some silly, some clumsy, some revolting.

The precise boundaries of what constitutes 'erotic writing' are fairly porous, though a text that deals with strong affection but makes no reference to bodily functions and physical desire would arguably fall outside the category. For example, one could argue that Shakespeare's Sonnet 18, 'Shall I Compare Thee to a Summer's Day', is not strictly speaking an 'erotic' poem, though it is a poem that clearly expresses powerful attraction. On the other hand, John Donne's Holy Sonnet 14, 'Batter My Heart, Three-Person'd God', could arguably qualify, given its powerful metaphors of penetration and rape – even though the primary context is spiritual rather than physical. But disputes over particular poems in many ways miss the point. As I have argued elsewhere, eroticism in early modern culture is not confined to precise limits but appears in many contexts – private and public, personal and political, secular and religious.[12]

This is nowhere better demonstrated than in manuscript miscellanies themselves. Although these collections contain much erotic material, and are a great resource for understanding early modern erotic culture and attitudes, they rarely have an exclusively erotic focus.[13] With a few exceptions, early modern manuscript miscellanies are miscellaneous in every sense of the word; collections devoted to the work of a particular author, or even to a particular genre or subject, are rare. Most surviving volumes collect whatever was of interest to their compilers, from masterpieces of lyric to verses on public affairs or political scandals; rude epigrams; copies of correspondence; jests and riddles; recipes for food, medicine, and ink. While some volumes were compiled by individuals, others were communally produced – some by groups of people adding material to a shared collection, others that were passed from one person to another over time. Over 250 manuscript miscellanies containing poetry have survived from the period 1560–1660, each one a unique record of their compilers' engagement with the literary culture of their time.[14] Much erotic material can be found in these volumes, and generally speaking it is integrated with a wide range of writing on other subjects.

Although these collections document an astonishing diversity of material, it is important to note that in other ways they offer a relatively restricted sample of early modern English culture. While the provenance of many of the volumes is unknown, the vast majority of surviving miscellanies were kept by a comparatively small, specific section of the population: young men from wealthy families, studying at either Oxford, Cambridge or the law schools at the Inns of Court in London. Many poems explicitly address student life – as, for example, the following epigram, entitled 'The Curse', found in a manuscript from Cambridge:

> May he
> Be by his father in his study tooke
> At Shakespeares Playes instead of the Lord Cooke[15]

Sir Edward Coke's *Institutes* (1628) was a standard legal text of the period. The days when Shakespeare's plays were a fit subject for study at university were far in the future.

It is worth remembering that, during this period, students entered university university between the ages of 13 and 16; this may account for the juvenile tone of some of the material collected in these volumes.[16] And yet the same manuscripts that contain poems mocking Henry Ludlow's unfortunate fart in Parliament in 1607 also collect much moving and erudite verse on topics ranging from love to the death of friends.[17]

Some surviving miscellanies, like Constantia Fowler's, were compiled by women, but their number is relatively small.[18] Whether their compilers were male or female, most surviving volumes have some connection either to institutions of higher learning or to aristocratic households.[19] Such documents were often the product of a coterie – or rather, of a series of interconnected coteries: groups of students at a college, family members in a large household, aristocrats at the royal court.[20]

Early modern England was very much in transition between print and manuscript culture.[21] Longer texts were most commonly circulated in the form of printed books, but shorter texts – lyric poems, jests and similar pieces – were still primarily circulated in manuscript. Written on loose sheets by their authors, they were shared and copied, some eventually finding their way into blank bound volumes. Take the case of John Donne, the most popular individual poet in manuscript culture. While only one copy of one poem survives in Donne's own hand,[22] over four thousand seventeenth-century manuscript copies of poems by Donne survive in the hands of various compilers, most of whom were personally unknown to Donne.[23] Only three of Donne's poems were printed during his lifetime.

While poetic miscellanies were compiled in the sixteenth century, most surviving collections date from the first half of the seventeenth century. This probably suggests that the practice of compiling poems was more widespread in the later period, but it may also be the case that a lower percentage of manuscripts has survived from earlier periods because of patterns of use and of collection. It is certain that only a small percentage of collections have survived from the sixteenth or seventeenth centuries. Presumably, most practising poets would have kept manuscript collections of both their own poems and those of other poets, but almost no autograph volumes by known poets have survived.[24] Mary Hobbs convincingly suggests that the relative abundance of early-seventeenth-century manuscripts reflects the increase in the numbers of minor gentry by 'prosperous merchants, lawyers, and doctors, many of whom had bought knighthoods and baronetcies from the impecunious James I... Their sons went to Oxford, Cambridge, or the Inns of Court, as befitted their new rank.'[25] For these young men, sharing poems at university could be a way of claiming membership in a community of wealthy, well-educated and leisured gentlemen.

Authors circulated their texts in manuscript for a variety of reasons. Much subliterary material of a scurrilous nature was shared in manuscript. But so were texts of great sophistication and seriousness. Before their publication in 1608, Shakespeare's sonnets circulated 'among his private friends'.[26] John Donne not only circulated all his poetry in manuscript but also kept his prose treatise *Biathanatos* out of print because it questioned whether suicide was sinful.[27] Printed books had to be licensed and approved by state authorities,[28] so texts likely to elicit censorship or disapproval naturally circulated in the more discreet medium of manuscript. Formal censorship by the authorities was directed primarily at suppressing political and religious dissent, not sexually explicit material.[29] Nonetheless, the relatively restricted nature of manuscript circulation allowed more freedom to use a crude tone or to address lewd subjects. Political satire was often bawdy and rude as well as subversive of established order, and it thrived in manuscript, as did other obscene, erotic or potentially offensive texts.[30]

Texts that circulated freely among an elite group could be censored if they moved beyond that group to a broader readership. Christopher Marlowe's English translations of Ovid's *Amores* circulated in manuscript, but when an edition appeared in print, it was included in a list of 1599 books the Archbishop of Canterbury and Bishop of London issued to be called in and burned.[31] This one-time ban was generally ineffective and may have been aimed more at John Davies' satirical epigrams, published in the same volume with Marlowe's Ovid. Nonetheless, classical poetry dealing with sexual subject matter was arguably seen as subversive when printed in English and thus accessible to women and to lower-class men. Martial's lewd Latin epigrams from second-century Rome refer to all manner of sexual activity: masturbation, oral sex, anal sex, homosexual relations (between both men and women) and all kinds of heterosexual coupling. Early modern editions of Martial published in Catholic countries were broadly expurgated in an effort to separate the poet's impeccable wit and diction from his often salacious subject matter.[32] But an unexpurgated Latin edition of all Martial's epigrams, with extensive scholarly commentary, was printed in England in 1615 and dedicated to Sir Robert Killigrew.[33] A second edition appeared in 1633. However, English readers could only read the unexpurgated Martial in Latin. An English translation by Thomas May published in 1629 removed all the sexually explicit poems.[34]

Fear of censorship was not the only reason authors avoided print. Much early modern verse was occasional – written for a specific occasion and often addressed to a specific person.[35] Such poems had no need of being printed; they could be given to their intended recipients directly. If the poem was witty or significant, it could be copied by third parties and spread from one compiler to another. Once removed from their initial recipients, occasional verses often needed a line or two explaining their context, as with this short poem by Richard Corbett describing a flirtation (whether actual or imagined):

> upon one comminge to visit his Mistress and shee being
>   absent hee wrote upon her lute thus
>
> Little lute when I am gone
> Tell thou thy Mistress heere was one
> That did come with full intent
>   to play upon her instrument
>
> The said Mistress going to visit him
> in his chamber in his absence
> shee wrote on one of his bookes thus.
>
> Little booke when I am gone
> tell thou thy maister heere was one
> that in her heart would bee content
> to be at his commandement[36]

Enough miscellanies have survived to allow one to generalize about which
texts were most popular in the communities of literate gentry that compiled
the volumes.[37] Poems on sex were much more common in manuscript than
print, as were political poems;[38] both of these types of poems could provoke
disapproval if they were printed. Poems dealing with death are also ubiq-
uitous in manuscript collections. There are serious epitaphs for particular
individuals, as well as poems lamenting untimely death – often the deaths
of children or youths. But one also finds a wide variety of bawdy mock epitaphs, such as the following, found in a miscellany compiled in the 1630s by
a man named Thomas Crosse:

> Heere sixe foote deepe in his laste sleepe
> The Lord Dubarius lies
> who lefte his breath and tooke his death
> betweene his Ladies thighes
> All through that hole to heaven hee stole
> I dare be bound to say
> hee was the last that that way paste
> and the first that found the waie.[39]

The identity of 'Lord Dubarius' is unclear – and other versions of the poem
name the deceased as Lord Lamport, the Lord of Dunsmore and the Lord
of Kilwicke.[40]

The wide variety of epitaphs circulating in manuscript is demonstrated
in a miscellany at Corpus Christi College, Oxford, which has a section of
almost 40 pages containing nothing but epitaphs – some on famous writers such as Shakespeare and Beaumont, others on prominent figures such
as Prince Henry, Queen Anne and the Archbishop of York.[41] There are also
many commemorating members of particular professions – a sexton, a scriv-
ener, a sailor, a lawyer, a physician, a butcher, a potter, a smith – even one on
'a scolding woman'.[42] Serious epitaphs appear side by side with humorous
ones. A popular bawdy verse lamenting the death of 'Mr. Prick of Christ
Church' is followed immediately by a somber verse on the death of Queen
Elizabeth.[43]

Beyond scandalous gossip about prominent individuals, manuscripts contained a large number of satirical poems on political issues more generally.[44]
These too could be sexualized, as in the song attacking the parliamentary
party in the Civil War, entitled 'A Roundhead', found in a collection from
the 1640s. The song's final verse reads:

> what's hee that met a holy sister
> And on a haycocke kindly kist her
> O thene his zeale abounded!

Twas underneath a shady willow
Her bible served her for a pillow,
And there springe up a Roundhead.[45]

Royalist poems often accused Puritans of being pious hypocrites in sexual matters, and attacked them for their unruly licentiousness.[46]

Like epitaphs, epigrams were very popular in manuscript collections – in part because their brevity made them ideal for filling up blank spaces in margins and at the bottom of pages. The following epigram, found in an Oxford manuscript compiled by one John Hopkinson (1610–80), criticizes a woman who tries to avoid getting pregnant by overindulging in sex:[47]

What madam Visna will you make your wombe
First a younge nurserie & then a tombe
Will you for pleasure be ridden into breath
And then for feare of paine ride the same to death?
You are to blame your knight will want an heire
And you the blessing of a mothers care
Ride softely madame & be ridden lesse
Soe shall your shame diminishe, you increase.[48]

Hopkinson's manuscript devotes several pages to a selection of epigrams, and similar collections are found in many other miscellanies.[49]

In early modern England, writing poetry was in many ways a social, even collaborative endeavour. Compilers not only collected poems but also responded to and in some cases reshaped them.[50] Poems making a particular point would often be answered by another making the contrary point. This habit may have been encouraged by the rhetorical training that boys received in school, where they were often asked to construct arguments on both sides of a particular question or issue.[51]

Among the most famous poems that provoked multiple answer poems is Christopher Marlowe's pastoral lyric, 'The Passionate Shepherd to his Love', in which a shepherd woos a young maiden.[52] Several other poets – including Walter Raleigh – wrote versions of the maid's reply to the shepherd.[53] Two of the most popular poems found in manuscript miscellanies were a pair of verses by Henry Rainolds and Henry King about an African woman in love with a young white Englishman,[54] probably written in response to the Latin poem 'Aethiopissa' by George Herbert. In Rainolds' poem, the 'blackamore wench' pleads with the white boy to love her, arguing that if his dark shadow can naturally follow and cling to him, she can too. In King's reply the boy rejects her, saying that 'mixed black and white / Portends more terror then delight'.[55] In a version found in a manuscript compiled by a man named Robert Killigrew,[56] the boy concludes by saying that his relationship with the black girl could only be consummated after death has made them equally 'dark':

> Else stay till death hath darkened mee
> And I'll bequeath my selfe to thee.

In this version, the conclusion of the poem is ambiguous: is the boy saying that after death racial differences will no longer exist and the two can love, or is he implying that death will sully his whiteness and bring him down to the woman's 'dark' level?

After circulating widely in manuscript for decades, Rainolds' and King's poems were finally printed in a collection entitled *Parnassus Biceps* in 1656.[57] In this printed version, the line reads 'stay till death hath blinded me', resisting the notion that the fair youth will become dark himself in time and insisting that love between the two of them would be a 'blind' error. This change increases the distance between the speakers, suggesting that the boy is right that black and white should not be mixed. Such textual variations, both minor and major, were a fundamental feature of manuscript transmission; poems could be edited or rewritten to suit the wishes of their compilers. More adventurous or unorthodox versions of poems tend to be found in manuscript than in print. In at least one manuscript from the 1630s, the genders of the speakers in this pair of poems are reversed, and the poems are entitled 'On a blacke boy in love with a faire maid' and 'The faire Maides answeare'.[58]

Poems on a specific theme could also generate poems that took the same theme and modified it in some way. To take a well-known example, Donne's poem 'The Bait' is a reworked version of Marlowe's popular 'Passionate Shepherd' poem; it takes the same opening line, 'Come live with me and be my love', as the starting point for a new text on the same topic. Compilers added lines and stanzas to poems, cut passages and reworked the poems in various ways.[59] These practices may have also been encouraged by the educational system, which taught the writing of imitative verse in many styles. This kind of imitative writing is evident in all sorts of poetry, including erotic poems.

Despite the specificity of individual manuscripts, one may make some large generalizations about erotic writing in manuscript miscellanies. It almost all tends to be from a male heterosexual point of view, for one thing. Though homoeroticism played an important role in early modern English culture, and both Shakespeare and Barnfield wrote poems on the erotic attractiveness of young men, poems expressing homoerotic desire are rarely found in surviving manuscript miscellanies. Most manuscript erotic poems tend to marvel at the female body, fantasize about seeing a woman naked or describe heterosexual intercourse. Poems glorifying (and objectifying) women's bodies are mirrored by blatantly misogynist texts that express fear and loathing of women. Both attitudes reflect the all-male and somewhat immature environment in which many poems were circulated and miscellanies compiled. Women are imagined objects of desire or threatening alien beings rather than companions, partners, friends or family members. Of course, there are exceptions – Donne's 'Canonization', 'Valediction: Forbidding Mourning' and many other poems popular in manuscript describe complex, affectionate relationships between men and women.[60] But poems either marvelling at female anatomy or denigrating women in some way are commonplace nonetheless.

Blazon-like descriptions of women's bodies are common, featuring lists of attractive body parts, generally starting with the face and ending with the genitalia. The following example is found in a manuscript compiled in two different hands in the early years of the seventeenth century:

> My love is full of pleasure
> hir haire is golden treasure
> her eies are starres hir forehead snow
> in her Temples Saphire growe
> Her Cheekes are milk & roses
> Lipps Rubies pearles discloses
> A silver tongue, an Ivory chinne
> Faire lookes most fairest skinn
> Hir Breastes firme ripe & round
> where Nector should abound
> If I might have the pressinge
> I would crave no othr blessinge
> Hir belly Lillyes staynes
> and moved it fills the vaines
> full of joye & rareness
> to see (oh see) hir bareness
> Hir thighes are sleeke & tender
> hir waiste is straight & slender
> These parts adjoyninge next the backe
> no faire proportion lacks
> Which bare out large & swellinge
> for Natures chiefest dwellinge
> is seated nere & richely made
> the entrance through a shade
> Where lukewarme water runs
> Like golde on morninge sun
> full of sweete contentment
> wth oyle & pretious ointmt
> Oh there I leave to speake
> no witt is but too weake

for who can feele that wonder
lyes hidden richely under[61]

Related to such crude blazons are poems dealing with voyeurism – a man (usually a young scholar) comes upon a beautiful maiden bathing. Who knows not what ensues? The following example comes from a volume used as a notebook by Simon Sloper of Magdalene Hall, Oxford:

Upon a summer day 'bought middle of the morne
I saw a lass that lay stark nak'd as she was borne
Twas by a raning poole with in a meadown greene
O there she lay to coole, not thinking to be seene

Straite did she by degrees, washe every limbe in ranke
Her breast her armes, thiges, her belly, & her flanke
Her leggs she opened wide. I let my eyes downe steale
Till that I had espied dame natures privy seale

I stript me to the skin & boldly leapd unto her
So thinkinge her to win. I thus began to woe [woo] her
Faire maide be not so quoy, times sweet in pleasure spent
Fie fie quoth she away, yet smiling gave content

Then winkskinge downe she glidd, seeming to be amazed
Yet heaving up her lid, againe on me she gazed
I seeing that laide downe, and boldly gan to kiss
O she did smile & frowne, so we fell to our bliss.[62]

Another example of this genre, entitled 'On a Gentlewoman Puttinge On a Cleane Smocke' is found in a Cambridge collection.[63] Arguably the most popular and sophisticated of such poems was Donne's Elegy 19 'To His Mistress Going to Bed.'

Rather than describing the act of disrobing or fantasizing about erotic encounters, other poems simply focus on male or female genitalia. Take, for example, the following epigram on a well-endowed man:

A Countrey Ladie with a knight was dancing.
Quod she with straddling Sir you marre your prancing.
Madam quod he 'twould make you stradle too,
Wore you between your leggs that which I doe[64]

Or the following poem from Oxford contemplating female organs and bodily functions:

On an Oxonlasse:

An Oxon lasse did take her coats up hiy
Course men her pritty legs & feet might spy

Thou hast a pritty leg sayd one sweet ducke
I'm Mary sir. sayd she or I have ill lucke
Their two indeed the twine I thinke, quoth he
they are and yet they are not – sir sayd shee
Their birth was both at once that Ile be sworne
And yet betwixt them both I sweare a man was borne:[65]

Early modern poetry was closely allied to music. Many texts that we now read as verse were intended to be sung, and may have been disseminated primarily as songs rather than texts. Many manuscript poems, including erotic and satirical poems, were written to be sung to a particular tune, just as printed ballads were. Take the following bawdy song found in a manuscript in the British Library:

A songe

1

Sitt thee downe, and wee'le prove
Ere we part the Acts of Love;
We will cull, and will kisse
Thankinge Cupid for the Blisse
That's created from the eyes
Of yor Mistress to her thighes

2

Glances that her eyes doe send
Fuell to yor fire doe lend;
Bellowes if you want, you know
She'ele blow upwards and below
Betwixt either Breath yor sence
Can discerne not difference

3

In the road if you're not skill'd
But through ignorance must yield
Ffollow her at her Commands
Sheele direct you with her hands.
But I know you cannot stay
Longe within the ready way.

4

ffor though tis not much about
You're not sooner in but out
The Daedalion Man [i.e. Daedalus] was thought
To this Labyrinth as naught

The Gate's allwayes ope yet tis
Ten to one but first you misst

5

If that you have wearied binne
Travellinge a while within
And the paines you tooke be great
Till that you art Bath'd in sweate
You may take your fill of rest
On that place of Downe, her breast.

6

Then if Perfumes be but scant
And such amorous sweets you want
Put yor nose into her tayle
There are sweets, that ne're will fayle
Smelt but sometimes 'ore and 'ore
There's not need of any more.[66]

The reference to smelling the woman's 'tayle' in the final stanza may refer to oral sex, but is more likely to suggest a disgust associated with excrement. Early modern discourse seldom openly refers to oral sex, and it is almost always seen as a degrading act for the person giving pleasure; they are being forced (or worse, choosing) to place their face near someone's ass – the ultimate in bodily submission and shame.[67]

Many manuscript poems in all genres are humorous, recording jokes, jests, riddles and plays on words. Simon Sloper's miscellany includes an antifeminist epigram that matches stereotypical female characteristics to English place names:

On Wemen

Weomen ar borne in Will-shire
Brought up in Cumberlande
Lead theire lives in Bedfordshire
Bringe theire husbands to Buck-in-game
And die in Shrewsberrie.[68]

Besides their general misogynist offensiveness, the jokes here are a bit creaky due to the passage of time. Briefly: Will-shire = willful or stubborn; Cumberlande = encumbrance, i.e. a wife; Bedfordshire = in bed (are women being attacked as lazy or sexually demanding?); Buck-in-game = sex, a pun on Buckinghamshire; and Shrewsberrie = shrewish or ill-tempered. The adolescent quality of manuscript culture comes through here quite strongly.

Other more aggressive examples of misogynist verse are common, such as the following contemptuous epitaph:

> Here lyes one enclosed under this Bricke
> Who in her life time Lov'd a P___
> You that passe by pray doe hir your honoure
> To pull out the P. and pisse uppon hir.[69]

Miscellanies also contained jests in prose, both sexual and scatological.[70] The following are all found in a manuscript containing a wide variety of texts in verse and prose, compiled around 1620, probably in Cambridge.[71] The first jest vividly dramatizes the perennial conflict between university students and 'uneducated' members of the local community:

> A miller seeing a scholler in Camb: looke out of his studie window as he past by him let out a monstrouse farte & bid the scholler cracke him that nut. The next day the miller was to passe the same way the scholler called to him & told him that he had crackt the nut & with that he flunge a foule filthie turde in his face holde quoth he there is the kernell.

As far back as Chaucer, millers were often the butt of jokes because of their supposed corruption and the fact that agricultural communities resented their dependence on millers to process their wheat into marketable flour.

Another jest suggests that the anus might also have its attractions:

> A company of gentlemen in theyre table talke had this in quaestion what was the rarest thing in ye world every one having given his opinion as it pleased him best at the length one merry companion amongst the rest step me fourth and told them that in his conceyte the rarest and strangest thing in the world was a sweet arsehole.

Like many others, this jest is founded on paradox: 'Sweet' here means clean and sweet-smelling; a sweet-smelling anus is thus the ultimate oxymoron. All the same, the idea that one member of a company of gentlemen would find an arsehole the rarest thing in the world cannot help but suggest a preference for anal sex; 'rarest' could mean 'most valuable' as well as 'most difficult to find.'

As one would expect from a culture made up primarily of adolescent boys and young men in which misogynist verse was common, many jests are made at women's expense. The following is a relatively mild example:

> It was the opinion of a clowne that a woeman was nevere past marriage till she waxed so old that she scracht the stoole she sat on in stead of her tayle.

And yet, one also finds jests that record women's witty responses to male taunting:

> A merrie gallant walking in London espying a gentlewoman readie to pas by him in the streats apparayled in a gowne of the olde fashion came to her and told her that he could not passe by her but he must needs for antiquitie sake kisse the hem of her garment why quoth the gentlewoman if you be so in love with antiquitie you may rather kisse my tayle which is far ancienter than that.

Another makes fun of a well-endowed man who is not able to satisfy his female lover:

> A married wife that loved the flesh well on a certayne tyme had a fellow of an extraordinary bignesse to deale with her but he by reason that he had wearied himself in such like affayres a little before could not give her her due as she expected whereupon being scarce well pleased she spake thus merrely unto him I never had quoth she more flesh to feed on and yet never lesse sauce to digest it.

Yet another not only has the woman getting the better of her male antagonist but also specifies that the audience of the jest supports her in shaming the abusive gallant:

> A lustie gallant that was in companye with certayne gentlewoemen being merrely disposed began to jeast with them and amongst many matters that they did reason of he tooke occasion to speake of some quallityes and propertyes belonging to the faemall sexe but above all quoth he this is the most peculiar which I doe most pittie that they are subject to so often falling and stumbling quickly downe no mervayle answeared one of the gentlewoemen in the companye for if such great blocks as you lye before them they must needs stumble and fall whereat the rest of the companye laught heartelye and he himself put to silence.

As Pamela Allen Brown has argued, whether originally written by men or not, jests like these functioned as 'cultural scripts that women could use as prompts for their own performances, or could spur their laughter when enacted by others'.[72]

While misogyny is a standard feature of manuscript culture, more positive views of women are also expressed. As in more general scholarly debates about women (indeed about any topic), varying points of view were often set against each other – as they were in school debates and exercises. Take for example this pair of poems on wives, found in a series of 87 poems on the subject of women in a 1630 manuscript owned by a man named Robert Bishop:

A wife

The w is woe
The J is nought but Jealousie
The ff is fawning, flattering woe

The E is nought but enmity
W J ff E spell nothing else but misery,
And therefor God grant thou to me
That I may (never) married be.

or thus

The w. is double wealth,
The J is everlasting Joy
The ff a frend unto the death
The E end of all annoy
wherefore good Lord grant thou to mee
That I may once well married bee

Marriage, a merry=age[73]

Some poems played with acrostics and other forms of word games:

A Question

When / sturdy stormes at seas arise
Shall / pleasant calmes agayne
I / see that under ashes doe
Lie / Hidden coles of fire
With / Heede so if you marke my minde
You / May a secret question finde[74]

A poem on the same page is written so that the first letter of each line spells out the words 'a prick'.[75]

One also finds poems that play with rhyme to create an expectation of a lewd word that does not appear in the text itself. The following is a particularly elaborate example:

A youthful Ladde, but in his language blunt
Was too familiar with a Ladyes _____
gentlewoman ffor which reprov'd he waxed wondrous sicke
was often visited, but his longe standinge _____
Sicknesse made him as stiffe, as any stocke
when yonge mayds came, he would take up their _____
words at the shortest, and with greivious groanes
would say, I pray you, but handle my _____
Head that doth burne, this prithee with thy handes
Though wouldst not thinke, how terribly it _____
Troubles my hart, my body is so duckt
All one with sweat, as if I now had _____
Threst all the day, two things as big as egges

Do vilely trouble me, between my _____
Thigh and my body, all my skin doth wrinkle
Pray let thy tender hands but feele my _____
Flesh how it trembles, have I not ill lucke
So many maydes to know, and none to _____
Have to my sweetheart, that might yield me some succour
Yea she would mend me soone, if I could _____
Gaze on her beauteous face, and starrelike eyes
And dally with the thinge between her _____
Chin and her nostrills, I meane her lips like jelly
I have a bodkin to put in her _____
Stringes to her apron; tis exceeding good
The only thinge to lett you maydens _____
Chase away a Louse. Tis worth summs of money
They often wish it were within their _____
Haire when it dangles, such a thinge as Mars
Did give to Venus, tis a good longe _____[76]

While most of the suggested words are still obvious to a modern reader, the last one – 'tarse', meaning 'penis' – is less familiar.

The practice of keeping manuscript miscellanies seems to have declined somewhat after the mid-seventeenth century. As the Puritan interregnum drew to a close and people began to anticipate a restoration of the monarchy, several verse anthologies were published that brought many poems popular in university manuscripts into print for the first time.[77] These volumes tended to be royalist in tone, presenting their poems as reminders of an elite cavalier culture at the universities in the good old days before the Civil War. Some bawdy verse was published in these collections, but much more remains unpublished to this day.

In the past, scholars have largely seen manuscript miscellanies as potential sources for texts by canonical writers. As such, they have been largely dismissed because the texts they contain are often considered 'corrupt' – that is, they have been subjected to changes (both intentional and accidental) by compilers and no longer represent the intentions of the original author. But it is precisely the communal and social nature of these collections that makes them so valuable as sources for discourse on early modern eroticism. They are not necessarily intimate or private documents, which later diaries might be, but they provide valuable insight into a network of early modern thoughts, feelings, attitudes and desires that printed texts do not preserve or communicate. The place of eroticism and sexual desire in these texts helps us understand its place in early modern culture more generally.

NOTES

1 Bodleian Library, Ashmole MS 47 f. 54r-54v. Crum D439. Manuscript poems are cited by manuscript call number and folio number with recto (r) and verso (v). If the poem is found in a Bodleian Library manuscript, the citation gives the identification number from Margaret Crum, ed., *First-Line Index of Manuscript Poetry in the Bodleian Library*, 2 vols. (Oxford: Oxford University Press, 1969). Transcriptions from manuscripts preserve original spelling, but common abbreviations are spelled out in full ('that' for 'yt,' for example). Passages in square brackets are my own conjectural interpolations for missing or illegible material.

2 Description from *A Descriptive, Analytical, and Critical Catalogue of the Manuscripts Bequeathed unto the University of Oxford by Elias Ashmole* (Oxford: Oxford University Press, 1845), 75.

3 A bawdy epigram attributed to Donne f. 36r: 'You say I lie; I say you lie judge whether / But if we both lie let us lie together' (Crum Y336); a six-line poem beginning 'It is not I that dye, I doe but leave ye inn' (Crum I1846) attributed to Sidney, f. 40v; William Strode's 'On a gentlewoman which sung and played on a lute', misattributed to Jonson, f. 92v.

4 Arthur Marotti, *Manuscript, Print, and the English Renaissance Lyric* (Ithaca, NY: Cornell University Press, 1995), 30–48.

5 Marotti, *Manuscript, Print*, 10–30.

6 British Library Add. MS 36452, f. 30v. Peter Beal, ed., *Index of English Literary Manuscripts*, vol. 2.1 (New York: Bowker, 1980), 500; and Mary Hobbs, *Early Seventeenth-Century Verse Manuscript Miscellanies* (Brookfield, VT: Ashgate, 1992), 2.

7 Huntington MS HM 904.

8 Beal, *Index*, 1.2, 356, and Ian Frederick Moulton, *Before Pornography: Erotic Writing in Early Modern England* (New York: Oxford, 2000), 168–93.

9 Found in 64 manuscript copies, Beal, *Index*, 1.1, 493–8.

10 Found in 29 manuscript copies, Beal, *Index*, 2.1, 83–5.

11 Moulton, *Before Pornography*, 3–15.

12 Moulton, *Before Pornography*, 35–40.

13 Collections with a primarily erotic focus include British Library printed book C. 39 a. 37; Bodleian Library MS Rawl. poet. 216; Dyce MS (44) 25 F 39 at the Victoria and Albert Museum; and Rosenbach MS 1083/15. Moulton, *Before Pornography*, 44.

14 Marotti, *Manuscript, Print*, 345–8.

15 British Library MS Add. 22603, f. 11v.

16 Hobbs, *Early Seventeenth-Century Verse*, 28.

17 Marotti, *Manuscript, Print*, 113, and poem D435 in Margaret Crum, ed. *First-Line Index of Manuscript Poetry in the Bodleian Library*, 2 vols. (Oxford: Oxford University Press, 1969), 1.206.

18 Miscellanies owned by women include Bodleian Library MS Rawl. poet. 108; British Library Add. MSS 4454 and 10309; Folger MSS V.a. 89, V.a.125, and V.b.198. Marotti, *Manuscript, Print*, 48–61; Hobbs, *Early Seventeenth-Century Verse*, 2; Moulton, *Before Pornography*, 54–64.

19 British Library Harley MSS 6917 and 6918 compiled by Peter Calfe, a Dutchman who had settled in London, are exceptions,.

20 Arthur Marotti, *John Donne: Coterie Poet* (Madison, WI: University of Wisconsin Press, 1986).

21 Harold Love, *Scribal Publication in Seventeenth-Century England* (New York: Oxford University Press, 1993).

22 Bodleian MS Eng. poet. d. 197. A verse epistle beginning 'Here where by all the saints invoked are', sent in a letter from Donne to Lady Carey and Mrs Essex Riche. Beal, *Index*, vol. 1.1, 243.

23 Beal, *Index*, vol. 1.1, 243–564.

24 Exceptions include British Library MS Egerton 2711 (Thomas Wyatt) and Corpus Christi College, Oxford, MS 325 (William Strode).

25 Hobbs, *Early Seventeenth-Century Verse*, 23.

26 Francis Meres, *Palladis Tamia* (London, 1598), 281–2; Beal, *Index*, 1.2, 450–4.

27 Love, *Scribal Publication*, 39–40, and Ernest W. Sullivan, 'The Genesis and Transmission of Donne's Biathanatos', *The Library*, 5th series, 31 (1976): 52–72.

28 Susan Clegg, *Press Censorship in Elizabethan England* (New York: Cambridge University Press, 1997), 3–29; Susan Clegg, *Press Censorship in Jacobean England* (New York: Cambridge University Press, 2001), 20–67.

29 See Clegg, *Press Censorship in Elizabethan England*, 198–217 on the bishop's ban of 1599. She suggests convincingly that it was an action taken against politically disruptive satire rather than against the representation of sexuality.

30 Marotti, *Manuscript, Print*, 75–6.

31 Moulton, *Before Pornography*, 102–8.

32 See, for example, *Martialis castus, ab omni obscoenitate perpurgatis* (Paris, 1554), and *M. Valerij Martialis Epigrammaton libri omnes* (Ingolstadt, 1602), edited by Matthaeo Radero, a Jesuit.

33 Martial, *M. Val. Martialis epigrammaton libri Animaduersi, emendati et commentariolis luculenter explicati* (London, 1615). STC 17492. 1633 edition: STC 17493.

34 Martial, *Selected epigrams of Martial. Englished by Thomas May Esquire* (London, 1629). STC 17494.

35 Marotti, *Manuscript, Print*, 2–10.

36 British Library Egerton MS 2421, f. 14v. Crum I392, I407, L446. This poem is crossed out with two large 'X's, as are several of the bawdier poems in this manuscript. Beal, *Index*, vol. 2.1, 185–6.

37 Marotti, *Manuscript, Print*, 126–33.

38 British Library Add MS 22601 mixes poems with letters and political petitions.

39 British Library Harley MS 6057; Crum H681, H1101, H1117. This section of Harley 6057 was compiled by Thomas Crosse in the 1630s. See Beal, *Index*, 2.2, 260.

40 Lamport: Bodleian MS Add. B. 8, f. 71v. Dunsmore: Bodleian MS Top. Oxon. E. 202, f.104r. Kilwicke: Bodleian MS Don. d. 58, f. 16v.

41 Corpus Christi College, MS CCC 328, f. 52r–70v: Shakespeare, f. 59r; Beaumont f. 66v; Prince Henry, f. 57v; Queen Anne, f. 62r; Toby Matthews, Archbishop of York, f. 67v.

42 Corpus Christi College, MS CCC 328, f. 58r.

43 Corpus Christi College, MS CCC 328, f. 62r. See Crum A1362, O1094, S984, T607, T1445, T1481.

44 Marotti, Manuscript, Print, 82–94.

45 Bodleian MS Rawl. poet. 153 (A), f. 23v–24r. Crum W422, W826. See Bodleian MS Ashmole 36/37: f. 77r for longer version that has a matching poem on cavaliers.

46 Marotti, Manuscript, Print, 118.

47 The notion that overindulgence in sex could lead to female infertility was a common one. See *Aristotle's Masterpiece* (London, 1684), Wing A3689, and Roy Porter and Lesley Hall, *The Facts of Life: The Creation of Sexual Knowledge in Britain, 1650–1950* (New Haven, CT: Yale University Press, 1995), 46–7.

48 Bodleian Library, MS Don. d. 58, f. 32v. Crum W578.

49 Bodleian Library, MS Don. d. 58, ff. 31r–40r. Also British Library MS Harley 7392, ff. 1r–9v; British Library MS Harley 1836, ff. 2r–10v; Bodleian MS Add. B. 97, ff. 41–60v; Bodleian Library MS Rawl. poet. 212, ff. 66v–57r rev.; Rosenbach Foundation MS 1083/15, ff. 2v–9r.

50 Marotti, *Manuscript, Print*, 152–9.

51 Joel B. Altman, *The Tudor Play of Mind: Rhetorical Inquiry and the Development of Elizabethan Drama* (Berkeley, CA: University of California Press, 1978), 31–46.

52 Found in 10 manuscript copies. See Beal, *Index*, 1.2, 326–7.

53 Raleigh's reply, 'The Nymph's Reply to the Shepherd', is found in 11 manuscript copies. See Beal, *Index*, 1.2, 393–4.

54 Kim Hall, *Things of Darkness: Economies of Race and Gender in Early Modern England* (Ithaca, NY: Cornell University Press, 1995), 116–122, 273–6. Gerard Previn Meyer, 'The Blackamoor and Her Love', *Philological Quarterly* 17 (1938): 371–6. Elliot H. Tokson, 'The Image of the Negro in Four Seventeenth-Century Love Poems', *Modern Language Quarterly* 30.4 (1969): 508–22.

55 Quoted from British Library MS Sloane 1792, f. 116r. The printed version in *Parnassus Biceps* reads 'Pretends' instead of 'Portends'. Printed versions do not always have the best texts.

56 British Library MS Sloane 1792, f. 116r.

57 Abraham Wright, ed., *Parnassus Biceps: Or Severall Choice Pieces of Poetry, Composed by the Best Wits that were in Both the Universities Before their Dissolution.* (London: 1656), sig. G5v–G6r. Wing W3686.

58 British Library MS Harley 6931, f. 6v–7r.

59 Marotti, *Manuscript, Print*, 135–208.

60 'The Canonization' is found in 35 manuscripts, 'A Valediction: Forbidding Mourning' in 54. See Beal, *Index*, 1.1.

61 British Library MS 22601, f. 82r–82v.

62 Bodleian Library MS Eng. poet. f. 10, f. 114r. Crum U164.

63 British Library MS Add. 22603, f. 8r–8v. Another copy is in Bodleian MS Eng. poet. e. 14, f. 77v.

64 British Library Add. MS 44963, f. 95.

65 Corpus Christi College, Oxford, MS CCC 328, f. 21. Crum A1230, B102, F28, M411.

66 British Library Add. MS 22603, f. 3r–4r.

67 Oral sex is seldom mentioned in early modern discourse, and attitudes toward it tend to reflect the ancient Roman idea that oral sex was particularly degrading because it brought the mouth into contact with the genitals. Marilyn B. Skinner, *Sexuality in Greek and Roman Culture* (Malden, MA: Blackwell, 2005), 18.

68 Bodleian MS Eng. poet f. 10, f. 95. Crum W2748.

69 Corpus Christi College, Oxford, MS CCC 327, f. 5v. Crum H890.

70 British Library MS Harley 6395, the jest book of Nicholas L'Estrange (d. 1655), contains 606 numbered jests.

71 National Art Library, Victoria and Albert Museum, MS Dyce (44) 25 F 39, f. 93v–95v.

72 Pamela Allen Brown, *Better a Shrew than a Sheep: Women, Drama, and the Culture of Jest in Early Modern England* (Ithaca, NY: Cornell University Press, 2003), 31.

73 Rosenbach Collection, Philadelphia: Rosenbach MS 1083/16, p. 15. Crum T506, T1509, T1510, T1511.

74 British Library Egerton MS 2421, f. 46. Crum W1478.

75 Moulton, *Before Pornography*, 47.

76 Bodleian Library, MS Rawl. poet. 153, f. 29r. Crum A599.

77 Marotti, *Manuscript, Print*, 265–81.

6

JAMES GRANTHAM TURNER

The Erotic Renaissance

In the beginning, Pietro Aretino created sex. So at least one would gather from innumerable references to 'Aretino's Postures', which became the generic brand name for illicit, pleasure-oriented, non-procreational, inventive and – above all – *visible* copulation. In the Italian, the French and later the English imagination, the entire programme of libertine representation could be summed up in the single word *Aretine*. Though Aretino himself only claims to have written sonnets post hoc, to accompany erotic 'figures' that he attributes to Marcantonio Raimondi after Giulio Romano (*c.*1524), reception history made him a universal artist and inventor, responsible equally for the pictures, the writings and the 'positions' they enact.

This influential myth of origins is, in fact, quite false. Classical antiquity invented sex, or at least literary genres that permit free allusions to genitalia and orifices: the epigram; the love elegy; the *Ars Amatoria*; the illustrated sex manual listing all the postures; the *Satyricon*; the medical treatise on generation. Or again, the Middle Ages invented sex. We are familiar with the lewd fabliau from Chaucer's *The Miller's Tale* and Boccaccio's *Decameron*, and specialists have identified a long tradition of carnival songs, anticlerical satires, burlesques of religion and sexual humour in vernacular and Latin poetry.[1] Aretino knew this; in a famous manifesto-letter justifying the *Modi* and proclaiming the nobility of the sex organs, he explains how classical art and literature inspired him: 'I was touched by the spirit that moved Giulio Romano to design them. And because poets and sculptors ancient and modern often write and sculpt lascivious things to amuse the mind ... I dashed off the sonnets on them that you see at their feet'.[2] (The originals are lost but Figure 6.1, crude as it is, preserves one of these images with its sonnet.) In his dialogues or *Ragionamenti* (literally pornographic, since the speakers are prostitutes and bawds), an entire story from Boccaccio – the one about the well-hung gardener in the nunnery – is transformed into a painting that adorns the convent parlour, along with other scenes showing 'all the various modes and avenues by which one can fuck and be fucked'.[3]

But classical, medieval and many Renaissance 'hardcore' texts operate within strong constraints of decorum and genre. Emphasis on the lower bodily functions, sex and excretion, is permitted in sophisticated epigrams about perverts (typified by the Roman poets Catullus and Martial) and in low styles devoted to broad humour or insult directed against base characters such as peasants, prostitutes and lascivious monks. We find abundant 'discourses of sexuality' – facetiae and vituperations, but also medical and didactic treatises – that we would hesitate to call *erotic*, if we reserve that term for literature that evokes the experience and the pleasure of sexual passion and not merely its mechanism or side effects. Of course, there are moments of sheer delight in deliberately coarse, comic texts, and educated humanists testified to the pleasure (*voluptas*) they derive from reading 'lascivious, naughty, playful' epigrams when they are written in brilliant Latin, though they describe disgusting bodies in rude words that are the ancestors of the modern *cunt* and *fuck*.[4] Overall, however, the hierarchy of genres that prevailed in 1500 separated the feelings of love from the workings of lust. Literature that was literally 'Erotic' – that is, dedicated to the god Eros, to the celestial Venus defined by Plato and his followers or to the Amor who rules the heart and poetry of Petrarch and the courtly Petrarchists – strictly repudiated the sexual body.

This chapter will explore exceptions: sixteenth-century texts, and episodes within conflicted texts, that bring sexuality and Eros together. Some are openly libertine or obscenely explicit; others develop the amorous sonnet and the philosophical love treatise in more elevated language, but all manifest an acceptance of passion and a corporeal turn away from strict Petrarchanism and Neoplatonism. In contrast to the 'separation of styles' that confined sexuality to the lower stratum of the fabliau and the joke book, I identify a broadly sex-positive phase of the Renaissance – when *lascivious* became a neutral or endearing term, sculpture was valued for 'filling every viewer's mind with libido' and beauty was discovered in earthly rather than 'celestial' love.[5]

Erotica Across the Genres

Two examples serve to illustrate this shift, each involving a single word. Writing in the 1460s, the Florentine Platonist Marsilio Ficino warns sordid earthly lovers, wallowing with the pigs in the pleasures of 'Bacchus and Priapus', to stay away from the 'celestial feast' of Plato's *Symposium*, where Socrates teaches 'true beauty' and 'legitimate love' – 'so great is the power of the amatory faculty! so great its sublimity!' ('*tanta sublimitas!*').[6] Writing in the 1520s, the Sienese academician Antonio Vignali flaunts the same concept,

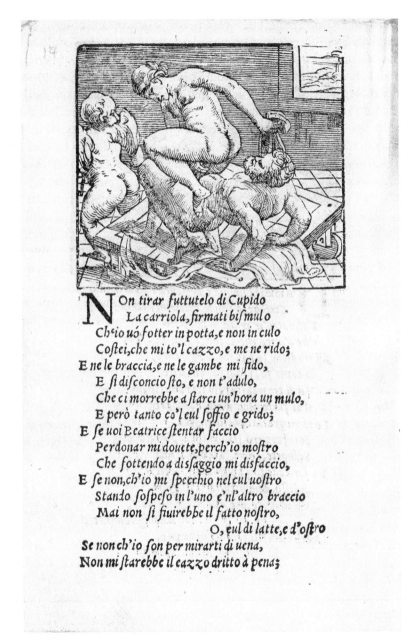

Non tirar futtutelo di Cupido
    La carriola, firmati bismulo
Ch'io uó fotter in potta, e non in culo
Costei, che mi to'l cazzo, e me ne rido;
E ne le braccia, e ne le gambe mi fido,
    E si disconcio sto, e non t'adulo,
    Che ci morrebbe a starci un'hora un mulo,
    E però tanto co'l cul soffio e grido;
E se uoi Beatrice stentar faccio
    Perdonar mi douete, perch'io mostro
    Che fottendo a disfaggio mi disfaccio,
E se non, ch'io mi specchio nel cul uostro
    Stando sospeso in l'uno e'nl'altro braccio
    Mai non si fiuirebbe il fatto nostro,
                    O, cul di latte, e d'ostro
Se non ch'io son per mirarti di uena,
Non mi starebbe il cazzo dritto à pena;

Figure 6.1 Unknown artist after copy of Marcantonio Raimondi's *I Modi*, 'Toscanini volume', f. B4v (T14). Woodcut. Milan, private collection.

sublimità, in an outrageous but inventive dialogue with the obscene title *La Cazzaria*. (Vignali's work has been translated by Ian Moulton, a fellow contributor to this volume, with the subtitle *The Book of the Prick*.) Arsiccio (Vignali himself) is training his student boyfriend Sodo in the arcana of sex, following a set of 'philosophical' questions that mimic the medical text *Aristotle's Problems*. The younger man had been embarrassed at a dinner party by the question 'why do the testicles never enter the vagina or anus during intercourse?' His ignorance and prejudice must now be corrected if he is to become a successful lover – an active seducer, rather than the passive catamite he is now. Noble women of 'elevated soul' prefer scholars for their secret lovers. Unlike working-class studs, students can entertain them 'between one fuck and the next' with 'lovely dialogues', wicked witticisms and 'a thousand *novellini amorose*' (little stories, like the *novelle* of Boccaccio), transforming sex from 'peasant feeding' into a delectable banquet – a *convito* (the usual translation of Plato's *symposium*). The amorous intellectual has learnt from books the 'good strokes and sweet lines'; since *colpi* and *tratti* are the marks made by brush and pen, he is an artist too – and a scientist, because due to his knowledge of genital anatomy he can 'find all the pleasurable and secret ways' to make love. What this hypothetical mistress values in a lover is precisely 'intellectual sublimity' (*sublimità d'ingegno*) – the ingenuity or genius able to 'find out the modes and secret ways', committed to acting out 'acute and subtle inventions'.[7]

Sublimità d'ingegno is not mocked here. Vignali's entire dialogue exemplifies it, however gross and misogynistic its material at times. Inverting and supplanting Ficino, it invites his private academy to a literary banquet in honour of Bacchus and Priapus, where genders and orifices mingle; where pigs have wings. As Moulton has discovered, despite all efforts to suppress or ignore this *Cazzaria* the great theorist Benedetto Varchi still praised it for *arte e ingegno*.[8]

Latin was still the preferred medium for expressing *ingenium* in stylish sexual slander, tales of erotic adventure and unabashed tributes to arousal. Arsiccio claims he is gathering material for a Latin treatise called *The Light of the Pudenda*. Catullus and Martial famously insisted that their poems *must* be sexually stimulating – cannot succeed unless they have 'a prick' (*mentula*) and make the reader 'itchy' in the erotic sense (*nisi pruriant*, an active verb with the text as its subject). Humanists made this a critical touchstone: Antonio Beccadelli defended his own 'lascivious' epigrams by evoking Sappho's verses, which 'excite *prurigo* in whoever reads them'.[9] (The poem might sport a phallus, but the author may be female and the 'itching' readers male – *cui* in the masculine plural.) The international reach of Latin allowed for ethnic slurs between Germans (drunks) and Italians (sodomites).[10] The

Dutch poet Johannes Secundus wrote an entire suite of poems on the kiss (expanding on Catullus), but also a brilliant epigram that sets conventional gender spinning: 'Tell me, grammarians, why *cunnus* is a masculine noun and *mentula* is a feminine noun' – that is, the penis is female and the vulva male, hence traditionally dominant.[11] The future Pope Pius II wrote his *Two Lovers* in Latin prose. In one of Girolamo Morlini's *Novellae* (pre-1520), written in a Latin that closely imitates Apuleius's *Golden Ass*, a woman describes herself walking through the market square on a moonlit night and feeling suddenly aroused by a splendid marble statue, which recalls her departed husband; she climbs the base, embraces the nude male figure and engages so deeply with '*erectus ille priapus*' that she cannot dismount, and remains as a public spectacle the next morning.[12] (Each of three women is competing for a valuable jasper, given to the one who tells the most humiliating story about herself.) This motif would later cross over into the vernacular: the French libertine dialogue *L'Escole des filles* invents a princess who commissions her own life-sized sex statue, complete with a 'member' that hardens and ejaculates at the throw of a switch.[13]

A favourite topic for humanists wishing to flaunt their Greek as well as Latin expertise is the 'bisexual' debate already explored by Plutarch, Achilles Tatius and Lucian – whether women or boys give greater pleasure (to the elite male, naturally). Beccadelli's book of epigrams is entitled *Hermaphroditus* and claims to possess the orifices and organs of both sexes, assuming that his readers will enjoy both. Poets like Pacifico Massimi and Théodore de Bèze or Beza (whose youthful erotica haunted him when he became the leader of the Calvinists in Geneva) flaunt their equal expertise with both sexes: Massimi threatens to perforate 'any boy, any girl' he encounters, Beza praises the 'little slit' of a lady and weighs the problems of satisfying boyfriend and mistress at the same time. But these Latin exercises in perverse antithesis don't necessarily count as 'erotic' in the subjective sense – dramatizing the joy or beauty of sex, expanding the imagination with new postures, augmenting the 'art' of love. Massimi praises the '*ingeniosi modi*' of his sexual partner, but this ideal mistress turns out to be his own hand; another poem, ending with an obscene pun on finding a blind woman's 'oculus', declares that he prefers a one-eyed lover because he hates to be seen.[14] As we move into the 'High Renaissance' of the sixteenth century, however, Latin poetry does raise sexuality to the aesthetic. In the homoerotic mode, Bartolomeo Leonico Tomeo complements Giovanni Bellini on finding a male lover whose marmoreal beauty will match and inspire his art and cause his 'work' to rise again. In a heterosexual vein, a Latin epigram in the voice of the recently discovered '*Cleopatra*' (later identified as Ariadne) celebrates the passion for statues; ending each line with a similar verb of desire (*arsit/amat*), the poet brings out the parallel between Julius Caesar (who 'burned' for Cleopatra in the flesh) and Pope Julius II (who 'loves' her in marble).[15]

In the sixteenth century, these topics also flow over into the vernacular, especially in writing intended for homosocial coteries. Lodovico Ariosto's comedy *I Suppositi*, performed at court in Ferrara and the Vatican, brought the house down with puns on its title, which means 'substitutes' but also 'sub-positions' in the sexual sense. After milking the sodomitic association (boys are often 'sub-posed' by older men, as the audience might have known), Ariosto assures us that he *doesn't* mean the notorious postures invented by ancient Greek courtesan authors.[16] In a later edition, Ariosto linked these explicitly to the sexual positions illustrated in the *Modi* engravings, which certainly do dramatize 'sub-position' (Figure 6.1). Popular carnival imagery of tools and fruits, always with genital double entendre, combines with the antique bisexual debate in the 'paradoxical encomium'. Normally written in chatty terza rima and labelled '*capitolo*' or chapter, these witty and erudite poems praise some abject or commonplace thing: a fig, an onion or a crude statue of Priapus. The painter Agnolo Bronzino celebrates the 'frying pan' that makes his eel spring back to life and the *pennello* (a paintbrush and a little penis) that creates 'a thousand and one diverse acts and extravagant modes, in front or behind'. Archbishop Giovanni Della Casa's *Capitolo del forno* debates the merits of two kinds of baker's oven – one hot and capacious, the other small, finely made and best suited for producing the perfect artisanal baguette – recognized immediately as a scandalous comparison of woman and boy. Others compare the square and the round, *quadro* and *tondo* – meaning vagina and anus, as well as picture formats and geometrical forms.[17]

The homoerotic poetry of the Italian Renaissance fills a book-length anthology, and much of it adopts the formal parallel of vaginal and anal sex, promoting *la delicatezza del tondo* as an art form or an improvement in taste: gourmet images for the 'two-loves' comparison involve the meat course (beef or kid, roast or boiled) and fruit (especially the fig versus the peach).[18] Vignali's prose *Cazzaria* belongs with these poems, since – despite its opening tribute to the noblewoman who values *sublimità d'ingegno* – it devotes most of its ingenuity to promoting sodomy. It is not merely facetious blasphemy when Vignali-Arsiccio defines 'Paradise' as the *dolcezza* experienced 'with your prick up a soft, white, boyish arse' (61).

In heterosexual poetry (and in courtly behaviour more generally), the Petrarchan pose still ruled: sublimely scornful, unattainable mistress, worshipful lover tormented by fire and ice, contenting himself with glances and sighs, pouring out sonnets. But more sensuous elements were being smuggled in. The painter Raphael drafted sonnets that for some scholars express 'conventional Petrarchism', but he evokes the pleasurable 'yoke and chain of your white arms around my neck' – a far more intimate embrace than Petrarch ever allowed.[19] Vignali typically wrote a poem that begins with conventional Petrarchan woes but ends with explicit genital action, skirts lifted and *cazzo in culo*.[20] A three-line 'tail' could be added to the noble sonnet: Aretino's comments on the *Modi* take this seventeen-line *caudato* form (already associated with scurrilous subjects), alluding to the 'tails' of the sexual performers whose dialogue is written directly into the poems. Several women, including Gaspara Stampa, took over the Petrarchan sonnet and fleshed out the portrait of love-suffering while switching the gender perspective. In France, Louise Labé wove into her Italian–French sonnet sequence the 'kiss-arithmetic' motif from the lustier Latin tradition:

Baise m'encor, rebaise-moi et baise:	Kiss me again, re-kiss me, and kiss
Donne m'en un de tes plus savoureux,	Give me one of your most savoury
Donne m'en un de tes plus amoureux:	Give me one of your most amorous
Je t'en rendrai quatre plus chauds que braise[21]	I'll give you back four hotter than
glowing coals.	

Pierre de Ronsard crafted many erotic lyrics that he collected under the throwaway title *Folastries* (*Frolics*), and probably authored a pair of sonnets that circulated in seventeenth-century anthologies like *Le Cabinet satyrique*, eulogizing the male and female genitalia.[22] (Moving from Italy to France, their number was reduced from three to two, with much less emphasis on the joys of heterosexual and homosexual sodomy.) Ronsard's penis is merely a 'lance'. But his salutation to the 'little crimson cleft' (*vermeillette fente*) with its soft 'velvet' hair is surprisingly respectful and beautiful. Ronsard is fulfilling what Vignali promised but botched with his grotesque obsession with vast, insatiable vaginas – to improve as a lover by learning intimate anatomy. English poets later exploit this expanded range for the sonnet: in Sir Philip Sidney's *Astrophil and Stella*, Desire growls 'give me some food' after a string of Petrarchan commonplaces; Shakespeare puns on *prick* and *will*, and runs the gamut from idealized homoerotic love to paradoxical encomium of the Dark Lady to bitter denunciation of 'lust in action'.

Another verse form associated with masculine sexuality and double entendre was also appropriated by a talented female writer, the Venetian courtesan Veronica Franco (or, as she preferred, Franca). In her hands, the terza rima '*Capitolo*' becomes a flexible instrument of challenge and seduction, request and lament. Exchanging ideas and verses with her aristocratic coterie, she tests the sincerity of their love and promises – to the one who convinces her with deeds rather than words – pleasures in bed 'so sweet and delicious' that all previous delights are confounded. She has learned her *modi* not from some book by Aretino, but directly from the god Apollo and the goddess Venus. Without ventriloquy, Franca proclaims herself a great artist in the 'opera' of sex, exceeding even the achievements of her singing voice and her pen – achievements that include this very poem.[23]

Meanwhile, the austere treatise on Ideal Love loosened up and made some room for physical sexuality. Ficino taught that lovers should communicate through gazing alone and despise the pigsty of corporeal intercourse, but as he works out the details these strict distinctions start to crumble. Rather than merely dismissing the 'vulgar' kind of earthly, passionate love, he analyzes it with vivid empathy and almost surgical precision. And he admits that, even in lofty Platonic love, 'the eye and the spirit *demand* the perpetual presence of a beautiful body' so that the soul 'is *forced* to desire' the same thing. And Ficino describes eyesight in notably sexual terms: the soul imprints images while couples are 'making babies'; a stream of 'sanguine spirits' shoots into the heart like sperm. The physiology is the same in 'vulgar love' as in the higher kind, where the image of the beautiful boy still 'flows through the eyes into the other' and 'generates' itself 'in the penetralia of his soul'.[24] The next generation of love theorists went further, admitting that the 'higher' Eros could be found in physical, even procreative desire, in the realities of marriage or the heterosexual affair with a courtesan – not merely in the cerebral man–boy crushes idealized by the Neoplatonists. Mario Equicola defined the ideal as the complete fusion of soul and body, and elevated touch to the highest rank among the senses. By aspiring to nobility and beauty, sex became compatible with art. Of course, these theories are mostly voiced by elite males, but important contributions to this 'sensuous turn' were made by the Jewish intellectual Leone Ebreo (Judah León Abravanel) and the courtesan Tullia d'Aragona. Leone recognized sex between man and woman as a natural effect of sacred Love, and traced parallels between the penis and the tongue, ejaculation and verbal expression. Tullia d'Aragona, in her dialogue on *The Infinity of Love* (1547), drew on her self-avowed 'experience' of intense passion to argue that corporeal, sexual union is *necessary* to achieve the highest stage of love: the fusion of two bodies and two souls. In this way, the 'lascivious' can become virtuous and honorable – and not necessarily within marriage. Even the 'vulgar' kind of Eros can be 'infinite' in its intensity, with its own space and breadth, rising in 'steps' like the Platonic initiation.[25]

Medical literature could also appeal to erotic pleasure, as opposed to the clinical detachment we expect today. Emanating from the medical school in Montpellier, the Catalan *Mirror of Fucking* or *Speculum al foderi* (c.1400) preserves a catalogue of ways (or *'maneras de foder'*) remarkable for its descriptive clarity and lack of moral comment, as well as passages derived from the *Kama Sutra* and from Arabic predecessors of the *Perfumed Garden*. Some of these 24 positions seem motivated by performative pleasure rather than the usual health or eugenics; for example, when the woman is advised to grasp the penis and guide it, to sit upon the man's legs or to brace her own leg against the furniture (all scenes later shown in the *Modi*).[26] Latin translations of Aristotle's *Problemata* speculated about 'the appetite of some men to be *suppositi* in the anus'. The papal physician Professor Giovanni Benedetto Sinibaldi defends his right to treat the subject of generation humorously and to 'arouse' the reader erotically, citing exactly Martial's line that writings about sexuality cannot succeed *nisi pruriant* unless they excite.[27]

Vignali's *Cazzaria* borrows a little from all these trends in erotic literature. Medical 'questions'; sodomy debates; folktales about women 'inventing the prick', endless political allegory and even Petrarch are woven into what the preface calls 'the greatest tangle of pricks there ever was'.[28] In this framing story, the reader loses himself in the 'excessively great pleasure of finding all the reasons and circumstances of fucking' and forgets about his actual date (38). Underlying all this is Vignali's new myth of the golden age and the Fall (134–5). Cazzo, Culo and Potta once lived happily together and 'did their deeds' openly, until shame destroyed everything. Intriguingly, for Vignali the same catastrophe generated the 'insatiable appetite' for new postures, 'other *modi*' that are 'disastrous' and 'constrained' or 'forced' (though *sforzato* also meant 'forceful' in the good sense, when applied to art). As proof, the speaker cites not the Giulio-Marcantonio *Modi* known to art historians but a different lost work of the 1520s – 'a little work called *La Cortegiana*', from which he rattles off a list of intriguingly named postures that rather undermines his pretended disapproval.

Aretino and Following

Though Aretino evokes Nature throughout the letter that accompanies and justifies the sonnets, the poems themselves express discontent with the 'natural' limitations imposed by mortality, time and biology. The women want to hold their favourite posture for an entire year, and both sexes long to perpetuate the moment of self-sufficient pleasure ('I care about nothing but fucking') and to refashion the body accordingly.[29] In the first sonnet, the lovers long to die 'fucking', to 'fuck Adam and Eve' in revenge for bringing death into the world – a variant on Vignali's libertine reinterpretation of the primal fall – and to fuse so completely that the testicles go inside: the impossibility that launched Vignali's dialogue

(T1). In another sonnet the woman on top 'would like to be all cunt, as long as you could be all prick' – a condition she recognizes as impossible; he replies, suddenly conscious of his 'poco cazzo', that if she pushes down hard enough they might achieve this transformation 'and I'll be prick, and you will be cunt'. To express this totalizing, self-enclosing desire in appropriate form, every line ends with cazzo or potta.[30] This virtuoso feat is repeated in a poem that steals Vignali's title, La Cazzaria del C. M., which not only describes but reenacts homosexual coupling by repeating cazzo and culo in each of its 144 lines in lieu of rhyme. Its companion poem, Effective Persuasion for Those who Dislike the Delicacy of the Tondo, imagines a literally homosexual state of blissful self-fusion: 'If Man could bugger himself in his own arse', the world would enjoy a new, peaceful golden age.[31]

A further irony lurks in that first sonnet and throughout the Modi writings. The genitalia are supposed to be honoured – indeed, celebrated – in festivals and displayed as ornaments according to Aretino's letter, and sex is valued as the supreme good. Without this fervent mingling of cazzo and potta (and culo for good measure), the world would be worth nothing – or rather, nothing but a cazzo. Like fuck in modern English, the same word signified the best of things and the worst of things.

Though the Modi themselves involve only heterosexual couples, Aretino's sonnets on them turn into dialogue–debates on the culo versus the potta, sodomy versus vaginal intercourse – relocating the 'two loves' debate to two openings in the female body. Both partners are imagined praising anal penetration as a sign of elite taste or true masculinity (with the occasional minority voice suggesting that it compensates for genital inadequacy). These constant calls for buggery – a triumph of will over physiology that overrides functional, mammalian definitions of human sexuality by expropriating forbidden areas – is frequently given to female speakers (though women were, in reality, more tightly bound to procreational ideology). But some of the males do try to live up to their definition of the 'real man', who defies zoological and patriarchal responsibility: 'Let my genealogy end with me!' ('Finisca in me la mia genealogia!'). Another poet, Francesco 'Coppetta' Beccuti, incorporated exactly the same line into one of his homosexual monologues in terza rima, proving that the trope can migrate easily between sexual kinds.[32]

Aretino exploits gender fluidity throughout his writings, drawing the visual, the literary and the sexual ever closer together. In letters and poetry, he begs the Marquis of Mantua to procure him the youth he was infatuated with, declares himself a 'born sodomite' – only converted to heterosexuality by miracle – and urges all boys to rejoice in this conversion; at the same time, he urges the Marquis to buy a statue of Venus 'so true and so alive that it fills with lust the mind of anyone who beholds it'.[33] By publishing many of these letters, Aretino promoted the sensuous and often gender-bending response as the right way to evaluate art. He appreciates the backside of a bronze 'Ganymede', archly hinting at his 'sin', and goes on to insist that even if the figure were female he would still prefer the rear view. Viewing Michelangelo's *Leda*, he confessed that he envied the swan. About Venus (in a companion piece to that *Leda*) he noted that, 'because a Goddess like that diffuses her properties into the desire of both sexes, [Michelangelo] made her the muscles of the male in the woman's body, just as she is moved by virile and female feelings with elegant vivacity of artifice'.[34] Aretino's disciple Lodovico Dolce praised Titian's 'Venus and Adonis' not only because Venus arouses every male viewer – 'there can be no one so chilled by age or so hard in his makeup that he does not feel himself growing warm and tender, and the whole of his blood stirring in his veins' – but because the 'lascivious charms' of Adonis combine male and female.[35]

In his prose *Ragionamenti* (1534–6), Aretino sometimes maintains the naturalistic, sex-positive stance that he used in the letter and sonnets on the *Modi*; the praise of the phallus in that letter, for example, had appeared almost verbatim in the final dialogue, recited by a midwife who broadens the encomium to include the vagina. His female characters describe orgies in the nunnery and ventriloquize what male customers see in the courtesan. But these voluptuary set pieces, erotic tableaux like the *Modi* in words, are embedded into a different kind of discourse – satire against the tricks and extortions of the prostitute and the brutality of her customers. Punitive and celebratory impulses struggle, even in the orgiastic first dialogue in which Nanna recounts her first experiences in the nunnery – a sequence that is supposed to be entertaining.[36]

Nanna sometimes transforms the naked into the nude in sensuous descriptions that emulate Aretino's friend Titian. She is particularly eloquent on the perfectly formed, 'gleaming' backside of the nun in the final orgy, seeing with the eyes of the prelate who 'softly opens the pages of the arse-missal' to 'contemplate *il sesso*' – sex itself. But at other moments her visual model is more Hieronymus Bosch. The display of interlocking bodies suggests Adam and Eve not in Paradise but amid their wretched descendants in limbo; souls roasting on a spit for Lucifer's carnival, malefactors impaled in Turkey, a sodomite in the mouth of the devil. And this satirical grotesque work brings with it a heavy-handed didacticism. After two women make love, they lecture each other on how much better 'the living' would be than this 'depiction'. Even the glorious wall paintings in this libertine nunnery spell out precisely whose pleasure must be served and who must be the servant: the nuns are 'obliged' to practice each posture in the painting before encountering their priestly lovers, to make themselves less awkward in bed, less like 'bean soup without oil and salt' for the men who come to consume them.[37]

Female instruction and male pleasure likewise dominate the posture-related episodes in the second set of dialogues, in which Nanna teaches her daughter the prostitute's art. Details of masculine arousal, though spoken through Nanna, seem drawn from autoerotic or homoerotic experience – compare Ronsard's heroic but generic 'lance' with the fascinated particularity of Aretino's description of that organ, straining and heaving 'like someone who wants to vomit but can't'. Even when Nanna's theme is the cruelty of men to sex workers, she occasionally floats off into the rapture she would feel 'if I were a man', or gives lavish details of the beautiful body about to be punished – a complicated intoxication of the senses mixed with excitement at her own powers of description and a streak of sadism.[38]

Remarkably, the tense combat of desire and punishment eases towards the end of the six *Dialogues*. The speaker is now the Midwife, who procures beautiful but virtuous ladies for her male clients. Her voyeuristic description of their undressing, caressing, wooing, climax and affectionate post-coital collapse deserves the label *erotica* rather than *pornography*. Sex here is uncoercive, untainted by grotesquerie or satire, polymorphous rather than phallocentric. The Midwife freely admits that the woman excites her to masturbation, and her friend the wetnurse gives her the ultimate compliment: 'a Sappho' could not have described her better.[39]

Numerous texts about illicit, non-reproductive sexuality were attributed to the mythic Aretino or claim his patronage. Most are too nasty to be included in a companion to erotic literature, but – as in the *Ragionamenti* – there are oases of imagination. Lorenzo Venier's *La Puttana errante* (c.1529), travestying the female knights-errant made popular in Ariosto's 'Orlando furioso', has a kind of epic grandeur-in-abjection, as the Whore-Errant enters Rome in triumph after the Sack or sets up her 'banner' to display 'fucking in such a strange manner, and in so many ways never fucked before' (42, 59, 81, 83–90). The 1535 *Tariffa delle puttane di Venegia* (*Price-List of the Whores of Venice*) – mostly a satirical, unglamorous exposé of sex workers, including Tullia d'Aragona – ends with a rapturous description of a sixteen-year-old 'garzonetta' (who performs 'now in one mode, now in another') with a precision of erotic detail that makes the 'gentleman' speaker sound like a procuress; orgasm in the arms of his favourite 'boy-girl' turns him into 'a nectar more precious than anything tasted by Jove in Paradise'.[40] Aretino himself promoted these poems by his younger friends. Dropping the names of the *Tariffa* and the *Puttana errante* into Nanna's dialogue created an instant canon; Nanna casually recommends 'reading the *Wandering Whore*' ('*la leggenda della Puttana errante*'), and within a few years, in remotest England, Gabriel Harvey misreads the passage and so adds 'the Legende of the Errant Putana' to Aretino's oeuvre.[41]

Collections of Aretino's 'capricious and delightful' *Ragionamenti* gather satirical dialogues by association. Matteo Bandello describes a pampered wife staying in her bedroom and reading 'the *Nanna* or the *Rafaella* of Aretino' (*Novelle*, I.34), even though the latter work (a dialogue of woman-to-woman advice about conducting a discreet affair) is really by the Sienese Alessandro Piccolomini, another member of the *Accademia degli Intronati* founded by Vignali. Robert Burton cites Aretino repeatedly to illustrate the most extreme forms of love in the *Anatomy of Melancholy*, but in almost every case he is actually quoting from a Latin translation of Rojas's Spanish dialogue *La Celestina* – giving Aretine paternity by default. Joachim Périon devotes an entire treatise to warning the French king and the Pope against the terrible influence of Aretino, citing at length from a text called *Capricium* that systematically defends sodomy. Périon must have had some title like *Cappricciosi e piacevoli ragionamenti* in front of him by 1550 – a pro-pederastic text (probably Vignali's *Cazzaria*) passed off as Aretino's and tacked onto his *Ragionamenti*. Périon's tract, in turn, convinced the Elizabethans that Aretino had indeed published an 'Apology for Pederasty' – a belief conspicuously displayed in E.K.'s notes to Spenser's *Shepherds Calendar*. Pierre de Brantôme quotes from 'Aretino' the idea that when lovers' tongues 'interlace' in a kiss they are sealing a pact to keep secret what goes on between them, but in fact this idea comes directly from Vignali's *Cazzaria*; again, Brantôme must have read some volume that bore Aretino's name on the title page, probably the same one that panicked the moralist.[42]

Of all these apocrypha, the most influential is the *Dialogo di Giulia e di Madalena* – the compilation that for centuries passed itself off as the authentic work of Aretino and the definitive list of 'postures'. Each of its three stages – the description of a successful and sumptuously dressed courtesan, the autobiography of Giulia and the catalogue of every known position – borrows heavily from those moments in Aretino when sex is least complicated by satire. The blason of the courtesan's body transcribes the prelate's response to the nun, lavishly reconstructed by Nanna on her first day in the convent. Her genteel manners are paraphrased from the training session Nanna gives her daughter, and Giulia's own initiatory moments, excited by the 'odour of pleasure' into masturbating with a glass dildo borrowed from her aunt, likewise come straight from the convent episode. The sixteenth-century French manuscript and the seventeenth-century printed versions shamelessly expropriate Aretino's name, though the most direct borrowings from the *Ragionamenti* vanished when the dialogue was printed in 1660 under the title *La Puttana errante* (a theft that effectively obliterates all trace of Venier's original poem). Nevertheless, a general air of cheerful hedonism is maintained, as if the *Ragionamenti* had been revised by the sex-positive Aretino of the sonnets.[43]

In Aretino's dialogues, the narrative impulse constantly threatens to submerge the 'sex effect' in a flood of satirical and punitive realism; in the more skeletal *Giulia e Madalena*, narrative is subordinated to taxonomy. Giulia's autobiography begins in response to the question 'what are the pleasures that the courtesan knows how to give?'. She narrates and catalogues the postures in arithmetically precise groups, as the speakers themselves point out ('I don't believe that standing on their feet the man and the woman can find any more modes of conjunction than the four you have tried'). Each of the 52 postures (36 in the printed version) is labelled by association with a physical object or action, forming a sexual Art of Memory. David Foxon correctly identified this dialogue as 'the first imaginative prose work which deals directly and exclusively with physical sexual satisfaction', but its single-mindedness is not far removed from simple-mindedness. Commentary and evaluation are limited to remarks like 'a woman can have no greater pleasure than the one she feels when a man joins with her carnally', or 'the greatest pleasure is when the tool is very big and very hard, and goes all the way in'. Except for a brief passage of pain and fear when her first masturbation draws blood (stolen from Aretino and removed in the printed version), and a brief reference to her dislike of oral sex, every new 'mode' inspires uncritical delight.[44]

Of all the early modern libertine texts, *Giulia e Madalena* (known throughout print culture as *La Puttana errante*) comes closest to twentieth-century descriptions of pornography as a sealed, claustrophobic genre – a 'pornotopia' wholly subject to masculine fantasy (though glimpses of quotidian reality appear from time to time). Giulia copies her own sexuality from the male models she observes – quite literally, through the various holes in the wall that convert domestic space into a 'camera obscura'.[45] First she sees her cousin Federico masturbating, then sits in exactly the same place and asks her sister Pippa to show her, with suitable finger movements, 'what men do to women' (59–61). In the manuscript she now imitates her aunt by borrowing her dildo, but the printed version moves directly to the next masculine object lesson – a remarkably detailed description of Federico and another youth buggering each other by turns. Perceiving Giulia's restlessness after witnessing this scene, her aunt argues that since men 'give themselves pleasure' women should 'do likewise'; aunt and niece then make love with equal abandon. (In the manuscript version, 63–5, this lesbian sequence is framed by reassurances that Giulia wants the 'real and natural' thing and that the aunt had 'too much of the man' in her face.) Even when the heroine discovers heterosexual coupling, masculine homoerotics are uppermost in her mind; she starts with Ruberto, her cousin's teenage lover, and when he fondles her 'like a boy' or takes her from behind she laughs delightedly at the thought of having seen him do the same with Federico (73–4). Her reality is effectively defined by a system of holes.

Beyond Italy

In France, the influence of classical and Italian erotica mingled with strong native traditions. Jean de Meun's continuation of the *Roman de la Rose* introduced into the allegorical romance cynical misogyny, deception, jealousy, the worldly advice of an old woman and an openly sexual 'plucking' at the climax. François Villon's Belle Heaulmière offers a blazon of her own sexual attractions, fine in her youth and now sadly withered. These medieval themes continue, but with a new twist, in Joachim Du Bellay's sixteenth-century poem *La Vieille Courtisanne*. The speaker claims to know 'everything that Aretino teaches', to 'put into practice all the secrets discovered in his book' (like Du Bellay himself, who borrows heavily from Aretino's *Ragionamenti*), but she uses this erotic training to establish her house as 'a public school of *honnesteté*', obligatory for all young men who wished to learn 'how to entertain the Ladies'.[46] François Rabelais also performs an erudite, inventive Renaissance transformation of popular tall tales and folk myths. His *Gargantua* and *Pantagruel* overflow with sexual language, lewd anecdotes (such as the 'ring' that guarantees the wife's fidelity, but only when it is round the husband's finger) and surreal genitalia – enough to rebuild the walls of Paris, according to his character Panurge. But is it erotic? Panurge's sexual humour always has a grotesque and misogynistic edge, and when Rabelais describes a true hedonistic Utopia, the Abbey of Thélème, the genital impertinence drops away and the lovers party in an atmosphere more like Castiglione's *Courtier* than Aretino's *Ragionamenti*.

My phrase 'genital impertinence' is taken from the greatest essay on sexuality of the sixteenth century: Michel de Montaigne's 'On Some Verses of Virgil' (*Essais* III.6). In some ways this is a male version of Villon's *Belle Heaulmière*, wistfully surveying his aged member and its fitful attempts to *gendarmer* or strut about like a policeman, recalling how 'impertinently genital' he was in his youth. Montaigne discovers in himself – and in the multitude of ancient and modern writers he channels, from Virgil to Beza – the whole range of contradictory passions that constitute Eros, from the bestial to the sublime. He rejects the idea of essential gender differences and denounces the hypocrisy of forcing women into strict chastity while

Cum priuilegio Regis

Figure 6.2 René Boyvin after Rosso Fiorentino or Léonard Thiry, detail of pepper holder from a design for a salt-and-pepper set. Engraving. London, British Museum.

granting sexual freedom to (French) men. Yet at the same time he maintains the old gendered polarization of female Nature and male Culture: men 'learn' their sexual know-how, by rather desperately reading Boccaccio and Aretino, while women 'engender' theirs, 'a discipline that is born in their veins'.[47]

Montaigne gives us a profound and encyclopedic meditation on sexual experience, then at the end claims it was nothing but *un flux de caquet* – a dribbling flow of gossip (typically the lewd chatter of women gathered to assist at a childbirth). Pierre de Brantôme's *Les Dames galantes* offers exactly the reverse: a comprehensive study of sexuality that is really a stream of bitchy gossip. Brantôme is fascinated by amorous 'secrets' that he thinks come from Aretino (as we saw earlier), and his vast, anecdotal *Dames* includes scenes in which ladies buy the 'postures of Aretino' from a Paris bookseller and gentlemen use this knowledge to seduce them. Compulsory heterosexuality comes to a climax in a sequence in which the royal duc d'Alençon, abetted by his chamberlain (Brantôme himself), presses ladies to drink from a goblet decorated with 'Aretine' scenes of copulation so that the male guests can tease out their reactions (Figure 6.2, a design for a luxurious table centre holding hot pepper, gives us a glimpse of such artefacts). But the result of such visual erotic stimulation is likely to be *donna con donna*, the Italian phrase he lifts from *Giulia e Madalena* (though he also uses the lacy word *fricarelles*). Brantôme finds himself compelled to imagine 'lesbiennes' everywhere at court and in the baths, where 'beautiful naked ladies ... intertouch [*s'entretouchoient*], fondle, handle, rub, intermingle and grope each other'. Brantôme assumes that erotic art inevitably reaches the inner core of sexual verity – 'so penetrating were these images, visions and perspectives' or 'figures of Aretino'.[48]

NOTES

1 Antonio Beccadelli, *The Hermaphrodite*, ed. and transl. Holt Parker (Cambridge, MA: Harvard University Press, 2010), xxv.
2 *Lettere*, ed. Paolo Procaccioli, 6 vols (Rome: Salerno Editrice, 1997–2002), vol. I, no. 308, dated 11 December 1537 in the first two editions but 19 December in later impressions. All translations in this chapter are mine.
3 *Aretino's Dialogues*, transl. Raymond Rosenthal, intro. Margaret F. Rosenthal (Toronto and Buffalo, NY: Toronto University Press, 2005), 16 (Part One, first day).
4 Beccadelli, *Hermaphrodite*, 2 (*Guarino da Verona*), 112–14 (*Poggio Bracciolini*).
5 For the parallel phenomenon in art, see my *Eros Visible: Art, Sexuality and Antiquity in Renaissance Italy* (New Haven, CT and London: Oxford University Press, in press).
6 *Commentary on Plato's Symposium on Love*, transl. Sears Jayne, 2nd edn (Dallas: Spring Publications, 1985), 107; original Latin from Ficino, *Commentaire sur le Banquet de Platon*, ed. and transl. Raymond Marcel (Paris, 1956), 199.
7 *La Cazzaria del Arsiccio Intronato*, ed. Pasquale Stoppelli, intro. Nino Borsellino (Rome: Edizioni dell Elefante, 1984), 44–5.
8 Antonio Vignali, *La Cazzaria: The Book of the Prick,* ed. and transl. Ian Frederick Moulton (New York: Routledge, 2003), 53.
9 *Hermaphrodite*, 118, and see 4 (Guarino); the classical texts cited are Catullus 16, Martial I.36, and a Latin ode imitating Sappho (not yet known in the original Greek).
10 Ingrid D. Rowland, 'Revenge of the Regensburg Humanists, 1493', *Sixteenth-Century Journal*, 25 (1994), 307–22 (texts on 321–2).
11 See my *Schooling Sex: Libertine Literature and Erotic Education in Italy, France, and England, 1534–1685* (Oxford: Oxford University Press, 2003, 2009), 6–10.
12 *Novelle e favole*, ed. Giovanni Villani (Rome: Salerno Editrice, 1983), 380–2.
13 See my *Schooling Sex*, 151–2.
14 *Les Cent Elégies: Hecatelegium, Florence, 1489*, ed. Juliette Desjardins (Grenoble: University of Grenoble Press, 1986), 122–6 (III.3, 'De Lusca'), 140 (III.7, 'De Palmera'), 200–2 (V.4, 'De pueros et puellas'); see also my *Schooling Sex*, 278.
15 Tomeo ('Fusco') quoted in my *Eros Visible*, 280; Evangelista Maddaleni Capodiferro quoted in Leonard Barkan, *Unearthing the Past: Archaeology and*

Aesthetics in the Making of Renaissance Culture (New Haven: Yale University Press, 1999), 241.

16 See my *Eros Visible*, 68.

17 *Il primo libro dell'opere burlesche di M. Francesco Berni, di M. Gio. Della Casa, del Varchi, del Mauro [etc]* (1548; repr. 'London', n.p., 1723), passim; Bronzino, *Rime in burla*, ed. Franca Petrucci Nardelli, intro. Claudio Mutini (Rome: Instituto della Enciclopedia Italiana, 1988), 24; G. *Guidiccioni, F. Coppetta Beccuti, Rime,* ed. Ezio Chiorboli (Bari: Laterza, 1912), 283, 288; Lorenzo Venier, *La puttana errante,* ed. Nicola Catelli (Milan: Unicopli, 2005), 59, 68, 77; for Della Casa see my 'Libertine Literature Forty Years On', *The Book Collector,* 54 (2005), Part I, 37 n.23 and Part II, Appendix.

18 Danilo Romei, ed., 5 September 2008, *Antologia di poesia omoerotica volgare del Cinquecento,* www.nuovorinascimento.org; compare Barkan, *Unearthing the Past,* 1999, 222; Venier, *Puttana errante,* 78, Adrienne van Lates, 'Caravaggio's Peaches and Academic Puns', *Word & Image,* 11 (1995), 55–60.

19 See my 'Raphael as Poet', *Source: Notes in the History of Art,* 32.2 (Winter 2013), 8.

20 Transcribed from ms. in Moulton, *Book of the Prick,* 65.

21 *Complete Poetry and Prose: A Bilingual Edition,* ed. Deborah Lesko Baker (Chicago: University of Chicago Press, 2006), sonnet 18 (my translation). Labé also contributed to the prose love treatise with *Le Débat de folie et d'amour.*

22 *Livret de folastries,* ed. Ad[olphe] Van Bever (Paris: Societe du Mercure, 1907), 104–5. Ronsard's gallantry is somewhat punctured when, ostensibly to show the power of the vagina, he declares that after having it for four nights the force of love is already diminished in him.

23 *Veronica Franco: Poems and Selected Letters,* ed. and trans. Ann Rosalind Jones and Margaret F. Rosenthal (Chicago: University of Chicago Press, 1998), 68–9 (*Capitolo 2*).

24 *Commentary,* 114, 115, 159–61 (*Commentaire,* 206, 207–8, 247–8); *De Vita* cited in Jacqueline Marie Musacchio, *The Art and Ritual of Childbirth in Renaissance Italy* (New Haven and London: Yal University Press, 1999), 129.

25 See my *For One Flesh: Paradisal Marriage and Sexual Relations in the Age of Milton* (Oxford: Oxford University Press, 1987, 1993, 2004), 68; *Schooling Sex,* 38–41; *Eros Visible,* 65–6.

26 *The Text and Concordances of Biblioteca Nacional Manuscript 3356, Speculum al foderi,* ed. Michael Solomon (Madison, WI: University of Wisconsin Press, 1985-1986), transcript pp. 37–43.

27 Paris, BnF, MS lat. 6540, f. 63v; Sinibaldi, *Geneanthropeia sive De Hominis Generatione* (Rome, 1642), title page, f. †5.

28 38; translation from Paula Findlen, 'Humanism, Politics and Pornography in Renaissance Italy', in Lynn Hunt, ed., *The Invention of Pornography: Obscenity and the Origins of Modernity, 1500–1800* (New York: Zone Press, 1993), 88.

29 There is no authorial text or full scholarly edition for the sonnets Aretino claims to have written in response to the *Modi,* though copies survive in print and manuscript at various removes from the composition date of *c.*1524–1527. They are cited by default from the 'Toscanini volume' of poems and

woodcuts (abbreviated 'T'), reproduced with translations and numbering in Lynne Lawner, *I Modi/the Sixteen Pleasures: An Erotic Album of the Italian Renaissance* (Evanston, IL: Northwestern University Press, 1988) and in Bette Talvacchia, *Taking Positions: On the Erotic in Renaissance Culture* (Princeton, NJ: Princeton University Press, 1999), Appendix B. I quote here sonnets T10 and T13.

30 Sonnet 6 ('Perch'io prov'or un sì solenne cazzo'), in Lawner, *I Modi*.

31 The unique copy, without author, place or date, is Paris, BnF, Enfer 562; see Lawner, *I Modi*, 56, n.22. Pascal Pia, *Les Livres de l'Enfer* (Paris: Coulet et Faure, 1978), col. 177, identifies the author as 'il Cavaliere Marino', who was accused of sodomy, but the imprint and the costume of the frontispiece figure are clearly earlier than 1609, when Marino gained that title.

32 Guidiccioni and Beccuti, *Rime*, 291, citing Aretino's *Modi* sonnet T8, line 5; compare Romei, *Antologia*, 267, 271, and Aretino, sonnets T2 ('huomo non è, chi non è bugerone'), 3, 7, 8, 10, 13, 16.

33 Alessandro Luzio, *Pietro Aretino nei primi suoi anni a Venezia e la corte dei Gonzaga* (Turin: Loescher,1888), 23–4, 76–9; *Scritti di Pietro Aretino nel Codice Marciano It. XI 66 (=6730)*, ed. Danilo Romei (Florence: Franco Cesati, 1987), 117–22; Aretino, *Lettere*, vol. I, no. 9 (6 August 1527).

34 *Lettere*, vol. V, no. 173 (January 1549); Vol. II, no. 5 (undated but *c.*1542).

35 Mark W. Roskill, *Dolce's 'Aretino' and Venetian Art Theory of the Cinquecento* (1968), (Toronto and Buffalo: Renaissance Society of America Reprint Texts, 2000), 10, 212–16.

36 The first day's dialogue is retroactively defined as incredible (*Dialogues*, 150) and as mere amusement (173).

37 All citations from *Dialogues*, 16–34; for the original Italian see Pietro Aretino, *Sei giornate*, ed. Guido Davico Bonino (Turin: Einaudi, 1975), 19–27.

38 Compare *Dialogues*, 55–6, 76–7 (Part One, second day), 165, 192–3 (Part Two, first day), 238, 257–60 (Part Two, second day); ambiguous passages that mix desire and violence are often associated with the 1527 Sack of Rome.

39 *Dialogues*, 342–3 (Part Two, third day).

40 Antonio Cavallino, *Tariffa delle puttane di Venegia*, ed. Guillaume Apollinaire (Paris: Bibliotheque des curieux, 1911), 122–8.

41 Cited in David C. McPherson, 'Aretino and the Harvey-Nashe Quarrel', *PMLA*, 84 (1969), 1554; compare Aretino, *Dialogues*, 12.

42 E.K., 'Glosse', *January*, line 59; Pierre de Bourdeille, seigneur de Brantôme, *Recueil des dames, poésies et tombeaux*, ed. Etienne Vaucheret, Bibliothèque de la Pléiade (Paris: Gallimard, 1991), 520; Vignali, *La Cazzaria*, 134; for Périon and his probable source, see my 'Libertine Literature I', 37–8.

43 *Il Piacevol Ragionamento de l'Aretino. Dialogo di Giulia e di Madalena*, ed. Claudio Galderisi, intro. Enrico Rufi, foreword by Giovanni Aquilecchia (Rome: Salerno, 1987), 23–35, identifies the main borrowings from Aretino, missing from *Cappricciosi e piacevoli ragionamenti di M. Pietro Aretino*, 'Nuova editione' (Leiden: Elzevier, 1660). The printed editions all reverse the names of the two dialogists.

44 'Aretino', *Giulia e Madalena*, 56, 62–3, 72–3, 85, 110; David Foxon, *Libertine Literature in England, 1660–1745* (London: Shenval Press, 1965), 27. The

posture-list from a seventeenth-century printed version is translated in Lawner, *I Modi*, 51–2.

45 A 'camera ... senza lume' (67); at one point Giulia actually squeezes through one of these 'holes' to join her lover (70–1).

46 *Œuvres poétiques*, ed. Henri Chamard, vol. V (Paris: Hachette, 1923), 162, 170.

47 See my *Schooling Sex*, 32; all citations are from Montaigne's *Essais*, vol. III, no. 6.

48 *Recueil des dames*, 261–3, 266–7 (describing a painting, however – not an actual lesbian scene he witnessed), 361–71; compare *The Lives of Gallant Ladies*, trans. Alec Brown, intro. Martin Turnell (London: Elek Books, 1961), 26–31, 128–37.

7

SARAH TOULALAN

Pornography, Procreation and Pleasure in Early Modern England

Discussing pornography and erotica in the past is not a straightforward matter, as many scholars have observed. Lisa Sigel has described scholars' attempts to distinguish between 'pornography', 'erotica' and 'obscenity' and to identify what past material might fall into these categories as characterised by a 'search for clarity collapsing into a confused wrangle'.[1] This is partly because, as Sigel points out, scholars have begun their discussions from different starting points. Some have focused on the classification of materials in law and examined prosecutions of producers and sellers, identifying developments in censorship and legalisation and shifting boundaries between what might be considered acceptable art or literature and that categorized as 'smut'.[2] Others have attempted to date 'the emergence of pornography as a form', or as a specific genre, which can be connected to shifting intellectual climates such as the Enlightenment or to nineteenth-century preoccupations with prostitution and morals.[3] When examining representations of sex that we might wish to identify as pornographic in the early modern period, we immediately encounter the problem of anachronism as we attempt to identify something in the past for which the word, and hence the idea as specifically conceived at the time the word was coined in the mid-nineteenth century – 'a description of prostitutes or of prostitution, as a matter of public hygiene' – did not yet exist.[4] The nineteenth-century term nevertheless has some resonance for early modern material, as its etymological meaning of writing of or about prostitutes encompasses not only one of its subjects – prostitutes and prostitution – but also its primary vehicle: the written word.[5] Today we largely understand pornography as a kind of visual material that presents explicit images of naked bodies and sexual acts through the media of digital and photographic images or film rather than as a type of written text, as the development of new technologies enabled the proliferation of pictures, first as still images and then as 'movies'. The advent of the internet in the late twentieth century further facilitated their distribution.[6] Although images of the sexual body and the body engaged in sexual acts circulated in early modern Europe, they did so frequently as illustrations to texts, or as engravings or woodcuts that might be selected and bound in with a particular item to a purchaser's individual taste or pocket.[7] The advent of the printing press in the mid-fifteenth century similarly boosted the production of texts that incorporated or focused upon the representation of sex and brought them into the orbit of a much wider audience, as literacy increased at the same time as the practice of reading to others continued.[8] The nature of pornography as a 'thing' and how it represents its subject matter has thus changed significantly over time. Consequently, it has been suggested that '"pornography" is arguably not a particularly useful category with which to describe the erotic writing of the early modern period', mainly because it is both 'imprecise' and 'notoriously hard to define'.[9]

Nevertheless, as I have previously argued in *Imagining Sex: Pornography and Bodies in Seventeenth-Century England*, the category of 'pornography' does provide a conceptual space in which texts and images of a sexual nature may be considered as they were understood to have a particular effect or purpose – the arousal of sexual feelings – whether intended to do so or not, and however different these representations may be to our modern understandings of it. A universally applicable definition is neither possible nor appropriate: we must examine our historical material both within its specific historical context and with an eye to its changing nature over time.[10] In this chapter, I will examine early modern medical writing about sex and reproduction in order to show how and why it could be understood, and responded to by contemporary readers, as a kind of pornographic writing. Following on from this, the chapter will then show how the contemporary context of medical knowledge and understandings about sex and reproduction infused other representations of sexual encounters in some of those texts that have, as Ian Moulton has pointed out, 'come to define the field for many readers and scholars' for this period.[11] These include Nicolas Chorier's *Aloisiae Sigeae Toletanae Satyra Sotadica de Arcanis Amoris et Veneris* (c.1659/60), which appeared in a French version as *L'Académie des Dames, divisée en sept entretiens satiriques* in 1680 and in an English adaptation as *A Dialogue Between A Married Lady and a Maid* by at least 1688 (if not earlier in 1684), and *L'École des Filles*, usually attributed to Michel Millot and Jean L'Ange and translated into English as *The School of Venus*.[12] Other English translations and adaptations of continental works, such as *Rare Verities: The Cabinet of Venus Unlocked, And Her Secrets Laid Open* (1658) and *A Treatise on the Use of Flogging in Venereal Affairs* (1718 [1639]), will also be mentioned, as well as texts originally produced in English, such as Charles Cotton's *Erotopolis* (1684) and *Aristotle's Masterpiece* (1684). Both these kinds of text represented the nature and purpose of sex in the same way – as having procreation as its outcome – and often did so in similar language and images and referencing the same examples and anecdotes from classical literature. Early modern writing that was perceived as pornographic – or erotic, obscene, lewd, licentious, lascivious, bawdy, filthy – did not tend to dissociate sex entirely from reproduction in the way that a modern reader would expect. This was a world in which it was not yet possible to deliberately avoid conception with any degree of confidence, and one in which the experience of sexual pleasure was still understood as connected to its procreative purpose. This is just one of the difficulties encountered in exploring this early modern literature of sex as pornography; others, such as authorial intention and the explicitness of representations, will also be addressed.

Pornography and Medical Writing About Sex and Reproduction

Medical writing about sex and the sexual parts of the body may be thought about as a kind of pornography at this time, as both those who wrote it and those who read it expressed or demonstrated a perception that it could be read as such. There was a contemporary understanding that reading about and discussing sexual matters, even in a medical context, was likely to be sexually arousing, and might therefore be condemned as unfit reading matter – or as suitable reading matter only for those who did not approach it with this intention. Although (as we have seen) the term 'pornography' was coined in the nineteenth century, two similar terms were used by some authors as pseudonyms when writing about sex; these authors included material from medical and semi-medical texts in the books they published. These terms were 'pornodidasculus' and 'erotodidasculus', the meanings of which were, respectively, teaching about prostitutes and teaching about matters of love or eroticism.[13] In this context, teaching about prostitutes meant teaching about sex, as prostitutes were considered to be experts in this subject: writing about prostitutes was understood to be, de facto, writing about sex. Medical writing about the parts of generation, sex and reproduction that explicitly represented itself as for the purposes of education and furthering knowledge was, clearly, teaching about sex. Authors and printers must have been playing on these similarities and ambivalences when producing books such as *Rare Verities: The Cabinet of Venus Unlocked, And Her Secrets Laid Open* (1658) which purported to be a text compiled from authors of Latin texts, including medical ones, for the purpose of educating its readers, and which similarly denied any obscene purpose – but the title of which clearly signalled its nature.[14]

Authorial intention, which some modern scholars have identified as a central component of pornography, was an issue of great concern to early modern medical authors. It also intersects with the idea that pornography is necessarily transgressive. Peter Wagner has defined pornography as 'the written or visual presentation in any realistic form of any genital or sexual behaviour with a deliberate violation of existing and widely accepted moral and social taboos'.[15] The *Oxford English Dictionary* similarly includes the idea of authorial intention in its definition, as it specifies that it is representation 'in a manner intended to stimulate erotic rather than aesthetic feelings'.[16] This definition simultaneously sets up an opposition between literary or artistic merit and sexual arousal that is difficult to sustain on closer examination (and especially in relation to early modern material produced as part of an educated literary or artistic culture).[17] It is evident that it was perceived by some as transgressive and a violation of contemporary moral boundaries to include descriptions of the sexual parts and discussion of the sexual act in early modern medical and midwifery books. Many medical authors presented justifications for their inclusion of this material, indicating that they understood that some readers would respond negatively and that their intentions could be regarded as questionable. The inclusion of this material can therefore be seen to be intentional and as violating moral and social boundaries, albeit with the expressed intention of educating readers rather than sexually arousing them. Such books may not therefore have been intended to *be* pornography, but their sexual content was nevertheless judged to be pornographic or obscene by at least some contemporary readers. Furthermore, authors were thoroughly aware that readers might be sexually aroused by their writing, whether or not this was their intention.

The Bible advised that God said: 'Be fruitful and multiply'.[18] Sermons and the prescriptive texts expanded from them preached that the primary (albeit not the only) purpose of marriage was to procreate, to fulfil God's commandment and to build a Christian society.[19] Contemporary medical ideas were not divorced from the pervading religious climate; authors of medical and midwifery books who wrote about generation (the contemporary term for reproduction) developed their explanations of how and why it took place, what might impede it and how such impediments might be remedied within this framework. They also drew on God's plan for mankind to propagate the species to justify their writing about a subject that was regarded as immodest. In the early seventeenth century, Helkiah Crooke (physician to James I) justified his description and explanation of 'the Naturall Parts belonging to generation' in book four of his major book of anatomy and physiology, *Microcosmographia: A Description of the Body of Man* (1615), by arguing that God had intended that 'those who are sober minded might knowe themselves, that is, their owne bodies, as well to give glory to him who hath so wonderfully Created them'.[20] Crooke's inclusion of the category of the 'sober minded' to define those who might be considered suitable to partake of this knowledge indicates his awareness that the nature of the subject matter was problematic, even for those medical men who he must have anticipated were likely to be the main audience for this substantial and specialised text.[21] It was also an acknowledgment that readers might potentially approach it with the wrong attitude or intention.

Early modern authors of medical books were thus clearly aware that they might be accused of 'obscene' purposes in writing about sexual matters, despite their ostensible concern to further extend the bounds of human knowledge by attempting to understand the workings of the body, and to celebrate the work of God in creating humankind. They therefore also further denied any obscene purpose by asserting that their work was only intended for the 'right' kind of reader who would approach the text with the 'right' attitude. Writing around seventy years after Crooke (towards the end of the seventeenth century), the anonymous author of the enormously popular work *Aristotle's Masterpiece* (1684) wrote in the preface to the reader: 'I not desiring this Book should fall into the hands of any obscene person, whose Folly or Malice may turn that into Ridicule that loudly proclaims the infinite Wisdom of an *omnipotent* Creator'.[22] Crooke went even further in his justification and challenged those who might accuse him of obscenity by asking whether the bad intentions or moral weakness of a few should prevent the higher purposes of those who, like himself, sought to fulfil God's will by learning about His creation in all its facets: 'but shall we therefore forfeit our knowledge because some men cannot conteine their lewd and inordinate affections?'[23] Crooke sought (ostensibly) to appease those who might suspect his purpose by reassuring the reader that the part of the book containing the discussion of the sexual parts of the body and the nature of the sexual act might be extracted, so that it could be read separately in private – thus removing it from the gaze of those whose intentions were not to educate themselves but to indulge their 'lewd and inordinate affections': 'beside we have so plotted our busines, that he that listeth may separate this Booke from the rest and reserve it privately unto himselfe'.[24] The implication is that such a 'sober-minded' individual reader will do so in order to protect others from possible 'sinful' reading while preserving his own education by reading the text in the 'right' way. But this suggestion for private reading also acts as a hint that it might be preferable to do so in order to hide any erotic response to the text – whether deliberately sought or incidental – from others who might detect it and consequently make an accusation of immorality.

Medical and midwifery books were thus recognised as having a potentially dual purpose: education in matters of sex and reproduction, but also,
through representation and discussion of the subject, the power to incite
a sexual response. Consequently, Nicholas Culpeper was accused of producing 'obscene' works by writing midwifery books, while another author
could confirm this judgement (albeit without the same intention of condemnation) by including his work, with others, as suitable reading for those
visiting or working in a brothel.[25] The author of *The Practical Part of Love*
(1660) included 'all sorts of books of Midwifery, as *Culpeppers Midwife,
the compleat Midwife, the birth of Mankind, Child-birth*, &c.' among reading matter and images suitable for 'Love's Academy'.[26] Such examples indicate that at least some of those who wrote and read these books were, like
Crooke and the anonymous author of *Aristotle's Masterpiece* (1684), aware
of the potential for readers to be sexually aroused by descriptions of the
male and female reproductive parts and their use during the sexual act to
propagate humankind, and thus were sensitive to the potential 'misuse' of
their work. However, examples of actual readers either seeking stimulation
through such texts, or finding them arousing despite their best intentions,
are rare. The exceptional recording by John Cannon of his reading of his
mother's midwifery book as an aid to masturbation enables us to see that
their concern was justified.[27]

Medical and midwifery books were clearly perceived and read as a kind
of pornography by some early modern people; they could be relied upon
to include sexual content, however briefly or prefaced with disclaimers
about intention. Another issue identified by modern scholars as crucial in
categorising representations as pornographic or obscene rather than erotic
(or aesthetically pleasing) is the degree to which they are explicit. Karen
Harvey has argued that pornography presents repeated representations,
using explicit language, of the sexual parts of the body and of the body
engaged in sexual activity, while erotica is more veiled, exploring its sexual
subject matter through the deployment of suggestion, implication, allusion
and metaphor.[28] Similarly, Philip Stewart identifies the difference between
decent and indecent images as consisting in whether they depict the sexual
act in progress or as either about to take place or having just been completed.[29] Medical books, whether discussing anatomy or the practice of
midwifery, must necessarily be explicit as they describe in detail the appearance, nature, function and composition of these parts of the body. However,
medical writing at this time also included more discursive content, including
allusions to classical and religious literature, and presented its content in a
style of writing that we might consider today to be more literary. The text
was not necessarily 'dry' and factual, but could be as beautifully evocative

of the body parts and acts it described as other literature. Such works could, then, be read for pleasure as much as to learn about the nature, function and operation of these parts – and we should not forget that the literature of sex, which apparently more obviously intends to arouse, also purports to be instructional.

There is a degree of intertextuality between medical books and others that testifies to both the overlapping of writing styles and to common cultural understandings of bodies and sex. We cannot be entirely certain, for example, that the French author Nicolas Chorier borrowed specifically from medical books for his descriptions and discussions of the sexual parts of the body in his originally Latin book, *The Dialogues of Luisa Sigea* (1659/60).[30] However, we can observe that there are passages in this work that are similar to those in contemporary medical books, including specific references to figures from the classics notorious for their sexual prowess or remarkable for having an unusual genital configuration that was understood to enhance their virility.[31] As a French lawyer, Chorier was an educated man who was highly likely to have been familiar with the same classical literature drawn upon by medical authors and those who wrote other kinds of literature, and was also likely to have read medical books.[32] It is therefore perhaps not surprising that Chorier named one of his main female characters Tullia, evoking – for readers steeped in classical learning – Juvenal's depiction in his sixth satire of the Roman matron Tullia's insatiable sexual appetite.[33]

Representations of Sex, Pleasure and Reproduction

It would perhaps be more surprising if early modern pornographic and erotic texts focused solely on sexual pleasure and ignored its outcome, unless we assume that a function of pornography is to provide a fantasy of sex disconnected from any moral or sociocultural context. While it may be possible for us in today's western world to think about sex in this way, because we have access to reasonably reliable contraception and safer pharmaceutical and surgical abortion – as well as living in a more secular society in which it has become more acceptable for women to bear children out of wedlock – this was not the world inhabited by early modern men and women. This was a period when both religious and medical discourses spoke of sex as having the primary purpose of procreation. The experience of pleasure in the act was recognised, but was understood to be God-given for the precise purpose of encouraging humankind to reproduce itself: without pleasure or the promise of children, people would have difficulty overcoming their 'natural' aversion to engaging in 'a thing so abject and filthy as is carnall copulation'.[34] Although it was observable that sex did not always lead to pregnancy, it must have been anticipated that this was an almost inevitable outcome. While childless couples might experience both personal despair and community derision at their inability to fulfil the marital duty of procreation, and so seek remedies for it, most marriages would have been quite quickly followed by the arrival of children.[35] Others may have deliberately sought to avoid conception through the use of contraceptive herbs, devices such as sponges and douching after intercourse and practices such as male withdrawal before ejaculation (coitus interruptus), but success in this endeavour was always uncertain.[36] The prevalence of illegitimacy (and its condemnation, prosecution and punishment) and pre-bridal pregnancy, as well as the experience of multiple pregnancies within marriage, all testified to the difficulty of disconnecting sex from reproduction at this time.[37]

Representations of sex in erotic and pornographic literature therefore imagined it in the context of that worldview and reproduced the understanding that the pleasure of sex was inextricably connected to conception, pregnancy and birth. Far from focusing on sex alone, ignoring its likely outcome, texts frequently reiterated the contemporary procreative imperative. For example, the first part of Charles Cotton's *Erotopolis* (1684), written as an extended topographical metaphor, frequently makes reference to the joys of fertility: 'Husbandmen generally take great delight in manuring either of these, for the Air is there generally wholsome, ... besides that, the husbandman shall be sure to have his penny-worth out of them, for they will seldom lye fallow'.[38] Fertility was an essential component of pleasurable sex; conversely, infertile sex could not be fully pleasurable sex. In *The School of Venus* (1655), sex without the ejaculation of seed was not desired, even if it allowed sexual pleasure without risk of pregnancy: 'Those whom you mentioned just now – the ones who never have an orgasm – are known as castrati, and have had their stones cut off: such men are good for nothing, except sometimes for an erection. But women in this country don't like that at all and one never hears of them showering their favours on men like that.'[39] These representations were underpinned by contemporary medical knowledge and understandings about the processes of reproduction, which connected both pleasure and fertility to heat in the classical humoural model of the body. In this model, the balance of the four humours – blood, yellow and black bile and phlegm – corresponded to the four qualities of hot, dry, cold and wet, and by analogy to four stages of life: infancy, youth, maturity and old age. The balance of the humours thus shifted as a person grew and developed, with heat increasing from infancy into maturity and then decreasing again as the body declined into old age. This change in heat was linked to reproductive ability: increasing heat as children grew towards adolescence precipitated the bodily changes of puberty and enabled production of the essential generative materials, seed and menstrual blood, while its decrease led to the cessation of menstruation in women in middle age and potential impotence and infertility in older men.[40] The rise in heat in adolescence also generated sexual feelings leading to the experience of lust and desire for sex.[41] Heat was also necessary during sexual intercourse to increase pleasure and incite orgasm. This was achieved through the friction of penetrative sex and the release of seed, which had to be sufficiently hot to be fertile and to itself cause pleasure.[42]

This conceptualisation of sex and pleasure thus underpins representations of the sexual body and sexual acts in a variety of different texts. In many medical and midwifery books that set out the signs of conception, this idea that conception brought the pinnacle of pleasure is reflected in the first sign of conception, where 'If a woman has ... taken more pleasure than usual therein, (which upon recollection she may easily know) it is a sign of conception'.[43] The connection between pleasure and fertility is also articulated in discussions about the size of the penis and which size is best. Those that are either too short or too long are not so good because the length affects the fertility of the seed when emitted, and thus reduces both pleasure and generative ability. Whether it is too short or too long, the seed will lose its heat before it can reach the womb (too far to travel in the vagina to the womb after emission if the penis is too short, too far to travel from the testicles through the penis in one that is too long) and therefore neither can excite a woman to the point of orgasm, so releasing her seed for conception: 'the short yard is the least of the two to be endured ... Because ... it reaches not so far as sufficiently to provoke a womans lust and seed'.[44] Authors of books about medicine, anatomy, generation and childbearing thus directly linked the pleasure of sex with conception. In the later sixteenth century, French surgeon Ambroise Paré wrote that sex was pleasurable precisely for the purpose of encouraging man to reproduce; the 'chiefest' cause of sexual desire was: 'That the kind may be preserved and kept for ever, by the propagation and substitution of other living creatures of the same kinde'.[45] However, the joys of sexual activity were not perceived as simply limited to inspiring a desire for sex – the outcome of which, if indulged, was likely to be pregnancy, and which would thus ensure the continuation of the human race – the pleasure of the act of sex itself was not seen to be complete *unless* conception occurred. Representations of sexual pleasure, in both medical and other writings, thus constructed the meeting of male and female seed through mutual orgasm as the pinnacle of pleasure and as the aim of the act of sex. Contemporary thinking about bodies and sex linked sexual pleasure and desire to fertility, and in so doing developed an erotic aesthetic in which sexually desirable bodies were bodies that were perceived as fertile. I have argued in publications about body size and reproductive health and about old age and infertility that ideas about ideal bodies and attractive, desirable bodies at this time were also connected to perceptions about the nature of a fertile body.[46]

Whether a particular text adhered to the contemporary Aristotelian one-seed model of generation (in which only men contributed seed for conception) or the Galenic–Hippocratic model (in which both men and women ejaculated seed at orgasm, which then mingled to form a conception), male seed had primacy. Men's seed was infused with vital heat, so was hotter and more active than women's cold, thin, watery and 'more imperfect seed'.[47] It was the vital principal that animated and gave form to women's generative matter, whether this was constituted of menstrual blood alone or of menstrual blood and seed: 'Mans seed is the agent and womans seed the patient, or at least not so active as the mans'.[48] Regarded as the most important element in conception, male seed was lauded in both medical books and in pornographic writing. Writers of both kinds of text echoed each other in extolling the virtues of copious quantities of male seed for its generative power. The overlap between medical books and pornography, noted earlier in this chapter, is particularly noticeable in the similarity between passages in Thomas Bartholin's *Anatomy* (1655) and Chorier's *Dialogues of Luisa Sigea* (1659/60). These refer to the Coleoni family and Agathocles, both of whom were well known for having, unusually, three testicles, which gave them not only enhanced prowess on the battlefield but also greater generative power: 'those that have three operators engaged at it ... flood of course the women with a still greater quantity than those who have only two'.[49] Similarly in *The School of Venus* (1655), Susanne tells Fanchon that those who 'produce more substance ... they give and receive the most pleasure'.[50] In both books of anatomy and the pornographic text, testicles are 'witnesses' to masculine virility and male potency.[51]

It was not only the quantity of the seed that was important but also its quality. Seed that was lacking the qualities that made it fruitful was, by definition, seed that could not provoke pleasure. For seed to be fertile and capable of generating conception it had to be 'copious in quantity but in quality well concocted, moderately thick, clammy, and puffed with abundance of spirits'.[52] Seed that fell short of these qualities, that was 'cold, thinne, waterie and feeble', would be both infertile and lacking in the qualities necessary to provoke pleasure.[53] Seed that was 'Prolifick' – that is, full of blood and spirits and hence capable of sparking conception – was understood to have vital heat in three elements: in addition to its natural, elemental heat it would also have heat from the father's soul and from the sun.[54] Heat was an essential component of the reproductive process at all stages and so its absence caused generative difficulties. Many remedies for generative dysfunction contained ingredients with heating properties intended to restore this missing element.[55]

In both early modern medical books and pornography, the virtues of male seed or semen were extolled – not only because it was understood to provoke and increase female pleasure in intercourse but also because its purpose was to spark conception. The qualities which gave male seed its generative power were the same qualities that meant women experienced pleasure in intercourse. Intercourse that resulted in conception was also the most pleasurable intercourse for women, because it fulfilled women's primary function: motherhood. Women were therefore represented in both kinds of text as eager for men's seed: it ignited and fanned the flames of female sexual desire and passion *and* engendered the offspring that would bring them the pleasures of both sexual and maternal satisfaction, fulfilling their role in marriage and society and so granting them status in their families and communities. Thus French physician Lazare Rivière, in his *Practice of Physick* (1655 [1640]), could describe how a woman's body responded during sex to receive the male seed: 'her womb skipping as it were for joy, may meet her Husbands Sperm, graciously and freely receive the same, and draw it into its innermost Cavity or Closet, and withal bedew and sprinkle it with her own Sperm, powred forth in that pang of Pleasure, that so by the commixture of both, Conception may arise'.[56] Others wrote that the womb greedily snatched the seed into the womb, or that, to enable 'the increase and multiplication of mankind', God had placed 'such a magnetick virtue in the womb, that it draws the seed to it, as the loadstone draws iron'.[57] Women in pornography long for this 'Liquor' and anticipate it as a 'Fountain of Joys'.[58] In *The Dialogues of Luisa Sigea* (1659/60), Tullia tells Octavia: 'I am indebted to this dew for my little daughter; I also owe it all my joys; the human race is indebted to it for its existence'.[59]

Even representation of acts that might initially be perceived as not straightforwardly generative in nature (because not penetrative), such as sexual flagellation, are presented as having conception as its ultimate end. The pain of whipping or beating is translated into sexual pleasure through raising heat, which precipitates the desire for copulation and increases the pleasure of the copulation that follows, bringing an intensified orgasm that enables the release of seed for conception: 'the refrigerated Parts, grow warm by such Stripes, and excite a Heat in the Seminal Matter, and that more particularly from the Pain of the *flogg'd* Parts, which is the Reason that the Blood and Spirits are attracted in a greater Quantity, 'till the Heat is communicated to the Organs of Generation, and the perverse and frenzical Appetite is satisfied'.[60] Sexual flagellation is represented as a means of raising desire and increasing pleasure for those who suffer a functional impairment that prevents conception – either the inability to achieve an erection for men (impotency) or barrenness caused by the inability to reach orgasm and release of the seed in women.[61]

A detailed medical explanation for how this was understood to work, Meibomius' *De Usu Flagrorum*, was first published in Latin on the continent in 1639, and subsequently in an augmented and corrected edition in Frankfurt in 1670. It circulated freely in England in the seventeenth century, but Edmund Curll was prosecuted for printing an English translation, *A Treatise of the Use of Flogging in Venereal Affairs*, in 1718.[62] While Meibomius' original text discussed sexual whipping as a stimulus only for male erection and a cure for impotence, Curll's edition included a letter from Thomas Bartholin to Meibomius' son Henry, dated 24 October 1669, which argues that women 'are rais'd and inflam'd by Strokes to a more easy Conception'. This explanation was undoubtedly in circulation prior to its publication, as we find it incorporated in those works of continental pornography that included scenes of whipping and beating for the purpose of sexual arousal. In *The Dialogues of Luisa Sigea* (1659/60), Ottavia declares that she is 'quite on fire' after being whipped by her mother, who reassures her that any pain 'will be soon turned into an inexhaustible source of pleasure'.[63] Tullia subsequently repeats an anecdote about a friend who previously had 'received no pleasure from Venus' but, after whipping intended to excite her, engaged in sex with her husband so that 'out of sheer voluptuousness she melted away into a prodigious flood' and finally became pregnant.[64]

Conclusion

The focus on the vital properties of male seed and its role in provoking female pleasure in intercourse also hints at another quality of this early modern pornography: the attention that is paid to the desirability of the male body. If the most likely readers of this material were other men (although female readers should not be excluded, both as imagined by male authors and in reality), then we also need to pay attention to how and why such representations may have been found pleasurable by readers – both male and female.[65] The overlap between medical writing about sex and other kinds of text exposes the importance of contemporary cultural influences on what is written, how it is written and how it is received. Medical and midwifery books could be read as a kind of pornography because they shared certain characteristics with other texts that represented sexual matters: they were explicit, they deployed similar styles of writing and description, they were instructional and they were perceived to transgress contemporary moral boundaries simply because they discussed sexual matters. They did so in the context of a contemporary procreative imperative: sex was intended for procreation and was God-given for this purpose. One of the significant differences between early modern pornographic writing and modern pornography, apart from the physical or material nature of the 'thing', is its relationship to reproduction. This is just one element – but a significant one – that has changed over time and that emphasises the importance of examining these texts in cultural context. We cannot assume that pornography inevitably only represents sex in isolation, divorced from any social, cultural or moral context. Early modern pornography not only recognises that procreation follows from sex but also conformed to contemporary understandings about the nature of sexual pleasure that saw it as indivisible from conception.

NOTES

1 Lisa Z. Sigel, 'Looking at Sex: Pornography and Erotica Since 1750' in Sarah Toulalan and Kate Fisher (eds.), *The Routledge History of Sex and the Body 1500 to the Present* (London and New York: Routledge, 2013), pp. 223–6, p. 224.
2 On early modern censorship and control of the book trade, see, for example, Annabel Patterson, *Censorship and Interpretation: The Conditions of Writing and Reading in Early Modern England* (Madison, WI and London: The University of Wisconsin Press, 1984); Nigel Smith (ed.), *Literature and Censorship* (Cambridge: D. S. Brewer, 1993). On sex and censorship, see Alec Craig, *The Banned Books of England and Other Countries: A Study of the Conception of Literary Obscenity* (London: George, Allen & Unwin, 1962); Alec Craig, *Suppressed Books: A History of the Conception of Literary Obscenity* (Cleveland, OH and New York: World Publishing, 1963); David Foxon, *Libertine Literature in England, 1660–1745* (New York: University Books, 1965); Ian Hunter, David Saunders and Dugald Williamson (eds.), *On Pornography: Literature, Sexuality and Obscenity Law* (Basingstoke and London: Macmillan, 1993); Geoffrey Robertson, *Obscenity: An Account of Censorship Laws and their Enforcement in England and Wales* (London: Weidenfeld and Nicolson, 1979); Donald Thomas, *A Long Time Burning: The History of Literary Censorship in England* (London: Praeger, 1969).
3 Sigel, 'Looking at Sex', pp. 223–6. See also Lynn Hunt (ed.), *The Invention of Pornography* (New York: Zone Books, 1993); Walter Kendrick, *The Secret Museum: Pornography in Modern Culture* (New York: Viking, 1987); Iain McCalman, *Radical Underworld: Prophets, Revolutionaries and Pornographers, 1795–1840* (Oxford: Clarendon, 1993).
4 See 'pornography, n.', in *Oxford English Dictionary Online* (Oxford: Oxford University Press, 2016), www.oed.com.
5 On use of the term 'pornographos', see Madeleine M. Henry, 'The Edible Woman: Athenaeus's Concept of the Pornographic', in Amy Richlin (ed.),

Pornography and Representation in Greece & Rome (New York and Oxford: Oxford University Press, 1992), pp. 250–68, esp. pp. 261–5.

6 Sigel, 'Looking at Sex', pp. 230–3.

7 See my discussion of images in Sarah Toulalan, *Imagining Sex: Pornography and Bodies in Seventeenth-Century England* (Oxford: Oxford University Press, 2007), chapter 7.

8 David Cressy, *Literacy and Social Order: Reading and Writing in Tudor and Stuart England* (Cambridge: Cambridge University Press, 2006); Adam Fox, *Oral and Literature Culture in England, 1500–1700* (Oxford: Clarendon Press, 2000); James Raven, Helen Small and Naomi Tadmor (eds.), *The Practice and Representation of Reading in England* (Cambridge: Cambridge University Press, 1996); Margaret Spufford, *Small Books and Pleasant Histories: Popular Fiction and its Readership in Seventeenth-Century England* (Cambridge: Cambridge University Press, 1985).

9 Ian Frederick Moulton, 'Erotic Representation, 1500–1750', in Sarah Toulalan and Kate Fisher (eds.), *The Routledge History of Sex and the Body 1500 to the Present* (London and New York: Routledge, 2013), pp. 207–22, p. 209.

10 Sigel, 'Looking at Sex', p. 225.

11 Moulton, 'Erotic Representation', p. 212. These are not, though, the only texts that might be included in the field. See also Toulalan, *Imagining Sex*, esp. pp. 15–31.

12 See Roger Thompson, *Unfit for Modest Ears: A Study of Pornographic, Obscene and Bawdy Works Written or Published in England in the Second Half of the Seventeenth Century* (London and Basingstoke: Macmillan, 1979), p. 28, and, for a description of the content, Moulton, 'Erotic Representation', pp. 213–14.

13 See, for example, Giovanni Benedetto Sinibaldus, *Rare Verities. The Cabinet of Venus Unlocked, And Her Secrets Laid Open. Being a Translation of Part of Sinibaldus his Geneanthropeia, and a Collection of Some Things out of Other Latin Authors, Never Before in English* (London: Printed for P. Briggs, 1658), p. 40. The British Library catalogue lists Sinibaldus as the author but it is an anonymously authored compilation that includes a translation of part of Sinibaldus' *Geneanthropeia* (1642) and other, unnamed, texts. *Rare Verities* is also listed in the British Library catalogue under the pseudonym 'Erotodidasculus', indicating that the author/compiler considered this presentation of a selection of choice sexual 'facts' as educating about erotic life.

14 This book was also included in the list of items suitable for 'Love's Academy' in Anon, *The Practical Part of Love* (London: n.p., 1660), pp. 39–40. See Peter Wagner's brief discussion of this book in *Eros Revived: Erotica of the Enlightenment in England and America* (London: Secker and Warburg, 1988), p. 11.

15 Wagner, *Eros Revived*, p. 5.

16 See 'pornography, n.', *Oxford English Dictionary Online*.

17 See my discussion in *Imagining Sex*, pp. 7–9, and in Moulton, 'Erotic Representation', p. 209.

18 Genesis 1:28, *King James Bible*. On Protestant reproductive polemic and its influence on vernacular medical and midwifery literature, see Kathleen Crowther-Heyck, '"Be Fruitful and Multiply": Genesis and Generation in Reformation Germany', *Renaissance Quarterly*, 55:3 (2002), 904–35.

19 See, for example, Henry Smith, *A Preparative to Mariage* (London: Printed by R. Field for Thomas Man, 1591). For a discussion of marriage and marital conduct books, see Anthony Fletcher, 'The Protestant Idea of Marriage in Early Modern England', in Anthony Fletcher and Peter Roberts (eds.), *Religion, Culture and Society in Early Modern Britain* (Cambridge: Cambridge University Press, 1994), pp. 161–81.

20 Helkiah Crooke, *ΜΙΚΡΟΚΟΣΜΟΓΡΑΦΙΑ[Microcosmographia]: A Description of the Body of Man*, 2nd edn (London: Printed by W. Jaggard, 1616 [1615]), p. 197.

21 For a discussion of Book IV, its author and reception, see Lauren Kassell, 'Medical Understandings of the Body, c.1500–1750', in Toulalan and Fisher (eds.), *The Routledge History of Sex and the Body*, pp. 57–74.

22 Anon, *Aristoteles Master-Piece, Or The Secrets of Generation Displayed in all the Parts Thereof* (London: Printed for J. How, 1684), p. 4 (italics in original). Mary Fissell has identified more than 100 editions of this text. It went through many new editions in the eighteenth century and continued to be published into the twentieth. See Mary E. Fissell, 'Making a Masterpiece: The Aristotle Texts in Vernacular Medical Culture', in Charles E. Rosenberg (ed.), *Right Living: An Anglo-American Tradition of Self-Help Medicine and Hygiene* (Baltimore, MD: Johns Hopkins University Press, 2003), pp. 59–87.

23 Crooke, *Microcosmographia*, p. 197.

24 Crooke, *Microcosmographia*, p. 197.

25 See Audrey Eccles, *Obstetrics and Gynaecology in Tudor and Stuart England* (London and Canberra: Croom Helm, 1982). Eccles quotes a contemporary writer who refers to Nicholas Culpeper's publication of midwifery books as producing obscene texts, p. 13.

26 Anon, *The Practical Part Of Love*, pp. 39–40.

27 See Tim Hitchcock, *English Sexualities, 1700–1800* (Basingstoke and London: Palgrave, 1997), pp. 28–9. For other examples of reading for sexual content see Andrew Taylor, 'Reading the Dirty Bits', in Jacqueline Murray and Konrad Eisenbichler (eds.), *Desire and Discipline: Sex and Sexuality in the Premodern West* (Toronto, Buffalo, NY and London: University of Toronto Press, 1996), pp. 280–95.

28 Karen Harvey, *Reading Sex in the Eighteenth Century: Bodies and Gender in English Erotic Culture* (Cambridge: Cambridge University Press, 2005), p. 20.

29 Philip Stewart, *Engraven Desire: Eros, Image & Text in the French Eighteenth Century* (Durham, NC and London: Duke University Press, 1992), pp. 318–19.

30 See Thompson, *Unfit for Modest Ears*, p. 28, and, for a description of the content, Moulton, 'Erotic Representation', pp. 213–14.

31 See my comparison in *Imagining Sex* (p. 14) of similar passages from the late-nineteenth-century translation of Chorier's text into English as *The Dialogues of Luisa Sigea* (Paris: Isidore Liseux, 1890), pp. 38–9 and Thomas Bartholin's *Bartholinus Anatomy* (London: Printed by Peter Cole, 1663), p. 55. The *Anatomy* was originally printed in Latin in 1655.

32 Nicolas Chorier (1612–1692) was a lawyer practising in Grenoble. Evidence of book ownership for England shows that men of this social status and education owned medical books. See Thompson, *Unfit for Modest Ears*, pp. 197–207.

33 Tullia is usually referenced in the context of representations of lesbian sex. See, for example, John R. Clarke, 'Look Who's Laughing at Sex: Men and Women Viewers in the Apodyterium of the Suburban Baths at Pompeii', in David Fredrick (ed.), *The Roman Gaze: Vision, Power, and the Body* (Baltimore, MD and London: John Hopkins University Press, 2002), pp. 149–81, p. 168.

34 Ambroise Paré, *The Workes of that Famous Chirurgion Ambrose Parey*, trans. Thomas Johnson, 2nd edn (London: Printed by Th. Cotes and R. Young, 1634 [1579]), p. 886.

35 Women's bodies, both married and unmarried, were scrutinised for the signs of pregnancy to detect either signs of incontinency or of infertility should they not quickly become pregnant once married. See Laura Gowing, *Common Bodies: Women, Touch and Power in Seventeenth-Century England* (New Haven and London: Yale University Press, 2003), chapter 4, esp. pp. 41–8, 71–3, 114–15.

36 On contraception and family limitation, see Angus McLaren, *Reproductive Rituals: The Perception of Fertility in England from the Sixteenth Century to the Nineteenth Century* (London: Methuen, 1984); Dorothy McLaren, 'Marital Fertility and Lactation 1570–1720,' in Mary Prior (ed.) *Women in English Society 1500–1800* (London: Methuen, 1985), pp. 22–53; E.A. Wrigley, 'Family Limitation in Pre-Industrial England', *Economic History Review*, 2nd ser., XIX:1 (1966), 82–109.

37 Patricia Crawford and Sara Mendelson, *Women in Early Modern England 1550–1720* (Oxford: Oxford University Press, 1998); Laura Gowing, 'Secret Births and Infanticide in Seventeenth-Century England', *Past & Present*, 156 (1997), 87–115; Martin Ingram, *Church Courts, Sex and Marriage in England* (Cambridge: Cambridge University Press, 1987).

38 Charles Cotton, *ΕΡΟΤΟΠΟΛΙΣ (Erotopolis): The Present State of Betty-Land* (London: Printed for Tho. Fox, 1684), p. 10.

39 Michel Millot and Jean L'Ange, *The School of Venus: or, the Ladies Delight Reduced into Rules of Practice*, trans. Donald Thomas (London: Panther, 1972 [1655]), p. 129.

40 On sexual development and infertility in old age, see Sarah Toulalan, '"Age To[o] Great, or To[o] Little, Doeth Let Conception": Bodies, Sex and the Life Cycle, 1500–1750' in Toulalan and Fisher (eds.), *The Routledge History of Sex and the Body*, pp. 279–95, and Sarah Toulalan, '"Elderly Years Cause a Total Dispaire of Conception": Old Age, Sex and Infertility in Early Modern England', *Social History of Medicine* 29:2 (2016), 333–59.

41 See my discussion in '"Unripe" Bodies: Children and Sex in Early Modern England', in Kate Fisher and Sarah Toulalan (eds.), *Bodies, Sex and Desire from the Renaissance to the Present* (Basingstoke and New York: Palgrave Macmillan, 2011), pp. 131–50.

42 In contemporary witchcraft belief, sex with the devil was sterile because it was cold and might also be painful rather than pleasurable. See, for example, Darren Oldridge (ed.), *The Witchcraft Reader* (London and New York: Routledge, 2002), p. 6.

43 W[illiam] S[almon], *Aristotle's Compleat and Experienced Midwife*, 12th edn. (London: n.p., 1764), p. 32.

44 Sinibaldus, *Rare Verities*, p. 40. See also, for an explanation of why a long penis is undesirable, various editions of *Aristotle's Problems*. From the first English edition at the end of the sixteenth century, this book was hugely popular and continued to be reprinted into the late eighteenth century. Anon, *The Works of Aristotle, in Four Parts ... III. His Book of Problems ...*, (London: n.p., 1792), p. 391.

45 Paré, *The Workes*, p. 886.

46 Sarah Toulalan, '"To[o] Much Eating Stifles the Child": Fat Bodies and Reproduction in Early Modern England', *Historical Research*, 87:235 (2014), 65–93; 'Unfit for Generation: Body Size and Reproduction', in Raymond Stephanson and Darren Wagner (eds.) *The Secrets of Generation: Reproduction in the Long Eighteenth Century* (Toronto: University of Toronto Press, 2015), pp. 301–18; '"If slendernesse be the cause of unfruitfulnesse; you must nourish and fatten the body": Thin Bodies and Infertility in Early Modern England', in Gayle Davis and Tracey Loughran (eds.), *A Handbook of Infertility in History: Approaches, Contexts and Perspectives* (Basingstoke: Palgrave Macmillan, forthcoming).

47 Crooke, *Microcosmographia*, p. 162.

48 Jane Sharp, *The Midwives Book, Or the Whole Art of Midwifry Discovered* (London: n.p., 1671), p. 62.

49 Bartholin, *Bartholinus Anatomy*, p. 55; Chorier, *The Dialogues of Luisa Sigea*, pp. 38–39.

50 Millot, *The School of Venus*, p. 100.

51 For a discussion of testicles as witnesses, see Raymond Stephanson, *The Yard of Wit: Male Creativity and Sexuality, 1650–1750* (Philadelphia, PA: University of Pennsylvania Press, 2004), p. 32.

52 Ambroise Paré, 'Of the Generation of Man', in *The Works of Ambrose Parey*, trans. Thomas Johnson (London: Printed by Jos. Hindmarsh, 1691 [1573]), p. 566.

53 Philip Barrough, *The Methode of Phisicke* (London: Printed by Thomas Vautroullier, 1583), p. 157.

54 Danielle Jacquart and Claude Thomasset, *Sexuality and Medicine in the Middle Ages*, trans. Matthew Adamson (Cambridge: Polity Press, 1988), pp. 52–60.

55 See Jennifer Evans, *Aphrodisiacs, Fertility and Medicine in Early Modern England* (Woodbridge: Boydell and Brewer, 2014).

56 Lazarus Riverius (Lazare Rivière), *The Practice of Physick*, trans. Nicholas Culpeper, Abdiah Cole and William Rowland (London: n.p., 1655 [1640]), p. 503.

57 Anon, *Aristotle's Compleat and Experienced Midwife*, trans. W[illiam] S[almon] (London: n.p., 1700), p. 21.

58 Anon, *A Dialogue Between A Married Lady And A Maid* (London: n.p., 1740), p. 33. This is an English adaptation of parts of the first five dialogues of Chorier's *Aloisiae Sigeae*.

59 Chorier, *The Dialogues of Luisa Sigea*, p. 39.

60 John Henry Meibomius, *A Treatise of the Use of Flogging in Venereal Affairs: Also of the Office of the Loins and Reins* (London: Printed for E. Curll, 1718 [1639]), p. 51.

61 See Chorier, *The Dialogues of Luisa Sigea*, pp. 189–94; Meibomius, *A Treatise Of the Use of Flogging*, p. 18 and elsewhere. See also my discussion of these representations in *Imagining Sex*, chapter 3.
62 Thompson, *Unfit for Modest Ears*, pp. 164–5.
63 Chorier, *The Dialogues of Luisa Sigea*, p. 149.
64 Chorier, *The Dialogues of Luisa Sigea*, pp. 193–4.
65 See my discussion of readers in *Imagining Sex*, chapter 1.

8

BRADFORD K. MUDGE

Novel Pleasure

Perhaps the most memorable scene of Jane Austen's most memorable novel is that in which Elizabeth Bennet turns down the proposal of Mr. Fitzwilliam Darcy. Readers general as well as professional will remember the excitement of Darcy's first proposal, its unexpected confirmation of his affections – however proud and haughtily expressed – and the passion and disdain of Elizabeth's response. Even students not accustomed to detailed remembrance are able to recall both Elizabeth's brilliant salvo – "You could not have made me the offer of your hand in any possible way that would have tempted me to accept it" – and her parting shot – "I had not known you a month before I felt that you were the last man in the world whom I could ever be prevailed on to marry."[1] Although the competition is fierce (and the question doesn't lend itself to a definitive answer), this scene could easily be among the most memorable of all of the romantic confrontations depicted in the first two hundred years of the English novel, a period beginning, say, with Aphra Behn and Delarivier Manley and ending with George Eliot and Charles Dickens. Yes, Elizabeth and Darcy would have to contend with the likes of Pamela and Mr. B., Catherine and Heathcliff, Dorothea and Ladislaw. But Austen aficionados would no doubt stake their claim. *Pride and Prejudice* is a most beloved novel, and nowhere as satisfying as those scenes in which hero and heroine match their wits. There, with passion aplenty, Elizabeth and Darcy each demonstrate feeling and intellect worthy of the other. There, too, readers are allowed inside a private moment unwitnessed by other characters and unconstrained by more formal protocols. It is, as far as Austen goes, a decidedly intimate moment. Would we, however, consider the scene "erotic"? Does Austen write "erotic" romance? What does the question itself suggest about the nature of novelistic pleasure and the tradition of which Austen is a part?

The answers, of course, depend on how the "erotic" is defined. Even a cursory knowledge of the English novel would suggest that Austen is among the most decorous of authors and proper to a fault.[2] She is ribald only occasionally and careful to treat sexual misconduct either by innuendo or by placing it offstage, where it is free to further plot and theme without direct description. Lydia's misbehavior in *Pride and Prejudice*, for example, is thematically central: she is the ignorant and independent daughter whose sexual indiscretions with Wickham come dangerously close to destroying the Bennet family. Those indiscretions, however, are represented in the novel only indirectly and certainly not for the purpose of arousing or titillating readers. Lydia's sexual body remains absent from our view. Her words, however, appear before us; after marveling at how oblivious she is to her own bad behavior, we note a variety of ungrammatical locutions, most significantly an ongoing failure to agree subject and verb. Through her bemused narrator, Austen is asking us to consider the relationship between linguistic and moral error. Should we really expect an appreciation for the protocols of courtship from one who is incapable of aligning two halves of a single sentence? Isn't it the case that the promiscuity of one sort lends itself to the promiscuity of another? But Austen also expects her readers to understand that Lydia's faults – grammatical as well as moral – are largely her father's responsibility, that he failed in his duty to educate her, and that her various misalignments could have easily been prevented. When Darcy steps in and buys Wickham off, he acts with a paternal heroism that saves the family, but he also creates a marriage the inequality of which is painfully obvious to Elizabeth. Like Mr. Bennet's own marriage, that of Lydia and Wickham dramatizes an imbalance crucial to the definition of romantic equality with which the novel ends.

It is entirely fitting, then, that the relationship between Elizabeth and Darcy should be marked by fluency, if not at first by agreement. Each demonstrates a linguistic sophistication worthy of the other; each is able to read complex verbal clues and make witty or pointed responses. Although of very different sensibilities, they both experience language as inextricable from character; they are both highly attuned to the words of others. So it is, then, when Austen has Elizabeth scorch her suitor's ears in that first proposal scene, modern readers immediately recognize a passion that extends well beyond the verbal arena in which it occurs and that signifies the exact opposite of Elizabeth's intended message. She rejects Darcy completely and unequivocally, but the narrative of which she is a part – the realist romance – has established conventions that encourage readers to recognize a romantic fate to which Elizabeth herself is blind, but of which she has just proven herself worthy.[3] Whereas Elizabeth acts unselfconsciously with equal parts eloquence and fury, Austen signals a passion recognizable by readers as that which can only be satisfied by the novel's resolution: a happy marriage between hero and heroine. In the case of *Pride and Prejudice*, this marriage not only brings together landed gentry and aspiring middle class in a none-too-subtle class allegory but also represents that union in terms of Darcy's home, Pemberley, of which Elizabeth will be soon made mistress. Treated throughout as a repository of cultural value, the preservation and reproduction of which are of the highest concern, Pemberley is distinguished by having a fine library. When Darcy points out that the library is "the work of many generations," he highlights the connections between physical and cultural reproduction, and in so doing explains the ends that Elizabeth's own passions will serve.[4] Put another way, Elizabeth's fluency aligns inner and outer – nature and culture – and confirms an emotional intelligence as authentic as it is irritated by Darcy's presumption. That fluency presents itself as disclosure, as an intimate revelation of the real, and Darcy is shocked – not only because the response is exactly the opposite of what he expected but also because the passion is both uncompromised and suggestive. Elizabeth's passion, her ability to be angry and independent and articulate all at the same time, suggests her capability for all of the various kinds of reproduction that Pemberley will require.

A case could be made, therefore, that Elizabeth's rejection of Darcy's proposal is erotically charged from beginning to end, that Austen uses one kind of conversation to suggest the passion of another, and that readers find the scene memorable in large part because Elizabeth performs the "no means yes" role with an intensity that demonstrates a realism remarkable for what it leaves to the imagination. Austen, of course, did not write in a vacuum. Her displacement of the sexual body from the realist romance and its refiguration as the passionate exchange of language has to be understood in terms of the history of the English novel and ongoing authorial experiments with the nature of novelistic pleasure. Late-seventeenth- and early-eighteenth-century novelists like Aphra Behn, Delarivier Manley, and Eliza Haywood had no qualms about describing the sexual body.[5] Nor were they adverse to experimenting with the ways their narratives might best share pleasure with their readers. Arousal was an effect devoutly to be wished, and authors borrowed from the stage, from continental romance, and from a variety of genres common to the libertine literatures of the day.[6] Behn's *Love-Letters between a Nobleman and His Sister* (1684), Manley's *The New Atalantis* (1709), and Haywood's *Love in Excess* (1719) all, for example, built upon French scandal fiction – imaginative renderings of real events – and titillated readers with seductions and assignations and intrigues brought to life by the magic of language. Such novels learned to peer into private places and reveal temptations and excitements that readers could share. Unsurprisingly, these early experiments with the form proved both popular and controversial.

Consider, for example, an intriguing but not entirely unusual moment in Manley's *The New Atalantis*. In the opening pages of her novel, Manley has one of her amorous protagonists visit a prospective lover. The scene, remarkable for all the various ways it is different from Austen's mastery in *Pride and Prejudice*, is nevertheless crucial to understanding the tradition of which Elizabeth Bennet was a part:

> The Duchess went to the Count's the next Day, immediately after she had din'd; she scarce allow'd her self time to eat, so much more valuable in her sense were the pleasures of love. The servants were all out of the way as usual, only one *Gentleman*, that told her, his lord was lain down upon a day-bed that joined the *Bathing-Room*, and he believed, was fallen a sleep, since he came out of the bath. The Duchess sofly enter'd the little *Chamber of Repose*. The weather violently hot, the umbrelloes were let down from behind the windows, the sashes open, and the jessimine, that covered 'em, blew in with a gentle fragrancy. Tuberoses set in pretty gilt and china pots, were placed advantageously upon stands, the curtains of the bed drawn back to the canopy, made of yellow velvet, embroidered with white bugles, the panels of the chamber looking-glass. Upon the bed were strew'd, with a lavish profuseness, plenty of *Orange* and *Lemon Flowers*, and to compleat the Scene, the young *Germanicus* in a dress and posture not very decent to describe; it was he that was newly risen from the *Bath*, and in a loose Gown of *Carnation Taffety*, stain'd with *Indian Figures*. His beautiful long, flowing hair, for then 'twas the custom to wear their own tied back with a ribbon of the same colour, he had thrown himself upon the bed, pretending to sleep, with nothing on but his shirt and night-gown, which he had so indecently disposed, that slumbering as he appear'd, his whole person stood confess'd to the Eyes of the Amorous Duchess; his limbs were exactly form'd, his skin shinningly white, and the pleasure of the lady's graceful entrance gave him, diffus'd joy and desire throughout all his form.[7]

In Manley's rendering of the moment, the Duchess is actively pursuing her own pleasure. Unexpectedly, it is the male body, rather than the female, that is carefully displayed and coyly described: Germanicus is objectified both by the Duchess, who is delighted by what she sees, and by Manley's narrative, which has no difficulty assuming that physical passion can be shared equally by men and women. The description highlights sensual details of all sorts, and sexual intercourse seems a perfectly reasonable outcome, not something reserved only for marriage or procreation. If one is tempted (foolishly) to consider early English novels as inherently more conservative and less provocative than their more recent predecessors, then here is evidence that the opposite is in fact the case. At the very moment, however, that we might be tempted to applaud the passage for its "realistic" content (doesn't it, after all, celebrate female sexual empowerment?), we also recognize something drastically different from Austen's passionate conversation.[8] Unlike Austen, who uses verbal exchange to mark and measure passions of various sorts, the Duchess serves exclusively the visual: she allows the reader to see through her to the beauty of objects – flowers, fabrics, bodies – that she intends to enjoy. In other words, Manley's eroticism seems to function within an entirely different narrative economy.

To juxtapose Manley's amorous Duchess to Austen's irate Elizabeth is to consider what the history of the English novel might reveal about literary pleasure generally and erotic pleasure in particular. It is also to be reminded that the majority of novels in eighteenth-century England were both written and read by women, and that romance of one sort or another dominated the generic field. Although readers began the century preferring continental romances like *Amadis de Gaula* (1508) or *La Princesse de Cleves* (1678), which relied heavily on chivalric fantasy, they ended the century preferring novels about more ordinary characters set in their own contemporary moment. What scholars refer to as "the rise of the realist romance" was inextricable from the beginnings of the Industrial Revolution, the expansion of the middle classes, and increased literacy rates.[9] Prosperity for the middle class meant more leisure time, and the novel – however much it was disparaged by arbiters of taste – quickly became a popular mode of entertainment. Its advantages were many: it was a private, portable delivery system for a kind of fiction that allowed readers to contemplate the transformative powers of love and marriage.[10] Moreover, it could pleasure its readers with voyeuristic glimpses into forbidden territories or with passionate conversations between soon-to-be consenting adults. As the late-seventeenth- and early-eighteenth-century novelists soon discovered, prose fiction was a kind of magic mirror, uniquely capable of seeing or speaking readerly desire.

The lavishly detailed room in which the Duchess helps herself to Germanicus thus stands in dramatic contrast to the room in which Darcy meets his stinging rebuff. Austen had no use for exotic fabrics, redolent flowers, or suggestive window coverings. In fact, she had no use for details of any sort other than those that attend what her characters think, feel, or say. The room in which they speak remains invisible. Darcy, like the unsuccessful Collins before him, cannot believe that Elizabeth will refuse. As a result, we witness arrogance give way to surprise, disbelief, and anger. The space to which Austen devotes her attention is thus entirely psycholinguistic. Her focus on conversation needs no competing verisimilitude; there are no props, no metaphors, no suggestions. Above all, there are no bodies, no details of dress, skin, or countenance. When the emotional drama pops in the foreground, in other words, bodies become as irrelevant to Austen as window coverings or potted plants. What *is* relevant is what her characters know, and are struggling to understand, about each other. Intimacy is first and foremost about knowledge. Yes, the unclothed body is traditionally treated as that about which we *most* want to know, but Austen's genius lies precisely in her ability to convince us otherwise. Her rooms remain undescribed, her bodies unmarked – not because the rooms were empty or the bodies unpleasing, but because her focus is instead on conversation, on the drama of voice in which one human being reaches out to another. Whether it is Willoughby explaining himself to Elinor, Fanny Price saying "no" to Sir Thomas, or Anne Elliot reconciling herself to Wentworth, all of the great moments are moments of self-disclosure and appeal. In these moments, Austen's genius transforms the private truth-telling of intimate conversation into a much-needed, public virtue. This is nowhere more evident, of course, than in the conversations between lovers. There, usually at the novels' end, we witness such perfect communication – linguistically, emotionally, intellectually – that we cannot help but believe in the happily-ever-after of marital bliss.

Manley's amorous Duchess, of course, remains interested in conversation of an entirely different sort. As its title page insists, *The New Atalantis* is a "secret" memoir, offering up previously undisclosed intimacies for the entertainment of its readers. It is not afraid to describe bodies in various stages of undress; nor is it reticent to acknowledge sexual intercourse as a perennially popular activity among consenting adults. Is it, however, generally speaking, any more "erotic" than Austen's *Pride and Prejudice*? At first glance, it might seem so. But many of today's readers would disagree, preferring Austen's passionate conversations to Manley's sensual descriptions. Eros, they would argue, attends mystery, and Austen knows the mystery of the human heart. Her fiction, they would claim, is psychologically the more "real." What, then, are we to make of the fact that on October 29, 1709 – nine days after the publication of the second volume of *The New Atalantis* – Manley was arrested? Prosecutors were not interested in parsing the "erotic" from the "obscene," or the "literary" from the "pornographic." They were not concerned about whether one kind of fictional pleasure was more or less legitimate than another. They were concerned instead with the question of libel. They were interested in the fact that the novel had a "Key" that identified the "Duchess" as Barbara Palmer, Countess of Castlemaine, and "Germanicus" as Henry Jermyn, first Baron of Dover. Today's readers may well find Austen's proposal scene passionately "realistic," but Manley's Duchess – thanks to the "Key" – could not have been more "real."

Exercising a power now more common to the tabloids, scandal fiction of the late seventeenth and early eighteenth centuries reveled in its ability to make the private public, and took some risk in doing so. Manley knew Aphra

Behn's own attempt at scandal fiction, *Love-Letters Between a Nobleman and his Sister* (1684), and borrowed her seduction scenes, her treatment of temptation and arousal, and her interest in the liminal spaces of court-yard and garden. Manley also knew Behn's plays, restoration comedies that featured risqué subject matter, witty dialogue, and strong female charac-ters. In *The Rover* (1677), for example, the exchanges between Helena and Willmore pop and crackle in ways that might seem to anticipate Austen's Elizabeth and Darcy. Helena's intelligence moves beneath the surface of her language, always playful, always irreverent, always unexpected. "Helena the Inconstant," as she proclaims herself, refuses to pledge either body or heart. Like desire itself, Behn's heroine resists being fixed or formulated – by Willmore, who loves her certainly, by marriage, which she most decidedly chooses, or by "troth," to which women generally are asked to submit.

Helena's impertinence – linguistically and morally – reaches out both forward and back. Her bawdy punning not only reminds us of the well-established connections between obscenity and satire – connections in evi-dence from Juvenal to John Wilmot, Earl of Rochester – but also represents a certain immorality for which restoration drama is famous, and which proved profoundly influential on the amorous fiction of the early English novelists. Behn, Manley, and Haywood were free to experiment with novelistic pleasure because, like restoration playwrights, they assumed an adult audience. They assumed that their readers could negotiate mature themes, and that they them-selves were only in danger from obscene libel or political misstep. Very few at the time were concerned about the "erotic," the "bawdy," or the "libertine." The word "pornography" – naming as it does a category of "anti-literature," the only purpose of which is readerly arousal – had not yet been coined.[11] This general lack of concern for the effect of sexual material is a key feature of the early eighteenth century, and it would change forever with the appearance of Samuel Richardson's *Pamela* (1740). Richardson wrote an epistolary romance in which a devout housemaid resists and then transforms her predatory mas-ter. But, in addition to penning a novel of unprecedented popularity, he used both his title page and prefatory material to confront and fuel a controversy about pleasure and the novel that would continue unabated until the middle of the twentieth century. Richardson made clear that the pleasures of prose fiction should serve a moral end. Most important, he emphasized a new real-ity for the English novel: that it possessed a large and enthusiastic following, composed to a significant degree of readers – either young or female or both – who were in danger from immoral books. Should these readers be corrupted, Richardson emphasized, English culture would suffer.

In the ensuing controversy, the strengths and weaknesses of Richardson's novel were hotly debated, the anti-Pamelas most famously represented by

Henry Fielding's *Shamela* (1741) and *Joseph Andrews* (1742). Fielding thought Richardson a prig, and critics have carefully and repeatedly dissected all of the various points of contention.[12] Too often lost, however, is the degree to which this mid-century debate about morality and the novel was actually a key moment in a much larger controversy about literary pleasure and the modern state. While it was easy to enjoy an authorial squabble that pitted a moral reformer against a bemused and clever cynic, it was less easy to recognize the beginning of the end for the world that Behn, Manley, and Haywood had created. Fielding writes with such humor and insight, in other words, that it is hard to see that he was on the losing end of this cultural debate. When, for example, in the prefatory material to *Shamela*, the aptly named Parson Tickletext is suddenly moved by a vision of Richardson's heroine – "Oh! I feel an Emotion even while I am relating this: Methinks I see *Pamela* at this Instant, with all the Pride of Ornament cast off" – we immediately recognize a jab at Richardson's peculiar blend of sanctimonious morality and self-indulgent sensationalism.[13] Although *Pamela* is unrelenting in its celebration of female chastity, for example, its narrative energy is utterly dependent on voyeurism and the ongoing threat of rape. The epistolary format does indeed provide the heroine agency – she is a formidable author in her own right, as well as genuine in defense of her "virtue" – but it also sexualizes that agency for its male readership, teasing with intimate glimpses into private, female places. Thus, when Parson Tickletext envisions a Pamela disrobed at once of both her worldly pretense and her clothes, we laugh because Fielding has nailed the joke: he has caught Richardson – together with his adoring readers – trying to have it both ways at once. Exposing Pamela as a "sham," Fielding's satire makes fun of uneducated schemers and pretentious novelists alike, in the process suggesting one kind of whore has much in common with another.

However tempting it might be to sympathize with Fielding, it was Richardson's priggishness that proved prescient. The novel was increasing in popularity, and so too were fears that readers were in danger from passionate and unreasonable fictions. Novels, in other words – like women generally – could tempt the innocent and corrupt the unsuspecting. The mature themes so much a staple of the fiction of Behn, Manley, and Haywood became an emblem for other fears about increased literacy, social mobility, and chaos. In the face of all this, Pamela seemed like just the heroine to save the day. Never flirtatious, never coy, she speaks only the truth. Like the novel in which she appears, she tells Mr. B. over and over again, "I am in earnest; trust me." He can't, and doesn't, accusing her of both using and being duplicitous fiction. He calls her "an artful slut," "a speaking picture," "a saucebox."[14] He believes that her resistance is part of the negotiation, and when he fails to gain her favors by force, he offers a contract specifying the sums he would provide once she agrees to become his mistress. It is not until he finally reads her letters – as we have been doing all along – that he becomes convinced of her virtue.

Little wonder that *Pamela* fueled a mid-century debate about women and pleasure and fiction. Soon after Fielding offered up his good-natured alternatives, John Cleland upped the erotic ante. He published *Memoirs of a Woman of Pleasure* (1748), the heroine of which, Fanny Hill, sets out to tell the "stark, naked truth" of her sexual experiences.[15] "I will not," she tells us, " ... bestow the strip of a gauze wrapper on it, but paint situations as they actually rose to me in nature."[16] Aware of the French antecedents and unwilling to use obscene language in his descriptions, Cleland wrote the most famous erotic novel in English. Like Fielding, he mocked Richardson and the male preoccupation with virginity and defloration. In an ingenious scene with a Mr. Norbert, for example, Fanny feigns innocence – for a large sum – while Norbert happily fantasizes himself a virile ravisher.[17] Not content simply to enact this well-known whorehouse trick, Cleland captures the solipsism of the male sexual imagination and the degree to which female 'virtue' had become a fetish. Although Fanny's adventures are clearly intended to arouse his readers, even in the Norbert scene, Cleland never leaves off satire for long. His heroine's progress from country innocent to kept woman to experienced whore and finally to happily married wife and mother parodies the conventions of the romance novel while offering itself as a more amusing, and more "natur[al]," alternative. Like Richardson, Cleland enjoyed demonstrating the ability of the novel to "see" forbidden pleasure: over and over again, the reader is allowed to peer into private spaces. To Richardson's moral self-assurance, however, Cleland laughingly responses with the irreducible "truth" of the human body. Rich and poor, male and female, young and old, bodies seek out and respond to physical beauty. At what cost, Cleland jokes, does the novel ignore that reality?

As its title suggests, Cleland's novel focuses on Fanny's sexual pleasure. In what we might be tempted to consider already a cliché among erotic novels, Fanny's adventures begin with voyeurism, lesbianism, and simple intercourse, before progressing to more advanced experiments with group sex, flagellation, and other so-called perversions. These sexual encounters are evenly paced throughout; the first volume covers Fanny's experiences as a mistress, while the second catalogues those that occur during her employ in Mrs. Cole's house of ill repute. Bookending these adventures are brief episodes with Charles, Fanny's one true love, who takes her virginity early in the first volume and then returns to marry her at the end of the second. Of this varied menu of sexual possibility and its relationship to romantic love, Cleland's novel makes two crucial points. The first is offered by Mrs. Cole, who, as Fanny relates, "considered pleasure of one sort or other as the universal port of destination, and every wind that blew thither a good one, provided it blew nobody any harm."[18] The second is from Fanny herself, who, at the end of her adventures, concludes with a "tail-piece of morality" that insists that the most pleasurable kind of sex is that between participants who truly love each other.[19] The two positions are not mutually contradict-ory. The first admits to a menu of possibility that normalizes the abnormal while keeping everyone safe; the second selects from that menu a preference for a physical pleasure enhanced by a genuine emotional attachment. As Fanny herself insists, she has been "perfectly consistent" throughout in cele-brating the superiority of "true" love.

Fanny's genial approach to the many kinds of sexual pleasure knows only one exception: male homosexuality. In what seems an odd scene towards the end of the novel, Fanny is horrified by and rails against two young men who pleasure themselves in the next room. The activities, she tells us, are "crimi-nal," and after watching at some length – secretly – and recounting all of the details, she "burn[s] ... with rage and indignation."[20] Then, on her way to "raise the house" upon the men, she accidentally falls and knocks herself out, allowing them to escape. Afterwards, commiserating with Mrs. Cole about these "miscreants," Fanny is asked by her advisor to consider that this "infamous passion" robs hardworking women of the opportunity to profit and that male effeminacy is a "monstrous" insult to women everywhere.[21] Of course, Fanny's outrage and Mrs. Cole's corroborative insights provide Cleland exactly the insurance policy he needs. Although Fanny herself might not like what she sees, her creator has gone to some trouble to let readers decide for themselves

Memoirs of a Woman of Pleasure catalogues the pleasures of the body in prose that carefully avoids the use of obscene language and within a narra-tive that duplicates many of the conventions of the romance novel. Fond of voyeurism but self-conscious about its dependence on metaphor, Cleland's eroticism positions itself as a more realistic version of the most popular novels of the day, making use of satire in part to protect itself from those who may have been seriously offended. Like Fielding, Cleland presupposes a mature, educated reader, one inclined to appreciate the humor of sex. In fact, Fanny concludes her story with a narrative moment that recalls the amusing Parson Tickletext. While describing the climax of her passionate reunion with Charles, she is overcome by her own imagination: "oh! – my pen drops from me here in the ecstasy now present to my faithful mem-ory!"[22] Like the good parson imagining Pamela without ornament, Fanny remembers an ecstasy so ecstatically that it recurs. Although it might seem that both Fielding and Cleland are demonstrating the power of the literary imagination, which of course they are, they are also poking fun at those moralists like Richardson who can't seem to tell the difference between a book and a body.

In time, the mid-century debate relinquished its urgency, replaced in due course by the critical commonplace that bad novels were proliferating unchecked and that bad readers endangered themselves and others. When, in the 1760s, the Gothic novel began to get traction, moralists were provided a convenient scapegoat. Virginal heroines wandered through exotic landscapes, and readers thrilled to ruined castles, mysterious hauntings, and the ever-present threat of rape. Commentators feared that these implausible fantasies did nothing to inculcate duty, responsibility, and hard work. Once again, women readers were thought to be the most susceptible. In novels by Ann Radcliffe, heroines struggled to understand mysteries that were explained eventually by rational, rather than supernatural, means. Not so in Matthew Lewis's *The Monk* (1796). There, actual ghosts and devils proffered temptations large and small. Either way, the eroticism of the Gothic novel preferred to do its magic in exotic locales, at historically vague cultural moments, and over the length of its entire narrative – not just in highly charged, individual scenes.

Consider Ambrosio, the title character of *The Monk*, who ends his adventures married to the Devil. Threatened with the awful justice of the Inquisition, he follows Matilda, his former lover and partner in crime, into a pact with a demon who promises escape. Given the intensity of the scene, it is easy for the reader to miss that Ambrosio's final action – the last in a long line that includes rape, murder, and incest – is verbal. When he says, "I do! I do!" after having already signed a "fatal contract" with the Fiend, he marries himself to an evil he can only barely imagine.[23] Thinking himself soon to be reunited with Matilda, he discovers that she was an agent of the Devil all along. Instead of conjugal bliss, he can expect a worse punishment than that he sought to avoid. Yes, the Devil tells him, he will be reunited with Matilda, but in Hell, where she will be torturing him for the rest of eternity. After this dreadful "marriage" – a perverse inversion of Radcliffe's "happily-ever-after" – Ambrosio is then seized by the bird-like demon, carried to "a dreadful height," and dropped to the rocks below. There, his "bruised and mangled" body clings to life; it is tortured by birds and insects for six straight days, before being carried off on the seventh day to the everlasting torments of hell. Lewis, having enjoyed rewriting Radcliffe, concludes his novel by rewriting Genesis as well.

The Monk is an erotic masterpiece, extravagant and excessive and brilliantly self-aware about its own novelistic pleasures. Matilda, agent of the

Devil and instrument of the monk's ruin, provides a case in point. She is easily among the most interesting characters in English fiction, and not because she provides the latest iteration in a long line of temptresses who engage, define, and placate the male imagination. As I have argued in detail elsewhere, Lewis uses "Maltida" not as a conventional literary "character," a representation in words of an individual "self" that may or may not carry an assortment of symbolic freight, but instead as the condition of possibility for desire itself, first and foremost that of the amorous monk who will be tempted and will fall – over and over and over again – but also that of the reader who, thanks to Lewis's genius, participates as well in the magic the ensnares the main character.[24] In other words, "Matilda" is a narrative strategy, a protean figure always contingent on fiction of one kind or another. Consider that "she" appears first as "Rosario," a devoted male acolyte; becomes "Matilda," who then assumes a variety of distinct personalities; and finally, at the novel's end, is revealed to be an agent of the Devil, whose every action was intended to exploit Ambrosio's vanity and pride. Consider too that her weapon of choice is fiction: not only is "she" herself a protean shape-shifter, a fiction, but "she" also deploys a wide variety of fictions to ensnare her victim. As "Rosario," she uses stories; as "Matilda," a painting, a song, a magic mirror, etc. Each fiction has its own truth or beauty with which the monk can sympathize or by which he allows himself to be affected. Using that time-honored connection between women and fiction, therefore, Lewis creates in "Matilda" a strategy by which the reader is forced to confront the pleasures of the novel generally and the Gothic novel in particular. "Matilda" says repeatedly to the monk and the reader alike: "What is it that you desire? What is it that you would like me to procure?" Appropriately enough, the Devil is everywhere to be found, and God is conspicuously absent.

It is significant that Austen's first published novel was *Northanger Abbey* (1817), a parody of Gothic fiction in which the heroine, Catherine Morland, learns to put aside irrational fantasies in favor of a realistic commitment to Henry Tilney and his family. Making fun of the Gothic proved an efficacious way for Austen to develop her own realist romance, where women could be reasonable and clever and, like Elizabeth Bennet, passionate conversationalists. Not all of her heroines are rewarded with Pemberley, but they all find marriage – and most, in addition to their perfect mates, are also provided with an attending patriarch newly chastened by events and now amenable to the right kind of female influence. Although she has no use for the Bleeding Nun or the Wandering Jew, Austen pleasures herself and her readers with unlikely encounters of her own. Repeatedly, she devises situations so socially and emotionally awkward that it seems language itself will have to collapse under the stress. Edward walks in on Elinor and Lucy Steele; Lady Catherine confronts Elizabeth Bennet; Edmund encourages Fanny to marry Henry Crawford – each scene so fraught that the Devil himself would have trouble finding the right words. Yet, against all odds, heroine and author together find a way, their collaboration proof that romance – even that faithful to the verisimilitudes of ordinary life – had magic all its own. Clearly avoidant of the sexual body, indeed of most bodies altogether, that magic was nevertheless capable of using its skills in service of readerly pleasure. Never, in fact, Austen aficionados would insist, has the language of the novel revealed so much while pleasuring so many.

Of course, Jane Austen may have set a standard, but hers was not the last word. Catherine and Heathcliff share a romantic passion strong enough to haunt generations; Dorothea and Ladislaw manage to love each other and reform the body politic. The Gothic novel followed Shelley and Stoker and Wilde in one direction, and Brontë and Forester and Lawrence in another. Yet this is only the story canonical novels tell. There is another story no less relevant to the understanding of erotic fiction and the lessons that fiction proffers about our own cultural moment. The first two decades of the nineteenth century – the same period that saw the publication of Austen's six, great novels – also witnessed a transformation in what Aphra Behn or Delarivier Manley or John Cleland would have referred to in their day as "libertine literature." In Cleland's world, for example, sexually explicit material came in many different shapes and sizes: street ballads, whore dialogues, trial accounts, travelogues, medical manuals, etc., as well as prose fiction. That material, generally speaking, served diverse functions and circulated freely among mature, educated adults. By the time Austen published, however, libertine literature had effectively given way to something that would soon be called "pornography": sexually explicit fiction intended to arouse its audience and to appeal to a broad, rather than select, readership. Historians have explained this emergence as having been facilitated by a small number of radical publishers whose obscenities originally served political purposes.[25] After the end of the Napoleonic Wars, these obscenities took on a sexual life of their own, morphing into something so dangerous as to require legislation. With the passage of the Obscene Publications Act of 1857, legislators stepped to continue what Samuel Richardson had begun: not only did they acknowledge that the pleasures of fiction needed to be policed by the modern state, but in so doing they also established a Manichean drama between "literature" and "pornography" that would continue for the next hundred and fifty years and would engage many of the finest writers of the period: Gustave Flaubert, Charles Baudelaire, Algernon Swinburne, Oscar Wilde, D. H. Lawrence, and James Joyce, among them. If "literature" came to mean a collection of national gospels crucial to citizenship and collective identity, then "pornography" became its demonic counterpart, Devil tales that seduce readers away from family, church, and state. "Literature" came to mean that which we all need to remember, "pornography" that which we would do best to forget.

"Eroticism" names the middle ground, the place between. Happier as an adjective than a noun, it connotes approbation, albeit of a grudging sort. It is, as we have seen, notoriously hard to define, blurring boundaries and wreaking havoc with the apodictic tendencies of both literature and pornography. Yet that difficulty is salutary. It forces historians of the novel to consider literary pleasure in all its myriad forms. Sometimes eroticism attends the visual, happy, like Manley's Duchess, to gaze upon the beloved splayed out before, or happier still, like Cleland's Fanny, for a hole in the bedroom wall. Sometimes, however, eroticism prefers language, a witty conversation between flirtatious adults, as in the case of Helena and Willmore, or a passionate exchange between the indignant and the misunderstood, as that between Elizabeth and Darcy. Either way, as the novel demonstrates repeatedly, authors experiment and readers enjoy, the proffered dreams of fiction beckoning, like Matilda, with pleasures at once familiar and not.

NOTES

1 *Pride and Prejudice* (New York: Norton Critical, 1966), ed. Donald Gray, 130–34. The scene occurs in Volume II, Chapter XII.
2 For a detailed account of Austen's ribald humor, see Jill Heydt-Stevenson, *Austen's Unbecoming Conjunctions: Subversive Laughter, Embodied History* (New York: Palgrave, 2008). For Austen and erotic love, see Robert Polhemus, *Erotic Faith: Being in Love from Jane Austen to D. H. Lawrence* (Chicago: Chicago University Press, 1990). Arguing the other side, that Austen calculatingly withholds the erotic, is Elaine Bander's "Neither Sex, Money, nor Power: Why Elizabeth Finally Says 'Yes!'" *Persuasions: The Jane Austen Journal* 34 (2012), 25–41.
3 For a classic study of the novel's development and Austen's somewhat odd position therein, see Ian Watt, *The Rise of the Novel: Studies in Defoe, Richardson, and Fielding* (Berkeley: University of California Press, 1957). See also, among others, Nancy Armstrong, *Desire and Domestic Fiction* (New York: Oxford, 1987); Margaret Ann Doody, *The True Story of the Novel* (New Brunswick: Rutgers, 1997); Terry Lovell, *Consuming Fiction* (London: Verso, 1987); Deidre Lynch, *The Economy of Character: Novels, Market Culture, and the Business of Inner Meaning* (Chicago: University of Chicago Press, 1998); Michael McKeon, *The Origins of the English Novel* (Baltimore: Johns Hopkins University Press, 1987); Steven Moore, *The Novel: An Alternative History* (London: Bloomsbury, 2013); Bradford Mudge, *The Whore's Story: Women, Pornography, and the*

British Novel, 1684–1830 (New York: Oxford University Press, 2000); Thomas Pavel, *The Lives of the Novel* (Princeton: Princeton University Press, 2013); Michael Schmidt, *The Novel: A Biography* (New York: Belknap, 2014); Dale Spender, *Mothers of the Novel* (London: Pandora, 1986); and William Warner, *Licensing Entertainment: The Elevation of Novel Reading in Britain, 1684–1750* (Berkeley: University of California Press, 1998).

4 *Pride and Prejudice*, 25.

5 See Ros Ballaster, *Seductive Forms: Women's Amatory Fiction, 1784–1740* (Oxford: Oxford University Press, 1992); and Catherine Gallagher, *Nobody's Story: Vanishing Acts of Women Writers in the Marketplace, 1670–1820* (Berkeley: University of California Press, 1994).

6 See Bradford Mudge, *When Flesh Becomes Word: An Anthology of Early Eighteenth-Century Libertine Literature* (Oxford: Oxford University Press, 2004).

7 Manley, *Secret Memoirs and Manners of Several Persons of Quality, of Both Sexes. From the New Atalantis, an Island in the Mediterranean*, ed. Rosalind Ballaster (London: Penguin, 1991), 20–21.

8 Enthusiasm for what might appear modern in this scene has to be qualified by the fact that the Duchess is being duped. Because he has grown tired of her, the Duchess's former lover contrives to have her fall for another, thereby facilitating their separation. Her lust is therefore less a marker of power and independence, and more an appetite which he can count on and take advantage of.

9 Among the numerous studies of the evolution of England's cultural marketplace, see in particular John Brewer, *The Pleasures of the Imagination: English Culture in the Eighteenth Century* (Chicago: University of Chicago Press, 1997).

10 See Nancy Armstrong, *How Novels Think: The Limits of Individualism from 1719 to 1900* (New York: Columbia University Press, 2006).

11 The key argument here is that of Walter Kendrick in *The Secret Museum: Pornography in Modern Culture* (New York: Penguin, 1987), 1–32.

12 See, for example, Sheridan Baker's summary in his 1972 critical edition, *"Joseph Andrews" and "Shamela"* (New York: Crowell, 1972), xi–xxx.

13 *Shamela*, 11.

14 *Pamela Richardon, Or Virtue Rewarded*, eds. T. C. Duncan Eaves and Ben D. Kimpel (New York: Riverside, 1971), 39–43.

15 *Memoirs of a Woman of Pleasure*, ed. Peter Wagner (New York: Penguin, 1985), 39. See also *Launching Fanny Hill*, eds. Patsy S. Fowler and Alan Jackson (New York: AMS, 2003).

16 *Memoirs*, 39.

17 *Memoirs*, 168–72.

18 *Memoirs*, 181.

19 *Memoirs*, 217–23.

20 *Memoirs*, 195.

21 *Memoirs*, 196.

22 *Memoirs*, 220.

23 Matthew Lewis, *The Monk*, eds. D. L. Macdonald and Kathleen Scherf (Toronto: Broadview, 2004), 359.

24 Bradford K. Mudge, "How to Do the History of 'Pornography': Romantic Sexuality and Its Field of Vision," in Richard C. Sha ed., *Praxis: Romantic Sexualities*. www.rc.umd.edu/praxis/sexuality/mudge/mudge.html

25 Ian McCalman, *Radical Underworld: Prophets, Revolutionaries, and Pornographers in London, 1795–1840* (Cambridge: Cambridge University Press, 1988).

9

RICHARD C. SHA

Erotic for Whom? When Particular Bodies Matter to Romantic Sexuality

The term "erotic" sometimes assumes the stance of a particular body/subjectivity and sometimes appears as a view from nowhere. The question "erotic for whom?" attempts to put a particular subject back in the foreground, thereby replacing a universalizing – if masculine – body with specific bodies. Laura Mulvey famously diagnosed what happens when a particular stance claims universality when she called out the eye of traditional filmic pleasure as the scopophilic voyeuristic male gaze that can only see woman as castration.[1] How then does eroticism negotiate the competing demands of individuality and universalism?

In Sade, the libertine model is taken to its logical conclusion: as sexual and moral restraints go by the wayside, one lover takes another's place, one hole is exchanged for another hole, and it seems as if desire is indifferent to different bodies. And yet when an individual body has the greatest power to flout social and religious convention – say the mother's body, or the body of a young female child, or even a she-goat – it is particularized for its shock value. What is the relation between eroticism and embodiment in Romanticism, and what are the stakes of this relation? Another way to put the question is: when are erotic bodies particularized, how do particularities stick to bodies, and when are the particularities fungible? When is the desiring body an abstract body and when does it demand a particular kind of embodiment?[2] And can the particularities be systematized? As the Romantics recognized, there remain significant downsides to particularity, since particular differences can remain an obstacle to mutuality and egalitarianism on the one hand, and thwart the simplicity and authenticity that reconciles eroticism with art on the other.[3]

To set the stage for reflecting upon how and why erotic particularities appear and disappear, I turn to the Ancient Greek tradition of eros. The problem is made more difficult by a split in eros itself: in ancient Greece, the term eros covers such multitudinous sins as love, desire, or sexual passion. So much of it, we may tend to forget, went down between men in the gymnasium. Eros is simultaneously an abstract ideal associated with a striving for beauty, and a real physical violent force of attraction.[4] One must not assume that the physical feeling is the ideal; furthermore, any undoing by desire of the self's mastery of itself is to be mourned, not celebrated. Here eroticism requires the measuring of the costs of autonomy and the price of its loss. Writ large, then, eros sits at the gap between physical acts/bodies and the emotional and political meaning of those acts, a point that Sade underscores when he locates philosophy incongruously in the bedroom. Eros thus has always been about the problem of connecting the particular experience to the universal, a skill that Kant would later call judgment.

Greek eros is further linked to *agon*; eros is a form of athletic contest. To wit, in Ancient Greece, erotic reciprocity (*anteros*) is the enemy of eros.[5] I raise this because so many writers of the Romantic period knew of this tradition owing to a deep education in the classics, and it poses an obstacle to thinking that eros can simply be enlisted for any single political aim, or mindlessly conflated with mutuality. Eros in the Greek tradition works through violent contest, but to do that, any mutuality between men must be the outcome of struggle, and the question is: what differences have to be left on the gymnasium floor, and how are they to be cast off? Within pederasty, of course, beauty is exchanged for knowledge, thereby underwriting a mutuality that is concretized by the physical intercourse between the passive male object of beauty and the active male lover. In "Sokrates and Alcibiades," Hölderin questioned Socrates for the reasons underlying his deference to the beautiful Alcibiades. He concluded, "*Und es neigen die Weisen / Oft am Ende zu Schönen sich.*" Hamburger translates this as: "And the wise in the end will / Often bow to the beautiful."[6] Hölderin's upshot is that even Socrates cannot have wisdom beyond the beautiful, and the German underscores beauty's overwhelmingness with consonance of "s" and "z" sounds. Insofar as the verb "*neigen*" suggests "to bend" and "*Ende*" can mean "tail," Hölderin also provides an answer by flashing Alcibiades' ass. In a larger view, the exchange between the *erastes* (the adult active male) and *eromenos* (the younger passive male) only counts as exchange if the actors play their required contingent roles; but does this exchange have the power to lastingly level power differentials, decontextualize the actors, and attenuate violence? Note how this exchange is predicated on a kind of taste capable of recognizing the terms by which exchange is possible.[7] Is erotic desire ever between bodies, or does it constantly risk asymmetricality? In the Romantic period, the effacement of erotic particulars might furthermore be necessary for literature not to be mistaken for pornography. Byron, we recall, thought that Keats' sensuousness made his work "the very onanism of poetry."[8]

Other complexities ensue for Romantic writers. When phrenologists Gall and Spurzheim locate the organ of amativeness in the mind, the possible specific forms of erotic embodiment shift. The mind now potentially erases or negates corporeal specificity even as Gall and Spurzheim break down heterosexual reproduction by separating the organ of amativeness from the organ of philoprogentiveness, or the organ of parenting, thereby making all eroticism potentially perverse and thus separating perversion from particular bodies.[9] Another complication: desire, in the Romantic period, changes from being based in similarity – as in Voltaire's insistence that "Amour Socratique" can be explained by the resemblance of a young boy with a girl, and in Percy Shelley's definition of passionate love as a thirst for likeness ("On Love") – to requiring of those bodies differences of sex and gender and certain degrees of filial relation.[10]

Thomas Laqueur has thus argued that the one-sexed Galenic body – whereby females are an inferior and inverted version of male – is replaced by a two-sexed body in the final decades of the eighteenth century, which in turn makes desire begin to turn on sexual difference.[11] In this view, the universal body gives way to sexed forms of embodiment, even as particular embodiment dissolves into something like Blake's masculine and Michelangeloesque females, perhaps in the name of egalitarianism. Lord Byron's Don Juan is emphatically a boy; by highlighting puberty, the poet chooses a moment before sexual difference is fully inscribed, and thus desire begins as a form of resemblance. Unlike the lothario he is supposed to be, Juan is more acted upon than acting, and thus he interrupts laws of gender by showing how the body will not support a crude binary.[12] The Romantic fascination with Ganymede and hermaphrodites can be explained in part by the lingering influence of the one-sex model because it stipulated all desire to be a form of resemblance. In "Ganymed," Goethe ejaculated, *"Du kühlst den brennenden/Durst meines Busens."*[13] Middleton translates this as: "You slake the burning thirst in my breast." Goethe's enjambment, however, suggests that the process of slaking is not yet complete. In his "Notes on Sculptures," Percy Shelley thought "A Ganymede" was "a statue of surpassing beauty."[14]

The fallout of this shift from one sex to two extends both to the development of female modesty and moral ethics.[15] William Blake insisted there was nothing wrong with pleasure, and worried about how sexual morality taught others to distrust pleasure and falsely contain it within modesty. He put it succinctly in his *The Marriage of Heaven and Hell*: "sooner murder an infant in its cradle than nurse unacted desires."[16]

As Laqueur and Blake already suggest, historically, certain forms of sex get politicized. The French Revolution framed middle-class sex as productive, while the *Ancien Régime* became associated with sterility and perversion. In Scotland, Robert Burns' 1792 "Why shouldna poor folk mowe" pits working-class fecundity against the sterile sexuality of the aristocracy, which wantonly turns to brass dildoes and sodomy.[17] Since poor "bodies hae naething but mowe," "mowe" being the Scots for to copulate, their reproduction far exceeds that of the upper classes, and Burns argues that the poor will literally overrun the rich. His repetition of "mowe, mowe, mowe" hints at a geometrical versus merely mathematical increase. Indeed, in his *Essay on the Principle of Population*, Thomas Malthus makes working-class sexuality the precise problem when he blames them for having children before they can afford them, but also denies them the possibility of birth control because that would be immoral.[18]

Romantic eroticism often approaches the aesthetic of the sublime, and aesthetics further complicates the relation of erotic particulars to universals. Insofar as aesthetics itself is the wedding of the sensuous to the intellectual, it is about how sensation gets generalized into ideas. If the hallmark of the sublime is transport outside of the self, the problem is both the degree to which the self is meaningfully disrupted so that it can strive for mutuality, and the fact that the ensuing disruption of the self can be tantamount to death of that very self.[19] Simply put, when love aspires to the condition of intersubjectivity, particulars must be shed. In this view, eroticism provides a sensuous embodiment for an otherwise potentially arid intellectual sublime. When Byron lost his love, John Edleston, he wrote in "To Thyrza": "Relenting nature vainly gave / My life, when Thyrza ceas'd to live." Intersubjectivity means that the death of one must be a mutual death, and the only consolation in the lyric speaker's death is that "my life" has been vainly given by nature. Here, the self is disrupted by nature, so much so that it becomes nature's object, yet it paradoxically remains self. Yet this self is an evacuated self, which explains why nature "vainly" gives it up. If Byron's turn to nature universalizes his situation, it also claims that the love between the poet and Edleston is likewise natural, and not a perversion.[20] Philip Cardinale has argued that Thryza is a Virgilian nod to Thyrsis, who is pitted against Corydon in a singing match, and it was Edleston's voice that first captivated Byron (65). Thyrza is the feminized form of Thyrsis. Corydon, of course, is famous in Virgil, for pining for a young boy.[21]

At times, Romantic eroticism draws upon the logic of organicism to tame the tendency of difference to legitimate hierarchy by returning the body to homeostasis; in this regard, insofar as these writers equated love with the life force, they made it possible to believe that love had the power to heal the self. If organicism reminds us of a universal human body and suppresses particulars, it does so either by making identity exceed any one set of particulars, or by making the boundaries of the self permeable so that the self as organism can interact with its environment and yet remain itself. In his 1799 poem, "Love," Coleridge waxed:

> All thoughts, all passions, all delights,
> Whatever stirs this mortal frame,
> All are but ministers of Love,
> And feed his sacred flame.[22]

In making love that which feeds the sacred flame of the mortal frame, Coleridge credited it with being the engine of life. This organic language enables it to incorporate and tame difference. Note that by homogenizing anything that disturbs the mortal frame 'ministers of Love,' Coleridge limits difference, which, in turn, is further reduced to the life force that drives this individual and every self. The logic of organicism allows the individual experience to speak for the universal.

Notwithstanding such organic language, the erotic sublime encounter in Romanticism can be very traumatic and leave lasting scars. Lauren Berlant remarks that desire only becomes memorable when it finds an object of attachment, and that repetition is the means by which our desires become known to us.[23] The problem is that repetition can both perpetuate identity and mark trauma, and trauma can either subsume identity or shatter it beyond recognition. Even worse, the repetition can be compulsive and control the person who thinks he or she is in control of it. Marchand argued long ago that the loss of Edleston was Byron's most profound loss.[24] In Byron's case, those scars are mitigated by the fact that Edleston's death becomes one example of human mortality, and thus one body becomes the fate of every body. In "Edleston," Byron goes so far as to insist: "*Mortua amicitia Mors sit amica mihi.*" McGann translates this line to be: "Since our friendship is dead, let Death be my friend." Byron replaces his particular friendship with the leveling powers of death. Indeed, Edleston's death has made Byron's life a living death. In "Euthanasia," the poet comments: "To be the nothing that I was / Ere born to life and living woe!"[25] If desire giveth the subject, it also taketh it away, and with it particularity itself.

Sexuality takes on a central role in the Romantic sublime rupture of the self. If existence is becoming "sexistence" in this period (to use Arnold Davidson's resonant phrase), sexuality becomes the sign of the ultimate rupture of the self.[26] That Andrew Elfenbein links the rise of Romantic genius with the ability to trouble categories of sex and gender provides further evidence that eroticism is being tied to both individual bodies and minds.[27] Blake's concept of self-annihilation acknowledges how far the rupture of the self can go. Katrin Paul has argued that transport ruptures the inside/

outside binary because it registers an ecstasy that cannot be located inside the self, but the full consequences of this rupture cannot be predicted in advance.[28] In ancient Greece, soma or body is personhood, thereby, stitching together bodily acts and identities even as psyche is the medium that connects the two.

In Romanticism, the correlations between a universal body and individual personhood have loosened considerably, largely because of a discourse of sensibility that allows personal experience to write itself on the body. But of course, not every experience can be written on the body, or else we have Hume's bundles of sensations and nothing empirically recognizable as a self. The net effect of this loosening is that some particularities become fungible both to eroticism and identity, and by extension desire now has multiple forms and objects of satisfaction that undermine the neat nascent binary and norm of two sexes. Enter the Romantic imagination, the arousal of which was often the precondition of eroticism, and all bets are off. That this origin of erotic thoughts hovered between transcendence and embodiment even further vexed the value of particularity within Romantic eroticism.[29] How would desire stick to a body hovering between physicality and psyche?

We witness the complication of eros in Anna Seward's opening lines to Erasmus Darwin's *The Botanic Garden*: she imagines a maid who has experienced disastrous love finding solace in a meadow of plants. It was Seward who prompted Darwin to write a poem about the Linnean taxonomy of plants, and he took verses that she sent to him privately, modified them without her permission, and used them to open his poem. Linneaus had categorized plants by counting their sexual organs: by the numbers of their stamens and pistils. The problem of course was the proliferation of erotic particulars: as five husbands or plants with pistils consort with other plants, one needs an algorithm to keep track of the various possible partners, and erotic difference and pleasure greatly exceeds the needs of sexual function while polyamorousness flouts conventional marriage. What solace, then, can such erotic diversity provide? The lushness of the garden reminds us of how bowers function in literature as sites of erotic excess. Seward opens her poem likening "the fair flower" with "lucid form" (line 13), but as the cataloguing of erotic differences mounts in Darwin any such lucidity seems a dream, especially given that sexual acts are referred to as "marriage." Under what universe is "marriage" a lucid form for plant eros, much less human eros? That Seward has Philomel, "sing[ing] to the night, reclining on a thorn," preside over this meadow reminds us of its penetrating violence. Philomel, of course, had her tongue cut out so she could not name her rapist.[30]

The story we have come to accept is that desire undoes: in its wake, identity collapses along with social and religious mores, not to mention the normal. In the Romantic period, several developments complicate such a narrative. The theory is that identity based on desire is necessarily incoherent, and once this is recognized, desire can be rerouted towards more progressive social aims. To what extent does history and the historical rise of two sexes enable desire to undo? Is the cause an ahistorical bodily drive or historical changes that frame the drive? Must desire's causal powers come at history's expense? Is undoing necessarily good? What are the particularities that are being undone? And can this undoing be in any way controlled? Hence I approach the problem from a different direction. Does the movement from both particularity to abstraction and similarly to difference and back again within Romantic eroticism allegorize, if not explain, how desire's alleged disruptiveness acquires its persuasive and causal powers? My larger goal here is to help us think about why Romantic desire as the ground of liberation and egalitarianism brings with it such trouble. My wager: desire's powers to negate or transcend particular forms of embodiment stem less from any actual destabilizing powers of desire itself, and more from the competing needs of what a sexuality that aspires to mutuality or egalitarianism demands. In other words, sometimes particularity is helpful to the cause, while at other times the effacement of particularity lends the appearance that the very rules have been transcended when in fact they may have only been temporarily suspended. A further complication is that sexual ecstasy can be papered over by a language of religious exaltation or platonism, as when Percy Shelley writes a "Hymn to Intellectual Beauty" and attempts to expand the congregation to "all human kind."[31]

This select effacement and highlighting of particularity is further screened by the difference between the universal body and particularized embodiment, and especially so once bodies are divided into two sexes. That bodies seem both universal and stubbornly particular can thus insinuate a judgment that reconciles the two without having a demand that such reconciliation be earned. The fact that Romantic desire at times needs to hold onto the very particularities it will claim to efface means that they and we are demanding more of desire than it can actually do, for desire cannot logically have its cake and eat it, too. Keats recognized this fact when, referring to Madeline's about-to-be-lost virginity in "The Eve of St. Agnes," he remarked: "as though a rose should shut, and be a bud again" (line 243).[32] If Fredric Jameson is right that the intensification of the body brings with it a reduction of temporality to present experience, Romantic eroticism runs the danger of falsely extending the immediacy of experience into the future.[33]

In their skeptical moments, Romantic writers were aware of the dangers of predicating a politics upon desire – and yet they did it. The sobering fact was that once desire erases boundaries, it is not clear how to arrest such erasure. Moreover, to the extent that erotic desire demands the giving up of absolute autonomy (lest desire be expressed as contest – or even worse, rape), the fact is that it can be helplessly one-sided and unreciprocated. To wit, Mary Robinson's sonnet sequence "Sappho and Phaon" not only empties out the sequence of its culminating epithalamion or wedding song but also insists that the force of desire is uncontainable. Sappho's love for Phaon is unrequited, but this does not attenuate her desire. If Sappho jumps off a cliff to end her misery – so much for the vaunted powers of fecundity behind heterosexual desire – the words "fly," "o'er," and "raptures" in her final sonnet leave us dangling in mid air. Any transcendence literally requires the abolishment of the body, and if Robinson's camera pans away from the ground in the final sonnet, we do know that gravity cannot be ignored and Sappho's body will be found there. Even worse, Robinson comments that "reflection pours the deep and frequent sigh, / O'er the dark scroll of human destiny."[34] If the repetition of the sigh marks the ability to identify desire as one's own, the fact that the best that "human destiny" can do is sigh hardly inspires confidence that desire and personal agency can be causally linked. Yet the fantasy of transcendence allows even failed Romantic love to thrive in spite of the misery it engenders.

Robinson makes Sappho's heterosexual passion feckless, and she insinuates the cause of this to be her "ungovernable passions," which obliquely refers to her passions for women.[35] Robinson likewise erases Sappho's body, noting that when the Greeks "paid adoration to Sappho, they idolized the MUSE, and not the WOMAN" (153). Robinson herself was known as the "English Sappho," and thus she turns to the sonnet form precisely to govern the ungovernable while simultaneously replacing her own body with a textual body in order to refute the charge. Robinson concludes: "Yet shalt thou more than mortal raptures claim, / The brightest planet of th'ETERNAL SPHERE." Indeed, if the sestet in the final sonnet of the sequence flirts with trochaic substitutions, the final line rigorously reasserts order and materiality through its unyielding iambic pentameter. Coupled with the sonnet's insistently punctuated end-paused (if not stopped) lines, Robinson insists upon an artistic control that has no power to instrumentalize the fury of erotic desire. Nonetheless, by then eroticizing the relationship between poet and audience as Sappho's body gives way to Robinson's poems, Robinson implores her readers to be a better and more appreciative audience than Phaon ever was.[36]

Leo Bersani worries about the ruthlessly exclusionary nature of desire, and argues that sexuality's antisocial nature undermines any attempts to redeem it.[37] And yet must sexuality be fundamentally antisocial? Robinson's Sappho's suicide would seem at least partly to support the antisociality of desire, and the same holds true for Goethe's Werther. Consider, too, Keats's "Isabella; or, The Pot of Basil." The title makes equivalent the protagonist and the buried severed head of her lover, and Keats's synechdoche warns readers that mutuality can be taken too far. The poet comments, "If Love impersonate was ever dead, / Pale Isabella kiss'd it, and low moan'd / 'Twas love; cold, – dead indeed, but not dethroned" (stanza 50). By raising the issue of precisely how we personate or personify love, Keats worries about how abstract ideals get located within specific persons, and the degree to which the figure of personification can do the work of stitching together particulars and ideals. "Impersonate" suggests the substitute is illicit and, according to the *Oxford English Dictionary*, is aligned with personify (definition 2A). His verb, "dethroned," reminds us of the tendency to idealize when we "impersonate" love. Even the dead object – the "it" – carries Isabella's love, and so one worry is the obsessiveness of erotic fixation that cannot see that perhaps it is only the dead that can live up to the ideal. Othello said this best as he stands over the sleeping Desdemona: "Be thus when thou art dead, and I will kill thee, / And love thee after."[38] By the poem's end, there is a further metonymy when the "lost basil" Isabella asks for "amorously" (stanza 62) substitutes for the head of Lorenzo, and in so doing Keats connects eroticism with fetishism. "Amorously" is an awkward adverb, and the basil stands in for the person to be addressed. That the poem is in ottava rima, a form associated with Italian heroic romance, further insists upon whether the vehicle of the poem can do the relentless work of love. The danger of eroticism, then, is the loss of autonomy, and here autonomy has been sacrificed for a thing (basil plant) that is a substitute for the thing (Lorenzo's head). When the dangers of necrophila and fetishism can be papered over by something as clichéd as love transcends death, Keats gives us a sense of how the cure is itself a poison.[39]

In "Laon and Cythna," Percy Shelley has his own version of dealing with the tension between erotic particularity and abstraction.[40] On the one hand, he relocates the meaning of incest from the act to the intention behind the act; on the other hand, by insisting on the brother and sister and on the physicalism of their union, he demands the contingencies that come with sibling embodiment and incest. To get to the physical intensity of their union, he has to posit that growing up together enhances rather than suppresses desire. The Westermarck hypothesis about why siblings do not engage in incest has made this claim difficult to believe in, because it argues the precise opposite: in this view, familiarity makes sexual desire impossible.[41] Moreover, the Latin root of "incest" means "impure";[42] thus, Shelley's relocation of the meaning of the sexual act from the bodily act to the mind behind it psychologizes the act, rendering it potentially transcendent of any particular body. In other words, Shelley insists that the psychology behind the act is the source of its meaning, and in doing so erases the very etymology of incest as impure even as he interrupts a connection between bodily act and moral meaning. And yet, carried too far, this erasure of particular bodies might threaten to get rid of difference between sibling incest and intergenerational incest, which would void any proffered egalitarianism because significant generational difference often correlates with hierarchy. And by moving the ground of meaning to psychological differences, which in turn ground ethical choices, Shelley actually forsakes egalitarianism for who has the most developed morality; however, the radicalism of the move is to suggest anyone might be a candidate for such development. Like Sade, the particular forms of sibling embodiment matter, especially for its shock value and the hope that such shock will remove the shackles of custom from his audience. In his preface, he claimed: "it was my object to break through the crust of those outworn opinions on which established institutions depend" (xxi).

What happens, then, when we track when difference is cited and when it is effaced within Romantic eroticism? Take these lines from Canto 6, Stanza 34, of "Laon and Cythna":

> The beating of our veins one interval
> Made still; and then I felt the blood that burned
> Within her frame, mingle with mine, and fall
> Around my heart like fire; and over all
> A mist was spread, the sickness of a deep
> And speechless swoon of joy, as might befall
> Two disunited spirits when they leap
> In union, from this earth's obscure and fading sleep.

Two bodies unite to form an intersubjectivity that is a literal breaking down of the borders between two bodies. Their veins, after all, beat to one interval, and Shelley's trochaic substitution of "made still" gives us the lingering trace of the contest between two different beings. The simile of "two disunited spirits" reminds us of a primal and originary unity between two spirits that have once again become one, but the turn to spirit and the making of spiritual unity ontologically prior to corporeal unity threatens to make the union of bodies an epiphenomenon. And if intersubjectivity is being reachieved, why does Shelley use the term "sickness" here, and what is this sickness? Donovan reads this moment as ejaculatory; certainly, the expenditure of semen was always suggestive of disease, not to mention effeminacy.

"Sickness" hints that the loss of individual corporeal boundaries is not without significant cost. Shelley's choice of "befall" further undermines any simple equation of eroticism with agency: befall insists upon contingency without agency. Shelley's final two lines flirt with chiasmus, and if the three syllables of "when they leap" can be crossed with "in union," thereby enacting the leap, the extra syllables of the final alexandrine function as a vestige of inequality. Yet, like the male nipple, it is present. The pronoun "they" further highlights Shelley's skepticism, indicating as it does authorial distance.

Shelley's traverse from erotic intersubjectivity to erotic particularity grows more vexed just five stanzas later:

> There we unheeding sate, in the communion
> Of interchanged vows, which, with a rite
> Of faith most sweet and sacred, stamped our union. –
> Few were the living hearts which could unite
> Like ours, or celebrate a bridal night
> With such close sympathies, for to each other
> Had high and solemn hopes, the gentle might
> Of earliest love, and all the thoughts which smother
> Cold Evil's power, now linked a sister and a brother.[43]

On the one hand, Shelley merely stipulates "a sister and a brother," which does not demand that they be siblings. His enjambment facilitates the blurring of one body into another so that both can intertwine around a we. On the other hand, siblinghood and the "gentle might of earliest love," and not rapturous desire, is what provides the foundational alexandrine of the Spenserian stanza its anchoring permanence. The two are closely sympathetic, and have been since their earliest love – a love whose original relation to sexuality is at best unclear. This link of sympathy is solidified by the "bridal night," but the foreclosed temporality of that one night must be offset by the more durable link between brother and sister.[44]

Egalitarianism, of course, raises the very problem of what to do with difference. That there are differences between people means that political equality must on some level remain indifferent to those differences. But are differences in gender and sex and orientation always fungible, and should we remain indifferent to them? While it is true that difference often licenses differences of treatment that are unethical, that does not mean that all differences warrant the same indifference. Egalitarianism further threatens to drain eros of the contest that makes it dynamic and destabilizing. To the extent that eroticism frames the self as fungible in order to get to intersubjectivity, difference is left as a trace. Its erasure threatens to make the work of getting to possible mutuality invisible, and with it the violence of that work. In the Victorian period, as homosexuality reasserted eroticism based on sameness, the inequality of partners simply disappeared, along with the specificity of the sexual act.[45] Of course, getting rid of differences of sex within homosexuality does not necessarily get rid of gender and its reassertion of difference in terms of hierarchy.

From the perspective of the standard history of sexuality, we might understand this traverse from erotic egalitarianism to contingency in terms of the shift from acts to identities, the ways in which sexuality becomes psychologized, with sexual identity thereby transcending biological sex. But if sex was about self-mastery even in ancient Greece, then how the subject acquires such mastery must be part of the story. That is, some component of psyche must be involved in the management of the self, even if the discipline of psychology was not yet developed. My larger point here is that historians of sexuality have been selective in the particulars they emphasize to make the claim that sex as acts is replaced by sexuality as identity.

In *Indifference to Difference: On Queer Universalism*, Madhavi Menon recently argued the problem with difference is that, while the multiplicity of differences are undeniable, difference is too often fetishized into one form of it. As she aptly puts it, "lived reality is at odds with identity politics".[46] To counter this, she proposes a queer universalism predicated on desire, but one that exploits the negativity of the universal to annihilate the need for particularity itself, thereby making us productively indifferent to any form of it. Menon argues, "I want to use universalism's fury to destroy our investment in difference as the basis of identity" (11). Nonetheless, if the violence of desire cannot be controlled, what makes it possible to contain the violence of universalism and prevent it from eradicating difference instead of encouraging indifference to it? To rescue "indifference" as a meaningful political category, Menon must make differences a fact of life (she cites Badiou to claim that there is no getting away from difference (11)), but to do that the violence of universalism must on the one hand be strong enough to empty out content itself yet on the other hand not so strong that it obliterates difference itself in its inescapable multiplicity. She submits that "traversing differences while in the grip of the universal models a way of being in which people need not give up differences" (12). Can desire both ground violence and limit its effects? My point is that the connections of desire to agency are more complex than any single theory can explain.

To return to the motivating question of this essay: why are Romantic erotic particularities selectively cited, and when does eroticism seem universal? I have suggested that the figural relay between particularity/contingency

and egalitarianism/universality surrounding Romantic desire enables a met-
alepsis between cause and effect that allows desire to acquire disruptiveness.
To make the cause of disruptiveness desire as opposed to historical contingencies, moreover, desire must be universalized – even as only certain repetitions of desire are counted. The Romantics worry about how one controls
the effects of this disruptiveness, once unleashed. They also worry about the
asymetricality of desire; about the violence or contest that must take place in
order for the self to aspire to mutuality. Yet they do not go so far as to reject
in advance the possibility that desire can have meaningful social effects.

What does all this mean for the understanding of Romantic eroticism? To
make desire the cause, must history be expunged? One answer would be to
suggest that these writers insist upon the rhetorical force of disruptive desire
and turn to desire as a strategy rather than as an essence that has the power
to undo. John Keats considered love: "A thing of soft misnomers, so divine
/ That silly youth doth think to make itself / Divine by loving."[47] Love here
is a misnomer that lacks a metaphysics capable of underwriting any particular strategy; though, of course, Keats makes love essentially rhetorical and
strategic. Certainly, Percy Shelley insists upon the shock value of brother
and sister incest when he not only stipulates its motivations to be pure but
also has those motivations erase the impurity incest has acquired. While
the solidity of the bond between brother and sister withstands the test of
time, the eroticism of their connection is necessarily both momentary and
ancillary. In this view, the particular eroticism could systematically be yoked
to the universal only insofar as the selection of the particular were rhetorical. Any systematizing judgment, then, would derive not from the leveling
effects of desire (which cannot be controlled) but rather from the need to
consider one's audience, and the always already contingent relation between
speaker and audience.

What theories are available to explain how desire sticks to the body, and
how best to harness them? The ways in which Romantic bodies and desires
hover between universality and contingency, abstract bodies and particular
forms of embodiment, help to occlude the shaping force of history. In this
view, the erotic provides a force field of particularities, waiting to be opera-
tionalized by either narrative or the lyric speaker.

NOTES

1 Laura Mulvey, "Visual Pleasure and Narrative Cinema," in *Visual and Other
Pleasures* (Bloomington: Indiana, 1989), 14–29. See Fred Burwick on Romantic
eroticism in *Romanticism: Keywords* (Sussex: Wiley Blackwell, 2015),
73–79.

2 Berlant thinks about the ways in which desire is "zoned" to particular geographies and to body parts. She considers how desire creates a need for mapping. See Lauren Berlant, *Desire/Love* (Brooklyn: Punctum Books, 2012), 14–15. Are bodies archeologically inflected by discourse, or do bodies and desires speak their own sexual perceptions and bodily logic as Chris Mounsey suggests in *Developments in the Histories of Sexualities* (Lewisburg: Bucknell, 2013), vii–viii? The mere fact that this debate exists points to why eroticism has such a tangled relation to history.

3 I am thinking here of the ways in which Jean Hagstrum celebrates the authenticity of Byron's "Thyrza" lyrics so that "deeply felt experience becomes embodied in the permanent forms of art" (178). See *Eros and Vision: The Restoration to Romanticism* (Evanston: Northwestern, 1989).

4 Thomas Scanlon, *Eros and Greek Athletics* (Oxford: Oxford University Press, 2002), 204.

5 Scanlon, *Eros*, 6.

6 Friedrich Hölderin, *Friedrich Hölderin: Poems and Fragments*, trans. Michael Hamburger (London: Anvil, 2004), 104–105.

7 I challenge the common wisdom that aesthetics defines itself against the sensual in order to offer a discourse of disinterest that preserves community. Aesthetics can more profitably be seen as being about what to do with the sensual.

8 Leslie Marchand, *Byron's Letters and Journals* (London: John Murray, 1977), 7: 217.

9 My use of mind here is controversial. Gall and Spurzheim did seek to embody brain functions. However, as I have argued elsewhere, their localization was really an idea of localization since there was really no corroborating anatomical evidence other than the shape of the skull.

10 François Marie Arouet de Voltaire, "Dictionnaire Philosophique," in *Oeuvres complètes de Voltaire*, 42 Vols. (Paris: Garnier Frères, 1878), 17: 180; Percy Shelley, "On Love," in *Shelley's Poetry and Prose*, eds. Donald H. Reiman and Neil Fraistat, 2nd edn (New York: Norton, 2002), 503.

11 Thomas Laqueur, *Making Sex: Body and Gender from the Greeks to Freud* (Cambridge: Harvard University Press, 1990).

12 I am indebted here to Susan Wolfson, "'Their She Condition': Cross Dressing and the Politics of Gender in Don Juan." *English Literary History* 54,3 (autumn 1987): 585–617.

13 Johann Wolfgang von Goethe. *The Collected Works: Selected Poems.* Ed. Christopher Middleton. (Princeton: Princeton University Press, 1983), 30–31.

14 Percy Shelley, "Notes on Sculptures in Rome and Florence," in *The Complete Works of Percy Bysshe Shelley*, eds. Roger Ingpen and Walter Peck (New York: Gordian P., 1965), 6: 324.

15 David Sigler, in *Sexual Enjoyment in British Romanticism: Gender and Psychoanalysis, 1753–1835* (Montreal: McGill-Queen's University Press, 2015), reads Romanticism as struggling with the meaning of sexual difference. He argues that sexual enjoyment is the ground upon which the culture finds the unconscious.

16 William Blake, *The Complete Poetry and Prose of William Blake*, ed. David Erdman (Garden City: Anchor Books, 1982), 38.

17 Robert Burns, "When Princes and Prelates," www.bbc.co.uk/arts/robertburns/works/when_princes_and_prelates/#work

18 Thomas Malthus, *Essay on the Principle of Population* (London, 1800).

19 On transport, see Katrin Pahl, *Tropes of Transport: Hegel and Emotion* (Evanston: Northwestern, 2012).

20 Lord Byron, *Complete Poetical Works*, ed. Jerome J. McGann (Oxford: Clarendon, 1980), 1: 350–52.

21 Philip Cardinale, "Lord Byron, Virgil, and Thyrza," *Vergilius*, 48 (2002): 55–66.

22 Samuel Taylor Coleridge, *Poetical Works I*, ed. J.C.C. Mays (Princeton: Princeton University Press, 2001), 604–610.

23 Lauren Berlant, *Desire/Love*, p. 20.

24 Leslie Marchand, *Byron: A Biography* (New York: Knopf, 1957), 1: 296, note 3.

25 Byron, *Complete Poems*, 1: 352–354, 459.

26 Arnold Davidson, *The Emergence of Sexuality* (Cambridge: Harvard University Press, 2001).

27 Andrew Elfenbein, *Romantic Genius: The Prehistory of a Homosexual Role* (New York: Columbia University Press, 1999).

28 Pahl, *Tropes of Transport*, 80.

29 For further details, see Vernon Rosario, *The Erotic Imagination* (New York: Oxford University Press, 1997) and my *Perverse Romanticism: Aesthetics and Sexuality in Britain, 1750–1850* (Baltimore: Johns Hopkins University Press, 2009).

30 Anna Seward, *The Poetical Works of Anna Seward*, ed. Walter Scott (Edinburgh, 1810), 2: 1–4.

31 Shelley, *Poetry*, 96.

32 John Keats, *The Poems of John Keats*, ed. Jack Stillinger (Cambridge: Harvard University Press, 1978), 311.

33 Fredric Jameson, *The Antinomies of Realism* (London: Verso, 2015) 28.

34 Mary Robinson, *Mary Robinson: Selected Poems*, ed. Judith Pascoe (Toronto: Broadview, 2000), 180.

35 Robinson's biographer, Paula Byrne, insists that "the English Sappho" was "a compliment to her technical proficiency and her strong sensibility, not as a comment on her sexuality" in *Perdita* (New York: Random House, 2004), 324. Yet Robinson had met Marie Antoinette, who was pilloried for her Sapphic loves, and Marie was rumored to be infatuated with the beautiful Mary Robinson.

36 On how Robinson and other women writers eroticize the relation between poet and reader, see Kari Lokke, "Gender and Sexuality," *A Handbook of Romanticism Studies*, ed. Joel Faflak and Julia Wright (West Sussex: Wiley Blackwell, 2012), 316.

37 Leo Bersani, *The Culture of Redemption* (Cambridge: Harvard University Press, 1990). Bersani credits Freud for recognizing that sexuality is always a turn away from the other.

38 William Shakespeare, *Othello*, *The Complete Signet Classic Shakespeare*, ed. Sylvan Barnet (New York: HBJ, 1972), Act 5, Scene 2, 18–19, p. 1131.

39 Keats, *Complete Poems*, 245–263.

40 For William Ulmer, 'Shelleyan Eros is metaphorically constituted and struc-
    tured' (6). See *Shelleyan Eros: The Rhetoric of Romantic Love* (Princeton:
    Princeton, 1990).

41 See Alan Richardson's chapter on incest in *The Neural Sublime* (Baltimore: Johns
    Hopkins University Press, 2010).

42 John Donovan, "Incest in 'Laon and Cythna': Nature, Custom, Desire," *The
    Keats-Shelley Review* 2: 1 (January 1987), 57.

43 Percy Shelley, *Laon and Cythna* (London: Printed for John Brook 1829).

44 Ulmer warns that eros can only fulfill itself in this poem "under the auspices of
    a triumphant male power" (64).

45 Elisabeth Roudinesco, *Our Dark Side: A History of Perversion*, trans. David
    Macey (Cambridge: Polity Press, 2009), 57.

46 Madhavi Menon, *Indifference to Difference: On Queer Universalism*
    (Minneapolis: Minnesota, 2015) 3.

47 John Keats, "And What is Love—It Is a Doll Dress'd Up," *Complete
    Poems*, 288.

10

MARIANNE NOBLE

Emily Dickinson in Love (With Death)

Because I could not stop for Death –
He kindly stopped for me –
The Carriage held but just Ourselves –
And Immortality.

We slowly drove – He knew no haste
And I had put away
My labor and my leisure too,
For His Civility –

We passed the School, where Children strove
At Recess – in the Ring –
We passed the Fields of Gazing Grain –
We passed the Setting Sun –
Or rather – He passed Us –

The Dews drew quivering and Chill –
For only Gossamer, my Gown –
My Tippet – only Tulle –

We paused before a House that seemed
A Swelling of the Ground –
The Roof was scarcely visible –
The Cornice – in the Ground –

Since then – 'tis Centuries – and yet
Feels shorter than the Day
I first surmised the Horses' Heads
Were toward Eternity –[1]

In *Tanglewood Tales* (1853), Nathaniel Hawthorne retells six classical myths for children, among them the tale of Persephone, or Proserpina.[2] As he tells the story in "The Pomegranate Seed," Proserpina was picking flowers when she saw emerging from a hole in the ground:

> a team of four sable horses, snorting smoke out of their nostrils, and tearing their way out of the earth with a splendid golden chariot whirling at their heels ... In the chariot sat the figure of a man, richly dressed, with a crown on his head, all flaming with diamonds. He was of a noble aspect, and rather handsome.[3]

" 'Do not be afraid,' " said he, with as cheerful a smile as he knew how to put on. " 'Come! Will you not like to ride a little way with me, in my beautiful chariot?' " But when Proserpina cried for her mother, "the stranger leaped to the ground, caught the child in his arms, and again mounted the chariot, shook the reins, and shouted to the four black horses to set off." She was terrified, but "as they rode on, the stranger did his best to soothe her."

> "Why should you be so frightened, my pretty child?" said he, trying to soften his rough voice. "I promise not to do you any harm." "My home is better than your mother's," answered King Pluto. "It is a palace, all made of gold ... "

> ... she happened to cast her eyes over a great broad field of waving grain – and whom do you think she saw? Who, but Mother Ceres, making the corn grow, and too busy to notice the golden chariot as it went rattling along.

The correspondences between these passages and Emily Dickinson's famous poem "Because I could not stop for Death" are striking. In both, Death is personified as a kindly gentleman caller, who forces an unwilling girl to give up her own self-determined actions and instead ride in his chariot with him. Both plots suggest sex and marriage: a girl is separated from the familiar and wed to Death, who takes her to a new home underground. In both, the sun is an important witness. In Hawthorne's story, Proserpina's mother searches for her until finally Apollo, the sun God, admits he saw her being carried off by Pluto. Dickinson writes, "We Passed the Setting Sun, / or rather – He Passed us –." Both particularly emphasize the horses' heads. And finally, and most strikingly, Dickinson appears to be echoing Hawthorne's image of "a great broad field of waving grain," when her speaker comments, "We passed the Fields of Gazing Grain –." In personifying "grain," the poem nods towards the fact that Persephone's mother, Ceres, is goddess of the harvest and is unfortunately gazing elsewhere. The reference to "fields of waving grain" does not appear in any of the other versions of the tale that Dickinson may have read, which therefore suggests that "The Pomegranate Seeds" is an important and unacknowledged source of Dickinson's famous poem.[4]

I am not the first to notice that Dickinson's poem alludes to the myth of Persephone, though I am the first to claim that Hawthorne's version of the myth is significant. In a 2001 article entitled "Because I, Persephone, Could Not Stop For Death," Ken Hiltner makes this connection, arguing that Dickinson's source is Charles Anthon's version of the Hymn to Demeter.[5] Anthon's version focuses on the anguish of the mother whose child is abducted, and Hiltner claims that the poem itself is about ruptured mother–daughter bonds, which are uneasily restored at the end of the poem through the pregnancy of Persephone, who reconnects with her mother through the eternal feminine and with immortality through her participation in the cycle of procreation. Hiltner explicitly rejects Hawthorne's version as a source because it eroticizes the abduction, which Dickinson does not, he says. But in fact, I – like many readers – find a subtle, macabre eroticism in the speaker's attraction to the "Civil" and "kind" bridegroom who seduces the speaker to her death.[6] In this chapter, I argue that the poem responds to the erotics of Hawthorne's version, in particular to the discourses of sentimental masochism he employs. The poem does not celebrate the paradigm of eroticized domination, though. Instead, it exploits it, overlaying the erotics of seduction on top of a narrative of self-determination, in which the speaker claims poetic vocation and the existential freedom that inheres in accepting death as a central fact of life and in letting go attachments to conventional identity scripts. The brilliance of the poem lies in the way it depicts an act of female self-determination predicated upon such submission without reifying misogynist ideologies. Reading the poem in dialogue with the erotics of Hawthorne's story clarifies that, when the poem culminates in a place of emptiness and despair, that place suddenly proves to be full of possibility and pleasure.

Before we address Dickinson's citation and revision of Hawthorne's story, however, it is important to acknowledge that the poem is not simply and directly a revision of Hawthorne.[7] Years before she wrote about sex and death through the mediation of Persephone in "Because I could not stop for Death," Dickinson had been attuned to the motif of men carrying off women in chariots to deathly new homes. Indeed, Dickinson's early letters and select poems consistently voice trepidation about marriage by invoking the image of a gentleman who carries a girl off in his carriage and takes her on a ride to a new house, which in turn results in the death of the bride. A good example of such early engagements with the convergence of death, marriage, and carriages appears in an 1845 letter that fourteen-year-old Emily wrote to her intimate friend, Abiah Root. Allusions to this convergence pervade the letter.

It opens with a metaphor that correlates marriage with separation and also with the ravages of time:

> Dearest Abiah,
> As I just glanced at the clock and saw how smoothly the little hands glide over the surface, I could scarcely believe that those self-same little hands had eloped with so many precious moments since I received your affectionate letter ... [8]

Here, Emily links time and distance as elements that thwart her contact with Abiah, and she uses the metaphor of eloping to characterize this disruption. She and Abiah *would* have been together if the hands on the clock had not eloped with time. Their time together has been obstructed by a marriage.

Dickinson hones in on the way marriage disrupts time and space in the next paragraph. She responds to Abiah's request for news of their friend Helen Humphrey, who had recently married, by saying: "I really don't know what has become of her, unless procrastination has carried her off." When people get carried off to marriage, they are not heard from again; they procrastinate with their former friends, no longer making time for connecting. Marriage, understood as a matter of time, carries women off. Dickinson continues, "we regretted more than ever that she was going where we could not see her as often as we had been accustomed. She seemed very happy in her prospects, and seemed to think distance nothing in comparison to a home with the one of her choice." Here, marriage is distance and occlusion – "going where we could not see her" – yet surprisingly, the bride seems to like it, presumably because she gets her own home.

All of these thoughts associating marriage with death, separation, and the passage of time culminate in a carefully wrought conceit comparing time to a courteous yet alarming gentleman caller in a chariot:

> since I wrote you last, the summer is past and gone, and autumn with the sere and yellow leaf is already upon us. I never knew the time to pass so swiftly, it seems to me, as the past summer. I really think some one must have oiled his chariot wheels, for I don't recollect of hearing him pass, and I am sure I should if something had not prevented his chariot wheels from creaking as usual. But I will not expatiate upon him any longer, for I know it is wicked to trifle with so reverend a personage, and I fear he will make me a call in person to inquire as to the remarks which I have made concerning him. Therefore I will let him alone for the present.

Dickinson invokes the familiar trope of time as a chariot, but she then develops it into a marital conceit by personifying time as a gentleman caller coming in the chariot, a wooer who might "make [her] a call in person" – a visit she dreads because it might force her to leave home, or perhaps because it would lead to her death. Marriage makes her think of autumn and impending death: the phrase "autumn with the sere and yellow leaf is already upon us" is an allusion to the words of Macbeth, near the end of his life, when all hope is about to collapse:

MACBETH   I have lived long enough. My way of life
Is fall'n into the sear, the yellow leaf,
And that which should accompany old age,
As honour, love, obedience, troops of friends,
I must not look to have...⁹

Surprisingly, the fourteen-year-old Dickinson finds her feelings about mortality, time, and the collapse of hope voiced in Macbeth's meditation on his own imminent death and the collapse of his ambitions. The *Macbeth* passage suggests that the marriages around her imply the collapse of her own ambitions, her dreams of honor and accomplishment cut off by its duties. Life possibilities are destroyed when men carry women off to the swift decline and death of marriage.

It astonishes Dickinson that women readily exchange worldly ambitions for the dubious compensation of a home of their own. In another letter to Abiah, dated March 14, 1847, the now sixteen-year-old Dickinson reports that her teacher Miss Adams has left Amherst to get married: "'Are you not astonished?'"

> She seemed to be very happy in anticipation of her future prospects, & I hope she will realize all her fond hopes. I cannot bear to think that she will never more wield the scepter, & sit upon the throne in our venerable schoolhouse, & yet I am glad she is going to have a home of her own & a kind companion to take life's journey with her.¹⁰

She notes with surprise that her teacher willingly relinquished a position of power and public esteem in order to become someone's wife, yet she concedes that Miss Adams evidently finds ample compensation in a life journey figured as acquiring a home of her own with a "kind companion." To Emily, the exchange of scholastic scepter and throne for a private home seems like a diminishment of power and possibility.

In Dickinson's imagination, the lives of brides are not only diminished but also effectively eradicated. In a letter to her friend and soon-to-be sister-in-law, Susan Dickinson, Emily – now twenty-two – describes with dread "[t]hose unions, my dear Susie, by which two lives are one"; "it will take us one day, and make us all it's own, and we shall not run away from it, but lie still and be happy."¹¹ This union erases the single life of the woman, and yet the woman cannot run away from it. Emily thinks, "it is dangerous, and all too dear, these simple trusting spirits [women], and the spirits mightier which we cannot resist [men]! It does rend me, Susie, the thought of it when it comes, that I tremble lest at sometime I, too, am yielded up." Women are so "simple" and "trusting," seemingly unaware that they are being rent and yielded up. Later, Dickinson more succinctly notes to Emily Fowler that "some day a 'brave dragoon' will be stealing you away and I will have father to go to discover you."[12] As Judith Farr notes, this "brave dragoon" of 1851 morphs into a "bold Dragon" in a letter of January 21,1852: "what would become of me when the 'bold Dragon' shall bear you both away, to live in his high mountain – and leave me here alone."[13] Marriage is a "Disaster" associated with abduction, as the phrases "stealing you away," "bear you away," "take us," "going where we can not see her," and "carried off" indicate. The same phrases characterize death. As a single example: "I think of the grave very often ... and whether I can ever stop it from carrying off what I love."[14]

As this brief epistolary survey demonstrates, Dickinson's revision of Hawthorne's rendition of the Persephone myth is informed by a long prehistory of associating marriage with abduction, a ride in a carriage, and death. But where she voices this association with alarm in her letters, Hawthorne develops it enthusiastically, within a sentimental framework that makes the violation of the female in marriage seem natural and erotic. Hawthorne gives the story the fullest patriarchal spin, depicting the ravaged girl's experience as weirdly good. His gentleman caller, Pluto, is benevolent, rich, and aggressively masculine. He is lonely, earnestly yearning for an alive and young girl to bring sunshine and vitality to his underground palace. He is awkward, unskilled in the norms of courtship, abruptly taking what he wants out of clumsiness more than bad intentions. He is smoky; a sexy and "rather handsome" suitor who carries Proserpina across the threshold of his huge bejewelled palace with a stream and a dog in front (though it's the stream of death and a three-headed dog).

Dickinson echoes this marital ideology in "Because I could not stop for Death." Like Pluto, her figure of death is "kind," attentive to the needs of the woman he seduces. Theirs is a pleasure drive – he "knew no haste"; he displays "Civility" as he drives the carriage past playing children and bucolic fields. Eventually, though, like Pluto in the Persephone legend, he takes her to his underground house, "a House that seemed / A Swelling of the Ground – / The Roof was scarcely visible – / The Cornice – in the Ground –." Dickinson defamiliarizes this house; it is only a "House that seemed." And its cornice is just sticking up from the ground, an image that jarringly literalizes the trope of Pluto's underground house. (The "swelling" of the house might suggest the groom's erotic desire.) The effect of such defamiliarization in Dickinson's poem is somewhat similar to a pattern of defamiliarization of conventions that Hawthorne also plays with, as, for example, when he writes:

"When we pass those gates, we are at home. And there lies my faithful mastiff at the threshold. Cerberus! Cerberus! Come hither, my good dog!"

So saying, Pluto pulled at the reins, and stopped the chariot right between the tall, massive pillars of the gateway. The mastiff of which he had spoken got up from the threshold, and stood on his hinder legs, so as to put his fore paws on the chariot wheel. But, my stars, what a strange dog it was! Why, he was a big, rough, ugly-looking monster, with three separate heads, and each of them fiercer than the two others; but fierce as they were, King Pluto patted them all. He seemed as fond of his three-headed dog as if it had been a sweet little spaniel, with silken ears and curly hair.[15]

Hawthorne is playing with the macabre, indulging the weirdness familiar things acquire when affiliated with death, and Dickinson echoes and also transforms his playful uncanny.

The carriage ride with death is the first Hawthorne motif that informs "Because I could not stop for Death." The second motif is the development of Proserpina's love for her abductor:

... the little damsel was not quite so unhappy as you may have supposed ...

"My own little Proserpina," [Pluto] used to say. "I wish you could like me a little better. We gloomy and cloudy-natured persons have often as warm hearts, at bottom, as those of a more cheerful character. If you would only stay with me of your own accord, it would make me happier than the possession of a hundred such palaces as this."

"Ah," said Proserpina, "you should have tried to make me like you before carrying me off. And the best thing you can now do is, to let me go again. Then I might ... come back, and pay you a visit."

... And then she burst into tears. But ... a few moments afterwards, Proserpina was sporting through the hall almost as merrily as she and the four sea nymphs had sported along the edge of the surf wave. King Pluto gazed after her, and wished that he, too, was a child. And little Proserpina, when she turned about, and beheld this great king standing in his splendid hall, and looking so grand, and so melancholy, and lonesome, was smitten with a kind of pity. She ran back to him, and, for the first time in all her life, put her small, soft hand in his.

"I love you a little," whispered she, looking up in his face.[16]

Passages like these reify the bedrock patriarchal assumption that women love their rapists and feel sorry for the needs that drive them to such desperate acts. Abduction and forced sex are depicted as signs of masculine favor, readily forgivable.

In Hawthorne's imagination, Proserpina is the angel of Pluto's house, and she comes to love Pluto because – as such – she privileges his subjectivity above her own. When Proserpina is finally leaving Hades, Hawthorne writes: "She even shed a tear or two, thinking how lonely and cheerless the great palace would seem to him ... after she herself – his one little ray of natural sunshine, whom he had stolen, to be sure, but only because he valued her so much – after she should have departed."[17] Proserpina becomes an object to herself. She speaks of herself in the third person, seeing herself through her husband's eyes as a little ray of sunshine that lightens up his house. From the man's point of view, which Hawthorne assumes Proserpina assumes, rape isn't so bad, really. He probably shouldn't have stolen her, but in keeping with the conventions of the angel in the house motif, Proserpina puts his needs ahead of her own.

Hawthorne develops the perverse erotics of the May–December romance he limns. Proserpina comes to desire Pluto sexually, as is suggested in a scene in which King Pluto – seeking to tempt Proserpina – offers her a pomegranate, the only one he can find:

> a dry, old withered pomegranate … Proserpina could not help coming close to the table, and looking at this poor specimen of dried fruit with a great deal of eagerness; for, to say the truth, on seeing something that suited her taste, she felt all the six months' appetite taking possession of her at once … somehow or other, being in such close neighborhood to her mouth, the fruit found its way into that little red cave.[18]

Six months of appetite render Proserpina eager to put the seeds of Pluto's withered fruit into her "little red cave." No one forces her; she eats them "with a great deal of eagerness." After all, she did love him a little.

In normalizing rape and abduction, and in investing readers in the erotic objectification of women, Hawthorne's story for children participates in and is informed by the discourses of sentimental masochism. It figures rape as a sign of erotic desirability, and it aligns female desire with erotic objectification. Ultimately, it suggests that a kind of erotic transcendence is available to the female who repudiates her own subjectivity and defines herself instead through the subjectivity of the man of whom she becomes a part. Stories like this find their fullest erotic flowering in books like *Jane Eyre*; *Wuthering Heights*; *Uncle Tom's Cabin*; *The Wide, Wide World*; *The Planter's Northern Bride*; *St. Elmo*; *The Hidden Hand*; and *Elsie Dinsmore*. Dickinson also engages this tradition in female writing. Her notorious and mysterious Master Letters – written to an unknown recipient, whom she names Master – can be read as a study in this popular ideology. As I have argued elsewhere,[19] one way of thinking about her uses of this discourse might be to approach them as aesthetic explorations of a culturally sanctioned discourse to give voice to erotic passion. The attraction to vulnerability and subordination in them is neither simply ironic nor a question of good-but-not-great discourses; instead, the discourse voices a passionate yearning for jouissance, for a shattering of the constraints of identity, for an ecstatic merge with totality, for orgasm. Subordination to a husband may not be an earnest wish for Dickinson, but an erotic sublime – an ecstatic surrender to an orgasmic, overwhelming flooding of sexual sensation – might well be.

The erotics of being mastered and forced are not uniquely female; they are only seen as such within a specific ideological formation. Walt Whitman compares the rising desire that culminates in orgasm to a feeling of being mastered by sexual sensations:

> On all sides prurient provokers stiffening my limbs,
> Straining the udder of my heart for its withheld drip,
> Behaving licentious toward me, taking no denial,
> Depriving me of my best as for a purpose,
> Unbuttoning my clothes, holding me by the bare waist,
> Deluding my confusion with the calm of the sunlight and pasture-fields,
> Immodestly sliding the fellow-senses away,
> They bribed to swap off with touch and go and graze at the edges of me,
> No consideration, no regard for my draining strength or my anger,
> Fetching the rest of the herd around to enjoy them a while,
> Then all uniting to stand on a headland and worry me.
>
> The sentries desert every other part of me,
> They have left me helpless to a red marauder,
> They all come to the headland to witness and assist against me.
>
> I am given up by traitors,
> I talk wildly, I have lost my wits, I and nobody else am the greatest traitor ...
>
> You villain touch! what are you doing? my breath is tight in its throat,
> Unclench your floodgates, you are too much for me.[20]

When Whitman imagines that all of the senses except that of erotic touch "desert every other part of me," he invokes the way sexuality feels like a hostile takeover that overwhelms and temporarily dissolves the "me." The "red marauder" of immersive sexual feeling suggests feelings of death, of being given up by traitors, of being taken over by external forces. But then the "floodgates" "unclench," the feeling of pressure erupts, and the self in the world returns with all of its five senses in balance. The feeling of threat to the self that Whitman associates with orgasm makes the act of yielding to sexuality feel like yielding to death, which is why metaphors of an external force that is "taking no denial," that is "depriving me of my best as for a purpose," are appropriate. The self would not do this to itself. So he imagines an alternative force assuming agency and forcing all of this erotic frenzy upon the self. And yet, with wild inconsistency, he concedes that it is he himself that has done this to himself. In short, Whitman identifies an erotics of being mastered intrinsic in the physical sensations of orgasm; it is neither gendered female nor coded sentimental.

Sentimental writers like Warner, Hentz, and Hawthorne – in *Tanglewood*, anyway – depict the pleasures of being forced to submit to passion as uniquely feminine. Dickinson challenges this misogynist ideology, noting, for example, that the Sun "passed us"; he saw this abduction and did nothing to help. It's a patriarchal conspiracy. Yet she also explores the aesthetically rich possibilities of an erotic sublime that the discourse of sentimental masochism affords. Her idiosyncratic and brilliant technique of intense compression infuses the erotic energy of the sentimental discourse into an opposed discourse, a counternormative one of self-determination and artistic self-creation. One way of understanding "Because I could not stop for Death" is in relationship to Adrienne Rich's persuasive claim that some of Dickinson's most renowned poems about eroticism and marriage are in fact "about the poet's relationship to her own power, which is exteriorized in masculine form, much as masculine poets have invoked the female Muse."[21] These poems are "about possession by the daemon, about the dangers and risks of such possession if you are a woman, about the knowledge that power in a woman can seem destructive, and that you cannot live without the daemon once it has possessed you." The female poet is euphoric to be possessed by her controlling poetic self, who gives energy, form, and focus to her passions and thoughts.

This is a compelling, comfortably feminist interpretation of some of Dickinson's expressions of pleasure at being possessed, or controlled, or forced, and I agree with it. But while Rich notes the danger that being possessed poses for a woman, she does not address the erotics of this self-surrender and the way that such poems provocatively voice a sexual self as well as a poetic one. In poems like "My Life had stood a Loaded Gun" and "Because I could not stop for Death," submission to the daemon implies an impending erotic jouissance: I could not shatter myself, so death did it for me. Dickinson constructs a kind of palimpsest by laying new plots on top of erased ones in a way that hijacks the erotic intensity of the patriarchal plot, associating that feeling with the alternative self-determining plot. The result is that, while the patriarchal plot is ironized and negated as a life choice, its affective energies are not. Instead, the culture's clichéd narrative of female submission is present under erasure; its expression of pleasure in submitting to hostile forces that assault one's coherent identity is put into the service of another plot involving the power and purpose of the identity of woman as artist, poet. *That* is an identity for which the culture offers few ready-to-hand discursive channels, and certainly none informed by orgasmic pleasures.

"Because I could not stop for Death" develops an erotic/poetic palimpsest of this kind in its engagement with Hawthorne's "The Pomegranate
Seed." The poem echoes his description of a carriage ride with a death-
dealing bridegroom, exploiting the affective energies of his sentimental
masochistic depiction of a protracted carriage ride that is pleasurable
precisely because it is fraught with impending self-annihilation. Like
Whitman, it describes a speaker increasingly vulnerable to destruction at
the hands of a malevolent yet attractive foe. The wooer in Dickinson's
poem is attentive and kind, yet also determined to have his way with her.
He creepily and systematically separates her from all of the stages of her
former life as he takes her to a new house where she will be his, and
dead. That house is "swelling," suggesting his desire, and perhaps her own
impending pregnancy. And all of this domination is packaged within a discourse of pleasure. Yet Dickinson overwrites on top of this plot an opposing counter-plot, one in which a female poet claims her artistic identity.[22]
Dickinson echoes Hawthorne's story of a ride with death that leads to
an underground marital residence. But while she portrays death-in-mar-
riage as "quivering and chill," she portrays the assertion of poet-self as an
action filled with triumphant self-expansion.[23] In her poem, the death of
the bride-self paves the way for an ecstatic possession of the poet-self, who
dilates into an uncharted orgasmic "Eternity" in the end of the poem. The
life lived towards this expansion feels like it is accompanied by immortality, a theme Dickinson refers to as "the flood subject," a concept that
unlocks her artistic energies.[24] Thus, it is a poetically generative life satu-
rated with desire. Dying to the bride-self enables the poet-self to dwell
in what she calls elsewhere a house of "Possibility," whose "Everlasting
Roof" is the "Gambrels of the Sky," rather than a house of conventional
marital death, whose "Roof was scarcely visible" and its "Cornice – in
the Ground."[25] The life of the poet is not a short ride towards a house
that buries its mistress alive, but a life lived always with reference to the
immortality of her words and the expansion of self that concept inspires.
The flood subject empowers the poet to create poetry for "Eternity" and
live in relation to that sense of self. And yet, Dickinson describes the act of
adopting this identity as not merely compensation for lost erotic pleasures
(sublimation). By depicting the vocation of poet through the mediation
of the Gothic erotics of Hawthorne's sentimental masochism, Dickinson
implies that the poetic vocation is seductive; it holds the promise of an
orgasmic, ecstatic expansion of being that is predicated upon yielding to
forces larger than the self-determining self.

In order to see how the theme of riding with death and immortality in
"Because I could not stop for Death" implies the birth of a poet-self, it is

helpful to consider it in comparison to a related poem that explicitly links being oriented towards immortality with the work of writing poetry:

> Some – Work for Immortality –
> The Chiefer part, for Time –
> He – Compensates – immediately –
> The former – Checks – on Fame –
>
> Slow Gold – but Everlasting –
> The Bullion of Today –
> Contrasted with the Currency
> Of Immortality –
>
> A Beggar – Here and There –
> Is gifted to discern
> Beyond the Broker's insight –
> One's – Money – One's – the Mine – [26]

The work of writing poetry, performed always with an eye on fame and immortality, is not a symbol of value ("Money"), not something acquired in order to buy something else that is truly valued. It is the valuable thing itself. It is meaning and purpose intrinsically. It is the source of goodness itself ("the Mine") rather than a check to be cashed, a promise of value. To be a poet is to be a beggar in the world's eyes, yet to be oriented towards the immortality of fame. The "Broker," by contrast, lives in time and only for its pleasures. To be a poet is to possess "insight," to be able "discern" an expansive frame of reference. It is to make value and immortality "Mine." The speaker of "Because I could not stop for Death" claims such a life; she lives in relation to immortality because she submits to the painful yet necessary death of conventional pleasures of selves in time.[27] And yet, while both poems address the same theme ("immortality"), they adopt different tones. "Some – Work For Immortality" depicts an active poet, deliberately and consciously pursuing a value higher than the norm, while "Because I could not stop for Death" describes a speaker who has "put away [her] labor." It is not determination or tenacity that orients her towards immortality in this poem, but yielding to the fact of death's superior power.

The motif of hard work in "Some – Work For Immortality" makes sense to a post-Puritan American reader. The motif of agency-in-submission in "Because I could not stop for Death," by contrast, does not; it is counter-intuitive, to say nothing of it being particularly problematic for a female speaker. That said, just its surprising claim – that an expansion in scope and power follows submission to death – lies at the heart of the poem. The speaker, with her busy self-focused "I," was missing something, something she gained when she yielded to death's seduction. As we scan the poem for clues to what this something was, our attention is drawn to the reorientation of the speaker's perspective on the things of this life. In the third stanza in particular, the actions of life are presented as part of a life-cycle that is always defined by death; the sun rises, shines and sets; children play, strive, and are buried. And yet, this perception does not trivialize the human, as it sometimes does in the hands of Puritan authors like Edward Taylor or Jonathan Edwards. In this Dickinson poem, understanding that all things are defined by death engenders feelings of expansion ("Eternity"), self-determination ("I first surmised"), and freedom (she rejects normative identity scripts). What strikes others as the bleak finality of the grave turns out to be a surprising possibility of opening.

The surprising openness of what seems to be utterly closed in this poem does not involve the Christian vision of immortality that it might have for Taylor and Edwards. There is no Heavenly City, no Christian frame of reference at all, only an endless movement of the horses' heads. The freedom of self-creation invoked in the expansiveness of death in this poem is closer to the existential agency in "being-towards-death" described by Martin Heidegger. Indeed, the central motif of life compared to a carriage ride with death strikingly anticipates Heidegger, and it is surprising that critics have not addressed this resemblance.[28] One of Heidegger's central claims is that, in making death a taboo subject, Western culture deprives individuals of the opportunity to confront their own death and to exist "*in the passionate anxious freedom toward death.*"[29] Most of us dread death and try not to think about it, with the result that we lose the opportunity to live and experience what our life really is, which is an experience of being that is always informed by its ultimate cessation. According to Heidegger, "being-towards-death" – confronting the anxious realisation that our own non-being is the condition of our being – creates feelings of freedom. One way that this is so involves the death of the conventional self, its habits and narratives of identity; this transition affords the freedom to choose how to be.[30] This is the death of the bride-self that we have discussed in this poem.

Heidegger also posits that death inspires feelings of freedom because of its personalness. Anticipation of death reveals "the possibility of understanding one's *ownmost* and extreme potentiality-of-being."[31] This inner-ness and own-ness of death suggests to us the possibility of a more authentic way of living, on our own terms. No one else can claim or grasp the moment in which a person ceases to be. Death is non-relational. Dickinson explicitly observes the singularity of our own death in another poem: "This Consciousness that is aware / Of Neighbors and the Sun / Will be the one aware of Death / And that itself alone."[32] And, whatever the self discovers in that moment, "Itself unto itself and none / Shall make discovery." Death is singular, one's own. Consequently, while the speaker in "Because I could not stop for Death" has a good bit of company – death, immortality, horses – it all disappears when she arrives at the cemetery. As Ferlazzo writes, "the lady is alone now; her gentleman friend has vanished unexplained."[33] At the moment of death, the speaker's aloneness is apparent: it is she on the journey, alone. Both Heidegger and Dickinson suggest that pondering this ownmost-ness of death suggests to us the ownmost-ness of our own life. It suggests that selves can choose how to make themselves be. This flash of realization releases selves from the grip of what Heidegger calls "the they," those conventional selves that impose norms of selfhood that package up identity in ways that foreclose possibilities for self-creation.[34] Dickinson unmistakably anticipates this rejection of the "they-self" in another poem that opens with this declaration: "I'm ceded [en] I've stopped being Theirs [en]. *Poems*, 353" She claims her own identity, on her own terms, by refusing to be the they-self any longer.

The mixture of anxiety and expansive freedom in Dickinson's story of an eternal ride with death anticipates Heidegger's concept of "being-towards-death," and the birth of the poetic self that the poem invokes is a result of the freedom engendered by confronting the anxiety of death. In the poem, riding with death orients the speaker towards the way that all the activities of the earth are time-bound. The journey of life is re-cast as a journey towards the grave. Death is the invisible and unacknowledged nature of all life. Children playing at school quickly become adults who pursue labor and leisure while the grain ripens, and then the sun sets, they grow chilly and are buried in the grave; all of these time-bound activities are part of one continuum. At first, the journey does not seem so doomed; it is pleasant and hopeful. The young play and they strive, fighting for control. The speaker uses the active voice to describe their actions. However, the fourth stanza contains a great reversal; the sun passes the speaker, and suddenly the verbs name the actions of other forces: "He passed Us"; "The Dews drew." Now, the speaker notes the encroaching cold and discovers her own remarkable lack of protection, her human vulnerability. Her clothing is pitifully thin, a frail barrier between her and hostile forces intent on her annihilation. No amount of striving can protect her from the looming disaster. She is about to be snuffed out. She is the acted upon. The carriage pauses before a swelling in the ground, and then, down she goes. It's over.

And yet, in opposition to this drama of futility, the poem counterposes the present aliveness of the speaker with her all-important freedom to "surmise." To "surmise" is not exactly to deduce or suspect or realize; it is to imagine or to form a notion on slight grounds. The word was important to the poets that Dickinson read, above all for its association with creative imagination. To exemplify its definition of the verb, the *Oxford English Dictionary* quotes Keats: "Show him a garden, and with speed no less, He'll surmise sagely of a dwelling house," and Robert Browning: "Can I know, who but surmise?"[35] The verb "surmise" also calls to mind Keats's "On First Looking Into Chapman's Homer," whose speaker mentions that he has visited Greece, yet never did he "breathe its pure serene" til he read Chapman's Homer – when, in an epiphanic moment, "with a wild surmise," he seemed to see new planets, new worlds, infinite possibilities. Keats's poem suggests that the power of the poet is that of surmise: making the world on one's own terms, imagining infinite possibilities, encountering the unknown. Analogously, when Dickinson's speaker "surmises" that the horse's heads are towards eternity, she is imagining without knowing, claiming her own cognitive and imaginative agency, in opposition to the prescripts of the "they." Hers is the kind of freedom that Heidegger relates to being-towards-death, that of inventing a self and inventing the world on one's own terms. In this poem, the speaker recalls the day she first surmised that death is eternal; at that moment, that day expanded exponentially. It felt like it contained centuries. Each stage of the journey from schoolyard to grave suddenly seemed not brief and doomed, but packed with time – centuries, to be precise. It may have expanded because eternity is only the totality of "nows," so that the context of each moment in the eternal continuum made the moment expand in significance and scope. Or it might be because on that day she awoke to the poignancy and intensity of the small things in life, precisely because of their ephemerality and rarity. Or it might be because the poet suddenly realized she was free to map the world on her own terms, to surmise freely, to bury her they-self. Or it might be because she conjured up a compelling personal system of cosmic structure.[36] Whatever the reason, she reports that, in opposition to the finality of death, her surmise expanded the richness or scope of her experience of time and contingency.

The encounter with death in this poem is more optimistic than some critics claim. To Helen Vendler, the poem registers the death of the dream of personal immortality and a resulting feeling of the devastating finality of death and the impersonality of "eternity."[37] Sharon Cameron argues that the poem aspires to transcend the temporality it observes but can only represent being in terms of time and change. Consequently, it registers the failure of the lyric itself, though it also acknowledges compensatory inspiration for artistry in the act of recording our failure to transcend contingency.[38] I agree with these critics that the poem registers the inescapability of history, time, and embodiment, but argue that the awareness of this fact is not so much agonistic as paradoxically liberating. Vendler and Cameron undervalue the erotics of this carriage ride, the seductive vulnerability of the knife-edge between life and death that infuses the poem with pleasure and anticipation. They also undervalue the way dread and freedom are not necessarily opposites, as Heidegger posits. The day on which the speaker "first surmised" expanded into something larger than centuries; it revealed her being in a different frame of reference. She grasped "the privilege of finitude," discerned the immensity of living things as they contribute their parts towards eternity. The finitude of human life is not simply a consolation prize to be milked for whatever it might have to offer. It is a condition that, when confronted head-on, expands the experience of life and floods the self with a relationship to eternity.

If one tries hard to have an orgasm, one may not get there. One must let go, yield the willing self to the other or to the body's own agenda. If one tries hard to be a poet, one also may not get there. Romantic poets stress that one must let go, yield to the daemon whose agenda will work its way through you. Analogously, to be a self-determined human being, one must yield to the inevitability of death. The resignation that other readers emphasize in this poem is there, but it is coupled with a self-expansion that the poem suggests cannot be controlled, only admitted. Once death defeats the self-will of the autonomous ego, the result is a feeling of participation in "eternity" through the very fact of physical being. As Dickinson reported to Thomas Wentworth Higginson, "I find ecstasy in living – the mere sense of living is joy enough."[39]

In conclusion, we can observe that "Because I could not stop for Death" rejects Hawthorne's misogynist ideology of sentimental masochism, which seduces women, encourages them to relinquish their subjectivity and locate their being in service to the needs of another, and glamorizes their death. The poem replaces this conventional, deathly script with an affirmative one, in which the woman claims her own subjectivity and vocation as a poet. There is a kind of death in this, since the bride-self must die for the poet-self to be born; but the exchange is worth it because it opens the freedom to surmise and awareness of the intense meaningfulness of life itself. A related poem written around sixteen years later crystallizes the way death inspires such an awareness:

> Death is the supple Suitor
> That wins at last –
> It is a stealthy Wooing
> Conducted first
> By pallid innuendoes
> And dim approach
> But brave at last with Bugles

And a bisected Coach
It bears away in triumph
To Troth unknown
And Kinsmen as divulgeless
As throngs of Down – [40]

In this poem, the buried-alive bride has no happy ending. Carried off to death – marriage – she is compensated by no life underground. But the contrast between deadness and aliveness in the poem emphasizes the value of the latter. The dead lack the exquisite aliveness of worldly relationships, in which kinsmen divulge themselves to one another. Contrasting their deadness to living kinsmen and clans and troths makes the brevity of life's relationships and intimacies seem all the more beautiful. Looking at life through the lens of death reveals beauty and freedom. Dickinson's romance with death turns out to be a romance with life.

NOTES

1 *The Poems of Emily Dickinson*, ed. R. W. Franklin (Cambridge: Harvard University Press, 1999), 479.

2 Nathaniel Hawthorne, *Tales and Sketches* (New York: Library of America, 1982).

3 *Tales and Sketches*, 1411–12. McPherson shows that Hawthorne's own source for this and other classical stories is Charles Anthon's *A Classical Dictionary* (Hawthorne as Myth-Maker) (Toronto: University of Toronto Press, 1969), 14.

4 Many versions of the legend were available to Dickinson, including not only source versions but also creative engagements with it. Virgil, Chaucer, Shakespeare, and Milton all treat the myth. Milton, for example, describes "Proserpine gathering flow'rs / Herself a fairer flow'r by gloomy Dis / Was gathered, which cost Ceres all that pain / To seek her through the world" (*Paradise Lost* IV 268–72). Anthon's *A Classical Dictionary* and Ovid's 'Metamorphoses' were widely read in her day and time, as was John Lempriere's *Classical Dictionary* (1788). Elizabeth Barrett Browning's *Aurora Leigh* engages with the theme by comparing seduction and sexual assault to a woman's death, and importantly comparing a love child to a "pomegranate." Mary Shelley wrote a mythological drama entitled *Proserpine* in 1820, though it was published only posthumously. On the numerous pre-Victorian iterations of this myth, see Andrew Rodopi, *The Lost Girls: Demeter-Persephone and the Literary Imagination, 1850–1930* (Amsterdam: Editions Rodopi B.V., 2007).

5 Ken Hiltner, "Because I, Persephone, Could Not Stop for Death: Emily Dickinson and the Goddess," *Emily Dickinson Journal* 10.2 (2001): 22–42. Hiltner argues that, in speaking in Proserpina's voice, Dickinson gives sympathetic yet exasperated voice to women who buy into the notion that a woman's happiness lies in being carried off by a domineering man, living in his house, being initiated into the mysteries of sex, and bearing his children. The speaker of the poem, Proserpina, believes all of this, but the poet does not. We hear the poet's

voice more clearly in the fourth stanza, which more starkly exposes the cold reality of a bride's rape and death. Hiltner argues that Proserpina longs for her sundered relationship with her mother, which is restored at the end when Proserpina *becomes* a mother and thereby participates in the eternal feminine. Anthon's source would suggest such a reading, since it only briefly renders the Prosperina story, enfolding it in a long encyclopedia entry about Proserpina's mother, and her outrage and grief. However, Dickinson's poem is not in fact about the mother's anguish, but about Proserpina, whose story is lushly imagined not in Anthon, but in Hawthorne's rendition. And her imagination rarely runs to the compensations of maternity. Ovid's rendition of the story attends even less to Proserpina's story than does the Homeric Hymn.

6   Allen Tate writes: "note the subtly interfused erotic motive, which the idea of death has presented to most romantic poets, love being a symbol interchangeable with death," in *Critical Essays on Emily Dickinson*, ed. Paul J. Ferlazzo (Boston: G. K. Hall, 1984), 88. Others who emphasize the erotics of the seduction in the poem include: Bettina L. Knapp, *Emily Dickinson* (New York: Continuum, 1989); Barton Levi St. Armand, "'Looking at Death, is Dying': Understanding Dickinson's Morbidity," *Approaches to Teaching Dickinson's Poetry*, eds. Robin Riley Fast and Christine Mack Gordon (New York: MLA, 1989), 155; and Robert McClure Smith, *The Seductions of Emily Dickinson* (Tuscaloosa: University of Alabama Press, 1996). Jerome Loving emphasizes the erotics of the poem, arguing that it is "about the day in every life when we realize that the desire for love is the desire for death," in *Emily Dickinson: The Poet on the Second Story* (Cambridge: Cambridge University Press, 1986), 47. On the other hand, Paula Bennett, Daneen Wardrop, and Helen McNeil read the poem as depicting "a form of rape" – see *Emily Dickinson Woman Poet* (Iowa City: University of Iowa Press, 1990), 74; *Emily Dickinson's Gothic: Goblin With a Gauge* (Iowa City: University of of Iowa Press, 1996), 88–95; and *Emily Dickinson* (London: Virago, 1986).

7   Critics have discussed other intertextual influences on the poem. Elizabeth Phillips summarizes: Robert Browning's "The Last Ride Together," Elizabeth Barrett Browning's *Aurora Leigh*, Keats's famous phrase "half in love with easeful Death." She also mentions biographical influences, emphasizing the death of a friend while on a carriage ride, a theme she refers to as "romantic" in *Emily Dickinson: Personae and Performance* (University Park: Penn State University Press, 1988), 86–87.

8   September 25, 1845. *The Letters of Emily Dickinson*, 3 vols, ed. Thomas H. Johnson (Cambridge: Belknap Press, 1958) 1: 19–21.

9   *Shakespeare: The Complete Works* (Baltimore: Penguin, 1969), 1132. See Paraic Finnerty, *Emily Dickinson's Shakespeare* (Amherst: Massachusetts, 2006).

10   *Letters* 1: 45–46.

11   *Letters* 1: 209.

12   *Letters* 1: 109.

13   *Letters* 1: 168–69. Judith Farr discusses this insight and the general dread of marriage in her essay "Emily Dickinson and Marriage: 'The Etruscan Experiment,'" *Reading Emily Dickinson's Letters: Critical Essays*, eds. Jane Donahue Eberwein and Cindy MacKenzie (Amherst: University of Massachusetts Press, 2009), 174.

14   *Letters* 1: 198.

15 *Tales and Sketches*, 1414–15.

16 *Tales and Sketches*, 1431–32.

17 *Tales and Sketches*, 1434.

18 *Tales and Sketches*, 1433.

19 Marianne Noble, *The Masochistic Pleasures of Sentimental Literature* (Princeton, NJ: Princeton University Press, 2000).

20 Walt Whitman, *Leaves of Grass* (New York: Norton, 1973), 57–58.

21 "Vesuvius at Home." *Parnassus* 5.1 (1976), 49–74. Rich also discusses the Demeter–Persephone legend in *Of Woman Born* (New York: Bantam, 1976), 237–40. Joanne Dobson and Joanne Feit Diehl also argue that the relationship between Dickinson's narrators and male lovers are meditations on the relationship between a poet and her creative imagination. See Joanne Dobson, *Dickinson and the Strategies of Reticence* (Bloomington: Indiana University Press, 1989); Joanne Diehl, *Dickinson and the Romantic Imagination* (Princeton: Princeton University Press, 1981).

22 Ruth Miller argues that in this poem, the speaker devotes herself to poetry: "What was Death-in-life came in the guise of that crucial encounter, but it tempered her soul and she survives as a poet." *The Poetry of Emily Dickinson* (Middletown: Wesleyan, 1968), 193–94.

23 Along these lines, William Galperin writes: "by redefining death so that it meant a woman's cooptation by culture, the poem similarly redefined immortality as a woman's self-possession, or the result, in turn, of a refusal to allow 'society' the prerogative of selecting her." "A Posthumanist Approach to Teaching Dickinson" in *Approaches to Teaching Dickinson Poetry* (New York: MLA, 1989), 113.

24 *Letters* 1: 319.

25 *Poems*, 466.

26 *Poems*, 536.

27 Daneen Wardrop reads the poem as claiming the birth of the poet self through the death of the bride self. See *Emily Dickinson's Gothic: Goblin with a Gauge* (Iowa City: University of Iowa Press, 1996).

28 I am indebted to Bruce Clarkson for his excellent essay reading of this poem in the context of Heidegger. The most important discussion of Dickinson in the context of Heidegger is Jed Deppman's "Astonished Thinking: Dickinson and Heidegger" in *Emily Dickinson and Philosophy*, eds. Jed Deppman, Marianne Noble, and Gary Lee Stonum (Cambridge: Cambridge University Press, 2013), 227–48.

29 Martin Heidegger, *Being and Time* (Albany: SUNY, 2010), 255. Italics and emphasis in original.

30 Michael Wheeler, "Martin Heidegger." *The Stanford Encyclopedia of Philosophy* (Fall 2015 Edition). http://plato.stanford.edu/entries/heidegger/#Death

31 Page 252, italics in original.

32 *Poems*, 817.

33 Paul J. Ferlazzo, *Emily Dickinson* (Boston: Twayne, 1976), 56.

34 Jed Deppman discusses Dickinson in the context of Heidegger's "they-self" in *Trying to Think With Emily Dickinson* (Amherst: University of Massachusetts Press, 2008), 143.

35 Keats, "Cap & Bells"; Browning, *La Saisiaz*. Both examples cited in the *Oxford English Dictionary*. www.oed.com.

36 Emily Budick proposes that this poem envisions time and eternity as two wheels, with the center of the wheel of eternity being located on the circumference of the wheel of time. These two wheels are at ninety degrees to one another. See *Emily Dickinson and the Life of Language* (Baton Rouge: Louisiana State University Press, 1985).

37 Helen Vendler, *Dickinson: Selected Poems and Commentaries* (Cambridge: Belknap Press, 2010).

38 Sharon Cameron, *Lyric Time: Dickinson and the Limits of Genre* (Baltimore: Johns Hopkins University Press, 1979), 135.

39 *Letters*, 474.

40 *Poems*, 1470.

11

DEBORAH LUTZ

Erotic Bonds Among Women in Victorian Literature

Anne Lister, an early-nineteenth-century lesbian, wrote in her diary about using Byron's poetry to seduce – or flirt with – pretty women.[1] She planned to give the fifth canto of "Childe Harold's Pilgrimage" (1812) to one young woman, who, when Lister asked her if she liked Byron's poetry, responded "yes, perhaps too well"; when the girl haunted Lister's "thoughts like some genius of fairy lore," she pondered sending her a Cornelian heart with a copy of Byron's lines on the subject.[2] Women she knew blushed when they "admitted" to having read *Don Juan* (1819–1824) and spoke of being "almost afraid" to read *Cain* (1821).[3] To one of her lovers, Lister read aloud *Glenarvon* (1816), Lady Caroline Lamb's melodramatic, fictionalized version of her affair with Byron; they found it a "very dangerous sort of book."[4] The novel's heroine cross-dresses, a practice women in Lister's social circle sometimes used to woo straight women.[5] Lister even played with performing Byronism in her romantic dalliances.[6] Like a bold Byronic hero, she gazed on attractive women with a "penetrating countenance," and looked "unutterable things" at them, which led them to confess to wishing she "had been a gent."[7] She tried to "mould" young women "to her purpose," treating them like toys.[8] But it wasn't only Byron who provided Lister with ways to act on her own sexual identity. Like many in the nineteenth century who had little access to information about "deviant" types of sexuality, she read classical texts for their descriptions of same-sex desire, especially Juvenal's *Sixth Satire*, with its famous lesbian orgy. She discussed them with other educated women as a covert means to figure out if they were lesbians.[9]

At the other end of the century, two lesbian poets wrote erotic texts, rather than merely reading them – or employing them for amorous purposes. Katherine Bradley and Edith Cooper, an aunt and niece who considered themselves married, developed a collaborative writing practice under the name Michael Field. As a "man," they wrote with passion about the lovely, sensual ways of women. In an untitled poem published in 1893, for instance, they seem to describe a girl's soul and countenance:

> Her soul a deep-wave pearl
> Dim, lucent of all lovely mysteries;
> A face flowered for heart's ease,
> A brow's grace soft as seas
> Seen through faint forest trees:
> A mouth, the lips apart,
> Like aspen-leaflets trembling in the breeze
> From her tempestuous heart.[10]

Yet the mystery of the face acts as a double for the girl's labia, both places linked to enigmatic nature – the deep sea and the shady forest – with an obscurity that beckons. Yopie Prins argues that Bradley and Cooper's collaboration itself had a sexual element, and that their poetry worked as "an eroticized textual mediation" between them.[11] Like Lister, Bradley and Cooper turned to the classical world to find images of their own sexuality. In their collection of lyric poems *Long Ago* (1889), they consciously imitate Sappho's fragments. Prins asks a question that will be important for this chapter: "How shall we read these poems written by two women writing as a man writing as Sappho?"[12]

Lister, Bradley, and Cooper are somewhat special cases, in that we have a strong sense of which texts they found erotic. Discovering what reading material Victorian women – or any historical individuals – used for erotic purposes is a difficult task. Women's sexuality has historically been subsumed under men's, which forces the reader to look through or underneath men's foregrounded desires to locate women's. While traces do appear in conventional, widely available literature of the period, women's desires and their bodies are mostly absent in the underground world of pornography, replaced by their representations by men.[13] Unearthing a lost library of Victorian women's pornography remains a dream, but I will try to pick up shadowy clues in this chapter. Terry Castle's remarks about writing the literary history of lesbianism apply also to women's erotic literature in the nineteenth century, in that this work means confronting, "from the start, something ghostly: an impalpability, a misting over, an evaporation, a 'whiting out' of possibility."[14] But, with the Victorians, this very ghostliness has sexual frisson. With such strict boundaries marking off gender roles, crossing them – making them blur or giving them a misty indeterminacy – took on its own eroticism, as we have seen with Lister performing Byronism, and Bradley and Cooper being Michael Field (being Sappho).

For Lister, books worked as erotic go-betweens; they provided a third element over which desire played between two people. Instead of risking a proposal such as "I desire you," she used the intermediate step of expressing appetite for a book and then wondered if another woman might also relish the same book (and then perhaps Lister herself). Byron's and Sappho's poems came to represent desire, and their role in the real world could be to further lust between two people, to make it manifest – make it, perhaps, physical. Reading space could become erotic or sexual space, as in the famous passage in Dante's "Inferno" (1314) in which a book draws Francesca and Paolo into bed together, rather than being an impetus for autoeroticism. Francesca explains that

> One day, to pass the time away, we read
> of Lancelot – how love had overcome him.
> We were alone, and we suspected nothing.
> And time and time again that reading led
> our eyes to meet, and made our faces pale,
> and yet one point alone defeated us.
> When we had read ow the desired smile
> was kissed by one who was so true a lover,
> this one, who never shall be parted from me,
> while all his body trembled, kissed my mouth.[15]

Seduction happened as a transfer: beginning with hunger for a book, and then from book to a second body. H.J. Jackson explores the regular practice in the nineteenth century of writing marginal notes in books in order to woo another reader – the handwriting (the "voice") of the writer seduced the reader as she read it alone. The poet Samuel Taylor Coleridge penned intimate comments in books he gave or lent to women, a romantic overture, a kind of whisper in the ear. Byron added marginalia in books for his lovers, such as Madame de Staël's *Corinne*, in which he professed his love for the owner of the book, Teresa Guiccioli.[16] John Keats wrote in an amorous letter to Fanny Brawne that he was "marking the most beautiful passages in Spenser, intending it for you."[17]

The theme of literature as a sexual device – to indoctrinate, flirt, tempt – runs through many nineteenth-century British novels. In Charles Dickens's *Our Mutual Friend* (1865), for instance, two men compete to teach the working-class beauty Lizzie Hexam to read. Another pretty girl, Maggie Tulliver in George Eliot's *Mill on the Floss* (1860), meets Philip Wakem among the Scotch fir trees, in a place called the Red Deeps. Even though she has given up books in order to subdue her will to her narrowed life, Maggie is convinced by Philip to borrow his novels, like those by Walter Scott and

Madame de Staël. He yearns to stir her passionate nature with literature, hoping to convince her to entertain his love. The young Catherine Linton in Emily Brontë's *Wuthering Heights* (1847) taunts and harasses her cousin Hareton Earnshaw with his oafish illiteracy. He steals away some of her beautiful books to learn to read, but she humiliates him when she discovers his clumsy efforts. Before long, the fighting becomes flirting over books. Eventually, the stranger Lockwood observes their growing desire:

> The male speaker began to read ... His handsome features glowed with pleasure, and his eyes kept impatiently wandering from the page to a small white hand over his shoulder, which recalled him by a smart slap on the cheek, whenever its owner detected such signs of inattention. Its owner stood behind; her light, shining ringlets blending, at intervals, with his brown locks, as she bent to superintend his studies; and her face – it was lucky he could not see her face, or he would never have been so steady.[18]

Passages in pornographic literature, as will be discussed shortly, make the book a vehicle for seduction more directly – an obviously stated link between body, book, and body.

If women who fancied other women found Byron's poems erotic, as Lister and her lovers did, then one wonders: what other literature excited these women? The most visible relationships that stirred women readers in mainstream novels and poems involved charged, heterosexual love narratives. Evidence in women's letters, diaries, and albums shows that Lister's was part of a wide-scale fixation on Byronic heroes, both in Lord Byron's poems such as "Childe Harold's Pilgrimage" (1812–1818) and *The Corsair* (1814), and as represented in popular novels such as Charlotte Brontë's *Jane Eyre* (1847) and Anthony Trollope's *The Eustace Diamonds* (1872).[19] In fact, sensual agitation in response to Byronism became so commonplace that it developed into a stereotype by the middle of the nineteenth century. Blanche Ingram of *Jane Eyre* tells Rochester that a "man is nothing without a spice of the devil in him" and that she desires something of a "wild, fierce, bandit-hero."[20] "An English hero of the road," she goes on, "would be the next best thing to an Italian bandit; and that could only be surpassed by a Levantine pirate."[21] While Brontë intends for the reader to understand that Blanche is "showy" and "not genuine" – "she was not original: she used to repeat sounding phrases from books" – her Jane also falls for the Byronic Rochester – who isn't exactly a bandit, but has his devilish, Bluebeard-ish side.[22] Trollope's Lizzie Eustace wants a lover who will "be rough with her" and have "fine Corsair's eyes, full of expression and determination, eyes that could look

love and bloodshed almost at the same time."²³ She longs for "manly properties – power, bigness, and apparent boldness" and to be "treated sometimes with crushing severity, and at others with the tenderest love."²⁴ Female
characters in Benjamin Disraeli's *Venetia* (1837), Emily Brontë's *Wuthering
Heights* (1847), George Eliot's *Middlemarch* (1871–1872), Oscar Wilde's
The Picture of Dorian Gray (1890), and many other Victorian novels yearn
for similar men with mysterious and potentially cruel selves, who might be
redeemed by a true love (usually the heroine who longs for him). Tales of
attraction to a Byronic hero are generally interlaced with failure – either
the hero loses his Byronism to become a proper mate (Rochester in *Jane
Eyre*), death interrupts (Catherine Earnshaw/Linton in *Wuthering Heights*
and Byron's heroines in *The Giaour* [1813] and *Manfred* [1817]), or the
Byronic hero turns out to be little more than a cad (*The Eustace Diamonds*
and Anne Brontë's *The Tenant of Wildfell Hall* [1848]). Byronic eroticism
involves hopeless longing – for what one can't have or what never existed.

Yet Byronism, as we have seen with Anne Lister, also came to represent
same-sex desire – as did Sappho, by the end of the nineteenth century, for
both men and women. Byronic literary characters found glory in transgressing codes of respectable behavior, especially those governing sexuality. In
Childe Harold, the hero *not* "in virtue's ways did take delight / But spent his
days in riot most uncouth / And vex'd with mirth the drowsy ear of Night."
What finds favor with him is "revel" and "ungodly glee," and he delights
most in "concubines and carnal companie."²⁵ In *Don Juan*, the hero commits
adultery, and when he dresses like a woman, men try to cajole him into sex.
From its publication until today, *Manfred* has been rumored to be about
incest, a reflection of Byron's own sexual relationship with his half sister. But
even deeper sexual "sins" are implied in many of Byron's poems, the heroes
ciphers on which to project one's own outlawed desires. Andrew Elfenbein
explores how homosexuality became part of the popular legend of Byron,
with the belief that he had "committed the most unspeakable sexual crimes."²⁶
Rumors about Byron being a sodomite connected his name and dandyism to
deviance and scandal, although this stance had a certain attraction for many.
Men like Benjamin Disraeli and Edward Bulwer-Lytton performed Byronism
as a potentially risky way to climb socially, to draw attention to their literary
raciness and drama.²⁷ Lister knew all of this; indeed, Byron's poem about the
Cornelian heart that she planned to use was originally written to attest to
his love for John Edleston.²⁸ Lister found Byron's representation of same-sex
love broad enough to include her own desire for her sex.

Somewhat paradoxically, the near-compulsory gender roles of the
Victorian era encouraged same-sex physical intimacies, especially between
women, so representations of these bonds proliferate. Victorian women

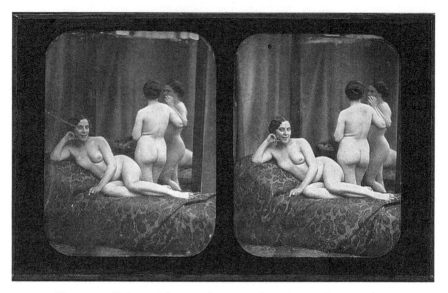

Figure 11.1 Unknown photographer, *c.*1850–1855. Stereo daguerreotype.
France. Indiana University Kinsey Institute.

were expected to develop close, devoted friendships with each other; expressions of the deep sentiment thought to be natural to their gender. In her exploration of female friendship, Sharon Marcus contends that anxieties about homosexuality did not emerge until the twentieth century, and the Victorians "saw no contest between what we now call heterosexual and homosexual desire."[29] A broader range of ways for women to be intimate with other women flourished. It was normal for women to kiss each other on the lips, to walk with their arms around each others' waists, to sleep with their limbs entwined, and to have lifelong partnerships – often described by them and others as marriages. Through her study of hundreds of their diaries and letters, Marcus charts Victorian women's passionate closeness to each other – their enjoyment with female friends of an amorous freedom not allowed with men who weren't their husbands.

Thousands of depictions of erotic fascination between women dot Victorian narratives, especially the novels of Elizabeth Gaskell, George Eliot, Charles Dickens, Anthony Trollope, and Wilkie Collins. Whether or not Victorian women readers felt this erotic heat themselves is unclear, but characteristics of these relationships were borrowed by pornographers of the time, who recognized their capability to excite sexually. Some of these passages also found their way into twentieth-century anthologies of lesbian literature, so they provide a fruitful intersection of literary eroticism and lesbianism. One significant example, used by Sharon Marcus as an exemplary text of female romantic friendship, is Charlotte Brontë's *Shirley* (1849). The novel focuses for much of its plot on two women smitten with each other, even though they ultimately marry men. Shirley's fellowship with Caroline fuels the story with a vitality absent from the heterosexual romances. Like Bradley and Cooper's interest in inhabiting male gender roles, Shirley (usually a man's name at the time) calls herself "Captain Keeldar" because she was given "a man's name; I hold a man's position." She goes on to say: "It is enough to inspire me with a touch of manhood … I feel quite gentlemanlike."[30] The two young women share a bed, gaze into each other's eyes, kiss, and grasp hands. Caroline informs Shirley that "no passion can ultimately outrival" their love for one another: "I am supported and soothed when you – that is, you only – are near, Shirley."[31] The friends marry two brothers, thus linking them forever as family. Caroline also participates in a second highly charged same-sex connection: Shirley's governess Mrs. Pryor showers a tender adoration on Caroline. Since neither the characters nor the reader know until the last quarter of the book that the older woman is Caroline's long-lost mother, their relationship appears to be an obsessive infatuation. With a typical gesture, Mrs. Pryor "swept Caroline's curls from her cheek as she took a seat near her [and] caressed the oval outline."[32] In a passage that closely mirrors heterosexual marriage proposals in other Victorian novels, Mrs. Pryor wants to set up her life with Caroline: "With you I am happier then I have ever been with any living thing … your society I should esteem a very dear privilege – an inestimable privilege, a comfort, a blessing … I hope you can love me?" She wishes to buy a house of her own and have Caroline "come to me then."[33] The eroticism of these passages manages to be both platonic and subversive, both revealing and cloaking a relationship that is unassailably pure and yet fully "queer."

The fervent physicality and gender flexibility of Shirley and Caroline's relationship had its counterparts in Victorian pornography. Steven Marcus, in his groundbreaking study *The Other Victorians*, explores pornographers' poaching of conventions from mainstream literature, such as sensibility from Jane Austen's novels, what he calls "Byronic trappings," and plot and characterization from Dickens and Thackeray. His argument can be extended to include representations of same-sex desire, especially women's. A passage from the pornographic *A Romance of Lust* (1873–1876), for instance, closely mirrors one from Christina Rossetti's "Goblin Market" (1862), a popular poem written for children and adults. In the former, a girl describes her sexual experience with an older woman: "she glued her lips to it [her clitoris], and after sucking a while began to play with her tongue … She licked me most exquisitely … She sucked it for some time … Her lips were wet with the moisture that had escaped from me … and I could not help licking the creamy juice from off her lips."[34] In the latter, Rossetti tells the story of a girl who becomes addicted to sucking the juices of fruit bought from sexualized goblins. She can only be saved by the sacrifice of her sister, who forces the goblins to cover her body with the sinful nectar. She runs home to her sister, who has been wasting away for the addictive drink, and calls to her to embrace her: "Hug me, kiss me, suck my juices/ ... Eat me, drink me, love me; / Laura make much of me."[35] The caressing consumption of this stickiness off skin works as an antidote to the girl's wasting illness. In pornographic texts, women also lick, kiss, and suck each others' bodies, but the context of sacrifice and addiction is replaced by the easy giving and receiving of pleasure.

In some cases, pornography also influenced the activities and writings of women who desired other women. Annamarie Jagose argues that Anne Lister, in her means of seducing women and in the language she used to describe her sexual activities in her diaries, draws on a "conventionally masculine pornographic tradition."[36] Lister had pretentions to being a writer, so she carried literary tropes – pornographic and otherwise – into her accounts of her love affairs. Yet, despite Lister's seeming access to it, almost all of the pornographic literature of the time that can be traced – either because copies still exist or we have descriptions of it in bibliographies such as Henry Spencer Ashbee's three-volume, approximately two-thousand-page list of erotic literature, which provides extensive plot summaries of many of the titles – was written for and by men.[37] These volumes' ephemerality – with their printing, publication, and sale heavily prohibited and policed, and authorities destroying them whenever they could (for instance, more than one-third of the titles on Ashbee's list no longer exist) – makes it even more difficult for us to know how many female readers had access to them.[38] If they did, did they enjoy them? Under what conditions did they read them?[39] We have some evidence that men read such texts aloud in pairs or larger groups, but did women (like Lister with *Glenarvon*)? And if so, with whom?[40] The only evidence I have been able to find of this is in pornography itself, where sophisticated women read aloud from pornographic works, usually in the company of men with whom they will then have sex. In *The Power of Mesmerism* (1880), for instance, Madame G. sits with two men and reads the Marquis de Sade's *Justine* (1791) and *Juliette* (1797) "in ten volumes, with their one hundred steel plates"; *Philosopie dans le Boudoir* (1795); *Fanny Hill* (1748); *The Romance of Lust*; and others.[41] A recurring character named Helen in the anonymous multi-volume memoir *My Secret Life*, published in the 1880s and probably mostly fictional, enjoys reading "baudy books" while the narrator, called Walter, "gamahuches" her.[42] Further on, Walter revels in "one or two chests full of the best and baudiest books in English and French" with a female lover.[43] In a

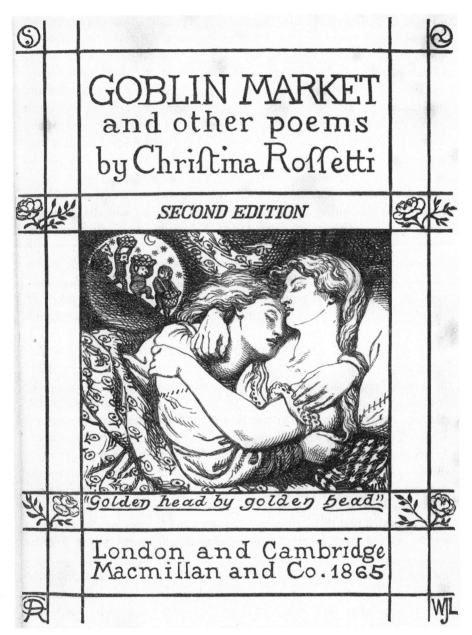

Figure 11.2 Title page, *Goblin Market and Other Poems*, Christina Rossetti. 1864.
Illustration,
Dante Gabriel Rossetti, 1862. London, The British Museum.

serial story in *The Pearl* – the complete title of which is "My Grandmother's
Tale or May's Account of her Introductions to the Art of Love: From an
Unsophisticated Manuscript Found Amongst the Old Lady's Papers After
Her Death, Supposed To Have Been Written About AD 1797" – two young,
inexperienced women on a ship spring a secret drawer in a man's cabin and
pull out books "full of coloured pictures of the most lascivious evolutions
of love," in which they read about "a doctor's exploits with a buxom young
widow."[44] They fondle each other, although the reader knows that a man
watches through a panel in the wall. Since the author of the work and its
likely readers are also men, this "watching" resounds in many ways.

As with "My Grandmother's Tale," Victorian pornography is rife with the
conceit that the author is a woman who describes her sexual experiences
with men – and often also women.[45] The male author speaks in a gendered
"female" voice, and what the female speaker does and has done to her tells
the reader what men want to do to, or with, women. Injecting male desires
into a female voice and body is a commonplace convention of pornography,
with one of the most famous examples being *Fanny Hill*, which takes the
form of a woman's letters to a female friend. Yet, by the early nineteenth
century, such narrative cross-dressing had also become so conventional in
literature of all sorts as to be almost invisible. Daniel Defoe's *Moll Flanders*
(1722) and *Roxana: The Fortunate Mistress* (1724) are "autobiographies"
by women whose lives are full of sexual scheming. Defoe's novels can be
seen as proto-erotic when placed in the larger history of narrative gender
play and erotic writing. Similarly, in *Pamela; or, Virtue Rewarded* (1740) and
Clarissa, or the History of a Young Lady (1748), Samuel Richardson wrote
letters in the guise of pretty young women. Many of his contemporaries saw
these books as licentious, and their heroines are unrelentingly pursued by
lecherous men – a theme exhaustively treated by pornographers of the time.

In some Victorian pornography, these cross-gender narratives can become
so complicated that they call to mind Bradley and Cooper writing as a man
writing as a woman. Layers of gender play appear most often in flagellation pornography, a formula so popular that most Victorian *sub rosa* texts
include the birching, whipping, or beating of men, women, boys, and girls.
The complexity of flogging narratives extends to their generic richness: novels; plays; poems; "histories," like *A History of the Rod;* "lectures," such
as the "Experimental Lecture by Colonel Spanker on the Exciting and
Voluptuous Pleasures to be Derived from Crushing and Humiliating the
Spirit of a Beautiful and Modest Young Lady; As Delivered By Him in the
Assembly Room of the Society of Aristocratic Flagellants"; "memoirs," such
as *The Spirit of Flagellation or The Memoirs of Mrs. Hinton, Who Kept a
School Many Years at Kensington* ... ; epistolary works, such as *Sublime of*

Flagellation in Letters from Lady Termagant Flaybum, of Birch-Grove, to Lady Harriet Tickletail, of Bumfiddle-Hall; and medical and scientific tracts. Byronic tropes appear in these texts more than in other pornographic writing – especially the cruel, aloof, and potentially abusive aspects of the Byronic character. Admirers in these tales exhibit a willingness to accept, and even enjoy, this dark side. Most often, female characters wield the rod and display Byronic masterfulness and aristocratic pride alternating with tender love. For instance, when the young charges of a flagellating governess in *Romance of Lust* first see her, they "marked the determined character of her countenance, and at once dreaded her becoming our governess, as we felt we should not only have one who would master us, but who would also be severe in every way."[46] The male speaker comments with fervent lust that she is "too stern and firm of purpose not to have bent any boy's will to her bidding."[47]

Many flogging narratives follow a formula that doesn't lead to intercourse – the use of the "rod" becomes the central interest. Erotic fascination focuses on the buttocks of the man, woman, or child being chastised, rather than the genitals of either sex. Lingering descriptions of the exposure and vulnerability of the "white angelic orbs" proliferate, and their preparation and uncovering follow ritualistic steps. A serial narrative in *The Pearl* that purports to be a woman confessing her experiences with other women serves as one example out of thousands: "Unfastening her drawers, Jane drew them well down, whilst Mrs. Mansell pinned up her chemise, fully exposing the broad expanse of her glorious buttocks, the brilliant whiteness of her skin showing to perfection by the dazzling glare of the well-lighted room.'[48] This obsession with a part of the body that doesn't vary much between the genders (men's buttocks garner the same type of description) allows for a gender mobility – readers can identify with and embody a wide array of characters, and their sexual enjoyment can move more fluidly among genders and body parts.

Steven Marcus remarks that, in flagellation pornography, "anybody can be or become anybody else, and the differences between the sexes are blurred and confused ... The ambiguity of sexual identity seems in fact to be part of the pleasure that this fantasy yields."[49] More than any other type of Victorian literature, these texts are peopled with characters who cross-dress, display androgynous or opposite-gender traits, or parade an unreal hypersexuality. A performative aspect pervades these stories, with both the flogger and the one being chastised taking on different roles, usually self-consciously so. A passage from *My Secret Life* provides a useful example. Set in a flagellation brothel in London, the scenario is arranged in advance by the narrator, Walter, with the "abbess" of the establishment. Masked, Walter enters a room in which a half-masked man, kneeling on a large chair, bends over the foot of a bed. The man wears a "woman's dress tucked up to his waist, showing his naked rump and thighs, with his feet in male socks and boots. On his head was a woman's cap tied carefully round his face to hide his whiskers." A woman standing behind him is dressed as a topless ballet dancer, and another – called Miss Yellow for the color of her hair, and naked except for boots and stockings – wields the rod. The man asks to see Walter's penis; Walter complies with this, but not with the man's desire to touch it. The abbess says to the man, "Now she shall whip you, you naughty boy."[50] As the man is being flogged, Walter sexually stimulates him with his hand, until he has an orgasm. A fourth woman in the room (Walter's current lover) watches, and later repairs to a different room with Walter for further sexual escapades.

What does this passage perform? For the first-person narrator Walter, the sexual tourist and voyeur, it is a theatrical tableau; he pays to watch the man being chastised perform his desire, which involves dressing up like a woman in a humiliating situation and being controlled by paid women who take masculinized roles (Miss Yellow, whom Walter describes as "a bold, insolent looking bitch," and the abbess; the ballerina is strongly feminized, but seems to signal the theatrical aspect of the whole). The "client" arranges to be watched by a man, who takes a masculinized, controlling role, and to interact with him sexually. Gender here feels dream-like, a magic lantern show that can be overlaid, like colored lights, onto bodies. The fourth woman holds an especially evocative place. Her position as a watcher on the sidelines of a drama not about her works figuratively for women's minimal role in the sexually explicit book trade. But Anne Lister also comes to mind, as a reader who transforms what she finds in books into an active identity, thus becoming an agent of her own desire.

As other critics have pointed out, Steven Marcus ignores women's desire in his writings on pornography.[51] He comments that the "entire immense literature of flagellation produced during the Victorian period, along with the fantasies it embodied and the practices it depicted, represents a kind of last-ditch compromise with and defense against homosexuality."[52] By this he means male homosexuality, of course, leaving out at least half of the population. Another odd quality about this argument – that flagellation pornography is a desperate attempt to mask, even while it represents, homosexuality – is that in much of the pornography of the period, same-sex acts – both male and female – flourished, completely unmasked. While most Victorians would not have understood these passages as "homosexual" – as defined in the twentieth century – they enjoyed them as titillating gender-cross play, similar to the pleasure found by Lister, Bradley, and Cooper with their gender-fluid writings and activities. In stories in *The Pearl*, for instance, two men have sex between each other's thighs while looking at pictures in

Fanny Hill (which has a famous passage of women having sex with each other); there is "An Adventure with a Tribade [lesbian]; Related in a Letter From A Young Lady to Her Sister"; and women use strapped-on India rubber dildoes (which they call "godemiches") that are "charged with a creamy compound of gelatine [sic] and milk" to penetrate other women at an all-female orgy.[53] *The Romance of Lust* is an especially rich source for same-sex activity. One Miss Frankland has a heavy pelt of hair covering her thighs and most of her torso, and such a large clitoris that she uses it to penetrate other women. The main character of the book has a sexual relationship with his uncle, who prefers men's anuses to any other sort of orifice: "Of course this was an old letch of his [anal sex with men], which his position as schoolmaster had given him so many opportunities of indulging in, and the still greater pleasure of initiating others in it."[54]

Walter, the narrator of *My Secret Life*, can hardly believe it when he meets a "sod," who tells him that some men are "fond of a bit of brown" and use dildos on each other.[55] But eventually he develops an obsessive craving to handle, "frig," and eventually suck another man's penis. Becoming acquainted with a young house painter in need of money, Walter suspects he is "an overfrigged bugger, who could no longer come," which bothers him. But then he indulges anyway, and "could not sleep for having frigged a man." Despite a feeling of queasiness with these acts, Walter continues to pay the man for sex. He dresses him in silk stockings, and eventually, in a sort of mad swoon of desire, "buggers" him.[56] At first Walter loathes himself and the painter, but for a long time his "mind ran on anus and nothing else," and he has sex with numerous men. One of Walter's earliest erotic experiences is spying on women having sex with each other. As a young man, he begins to understand that, just as he enjoys his cousin's penis, "some women find similar pleasures with their own sex."[57] He soon develops an interested knowledge in "the Lesbian games," especially what he calls "flat fucking."[58] Sometimes, when he meets women, he feels that his "observation, experience, and almost instinct" tells him that "they were tribades."[59] Unsure about the morality of such activities at first, he ultimately decides that pleasure has its own rules: "Why should not men have each other's bums if they liked, why not women rub cunts together if it's pleasure to them?"[60]

The libertine philosophy espoused by Walter runs through most Victorian-era pornography. This utopian vision of gender and sexuality – that gender and genitalia don't matter when it comes to pleasure – fits within Stephen Marcus's theory of "pornotopia." In this utopia, men always have erections when they want, women enthuse and are at all times ready for anything, and orgasms occur at the perfect moment (and repeatedly and simultaneously).[61] While situations, places, and persons might vary, sameness and repetition of acts and experiences rule. What is to be found in entering into the woman's (or man's) body should not be mysterious and unplumbable, but always more or less the familiar and expected. This literature of the finite and known contrasts sharply with the yearning for the unknowable that is part of Byronism. With the former, desire is satiated; but with the latter, desire remains open, variable, and constant.[62] In some ways, the utopia of pornography is matched by the homoeroticism of what Sharon Marcus calls the "plot of female amity" in Victorian novels, which runs alongside and promotes the heterosexual marriage plot. Compared to the misunderstandings and obstacles that spring up between the heterosexual lovers – which in some cases follow the dystopia of Byronism – "the bond between female friends, in contrast, is either established before the novel begins or coalesces almost instantaneously, intensifies almost effortlessly, and can be expressed clearly and openly."[63] Yet all three of these literary representations followed pre-established formulas, and readers consumed them to encounter the plots and emotions they already knew.

Victorian women who did read pornography probably found themselves identifying with a range of characters, genders, and positions – as did Lister, Bradley, and Cooper. Some creativity and imagination would have been needed to assume a part in this male world. Such active reading and gender mobility would not have been hard to sustain with Victorian pornography, with its active transgression of such rules and other taboos (such as incest). Equally important, however, are the passages of female homoeroticism to be found everywhere in Victorian novels, which didn't subvert social norms. As Sharon Marcus puts it, they were ways of exploiting the play of the system, openly and without subterfuge. If the library of Victorian women's erotic or pornographic fiction could be found, would it be dystopic? What role would friendship and collaboration play in it?

NOTES

1 Annamarie Jagose warns of projecting our understanding of lesbian identity onto nineteenth-century people or literary characters. She discusses Anne Lister in this light, and Miss Wade from Dickens's *Little Dorrit*, who sets up house with another woman and has been read as a lesbian by numerous literary critics. See Annamarie Jagose *Inconsequence: Lesbian Representation and the Logic of Sexual Sequence* (Ithaca: Cornell University Press, 2002), 14–23 and Chapter 2.

2 Anne Lister, *I Know My Own Heart: The Diaries of Anne Lister 1791–1840*. Helena Whitbread, ed. (New York: New York University Press, 1988), 42. See also *No Priest But Love: The Journals of Anne Lister from 1824–1826*, Helena Whitbread, ed. (Otley: Smith Settle, 1992) and Jill Liddington, *Female Fortune: Land, Gender and Authority: The Anne Lister Diaries and Other Writings, 1833–36* (London: Rivers Oram Press, 1998).

3 Ibid., 203.

4 Ibid., 296.

5 For instance, Lister tells of her friend "putting on regimentals and flirting with a lady under the assumed name of Captain Cowper" (290). See also 293.

6 Andrew Elfenbein, in his work on Lister, discusses her Byronic performances in the context of men signaling their desire for other men by being Byronic. See *Byron and the Victorians* (Cambridge: Cambridge University Press, 1995), 247–9.

7 Lister, 74, 78.

8 Ibid., 72, 192.

9 Ibid., 287. See also Margaret R. Hunt, "English Lesbians in the Long Eighteenth Century," *Singlewomen in the European Past, 1250–1800*. Judith M. Bennet and Amy M. Froide, eds. (Philadelphia: University of Pennsylvania Press, 1999), 276.

10 Michael Field, *Michael Field, The Poet: Published and Manuscript Materials*. Marion Thain and Ana Parejo Vadillo, eds. (Peterborough, ON: Broadview, 2009), 125.

11 Yopie Prins, *Victorian Sappho* (Princeton: Princeton University Press, 1999), 76.

12 Ibid., 74.

13 For women and eroticism in Charlotte Brontë's and George Eliot's fiction, see Kathryn Bond Stockton, *God Between Their Lips: Desire Between Women in Irigaray, Brontë, and Eliot* (Stanford: Stanford University Press, 1994), especially chapters 4–7.

14 Terry Castle, *The Apparitional Lesbian: Female Homosexuality and Modern Culture* (New York: Columbia University Press, 1993), 28.

15 Dante Alighieri, *The Divine Comedy*, Allen Mandelbaum, trans. (New York: Knopf, 1995), 80–1.

16 H.J. Jackson, *Romantic Readers: The Evidence of Marginalia* (New Haven: Yale University Press, 2005), 174–5.

17 Quoted in Jackson, 182.

18 Emily Brontë, *Wuthering Heights* (London, Penguin, 1995), 304–5.

19 William St. Clair explains that the majority of commonplace books of the period have excerpts of Byron's poems, showing that he was treasured, by women especially, as the poet of "long-suffering constant tragic love" (10). "The Impact of Byron"s Writings: An Evaluative Approach," *Byron: Augustan and Romantic*, Andrew Rutherford, ed. (Basingstoke: Macmillan, 1990), 1–25. See also Elfenbein; Francis Wilson, ed., *Byromania: Portraits of the Artist in Nineteenth- and Twentieth-Century Culture* (New York: Palgrave, 2000); and Deborah Lutz, *The Dangerous Lover: Gothic Villains, Byronism, and the Nineteenth-Century Seduction Narrative* (Columbus: Ohio State University Press, 2006).

20 Charlotte Brontë, *Jane Eyre* (New York: Norton, 2016), 202.

21 Ibid., 209.

22 Ibid., 210.

23 Anthony Trollope, *The Eustace Diamonds* (New York: Everyman, 1992), 2130.

24 Ibid., 2161–2.

25 Lord Byron, *Byron's Poetry*, Frank D. McConnell, ed. (New York: Norton, 1978), 26.

26 Elfenbein, 206.

27 See Elfenbein, chapter 6.

28 Ibid., 247.

29 Sharon Marcus, 58.

30 Charlotte Brontë, *Shirley* (New York: Harper, 1899), 207.

31 Ibid., 268. Anne Longmuir argues that the character Shirley was possibly based, in part, on Anne Lister. "Anne Lister and Lesbian Desire in Charlotte Brontë's *Shirley*," *Brontë Studies* 31 (2006), 145–55.

32 Brontë, *Shirley*, 243.

33 Ibid., 391.

34 William Simpson Potter and others, *The Romance of Lust* (London: n.p., 1892), 163.

35 Christina Rossetti, *The Complete Poems*. R.W. Crump, ed. (New York: Penguin, 2005), 17.

36 Jagose, 14.

37 Ashbee was the most prolific collector and bibliographer of erotic fiction in the Victorian era. His three bibliographies (published under the pseudonym Pisanus Fraxi) – *Index Librorum Prohibitorum* (1877), *Centuria Librorum Absconditorum* (1879), and *Catena Librorum Tacedorum* (1885) – provide the basis for all scholarly work on nineteenth-century erotica. For more on Ashbee, see Ian Gibson, *The Erotomaniac: The Secret Life of Henry Spencer Ashbee* (New York: Da Capo, 2001) and Steven Marcus, *The Other Victorians: A Study of Sexuality and Pornography in Mid-Nineteenth-Century England* (New York: Basic Books, 1964), chapter 2. Peter Mendes explores with great care what is known about the writers, printers, publishers, and distributors of sexually explicit fiction in Britain. All of the people involved that he can track are men, with one exception: the Paris publisher/bookseller Mlle. H. Doucé. See *Clandestine Erotic Fiction in English: 1800–1930* (Aldershot: Scolar, 1993). For more about the producers of Victorian pornography, see Lisa Sigel, *Governing Pleasures: Pornography and Social Change in England, 1815–1914* (New Brunswick: Rutgers University Press, 2002); Iain McCalman, *Radical Underworld: Prophets, Revolutionaries, and Pornographers in London, 1795–1840* (Cambridge: Cambridge University Press, 1988); and Deborah Lutz, *Pleasure Bound: Victorian Sex Rebels and the New Eroticism* (New York: Norton, 2011).

38 This policing occurred in multiple ways. Most Victorians accessed their books through subscription services, the most famous being Mudies. Such services developed a great power over publishers, and thus authors. If Mudies and similar companies refused to order a newly published book, it would have a difficult time reaching the public, leading publishers to carefully mark what Mudies preferred before they agreed to publish a manuscript. Mudies had a narrow sense of what was morally sound. Additionally, various laws and groups, especially the Society for the Suppression of Vice, led to publishers being prosecuted and even jailed for printing "indecent" material. See Sigel, especially chapters 1 and 3, and McCalman, chapter 10.

39 Sharon Marcus makes a case for Victorian women having some access to pornography. See *Between Women: Friendship, Desire, and Marriage in Victorian England* (Princeton: Princeton University Press, 2007), 141. See also Lynda Nead, *Victorian Babylon: People, Streets, and Images in Nineteenth-Century London* (New Haven: Yale University Press, 2000), 161–97, and Walter Kendrick,

The Secret Museum: Pornography in Modern Culture (Berkeley: University of California Press, 1987), especially chapters 3 and 4.

40 For instance, Algernon Charles Swinburne describes reading de Sade's *La Nouvelle Justine* aloud to Dante Gabriel Rossetti and George Boyce. See the letter Swinburne wrote to Richard Monckton Milnes (Lord Houghton) dated August 18, 1862, in *The Swinburne Letters*, Cecil Y. Lang, ed. (New Haven: Yale University Press, 1958), vol. 1, 54. A good deal of collective reading and collaborative writing of pornography happened among this group.

41 Anonymous, *The Power of Mesmerism, and Laura Middleton: Two Novels of the Victorian Underground* (New York: Grove Press, 1969), 29.

42 Anonymous, *My Secret Life* (1880s), 2 vols (New York: Grove, 1966), 1933.

43 Ibid., 2193. In another passage of *My Secret Life*, the narrator tries to seduce a young woman by showing her the frontispiece of *Fanny Hill* (with its sexually explicit pictures) and then lending the whole book to her (589).

44 Anonymous, *The Pearl* (1879–80) (New York: Blue Moon, 1996), 481–2.

45 A few examples, of many, are *Memoirs of a Russian Princess: Gleaned from her Secret Diary* (1890); *Love and Safety; or Love and Lasciviousness with Safety and Secrecy: A Lecture, Delivered with Practical Illustrations by The Empress of Asturia (The Modern Sappho), Assisted by Her Favourite Lizette and Others, To many Ladies, From Youngest to Oldest* ... (1896); *The Convent School, or Early Experiences of A Young Flagellant, By Rosa Belinda Coote* (1898); and *Confessions of Madame Vestris in a Series of Familiar Letters to Handsome Jack* (1899).

46 Potter, 153.

47 Ibid., 219.

48 *The Pearl*, 48.

49 Steven Marcus, 257, 259.

50 *My Secret Life*, 2196–8.

51 See especially Sharon Marcus, 142.

52 Steven Marcus, 260.

53 *The Pearl*, 41, 296, 198–203.

54 *The Romance of Lust*, 255. Other Victorian pornographic texts that depict same-sex sexuality openly include *Letters from a Friend in Paris* (n.d.); *The Sins of the Cities of the Plain* (1881); *Teleny, or the Reverse of the Medal* (1893); *Rosa Fielding, or A Victim of Lust* (1867); *Randiana, or Excitable Tales: Being the Experiences of an Erotic Philosopher* (1884); and the periodical *The Boudoir* (c.1880s).

55 *My Secret Life*, 1151.

56 Ibid., 1562–3.

57 Ibid., 334.

58 Ibid., 1847. One of the few English Victorian-era texts included in the anthology *The Literature of Lesbianism: A Historical Anthology from Ariosto to Stonewall*, Terry Castle, ed. (New York: Columbia University Press, 2003) is a passage from *My Secret Life*. See 542–7. Christina Rossetti's "Goblin Market" also appears.

59 *My Secret Life*, 2155.

60 Ibid., 2155.

61 Steven Marcus, 268.

62 See Kate Flint for a discussion of late-nineteenth-century short stories and poetry written by New Women, some of them lesbians, about one-sided same-sex desire on urban streets. "'The hour of pink twilight': Lesbian Poetics and Queer Encounters on the Fin-de-Siècle Street," *Victorian Studies* 51.4 (2009), 687–712.
63 Sharon Marcus, 82.

12

COLETTE COLLIGAN

The Making of the Enfer Bibliography

Guillaume Apollinaire, Eroto-Bibliography and the Enfer Collection

The Enfer collection is the restricted collection of erotic books in the National Library of France (*Bibliothèque nationale de France) (BNF)*. Its precise origins are unclear, but it is said to have been founded in the early nineteenth century as an instance of state censorship.[1] It is now a dormant collection; it stopped acquiring new materials in the early 1970s in response to more permissive cultural standards. The value of the collection lies not only in the rare works of erotic writing it holds but also in its unique assemblage of books, from the eighteenth-century French erotic classics to Olympia Press translations of Guillaume Apollinaire's *The Debauched Hospodar* (1953). It captures a culture's ideas and practices around erotic writing and publishing, censorship and sequestration over a roughly 150-year period, and is today an acclaimed part of France's cultural heritage.

The first emissaries for this collection were three young writers who worked purposefully to produce its first bibliography in 1913. Foremost among them was Guillaume Apollinaire (1880–1918), who was just over thirty when he took up this project, and already a key intermediary figure in French avant-garde artistic circles and editor of erotic books published by the Bibliothèque des curieux. He was joined by two slightly younger men, Fernand Fleuret (1883–1945) and Louis Perceau (1883–1942), both men of letters with deep interests in eroto-bibliography who later collaborated as editors of twelve erotic works.[2] The three men first met each other at the National Library. Fleuret recalled, years later, how he and Apollinaire would spend hours working side by side in the reserve section of the library, and then leave together feeling '*ivres de liberté*' (drunk with liberty).[3] According to Vincent Labaume, the men approached their task of eroto-bibliography differently. Apollinaire prioritised works that exalted the individual in revolt against moral order, Fleuret sought unique style above all else and Perceau – a confirmed socialist – revelled in liberating a subterranean literature that had been suppressed by censorship and surveillance.[4] Their 1913 bibliography, Labaume writes, prepared the cultural terrain for the liberation of morals to come.

Yet this bibliography, which was to bring the Enfer collection to visibility, was itself working under the constraints of censorship. In order for their work to be accepted, Apollinaire, Fleuret and Perceau had to suppress the contents of the books they catalogued, as well as information about the secret cultures that produced and circulated these books. They also had to suppress the passions of eroto-bibliophilia that sustained their interest in the collection. Their published bibliography, as well as unearthed archival sources pertaining to its production, reveal the extent to which this secretive print culture and the men's knowledge of the clandestine operations of bibliophiles, booksellers and publishers could not be publicised. Apollinaire, Fleuret and Perceau effectively became mediators of state censorship with their bibliography. Yet, if they only brought certain truths about the collection into sanctioned visibility, their work also cultivated a subterranean culture of collection around Enfer. This feedback loop recalls Judith Butler's theory that censorship is 'necessarily incomplete' and inevitably regenerates what it seeks to suppress.[5] This chapter uncovers for the first time this history of censorship, the secrets the bibliographers could not lay bare and the culture of erotic collection they inspired, revealing how a censored bibliography helped make Enfer a national emblem of France's liberal cultural heritage, as well as a secret emblem for eroto-bibliographers and collectors assembling collections outside the law.

L'Enfer de la Bibliothèque nationale, 1913

Before the 1913 publication of *L'Enfer de la Bibliothèque nationale* by the Mercure de France,[6] there was no catalogue of the National Library's collection of forbidden books, located on rue Richelieu in Paris. Bibliophiles certainly knew of its existence, and knowledge of the collection was part of public culture by the end of the nineteenth century. On 16 August 1896, *Le Gaulois* ran a report describing the cabinet that housed the collection of roughly 1,000 books, and explained how a special request to library administration, along with proof of serious purpose, limited access to roughly twelve patrons per year.[7] A few years later, a serial story published in *La Lanterne* featured a female reader of pornography asking her lover to get her access to the Enfer collection.[8] When Apollinaire began writing prefaces for erotic publications by L'Arétin, Nerciat and de Sade in 1909, however, there was no way to know which or how many books constituted the sulfurous collection.[9] It was his work editing books within the collection and his meeting of Fleuret at the National Library that helped them see the need for a bibliography.

The first preface for the bibliography introduces the absence of such a catalogue under the mantle of interdiction. Robert Yve-Plessis apparently began work on a catalogue around 1900, having been granted access to twenty volumes at the time, but library administration restricted his work, preventing him from taking notes and insisting a staff member watch him. His notes, the men explain in the preface, were the basis of their work, though they do not reveal how they were granted privileges previously denied. Although the preface frames the bibliography's work against this history of interdiction, its tone is not defiant; nor does it advocate for greater access. It simply states that the bibliography will be useful for historians, philosophers and men of letters. It concludes with a staid picture of how such a collection should be used, quoting Charles Nodier (1780–1844), the French Romantic writer, member of the Académie française and Director of the Bibliothèque de l'Arsenal, who claimed never to have read a bad book but to have consulted many for instructive reference.[10]

A second preface from the 1919 edition recycles some of the same material, but gives more information about the collection itself. It provides clarity about its size, describing it as a small collection of roughly 900 books, only a dozen of which pushed the limits of extreme licence. It also explains that these books had not been amassed at the library as a temporary holding site in anticipation of some great act of book burning, but were rather selected and kept as evidence of judgements against them, in the service of history. Selection, not seizure, was the operating principle behind Enfer. By bringing the collection under curatorial control and downplaying the number of its very worst books, the second preface builds on the first to dampen the flames of Enfer's hellfire and rationalise its existence for posterity.[11]

These prefaces set the tone for the bibliography entire, which is notable for its sobriety. Its primary function is to list all the books housed in the Enfer collection. It organises its entries according to item call numbers from 1 to 930, bringing the collection under enumerative control, to account for everything in Enfer up to roughly 1912. The individual entries vary considerably in length, depending on the book's reputation and available bibliographical knowledge, but each entry follows the same organisational and informational structure. Each starts with a header, which is the full transcription of the title page, followed by the collation with copy-specific details about the book (e.g. page length, paper type, binding, illustrations). For a good number of entries, this is the substance of the record. For other entries, where more information had been gathered, there are lists of judgements against the books, details about authors, printers and publishers, and histories of publication and textual transmission. In the case of active writers or dealers, names are masked with asterisks.

A closer look at some of the longer entries reveals how the bibliographers collected their information from diverse sources. For the court judgements against the books, they often consulted *Le Moniteur*, a weekly periodical that published judicial news. They also frequently cited other bibliographies, notably those by Jules Gay and Henry Spencer Ashbee, who had prepared the two most comprehensive bibliographies of clandestine erotic books available at the time. Other sources are quoted, although not cited, such as Apollinaire's own critical introductions for Arétin, Nerciat and de Sade.[12] In fact, their practice was to quote liberally from other sources – so much so that some entries are a series of quotations held together by threads of their own commentary. This was a work of bibliographic assemblage as much as bibliographic enumeration, a 'scissors and paste' gathering of hard-to-find, specialist knowledge about forbidden books.

What one does not find in these entries are racy excerpts from the books or titillating descriptions of their contents. Commentary, if provided, usually pertains to the work's literary merit or bibliographic quality, as in the case of its description of Arétin's *Dialogues* as a literary monument:

> *Cette verve endiablée, ces descriptions bigarées, cette imagination pittoresque, ce bons sens et cette liberté d' expressions n'ont pas été sans influencer le génie de François Rabelais et par la la culture générale des français.*

> [Such great liveliness, mixed descriptions, picturesque imagination, such common sense and freedom of expression surely influenced the genius of François Rabelais and thus the French people's general culture].[13]

While the syntax and rhythm of this sentence builds excitement, it hardly inflames the passions. The entry on Fleuret's book, *Le Carquois*, which was published around 1912 under the pseudonym Louvigné du Dézert and pretended to be a found manuscript, stokes the flames a little more by praising Fleuret's playful deception and libertinism and by quoting a reviewer who moralises against the book.[14] By and large, however, the tone of the bibliography is impersonal and uniform, without texture, signature or affect. It is, in fact, surprisingly methodical and serious-minded, given the literary facundity and fellowship of these three men and the license taken by other clandestine erotic bibliographies.

The Enfer bibliography, for example, is far different in look and tone from Ashbee's three-volume bibliography. Ashbee's work is a chaotic assembly of bibliographic description and metadata that moves between languages, incorporates excerpts with abandon, marks up every page 'with hiccoughing references and hieroglyphic citations', and digresses eagerly into personal stories and sexual arcana. The bibliography of this 'pornographer royal', Steven Marcus writes, is 'at once a monument of personal scholarship and a monument of his personal eccentricity'. Its form, Marcus argues, reflects both Ashbee's erotic obsessions and his moral prevarications about the material.[15] Jules Gay's *Bibliographie des ouvrages relatifs à l'amour aux femmes, au mariage, et des livres facetieux* (1894–1900) is restrained in comparison to Ashbee's bibliography, but is still far more inflamed by the erotic content of its list than the Enfer bibliography.

The Enfer bibliography took a more staid approach than these clandestine bibliographies, while also distancing itself from contemporaneous French practices of what might be called biblioeroticism. Octave Uzanne (1851–1931), advocate for the new bibliophilia movement in France and founder of periodicals and societies dedicated to the book, describes the passionate tastes for erotic books among bibliophiles – passions seemingly suppressed by the compilers of the Enfer bibliography. In Uzanne's short story, '*Le Cabinet d'un eroto-bibliomane*' (1878), he creates a portrait of a 'bibliophalliphile' [a lover of phallic books] based on the Paris-based English collector Frederic Hankey, who collects forbidden books and hides them deeper and deeper in his library according to their depravity.[16] Uzanne gave vision to not only the erotic collector but also the erotic collection. In his *Dictionnaire Bibliophilosophique* (1896), he refers to an enfer collection (which extended in meaning beyond the national collection to include private erotic libraries) as a site of transgressive collecting practices that included sequestration, masturbation, and secret fellowship:

> *L'Enfer c'est le coin maudit de toute Bibliothèque un peu éclectique, le Sadic'corner comme dirait un Anglais. C'est la vitrine spéciale, le rayonnage où sont les poisons, les excitants, les priapées; c'est là que dorment les traités érotologiques, les romans de Paphos, les épiphallies des de Sade, des de Nerciat, des Restifs, des Piron et de tous les cantharidés du XVIIIe siècle.*
>
> *Enfants, n'y touchez pas! … Craignez ces Livres qu'on ne lit que d'une main! Attendez l'âge viril auquel on prend plaisir à s'en griser les sens en galante compagnie.*

[The Enfer is the cursed corner of all eclectic libraries, the Sadic corner as the English would call it. It is the special showcase, the shelf where the poisons, the stimulants and the obscenities are kept; it is where erotic treatises are housed, Paphos' novels, the phallic imaginings of de Sade's, de Nerciat's, des Restifs', des Piron's and of all the aphrodisiacs of the XVIIIth century.

Children, do not touch them! ... Fear these books that you read with only one hand! Wait for the time of your manhood when you will enjoy it the fullest and in good company].[17]

Unlike Uzanne, the compilers of the Enfer bibliography do not create such portraits of collectors and collections; nor do they describe or assemble their record in such as way to suggest biblioeroticism. While Uzanne was said to have approached his bibliophilic passions with sperm in his eyes, the compilers of Enfer brought more science than passion to their bibliography.[18]

In brief, the scholarly look and content of the Enfer bibliography shows an effort to legitimise the men's work, normalise the collection and bring it under methodical control. They leveraged the legitimacy of bibliography – a discipline the French had mastered – to make public their catalogue through the auspices of the Mercure de France and spread knowledge about these books for immediate use and posterity. Such an approach was likely necessary to maintain access to the collection and connections with the National Library.

The Making of the Enfer Bibliography, 1909–1913

Behind the scenes, Apollinaire, Fleuret and Perceau were far more involved in their project than is evident in the official published version of their bibliography. Traces of their spirited working relationship and editorial process are found in their unpublished letters, journals, book proofs and personal libraries. More significantly, these sources disclose the men's deep ties with secret print networks, and new discoveries about Apollinaire's affiliations with these networks – including his attitudes toward his own erotic writing and his scruples about publicising it.

Letters between Apollinaire, Fleuret and Perceau, many of which remain unprinted, are among the most important documentary evidence of their work on the bibliography. Although the correspondence is uneven and incomplete (reflective more of what has been kept than what was exchanged), it is multidirectional and thus sheds some light on their three-way collaboration.[19] This correspondence resulted from distance: while Apollinaire was largely in Paris during this period, near the collection, Fleuret was frequently in the south of France and Perceau had fled to Brussels to escape arrest on account of his socialist activities. Over a three-year period, their letters document how they met at the Richelieu library to consult the books, how they prepared their bibliographical notices and combed through available sources, how they met with different people to gather first-hand information and how they felt about their protracted project carried across time and distances.

From the start, the letters reveal the deep ties of affection between the men. Fleuret and Apollinaire are the most expressive about their friendship and collaboration. When Fleuret leaves for the south of France in 1911, for example, Apollinaire writes:

> *Vous avez été pour moi un ami parfait, un compagnon charmant et délicat, et parfois un collaborateur dont la collaboration m'honorait infiniment*
>
> [You have been a perfect friend to me, a delicate and charming companion and sometimes a collaborator whose collaboration honoured me greatly][20]

He hopes they can continue working together from a distance on their bibliography. After a misunderstanding, Fleuret expresses similar affection for Apollinaire: '*mes liaisons sont fort rares, mais elles sont indénouables*' [my friendships are rare but they are unbreakable].[21] Fleuret is equally affectionate toward Perceau when writing to Apollinaire, calling him '*notre anarchiste*' [our anarchist].[22] Perceau does not appear as frequently in the correspondence; only a few letters of his to Apollinaire survive, but mention of him in Apollinaire's private journal from this period suggests the heterosexual nonconformism connecting these men in friendship. Apollinaire recounts how a quick sexual encounter with a dressmaker in a Parisian cul-de-sac led to discovery of Perceau's Italian mistress, Fleuret's discovery of her Italian lover, and Perceau's discovery of his duping.[23] Correspondence among the men also continued beyond their work on the bibliography into the First World War, as they exchanged erotic stories and poetry. Their letters and journals reveal the bonds of heterosexual fellowship, as well as erudition, that brought them together, sustaining and informing their bibliographical project.

At the same time, the letters show the considerable labour that went into the making of the bibliography and the tensions this created. Apollinaire's letter to Fleuret from March 1911 suggests the impetus for the project: a window of opportunity opened by a recent amnesty on certain older books in the Enfer collection.[24] Yet, while urging Fleuret to hasten with the work, Apollinaire realises the challenge of their task in face of the paucity of information. Worried about the incompleteness of the entries, he spells out a strategy to add copy-specific details about the books, such as providing descriptions of bindings.[25] On his side, Fleuret explains how he feeds in information from clandestine bibliographies by Ashbee and Pierre-Gustave Brunet, while extracting biographies from a variety of sources. He also exchanges bibliographical notes and records with Perceau, who sweats over the bibliography '*comme un paysan du Poitou*' [like a Poitou labourer].[26] As they update each other on their progress and begin correcting the book proofs their publisher sends them in increments, they intermix news about their other literary work, give each other encouragement and gossip about people they know. The whole affair is protracted and chaotic, apparently frustrated by Apollinaire not meeting deadlines and the Mercure de France's delay with publication. Fleuret, who expresses the most frustration, continually questions Apollinaire about its progress while writing to Perceau: *'Je crois que c'est un four noir'* [I think it is a flop].[27] When he finally sees a copy of their bibliography in a Nice bookshop in June 1913, roughly three months after its publication, it comes as a surprise and he is convinced the press has swindled them.[28]

Amid erotic encounters and bibliographical notes, we also find evidence of the men's ties to clandestine erotic print networks. They deliberately sought out collectors, booksellers and publishers for information. Fleuret had connections with Octave Uzanne, who frequently provided him with *'quelques lumières'* [some insights].[29] From Uzanne, he hears curious things about Ashbee and Hankey, the Paris-based English bibliographer and collector who are mentioned, but little described, in the bibliography.[30] Apollinaire, in a diary entry from June 1911, similarly reveals how he gleaned information from the bookseller Gustave Lehec about key dealers and collectors: Isidore Liseux, Gay and Doucé, and Ashbee and Hankey.[31] Neither Uzanne nor Lehec are cited as informers in the bibliographer, however; and the sober tone of the published bibliography suggests that any truly curious stories gleaned from these interviews – such as those found in Goncourt's journals – did not make it into the manuscript. Yet, their letters disclose still more professional ties with clandestine dealers. Fleuret writes to Apollinaire about his meeting with the publisher Brockhaus in Leipzig to see manuscripts for *The Memoirs of Casanova*, which leads to an offer to work on an edition with Apollinaire and Fleuret, though Fleuret initially assumes Brockhaus would be proposing sodomy.[32] In a later letter to Perceau in Brussels, Fleuret discusses some of the shops where clandestine books can be found and asks him to look for a publisher for his erotic book of poems *Le Carquois*, naming the exiled publisher Charles Carrington as a possibility.[33] The letters passed between these men thus provide a glimpse into the secret culture of print in which they moved, in sexual fellowship and literary partnership.

This secret culture of print, however, is hard to find in the published version of the bibliography, proofs for which show that Apollinaire actively suppressed information about the clandestine book trade that had been gathered and even written up. Three different sets of these proofs have survived: one located at the BNF, one at the Bibliothèque Jacques Doucet (BLJD) and one at the Bibliothèque historique de la ville de Paris (BHV).[34] As far as I know, these proofs have never before been collated for comparison. The three sets are incomplete, but show additions and deletions in Apollinaire's hand. They disclose how he inserted more detail over the course of his revisions, but also suppressed names, titles and opinion – stripping the bibliography of its passions and revelations, and apparently internalising the forces of censorship.

In the BHV proofs, for example, Apollinaire crosses out two paragraphs at the end of the entry on *Le Théatre Erotique de la rue de la Santé* that rail against the conservative French senator Réné Bérenger, known for his campaigns against the circulation of obscene works:

> *M. Bérenger, – l'odieux Bérenger, – n'avouait-il pas qu'il ne détestait pas les gauloiseries salées – c'est sous cet euphémisme que le père de Pudeur désigne les plaisanteries scatologiques.*
>
> *Et tous ces hypocrites saligauds, qui se délectent aux histoires de Foiromanie, s'ils le pouvaient, livreraient aux flammes les chefs d'oeuvre que sont les neuf dixième des ouvrages de l'Enfer.*
>
> [M. Bérenger, – the despicable Bérenger, – didn't he admit that he did not hate sick licentious jokes – it is under this euphemism that the father of modesty referred to scatological jokes.
>
> And all these bloody hypocrites, would have nine tenths of the Enfer's masterpieces be thrown into the flames].

In the BNF proofs, next to the entry on *Lesbia, Maitresse d'Ecole*, Apollinaire again had second thoughts about what could be included in the final version of the bibliography. He crosses out handwritten marginalia, which refers to the book as '*un des ouvrages les plus licentieux et les mieux écrits sur le tribadisme*' [one of the most licentious and best written works about lesbian sex]. Apollinaire connected the work to French thought about lesbian identities and practices, but suppressed his note, instead simply describing the book's physical features.

The BLJD proofs reveal a similar process of censoring references to lesbian practices. Apollinaire removes printed text that was intended to accompany the entry on *L'Ecole des Biches*:

> *L'Ecole des B. est une série de scènes où le tribadisme prédomine. Peu remarquables par l'orginalité, mais très érotique, sans crapulerie, ni grossièreté. Ce livre est assez bien écrit, mais monotone à la lecture. C'est la répétition de toutes les poses que l'on trouve dans les livres de ce genre. Manque d'évènements et d'intrigue.*
>
> [L'Ecole des B. is a series of scenes where lesbian sex is predominant. It is not a very original book but it is very erotic without any sleaze or crudeness. This book is fairly well written, but monotonous to read. There is a repetition of all the poses that you find in these types of books. A lack of events and plot.]

The final published version of the entry provides extensive detail about the book's banning and authorship, but no description of its content or inclusion of lesbian scenes. Hankey was one of the book's presumed authors, and a detailed description of an enfeebled man who relied on crutches is given, but again the BLJD proofs reveal a suppression of sexual information about the man. Removed from the published version, but still retained in the BLJD proofs, is the following description of Hankey's sexual tastes: '*devenue impuissant, il jouissait de la vue des objets érotiques, livres, bronzes, dont il avait une grande quantité*' [After he became impotent, he sought pleasure in the sight of erotic objects, books, bronzes which he had plenty of].

As the process of revision removed sexual content and sexual politics from the final version of the bibliography, it also established a code with which to mask the names of active dealers. In the final version of the bibliography, the names of certain publishers are partly obscured. Charles Carrington appears as C.rr.ngt.n, Charles Hirsch as H.rsch and Madame Roberts as R.b.rts. Where these publishers' identities are already known, the code is not difficult to break and thus functioned as a legal precaution; but where the publishers' identities remain unknown, the code has proven to be an effective mask. Comparison of the BHV proofs to the BLJD proofs reveals the careful work that went into the application of this code and suppression of information related to clandestine dealers. The names of the publishers are often intact in the earlier set of BHV proofs, partly encoded in the later set of BLJD proofs and systematically encoded in the final published version.

The editing and encoding of the entry for *Odor di Femina* across these two sets of proofs is especially revealing. This erotic novel by Edouard Démarchin, first published in 1890, was often reprinted. The Enfer copy bears the following publisher's imprint: 'G. Leboucher, libraire-éditeur, Montréal (Canada)'.[35] As Cécile Loyen and I have discussed in an article for *Histoires Littéraires*, the proofs divulge information previously unknown to bibliographers about the mysterious publisher who went by the name 'G. Lebaucher'.[36] In the BHV proofs, the entry gives the following information about the publisher:

> *Celle-ci est due à l'imprimeur G..., établi à Malakoff et beau-frère de l'éditeur H.rsch.*
>
> *Ce G... a surtout produit des contrefaçons, néanmoins il a édité quelques ouvrages originaux: quelques romans anglais et allemand et une excellente fantaisie*, Les onze mille verges, *par G.A. (Le spécimen porte*, Les onze mille verges ou les amours d'un hospodar, *et c'est ce double titre qui, parait-il, est le bon), roman français mêlé de vers, il contient, dit-on, les premiers poèmes libres en vers libres et c'est une des plus amusantes productions érotiques, il a*

été écrit aussitôt après la guerre russo–japonais, dont il parle, et l'on y voit le général Stoessel.

[This G... mostly produced pirate editions; however, he also edited a few original works: a few British and German novels as well as a great fantasy novel, *Les onze mille verges*, by G. A. (The original version reads, *Les onze mille verges ou les amours d'un hospodar*; this double title, according to some sources would be the right one). It is said that this French novel mixed with verses contains the first free verse poems and it is one of the most amusing erotic productions. It was written right after the Russian–Japanese war, which it discusses and the Général Stoessel is one of its character].

The publisher's name is simply printed as 'G...', but a few pages later in the BHV proofs the full name is printed as 'Gauché', a crucial piece of evidence for tracking down his identity. This spelling of his name, along with the details about his residence in Malakoff, have provided us with enough information to identify the mysterious publisher–printer of numerous clandestine erotic works from the late nineteenth and early twentieth centuries, including Apollinaire's stupendously violent erotic novel *Les Onze mille verges* (*c.*1907) and adaptation of a German novel *Les Exploits d'un jeune Don Juan* (*c.* 1907).[37] This publisher's name was Jules-Eugène Gauché (1854–1922), and he worked from his Malakoff printshop with his female partner Angélina Leboucher (1872–1918), who was also the mother of his children. Together, they published clandestine erotic novels under the imprint G. Lebaucher, which was an amalgam of their family names, a nod to their partnership and a secret record of their intimate lives and feelings.[38] In short, when written up in the BHV proofs, this entry provides enough clues for finding key people in the trade and the people behind the publication of Apollinaire's own erotic writing.

The later set of BLJD proofs adds a few minor hand corrections to this entry, the most significant being the reworking of the code from 'G...' to 'G...ch' (showing attention paid to the code) and the deletion of the initials 'G. A' (revealing misgivings about exposing Apollinaire's authorship of *Les onze mille verges*). Most of this information about the publisher and Apollinaire's novel, however, does not make it into the final published version of the bibliography, in which the portion of the aforementioned entry is reduced to the following sentences:

Celle-ci [Odor di Femina] *est due à l'imprimeur G...ch., qui était établi près de Paris.*

Ce G...ch. a surtout produit des contrefaçons, néanmoins il a édité un petit nombre d'ouvrages originaux.

[This is attributed to G...ch, a printer established near Paris.

This G...ch. mostly produced pirated books; however he also published a few original works.][39]

While the proofs show how Apollinaire wrote himself into his bibliography – including his secret work in the Enfer collection – by referencing it within another book's entry, the final published version shows how he ultimately wrote himself out, suppressing the most explicit connection he ever made about his authorship of *Les Onze mille verges* and removing his work from its place of 'honour' beside the 'masterpieces' of Enfer.

Les Onze mille verges was not Apollinaire's only foray into erotic writing. In addition to *Les Exploits d'un jeune Don Juan*, he is the presumed author of another work that has not survived. Although he was known for his erudite introductions to older works of French erotica, he had a pronounced taste for contemporary erotic fiction, demonstrated in his own writing and by the works found in his personal library. His collection of approximately 5000 books remains intact at the Bibliothèque historique de la Ville de Paris, and contains a significant list of erotic titles published in French and English during his day. His personal collection of erotic books included titles published by the principal clandestine publishers of his day: Auguste Brancart (1851–?); Aimé Charles Emile Duringe (1854–1913); Charles Carrington (1867–1921); Jules-Eugène Gauché (1854–1922); and Angélina Leboucher (1872–1918). Many of these titles circulated in very small print runs, including *Des Grieux (The Prelude to 'Teleny')* (1899), which was apparently restricted to only 200 copies. Apollinaire's copy is now one of just three surviving, and reveals the exclusive access he had to clandestine erotic books in Paris.[40]

The letters exchanged between Apollinaire, Fleuret and Perceau, the book proofs they reviewed and the erotic book collection Apollinaire built up in his own library are an important 'archive of feelings', to use Ann Cvetkovich's phrase for the heightened affects encoded in sexual archives.[41] Together, they chronicle the erotic interests, cultural politics and active print networks that drove the men to document the nation's sequestered collection of erotic literature. Little of this, however, made its way into the bibliography that helped make Enfer famous, at once revealing the constraints of official print and the importance of the archive for retracing an affective history of erotic literature conditioned by censorship.

L'Enfer as Emblem, 1913–

The Enfer collection's path to legitimacy began with the publication of its first bibliography. The sober, methodical approach of the bibliography, in its final version, normalised the secret collection for public respectability. As the first privileged intermediaries of the Enfer collection, Apollinaire, Fleuret and Perceau had to withhold its secrets to dampen its flames, but this withholding allowed the collection to enter official public discourse. Around 1500 copies circulated. The Mercure de France's catalogue worked to underscore the scholarly importance of the collection, noting that the value of the books lay in what they could teach about the history of morals.[42] Although reviews of the bibliography were sparse, they appeared in respectable periodicals. In *La Revue de Psychiatrie*, Jean Vinchon wrote about Enfer as an important source of historical documents on sexual perversions. Outside of France, reviewers presented things more sensationally, including one who wrote in a Berlin newspaper that the French National Library was trying to suppress the bibliography by taking action against the publisher (the reviewer wrote to Apollinaire apologising for the need to sensationalise).[43] That same year, the bibliography prompted the Englishman E.S.P. Haynes to write an article exposing the burying of erotic books in the Private Case collection of the British Museum, and advocating for open cataloguing and access around the pursuit of knowledge.[44] A second edition of the Enfer bibliography appeared in 1919, after Apollinaire had died, suggesting continued public interest in the collection. Apollinaire's widow even made inquiries in the 1920s about publishing another reprint of the bibliography, and correspondence between Fleuret and Perceau suggests that discussions about a new revised edition continued with publishers (although no such edition materialised).[45] All of this work initiated the gradual process of bringing the collection into public respectability and visibility. In 1969 – the year after the widespread student and labour protests in France, when it was '*interdit d'interdire*' [forbidden to forbid] – the library closed the collection, signalling that Enfer belonged to a less-liberal age. Only a few new books slipped into the collection after that date.[46] In 1978, Pascal Pia published an authoritative two-volume bibliography of *Les Livres de L'Enfer du xive siècle à nos jours* (1978), which accounted for the entire collection and furthered Enfer's transformation from a library secret to a historical collection of rich national importance.[47] In 2006, the National Library put Enfer on mass public display with a dedicated exhibition, advertised by a giant pink 'X' symbol on its east tower. As Alison Moore persuasively argues, this exhibition – which attracted 80,000 visitors – marked the incorporation of Enfer into the powerful discourse of French cultural patrimony, as a symbol of the country's battle for liberal ideals and reputation for erotic license.[48] The first Enfer bibliography, I argue, initiated this transformation of the moral and cultural landscape for erotic print – and partly by censoring itself.

Yet, if Apollinaire, Fleuret and Perceau figuratively brought Enfer out of the nation's closet into the public – and into state surveillance and regulation – their coded bibliography also cultivated a secret transnational culture of amateur collection around Enfer. When Apollinaire died in 1918 from the influenza virus that ravaged Europe's population, Fleuret and Perceau continued their work of erotic erudition, bibliographical activity and correspondence. Perceau in particular continued his bibliographical work, becoming the French expert of clandestine erotic literature and publishing the new two-volume *Bibliographie du roman érotique au XIXe siècle* (1930).[49] A rich archive of his manuscripts (which the French National Library bought) includes dozens of letters he received between the 1920s and the early 1940s from male collectors and bibliophiles across France and Europe, inquiring and providing information about erotic books and putting him into contact with erotic booksellers, collectors and other bibliographers – including his British counterparts, Alfred Rose and Charles Reginald Dawes. In these letters, correspondents repeatedly refer to their private collections of erotica, describing their size, contents and desiderata. In one letter, a French correspondent – who refers to himself as a 'bibliomaniac' – writes to Perceau about his desire to reconstitute his collection, which was destroyed by bombing in Auxerre during the Second World War. Another correspondent writes about lost books from his collection, including a magnificent copy of the nineteenth-century erotic classic *Gamiani*, which he inherited from an uncle and lent to a friend, who lost it in Tonkin. A Dutch correspondent writes to Perceau about his views on clandestine English works like *Teleny* and *My Secret Life* and on the German bibliographer Paul English, who lacks, in his opinion, the passion of an amateur collector of erotic books. He also exchanges information with Perceau about the purchase of Japanese Ben Wa balls in Paris.[50] In these letters, we find stories of loss and desire, feeling and fetishism concentrated around correspondents' small private collections and responsive to the bibliographic activity of the Enfer bibliographer, including the mysteries surrounding so many clandestine books. They speak of '*mon Enfer*' or '*mon petit Enfer*' [my (little) Hell], revealing how their collections and collecting practices grew in the shadow of the National Library's collection and gained meaning through eroto-bibliographic networks of communication. In the bibliographer's archive, we therefore uncover the ways in which the Enfer collection also became an emblem for an amateur transnational culture of erotic collection, organised around forbidden books, collecting, bibliography and sex. If a process of censorship initiated the emblematisation of Enfer as a cultural glory, it also vitalised its emblematisation as a secret cultural repository for private collectors of forbidden books, reminding us that censorship is never complete.

NOTES

1 Marie-Françoise Quignard, *'De l'existence de l'Enfer'* in Marie-Françoise Quignard and Raymond-Josué Seckel (eds.), *L'Enfer de la Bibliothèque: Eros au Sécret* (Paris: Bibliothèque nationale de France, 2007), 166.

2 Vincent Labaume, *Louis Perceau: le polygraphe, 1883–1942* (Paris: J.-P. Faur, 2005), 143.

3 Fernand Fleuret, *De Gilles de Rais à Guillaume Apollinaire* (Paris: Mercure de France, 1933), 286.

4 Vincent Labaume, *Louis Perceau: le polygraphe, 1883–1942* (Paris: J.-P. Faur, 2005), 142–43.

5 Judith Butler, 'Ruled Out: Vocabularies of the Censor' in Robert C. Post (ed.), *Censorship and Silencing: Practices of Cultural Regulation* (Los Angeles: Getty Research Institute, 1998), 249.

6 Guillaume Apollinaire, Fernand Fleuret, and Louis Perceau, *L'Enfer de la Bibliothèque nationale: icono-bio-bibliographie descriptive, critique et raisonnée, complète à ce jour de tous les ouvrages composant cette célèbre collection* (Paris: Mercure de France, 1913).

7 *Le Gaulois*, 16 August 1896.

8 *La Lanterne*, 10 November 1904.

9 Guillaume Apollinaire wrote bibliographical essays and notes for *L'oeuvre du Marquis de Sade* (Paris: Bibliothèque des curieux, 1909), *L'oeuvre du divin Arétin*, 2 vols. (Paris: Bibliothèque des curieux, 1909–10) and *L'Oeuvre du chevalier Andrea de Nerciat* (Paris: Bibliothèque des curieux, 1910–11).

10 Apollinaire, Fleuret, and Perceau, *L'Enfer de la Bibliothèque nationale*, 5–8.

11 Guillaume Apollinaire, Fernand Fleuret and Louis Perceau, *L'Enfer de la Bibliothèque nationale: icono-bio-bibliographie descriptive, critique et raisonnée, complète à ce jour de tous les ouvrages composant cette célèbre collection. Nouvelle édition* (Paris: Bibliothèque des curieux, 1919), 6–7.

12 See Pisanus Fraxi (Henry Spencer Ashbee), *Index librorum prohibitorum* (London: Privately printed, 1877); *Centuria librorum absconditorum* (London: Privately printed, 1879); *Catena Librorum Tacendorum* (London: Privately printed, 1885). Also see Jules Gay, *Bibliographie des ouvrages relatifs à l'amour aux femmes, au mariage, et des livres facétieux*, 4th edition, 4 vols (Paris: J. Lemonnyer: Ch. Gilliet; Lille: S. Becour, 1894–1900).

13 Apollinaire, Fleuret and Perceau, *L'Enfer de la Bibliothèque nationale*, 19.

14 Apollinaire, Fleuret and Perceau, *L'Enfer de la Bibliothèque nationale*, 381–84.

15 Steven Marcus, (1964), *The Other Victorians: A Study of Sexuality and Pornography in Mid-Nineteenth-Century England* (New Brunswick, NJ: Transaction, 2008), 53, 52.

16 Octave Uzanne, 'Le Cabinet d'un eroto-bibliomane,' in *Caprices d'un bibliophile* (Paris: É. Rouveyre, 1878), 127–46. Also see Willa Silverman, *The New Bibliopolis: French Book Collectors and the Culture of Print, 1880–1914* (Toronto: University of Toronto Press), 180.

17 Octave Uzanne, *Dictionnaire bibliophilosophique, typologique, iconophilesque, bibliopégique et bibliotechnique à l'usage des bibliognostes, des bibliomanes et des bibliophilistins* (Paris: Imprimé pour les sociétaires de l'Académie des beaux livres, 1896), 174–75.

18 See Edmond de Goncourt and Jules de Goncourt, 20 September 1887, in Robert Ricatte (ed.), *Journal: mémoires de la vie littéraire, 1851–1896, vol. 3: 1887–1896* (Paris: R. Laffront, 2014).

19 Apollinaire's letters to Fleuret are collected in Victor Martin-Schmets (ed.), *Correspondance générale: Guillaume Apollinaire* (Paris: Honoré Champion éditeur, 2015). I have also consulted manuscript letters exchanged among the men: letters from Fleuret to Apollinaire and Perceau, and letters from Perceau to Apollinaire and Fleuret, located at the Richelieu site, *Bibliothèque nationale de France*. For discussion of this correspondence, see Raymond-Josué Seckel, 'L'Enfer d'Apollinaire à Apollinaire', in *L'Enfer de la Bibliothèque: Eros au Sécret* (Paris: *Bibliothèque nationale de France*, 2007), 326–46.

20 Apollinaire to Fleuret, 1912, in *Correspondance générale*, 743–44.

21 Fleuret to Apollinaire, 1912, 'Guillaume Apollinaire. Correspondance' (Paris: *Bibliothèque nationale de France, Département des manuscrits*), f. 51.

22 Fleuret to Apollinaire, c.1913, 'Guillaume Apollinaire. Correspondance' (Paris: *Bibliothèque nationale de France, Département des manuscrits*), f. 93.

23 Guillaume Apollinaire, *Journal intime: 1898–1918*, Michel Décaudin (ed.), (Paris: Éd. Du Limon, 1991), 150.

24 Apollinaire to Fleuret, March 1911, in *Correspondance générale*, 743.

25 Apollinaire to Fleuret, April 1911, in *Correspondance générale*, 744.

26 Fleuret to Apollinaire, 1912, 'Guillaume Apollinaire. Correspondance' (Paris: *Bibliothèque nationale de France, Département des manuscrits*), f. 51.

27 Fleuret to Perceau, c.1913, 'Louis Perceau. Lettres de Fernand Fleuret et coupures de presse' (Paris: *Bibliothèque nationale de France, Département des manuscrits*).

28 Fleuret to Perceau, 13 June 1913, 'Louis Perceau. Lettres de Fernand Fleuret et coupures de presse' (Paris: *Bibliothèque nationale de France, Département des manuscrits*).

29 Fleuret to Apollinaire, 1912, 'Guillaume Apollinaire. Correspondance' (Paris: *Bibliothèque nationale de France, Département des manuscrits*), f. 61.

30 Fleuret to Louis, 26 March 1913, 'Louis Perceau. Lettres de Fernand Fleuret et coupures de presse' (Paris: *Bibliothèque nationale de France, Département des manuscrits*).

31 Apollinaire, *Journal intime*, 151.

32 Fleuret to Apollinaire, 24 August 1912, 'Guillaume Apollinaire. Correspondance' (Paris: *Bibliothèque nationale de France, Département des manuscrits*), f. 67.

33 Fleuret to Perceau, 1913, 'Louis Perceau. Lettres de Fernand Fleuret et coupures de presse' (Paris: *Bibliothèque nationale de France, Département des manuscrits*).

34 Hand-corrected proofs for the 1913 edition of *L'Enfer de la bibliothèque nationale* are located in Enfer, Bibliothèque nationale de France, RES P-Q-803; Fonds Guillaume Apollinaire, Bibliothèque Historique de la Ville de Paris, 4-APO-0176 (res); and Collection de Jacques Doucet, Bibliothèque littéraire Jacques Doucet, 1090, B VI 5.

35 See *Odor di Femina, Amours Naturalistes par E.D. Auteur de Mes Amours avec Victoire* (London: Londres Imprimerie de la Société Cosmopolite, 1890); *Odor di femina, amours naturalistes par E. D. auteur de Jupes troussées* (Montréal: G. Lebaucher, libraire-éditeur, 1890).

36 Colette Colligan and Cécile Loyen, 'Le mystérieux éditeur clandestin de Guillaume Apollinaire', *Histoires Littéraires* 69 (2017), forthcoming.

37 *Les Onze Mille Verges par G... A...* (Paris: En vente chez tous les Libraires, *c*.1907); *Les Exploits d'un jeune Don Juan par G. A.* (Paris: En vente chez tous les Libraires, *c*.1907).

38 Colligan and Loyen, 'Le mystérieux éditeur clandestin de Guillaume Apollinaire', forthcoming.

39 Apollinaire, Fleuret and Perceau, *L'Enfer de la Bibliothèque nationale*, 126–27.

40 *Des Grieux (The Prelude to 'Teleny')* Vol 1 (1899). Apollinaire's library is housed at the Bibliothèque Historique de la ville de Paris. For a bibliography of this collection, see Gilbert Boudar (ed.), *Catalogue de la bibliothèque de Guillaume Apollinaire*, 2 vols (Paris: Editions du CNRS, 1983).

41 Ann Cvetkovich, *An Archive of Feelings* (Durham, North Carolina: Duke University Press, 2003), 239–71.

42 'Apollinaire. *'Répertoire alphabétique utilisé pour confectionner le dossier de presse de* l'Hérésiarque, Alcools, l'Enfer de la Bibliothèque nationale *et* Le Manifeste de l'Antitradition futuriste' (Paris: Bibliothèque nationale de France, Département des manuscrits).

43 Raymond-Josué Seckel, 'L'Enfer d'Apollinaire à Apollinaire', in *L'Enfer de la Bibliothèque: Eros au Sécret*, 335.

44 E.S.P. Haynes, 'The Taboos of the British Museum Library', *The English Review* (1913), 123–34.

45 Briffaut to Perceau, 2 December 1925, 'Archives de Louis Perceau' (Paris: *Bibliothèque nationale de France, Département des manuscrits*).

46 Raymond-Josué Seckel, 'La fermeture de L'Enfer ...', in *L'Enfer de la Bibliothèque: Eros au Sécret*, 412.

47 Pascal Pia, *Les Livres de L'Enfer: bibliographie critique des ouvrages érotiques dans leurs différentes éditions du XVIe siècle à nos jours* (Paris: C. Coulet et A. Faure, 1978).

48 Alison Moore, 'Arcane Erotica and National "Patrimony": Britain's Private Case and the Collection de l'Enfer of the *Bibliothèque Nationale de France*,' *Cultural Studies Review* 18 (2012), 198, 208.

49 Louis Perceau, *Bibliographie du roman érotique au XIXe siècle*, 2 vols. (Paris: Georges Fourdrinier, 1930).

50 These letters to Louis Perceau date from 1931–1942, 'Archives de Louis Perceau' (Paris: *Bibliothèque nationale de France, Département des manuscrits*).

13

AMY S. WYNGAARD

Sade, Réage and Transcending the Obscene

In 1954, the first modern sadomasochistic novel written by a woman, *Histoire d'O*, was published in Paris, both in the original French (Editions Jean-Jacques Pauvert) and in English translation (*The Story of O*; Olympia Press). Not surprisingly, the novel sparked widespread cultural controversy. Readers and critics (as well as the French *Brigade Mondaine*, or morality police) were not only pulled in by the provocative storyline – featuring an eponymous protagonist who willingly becomes a sexual slave and submits to a number of painful and degrading acts in a chateau on the outskirts of Paris – but also by speculation about the identity of the author, the pseudonymous Pauline Réage, later identified as Dominique Aury (b. Anne Desclos). More than 150 years earlier, in the tumultuous years surrounding the French Revolution, the writings upon which Réage based her novel and the criminally deviant Marquis de Sade who penned them similarly shocked and intrigued the French public and government officials. Significantly, the works of both writers, linked by setting and theme, also share an important role in literary history. Each designates a pivotal moment in the history of pornography: Sade's and Réage's texts mark, respectively, the origin and the 'end' of the modern Western literary genre of pornography. Their closely intertwined publications, their similar critical receptions and their legal entanglements in the mid-twentieth century paved the way for the (relative) acceptance of sexually explicit literature in mainstream French and American culture.

For many, the Marquis de Sade is best known for inspiring the term 'sadism'. The term was popularized by Richard Von Krafft-Ebing in his *Psychopathia Sexualis* (first published in 1886), where he mined Sade's works to construct a pathology of the psychosexual disorder in which pleasure is derived from inflicting pain and humiliation on unwilling victims. Indeed, Sade's works are a veritable catalogue of sadistic acts. Overall, his pornographic works feature similar themes and content, and critics have long remarked on these repetitions and multiplications – within both his texts and his *oeuvre* as a whole –as a hallmark of his writing style.[1] In *Les Cent Vingt Journées de Sodome ou l'Ecole du libertinage* (begun in 1782), four procuresses recount 600 perverse 'passions' – divided into four escalating categories: 'simple', 'double', 'criminal' and 'murderous' – that four aristocrats commit over four months on 42 victims, including their wives and daughters, in a chateau in the Black Forest.[2] In *Justine ou les Malheurs de la vertu* – Sade's first published novel, which appeared anonymously in 1791 – the virtuous Justine, left poor and orphaned at the age of 12, is serially imprisoned, tortured, raped and victimized as she attempts to make her way in the world. Ultimately, she is saved from a death sentence and briefly finds herself safe before being struck by lightning and killed – a distinctly Sadean twist to the traditional moral ending. In composing such works, Sade not only drew from – and perverted – popular contemporary literary modes such as the sentimental novel, but also from his own actions and proclivities. Sade would flee France and be imprisoned numerous times due to his deviant acts, including two public *affaires* involving the sexual mistreatment and alleged poisoning of prostitutes; he would die at Charenton in 1814, incarcerated for his writings at Napoleon's order one final time.[3]

Like other pornographic works of the seventeenth and eighteenth centuries, which were known in French under the code name *livres philosophiques*, Sade's texts combine sexually explicit content with political and social critique. His novels famously target both church and state.[4] *La Philosophie dans le boudoir* (1795), presented in the form of a philosophical dialogue, stages the sexual initiation and moral corruption of an adolescent girl (Eugénie), undertaken at the request of her father by a libertine noblewoman (Mme de Saint-Ange), her brother (the chevalier de Mirvel) and his atheist friend (Dolmancé), culminating in Eugénie's participation in her mother's rape and deliberate infection with syphilis. Perhaps the most salient feature of the novel is the revolutionary pamphlet inserted into the story, '*Français, encore un effort si vous voulez être Républicains*', in which Sade expounds upon his theories concerning liberty, religion, the monarchy and morals and encourages citizens of the newly founded French republic to follow the laws of nature rather than social convention in committing acts such as suicide, incest, murder and sodomy. Similarly, in *L'Histoire de Juliette, sa soeur, ou les Prospérités du vice*, appended to *La Nouvelle Justine ou les Malheurs de la vertu* (dated 1797), Justine's libertine sister, Juliette, tells her life story in a first-person philosophical narration that highlights her own perverse and criminal acts as well as those of the libertines she encounters – including murder, mutilation, incest, cannibalism and torture. Juliette's message is to give free rein to individual desire without regard for the consequences for others. The extensive dual work, composed of 10 volumes with 100 engravings, is strongly anti-clerical; it features a detailed scene in which Juliette lists, for Pope Pius VI, all the immoral acts committed by his predecessors. Appropriately, the scene culminates in an orgy in which the Pope participates, and a number of the engravings depict ecclesiastics participating in deviant sexual acts in sacred settings (11.1).

While bearing the hallmarks of early modern pornography (a politically and socially motivated form written by members of the male elite and featuring the same aristocratic libertines who made up its target audience), Sade's works importantly – and perhaps paradoxically – evolved the genre. As Lynn Hunt has demonstrated, his texts designate a tipping point in the history of Western European pornography by signalling the development of a novelistic form that turned away from the classic critiques of church and state to focus on sexual pleasure 'as an end in itself' – what Hunt deems the salient characteristic of 'truly' modern pornography.[5] In the 1790s, at the time Sade was writing, 'politically motivated pornography reached its zenith … and then virtually disappeared, to be replaced by pornography that continued to test moral and social taboos without targeting political figures'.[6] Hunt argues that Sade's texts embody and enact this transition; by attacking 'every aspect of conventional morality', he 'undermined the use of pornography for political ends in the future'.[7] Sade's works gave way to the novels of authors such as Andréa de Nerciat, who furthered this transition by evacuating philosophical and political content and focusing on the depiction of bodily pleasures.[8] Significantly, in his 1806 *Dictionnaire critique, littéraire et bibliographique des principaux livres condamnés au feu, supprimés ou censurés*, Etienne-Gabriel Peignot defined 'pornography' for the first time as the category of books repressed for moral, rather than religious or political, reasons – and cited Sade's *Justine* as a particularly reprehensible example.[9] By the 1830s, pornography became a distinct genre of its own, no longer associated with subversive philosophy and politics.[10]

The explosive content of Sade's works caused him – and those associated with him – many troubles during his lifetime: his editions were seized on multiple occasions, his printer was arrested and Sade was imprisoned more than once for his writings.[11] In 1836, extant volumes and manuscripts of his works were closeted away in the newly formed *Collection de l'Enfer* (Hell) of the French National Library; Sade's works were thus officially relegated to the literary underground, with a few copies continuing to circulate among private collectors.[12] It was not until the early twentieth century – when Sade's works were rediscovered by sexologists, as well as the surrealists – that modern editions appeared, beginning with Dr. Eugène Dühren's (Dr. Iwan Bloch's) edition of *Les Cent Vingt Journées de Sodome*, which was published in 1904. Early editors such as Dühren and Maurice Heine

T. II. _ *P. 241.*

Figure 13.1 Illustration from *La Nouvelle Justine*. Courtesy of Houghton Library, Harvard University. FC7.SA152.B797N V. 2.

circumvented trouble with the law by producing limited press runs and restricting sales to subscribers.[13] Following these examples, in 1947, young Parisian publisher Jean-Jacques Pauvert boldly undertook the publication of Sade's complete works, resulting in him being brought to trial in 1956 for the publication of the first four volumes – *La Philosophie dans le boudoir*, *La Nouvelle Justine*, *L'Histoire de Juliette* and *Les 120 Journées de Sodome* – which were charged with crimes against morality.[14] During the trial, Pauvert defended his publications, pointing to their limited circulation and to Sade's literary importance; prominent contemporary French writers such as André Breton, Jean Paulhan and Georges Bataille similarly testified to Sade's import as a writer and philosopher in his explorations of man's capacity for evil.[15] Although Pauvert was convicted in 1957, his sentence was annulled and his conviction partially overturned following an appeal. Pauvert's victory, while mitigated, established that literary significance took precedence over explicit content, opening the doors to the free publication of Sade's works in the 1960s.[16]

The critical reappraisal of Sade in mid-twentieth-century France directly inspired Aury's composition of *Histoire d'O*, the publication and history of which are closely linked with Sade's works. As the story goes, in the early 1950s, Aury (Paulhan's mistress) was concerned that his passion for her was flagging, so she undertook writing *Histoire d'O* because she knew of his interest in Sade.[17] The novel stages the sexual exploits of a young Parisian photographer who enters into a submissive relationship with her lover, René, and later his stepbrother, Sir Stephen. In the course of the novel, O is violated by multiple strangers: chained, whipped, branded and pierced in service to the men she loves. Paulhan was impressed with the book and helped Aury to find a publisher: Pauvert, who in 1953 was in the midst of publishing Sade's complete works and had not yet fully encountered his troubles with the law.[18] Paulhan composed the book's preface, 'Le Bonheur dans l'esclavage', which defended the explicit novel's 'danger' by lauding its 'truth' and ultimate 'decency' without revealing its backstory.[19] Following Paulhan's lead, critics compared the book to the great classics of French eroticism and – citing its 'decent' and 'discreet' language, its 'purity of style' and its 'dignity' – declared the novel 'not pornographic' (to which I will return shortly).[20] The book attracted the French government's attention in early 1955, after it won the prestigious *Prix des Deux Magots*. Although Pauvert and Maurice Girodias, the publisher of the English translation, were threatened and harassed by police, legal action against the French edition was ultimately dropped.[21] Girodias's troubles lingered after he published a second, improved translation (completed by Austryn Wainhouse) under the title *The Wisdom of the Lash*. Although the police seized copies of the book, it was never officially banned, and the author's identity remained a well-guarded secret for forty years.[22]

The publication of Sade's and Réage's works in the 1950s and 1960s ultimately tied together three publishers on both sides of the Atlantic: Pauvert, Girodias and Barney Rosset of Grove Press. Their motivations for selling 'dirty books' were strikingly similar to those seen in Sade's era, combining daring, idealism and financial drive. Their tactics also recall those of eighteenth-century printers and booksellers, with their recourse to false publication addresses (in the case of Pauvert, that of his parents' garage) and manipulating the authorities (Girodias, for example, took advantage of a loophole in French law that treated publications in English with greater leniency).[23] The three publishers were collaborators as well as competitors. Inspired and aided by each other's success, they were also deeply invested in their own, which at times led to divisive contractual disagreements and legal battles. All three benefited from and cultivated the unique cultural climate of the post-war period – one that saw increased intellectual exchange between France and the United States, fostered by the growing expatriate community in Paris, which included writers and translators such as Wainhouse and Richard Seaver (who first collaborated on the English-language literary magazine *Merlin*, debuting works by writers such as Samuel Beckett). This climate also witnessed a public push for increased social and political freedoms, including freedom of the press. Significantly, both Wainhouse and Seaver would be employed by Girodias (as translators for his erotic *Traveller's Companion* series) and later by Rosset, playing key roles in carrying Sade's and Réage's texts – and their attendant cultural battles – from French to American soil.

Rosset's publication of Sade and Réage was an integral part of Grove Press's programme to challenge US obscenity laws and censorship practices with racy and provocative works.[24] Rosset published editions of D. H. Lawrence's *Lady Chatterley's Lover* in 1959 and Henry Miller's *Tropic of Cancer* in 1961, both of which were dragged through the courts. Grove lawyer Charles Rembar successfully defended the Press's right to publish and distribute the works based on a 1957 Supreme Court decision known as the Roth opinions, which established obscenity (and its corollary, pornography) as material appealing to prurient interest that was 'utterly without redeeming social importance' – a standard that Rembar transformed into the so-called 'cultural value test'.[25] Following these legal victories, Rosset looked to France – and ultimately to Pauvert and Girodias – for controversial works and authors. Rosset had published a volume containing carefully chosen excerpts of Sade's works – *The Marquis de Sade: An Essay by Simone de Beauvoir with Selections from his Writings Chosen by Paul*

Dinnage (1953) – and was aware of the landmark French legal decision involving Pauvert. Seaver, Rosset's managing editor, negotiated a plan with Wainhouse – who had translated Sade's *Justine, The Bedroom Philosophers, The 120 Days of Sodom* and *The Story of Juliette* for Olympia Press under the pseudonym Pieralessandro Cassavini – to bring out the first unexpurgated American translations of Sade's works with Grove.[26] The road to publication was far from smooth: Grove had to not only navigate various threats and demands from Girodias (who claimed ownership of Wainhouse's 'tightened and improved' translations) but also fend off competition from pirated editions based on the Olympia volumes – yet another striking parallel to eighteenth-century French publishing, in which copyright did not exist.[27]

Rosset and his translators carefully strategized in order to safeguard their Sade volumes from censorship. In the *Lady Chatterley* case, the format and composition of the volume, along with its advertising and promotion, were cited as proof that the book was a serious work of literature that did not 'pander to the lewd- and lascivious-minded for profit.'[28] Seaver and Wainhouse thus endeavoured to give their editions a serious and scholarly tone. The 1965 edition of *The Complete Justine, Philosophy in the Bedroom and Other Writings* featured a critical apparatus, including essays by Paulhan (touted as being a member 'of *l'Académie française*') and literary theorist Maurice Blanchot as well as prefaces by Rosset and the translators that asserted Sade's 'social value' at that particular cultural moment, amid the movements for civil rights and civic freedoms. The back cover of the volume displayed quotations from respected French authors and critics such as Charles Baudelaire, Guillaume Apollinaire, Pierre Klossowski and Simone de Beauvoir. It also included a notice stating: 'The Sale of This Book is Limited to Adults'. Grove's tactics paid off: *Justine* was met with widespread critical approval, making a number of 'best books of the year' lists. With the exception of a few rustlings of discontent when the cheaper mass-market paperback edition of *Justine* appeared in 1966, no serious legal threat to the Sade volumes emerged.[29] By the time *Juliette* appeared in 1968 (following the 1966 publication of *The 120 Days of Sodom and Other Writings*), it was denuded of critical apparatus, save for a brief foreword by the translator and a bibliography of Sade's works. Grove no longer needed to justify Sade's publication: Sade was an established part of the American literary landscape, as further evidenced by lagging sales and reviews in the popular press.

Concurrently with its production of the first Sade volume, Grove undertook the first American edition of *Story of O*, the English-language rights of which it had secured from Pauvert in 1961 following the US Federal Court of Appeals decision in favour of *Lady Chatterley*.[30] Grove prepped the terrain 'very carefully' for the publication of Réage's novel; the publisher launched a strategic plan, employing tactics very similar to those used in the Sade project, to shape public reaction.[31] Grove printed the first dozen pages of *Story of O* in the October–November 1963 issue of its literary magazine, the *Evergreen Review*, prefacing the text with 'A Note on *Story of O*' by translator Sabine Destré (later known as Sabine d'Estrée, a pseudonym for Seaver). This preface summarized the French reception of the novel and suggested that the French Minister of Culture, André Malraux, had intervened to prevent the police from investigating it – importantly, ending any 'censorship problems' in that country.[32] Seaver attempted to engage prominent author and critic Susan Sontag to write a preface that would accompany Paulhan's, hoping her imprimatur would ensure the novel would not be 'misconstrued' in the US. When she declined, he included instead a translation of André Pieyre de Mandiargues's 1955 *Critique* review. This review established *O* as a serious piece of literature, calling it 'a genuine novel' and 'a mystic work' showing the progress of woman, 'through the decline of her flesh, having become pure spirit'.[33] Grove also engineered the novel's presentation; the Press gave it a plain white cover, displayed the title in black type framed by a thin black line, and imprinted it with the same adults-only notice that had appeared on *Justine* 'to avoid any appearance of appealing to prurience'. The discreet design, along with Grove's record of defending its books in court, prompted bookstores to display the novel openly – a first for the publisher and its works.[34]

Strikingly, although Sade's *Justine* had appeared relatively uncontested the previous year, numerous critics declared *O*'s watershed impact on censorship laws as soon as it was published in March 1966. The novel – a 'serious', contemporary work of literature featuring hardcore sex – was perceived as upending the established legal definition of the obscene. Eliot Fremont-Smith's influential review in *The New York Times* stated that the novel, which 'uses ... erotic fantasies of the most perverted hard-core sort to elicit erotic responses in the reader as a means to traditional literary ends', ushered in 'the end of any coherent restrictive application of the concept of pornography to books'. According to Fremont-Smith (borrowing from critic Leslie Fielder), *O* shattered all of the distinctions that had defined pornography to that point – between sex and art, smut and high-class erotica, men and women – leading him to assert that 'pornography as a concept may soon disappear'.[35] Such declarations were subsequently echoed throughout the popular press: by shattering – or 'transcending', as one reviewer put it – the distinctions between the erotic (sensual, artistic) and the pornographic (prurient, commercial) upon which the Supreme Court standard of obscenity was based, the novel effectively brought about the 'end' of (literary) pornography and censorship. One critic wrote: '[t]he *Story of O* may be read as the obituary of pornography as a serious concern'; newspaper headlines decreed that 'Censorship Went Out With "O"'.[36] Indeed, the novel was never pursued on obscenity charges in a US court of law, and proved extremely popular with American audiences; it quickly became a bestseller and remained consistently in print for six decades after its initial publication.

It is significant that the publication of Réage's novel (not Sade's) was seen as marking pornography's 'end' in the 1960s. As critics such as Hunt and Walter Kendrick have shown, the regulatory category of pornography emerged in the early nineteenth century in response to fears about the democratization of the genre – specifically the access of women and the lower classes to sexually explicit material that had previously been the purview of the male elite.[37] At the moment of its modern inception, then, pornography was defined in opposition to women: as words and images to which they were denied access. Not surprisingly, the gender of O's author, which was hotly debated, had a direct impact on the reception and interpretation of the work – and whether or not it was seen as pornographic. French critics imbued the novel with the idealized feminine qualities of decency, purity and dignity (in contrast with the crude, vulgar and pornographic) – analyses carried over to the American press. As a reviewer in *Choice* wrote: 'There has been discussion ... as to whether or not [*Story of O*] was in fact written by a woman, the implication being that pornography is not a genre that has usually attracted women. It is, however, on this point that one can start to build a case for the book as a significant work of literature'.[38] If, for some, the novel's female authorship distinguished it from the pornographic by highlighting its literary qualities, for others the fact that the work was written by a woman made it non-pornographic through very different means. Several critics insisted on its failure to stimulate the male reader, calling it dull and comparing it to a recipe or the proceedings of a 'chicken dinner of a PTA'.[39] Some feminists unwittingly furthered such essentializing reactions by refusing to believe the novel could have been written by a female author due to its adherence to dominant male ideology and its portrayal of women as passive victims – stances that would necessarily be revisited following John De St. Jorre's unmasking of Pauline Réage as Dominique Aury in 1994.[40]

Réage's novel was widely credited with inaugurating a new form of explicitly erotic literature that defied existing categories by combining hardcore elements with highbrow narrative techniques – a genre that in fact had a long history in France (notably traced by writer Georges Bataille in his 1957 *L'Erotisme*), and that had already been introduced to the US thanks to Grove Press's efforts (and been dubbed 'grovepressy' as a result).[41] While owing in part to the author's style – which was spare, matter of fact and free of 'dirty words' – the perceived novelty of Réage's text was also coloured by the author's gender and the long-established moral and philosophical taboos pertaining to women and pornography – if a woman wrote it, it wasn't pornographic; if it was pornographic, a woman didn't write it. Réage herself, it would seem, was not immune to the weight of such judgments; *Retour à Roissy* (1969), the sequel to *Histoire d'O*, was seemingly more 'feminist' in tone and perspective, depicting an unhappy and introspective protagonist who contemplates freedom at the open-ended conclusion. In contrast, Réage's introduction to the volume underscored the traditional dynamics behind the composition of *O*, written by a 'girl in love' to please the 'man she loved' by building 'clandestine castles' peopled 'with girls in love, prostituted by love and triumphant in their chains'.[42] Although credited with being revolutionary, Réage's writing and its critical reception entrenched the stereotypes and prejudices surrounding women and sexual content, specifically the beliefs that sexual desire and fantasy are determined along clear gender lines and that female-authored erotic texts are necessarily an expression of 'what women want'. These attitudes were still in evidence in the first decades of the 2000s, which witnessed a dramatic rise in the number and popularity of explicit texts written by women, as illustrated by the cultural phenomenon surrounding E. L. James's *Fifty Shades of Grey* series.

Although purportedly *Twilight* fan fiction, *Fifty Shades of Grey* (2011) and its sequels owe much to *Histoire d'O* in their depiction of the relations of a young submissive slave, Anastasia Steele, and her dominant master, Christian Grey. Critical reactions to the *Fifty Shades* series have been largely negative: the books have been dismissed as being poorly written, offensive to feminist sensibilities and illustrative of the nascent genre of 'mommy porn', which caters to the safely subversive sexual fantasies of traditional suburban housewives. Both proponents and detractors of the series have emphasized that the books were originally self-published on the internet, a fact that has been used to advance claims about the books' role in liberating women (as the content can be downloaded anonymously and without shame), or – more frequently – to underscore the books' status as unsophisticated pap.[43] Such assessments, however, belie the books' appeal to a wide demographic – an appeal that not only inspired a successful successful film adaptation in 2015 and a sequel in 2017 (with another slated to appear before 2019) but also spurred a number of imitators, including Anna Todd's *After* series (also originally self-published on the internet), which similarly features the eye-opening sexual awakening of a naïve and inexperienced 'good girl' at the hands of a socially deviant 'bad boy'. The ongoing discussions and debates surrounding these books suggest that little has changed in the evaluation of explicitly erotic texts written by women in the half century since the publication of *O*. If Réage's novel was symbolically seen as lifting the legal restriction on pornography because it was written by a woman, paradoxically it did not erase the longstanding divides and prohibitions pertaining to women and the representation of sex – recast here as the belief that if a woman writes it (or consumes it), it must not be good (neither well written nor stimulating).

The histories of Sade's and Réage's texts and their receptions trace an evolution of terms and concepts that is very much ongoing in western society. From pornography's inception as a modern term, literary genre and regulatory concept (with Sade) to its end as a legal category distinct from the artistic and the erotic (with Réage), we have arrived at 'porn': a word used to evoke the sexually explicit imagery now widely available for consumption on the internet, the casual usage of which – in referring to sexual material as well as to glamorized or sensationalized visual presentations (i.e. 'food porn', 'weather porn') – indicates both its prevalence and its banality. Ironically, at a moment when access to sexual imagery could not be more open or democratic, we appear to be witnessing a reification of many of the same boundaries that have defined pornography in the past (although differently expressed). This can be seen in the emergence of internet sites that purport to cater specifically to women's sexual desires and fantasies ('sexy' and 'tasteful', featuring 'real passion' and 'intimacy', etc.). It can be seen in the explosion of 'erotic romance' fiction (à la E. L. James), which is also viewed as the purview of female authors and readers in its recourse to the imagination rather than to hardcore visuals. And it can be seen in the elitist disdain of such novels and their film adaptations, which surpasses the criticism launched at similarly themed (but far less explicit) popular books and movies such as the *Twilight* saga, ostensibly underscoring the discomfort still felt about female sexual agency and its expression – even if (or especially because) these texts and films perpetuate comfortable gender stereotypes.[44] Ultimately, it seems that – just as in the time of Sade and Réage – sex and its representation will always be regulated, if not legally then morally. Such regulation takes place under the guise of critical judgments and pronouncements, which – perhaps happily for consumers – are easily ignored and forgotten in the vast, anonymous world of internet porn.

NOTES

1 See, for example, Roland Barthes, *Sade, Fourier, Loyola* (Paris: Seuil, 1971); Lucienne Frappier-Mazur, *Sade et l'écriture de l'orgie: Pouvoir et parodie dans l'Histoire de Juliette* (Paris: Nathan, 1991).

2 Sade copied the text on a roll of paper when he was a prisoner in the Bastille in 1785 and left it hidden there upon his transfer to Charenton on 2 July 1789; it was finally published by Dr Eugène Dühren (Dr Iwan Bloch) in 1904. In 2014,

the manuscript, which had been illegally sold to a Swiss collector, was returned to France following a lengthy legal battle.

3　Donatien Alphonse François, Marquis de Sade, *Oeuvres*, ed. Michel Delon, 3 vols. (Paris: Gallimard, 1990–98), vol. l, xxiii–lxxix.

4　See Peter Wagner, *Eros Revived: Erotica of the Enlightenment in England and America* (London: Secker & Warburg, 1988), 59–112.

5　Lynn Hunt, 'Pornography and The French Revolution', in Lynn Hunt (ed.), *The Invention of Pornography: Obscenity and the Origins of Modernity, 1500–1800* (New York: Zone Books, 1993), 305.

6　Hunt, 'Pornography', 302.

7　Hunt, 'Pornography', 330.

8　Hunt, 'Pornography', 335.

9　The word 'pornography' comes from Rétif de la Bretonne's *Le Pornographe* (1769), a treatise on prostitution (from the Greek *pornê*: prostitute, and *graphein*: to write). See Amy Wyngaard, *Bad Books: Rétif de la Bretonne, Sexuality, and Pornography* (Newark, NJ: University of Delaware Press, 2013), 47.

10　Hunt, 'Pornography', 302–3.

11　Sade, *Oeuvres*, vol. 1, lxxviii–lxxix.

12　Roger Shattuck, *Forbidden Knowledge: From Prometheus to Pornography* (New York: St. Martin's, 1996), 236.

13　In his preface to *Les Cent Vingt Journées*, Dühren also insisted on the medical interest of Sade's text.

14　Jean-Jacques Pauvert, *L'Affaire Sade* (Paris: Pauvert, 1957), 9.

15　Pauvert, *L'Affaire Sade*, 44–65.

16　Elisabeth Ladenson, *Dirt for Art's Sake. Books on Trial from Madame Bovary to Lolita* (Ithaca, NY: Cornell University Press, 2007), 230–1.

17　John de St. Jorre, *Venus Bound: The Erotic Voyage of the Olympia Press and Its Writers* (New York: Random House, 1996), 211.

18　St. Jorre, *Venus Bound*, 203–12.

19　Jean Paulhan, 'Le Bonheur dans l'esclavage,' in Pauline Réage, *Histoire d'O* (Paris: Pauvert/Livre de Poche, 1999), 10, 11, 14, 21.

20　See 'Mystère d'O', *Carrefour*, 26 January; André Berry, 'Chambre rouge et chambre des supplices', *Combat*, 14 March (Syracuse, NY: Grove Press Records, Special Collections Research Center, Syracuse University Library, 1955).

21　According to Aury's account, the Minister of Justice dropped the charges after Aury had lunch with him—a mysterious action, which seems to have been based more on chivalry than on judicial principle. See St. Jorre, *Venus Bound*, 214–5.

22　St. Jorre, *Venus Bound*, 216.

23　See Ladenson, *Dirt for Art's Sake*, 229; Richard Seaver, *The Tender Hour of Twilight. Paris in the '50s, New York in the '60s: A Memoir of Publishing's Golden Age*, ed. Jeannette Seaver (New York: Farrar, Straus and Giroux, 2012), 60–1; St. Jorre, *Venus Bound*, 71–2.

24　For a detailed discussion of the history of Grove Press, see Loren Glass, *Counterculture Colophon: Grove Press, the Evergreen Review, and the Incorporation of the Avant-Garde* (Stanford, CA: Stanford University Press, 2013).

25　Charles Rembar, *The End of Obscenity: The Trials of Lady Chatterley, Tropic of Cancer, and Fanny Hill* (New York: Random House, 1968), 45–58, 453–68.

26 Due to legal concerns, explicit passages in Dinnage's volume were kept in the original French. See Amy Wyngaard, 'Translating Sade: The Grove Press Editions, 1953–1968', *Romantic Review* 104 (2013), 317–18.

27 See letter from Wainhouse to Seaver, 23 October (Syracuse, NY: Grove Press Records, Special Collections Research Center, Syracuse University Library, 1963). See also Wyngaard, 'Translating Sade', 321.

28 Rembar, *The End of Obscenity*, 485–6.

29 See Wyngaard, 'Translating Sade', 320–7.

30 See letter from Pauvert to Grove Press, 5 December (Syracuse, NY: Grove Press Records, Special Collections Research Center, Syracuse University Library, 1960).

31 See letter from Seaver to Pauvert, 1 October (Syracuse, NY: Grove Press Records, Special Collections Research Center, Syracuse University Library, 1964).

32 See Sabine Destré [Richard Seaver], 'A Note on *Story of O*', *Evergreen Review* 7 (1963), 32.

33 See letter from Seaver to Sontag, 19 February; letter from Sontag to Seaver, 18 March; letter from Seaver to Sontag, 7 April (Syracuse, NY: Grove Press Records, Special Collections Research Center, Syracuse University Library, 1965). See also André Pieyre de Mandiargues, xvi, xviii.

34 Seaver, *The Tender Hour of Twilight*, 363–4.

35 See Eliot Fremont-Smith, 'The Uses of Pornography', *The New York Times*, 2 March (Syracuse, NY: Grove Press Records, Special Collections Research Center, Syracuse University Library, 1966)

36 See Laurance Wieder, 'Erotic Fiction's New Form', *The Supplement, Columbia Daily Spectator*, 15 December (New York: Columbia University, 1966); 'Censorship Went Out With "O"', *San Francisco Sunday Examiner and Chronicle*, 20 March (Syracuse, NY: Grove Press Records, Special Collections Research Center, Syracuse University Library, 1966).

37 See Lynn Hunt, 'Introduction: Obscenity and the Origins of Modernity, 1500–1800,' in Lynn Hunt (ed.), *The Invention of Pornography: Obscenity and the Origins of Modernity, 1500–1800* (New York: Zone Books, 1993), 12–3, 36, 44–5; Walter Kendrick, *The Secret Museum: Pornography in Modern Culture* (New York: Viking, 1987), 26–31, 48–50, 57–8.

38 See review in *Choice*, July–August, 415 (Syracuse, NY: Grove Press Records, Special Collections Research Center, Syracuse University Library, 1966).

39 See Paul West, 'Flagelatinous', *Book Week*, 20 March; 'Story of a Female Sadist', *Washington Star*, 20 March (Syracuse, NY: Grove Press Records, Special Collections Research Center, Syracuse University Library, 1966).

40 See Amy Wyngaard, 'The End of Pornography: The Story of *Story of O*', *MLN* 130 (2013), 992–3; John de St. Jorre, 'The Unmasking of O', *The New Yorker*, 1 August 1994, 42–50.

41 See Tom Fensch, 'The Verdict: Shocking', *Iowan*, 7 March (Syracuse, NY: Grove Press Records, Special Collections Research Center, Syracuse University Library, 1967).

42 See Pauline Réage, 'A Girl in Love', in Pauline Réage (ed.), *Return to the Château, Preceded by A Girl in Love*, trans. Sabine d'Estrée [Richard Seaver] (New York: Grove, 1971), 1, 9.
43 See Wyngaard, 'End of Pornography', 995.
44 See, for example, Catherine Pearson, 'The Best Places to Find Porn for Women Online', *Huffpost*, 8 December 2015.

14

DAVID GREVEN

"Nothing could stop it now!"
Tennessee Williams, Suddenly Last Summer, and the Intersections of Desire

Tennessee Williams' one-act play *Suddenly Last Summer* opened off Broadway in 1958, along with another one-act, *Something Unspoken* (1958), in a double bill that was given the title *Garden District*. The heroine of *Suddenly*, a young woman named Catharine Holly, refers to the titular location in telling fashion. In the midst of her shocking story about her cousin Sebastian Venable's near-fantastical murder the previous summer and her participation in his homosexual cruising, Catharine gives her role in his affairs a definitive terminology. "Don't you understand?" she says to Doctor Cukrowicz, who has given Catharine a truth drug in order to hear her tale at last. "I was PROCURING for him!"[1] Distinguishing herself from Violet Venable, the poet's mother, Catharine makes her knowledge about her role clear: "I knew what I was doing. I came out in the French Quarter years before I came out in the Garden District."[2] While it is not clear that Catharine's assessment is correct, she claims that Violet procured for her son unwittingly, in contrast to Catharine's knowing complicity in Sebastian's sexual rites.

Williams anticipates as Catharine articulates the slippages between the incipient language of gay liberation (coming out of the closet) and the language of established social customs such as the debutante's coming out party. The gay male vernacular use of the term coming out "burlesqued the rituals of society women," notes historian George Chauncey. Gay men "developed a rich language of their own, which reflected the complex character and purposes of gay culture generally." Typically, "standard terms were given a second, gay meaning."[3] While the gay rhetoric of coming out of the closet emerged in the late-1960s Stonewall Riot moment, it is significant that Catharine understands her own autonomous and fully informed role in Sebastian's cruising in terms of institutionalized rituals of femininity. She draws a parallel between the young woman's coming out party, which signals her marriageability and implicitly her sexual availability, and her gay cousin's pursuit of illicit sexual encounters. But even more significant is Catharine's parodic view of the coming out party in terms of her own sexuality. As Violet Venable sneers, Catharine's behavior gave her a "notoriety" that left the older woman "disgusted, sickened," and unable to comprehend the fact that her son was "amused by this girl." Catharine's behavior leads to scandal; to being, in Violet's words, "dropped off the party lists, yes, dropped off the lists in spite of my position."[4] Catharine's pursuit of libidinal pleasure – improper social behavior for an unmarried woman in the South, or indeed for any woman – casts her outside of the ranks of polite society. And because she has herself been a transgressor, she understands – picks up on the secondary meanings of – Sebastian's behavior, actions, and language, and also empathizes with him. Catharine's empathy for Sebastian acknowledges him as a fellow traveler in the realms of sexual exploration. Women's sexual desire and gay male sexual desire, both seen as illicit, converge in Catharine's narrative and the theme of "procuring."[5]

Another desire haunts the text; one equally important to it and its author. Williams explicitly evokes Herman Melville when Violet refers to the author and his work *The Encantadas* (104). First published in *Putnam's Magazine* in 1854, *The Encantadas, or Enchanted Isles* consists of ten lyrical, philosophical sketches about the Galápagos Islands. Violet's reference evinces what I call *intertextual desire*: a longing to inhabit and surpass the work and achievement of an artistic precursor. Violet's narrative of *The Encantadas* figures Williams' effort to inhabit the exotic and sensual world of Melville's writing and to extend his knowing sexual themes. This effort depends on a certain degree of obfuscation. Melville's work often sensualizes and sexualizes its situations and language, and frequently illustrates Melville's homoerotic sensibility. Though it foregrounds sexuality at its most threatening and explosive, and links this thematization to Melville's writings, *Suddenly* references a Melville work that does not foreground sexuality. Williams creates a Melvillean atmosphere of illicit sexuality organized around homosexuality, but the linkages the playwright establishes with Melville's homosexual themes emerge indirectly and suggestively. As an example of this, *Typee* (1846; Melville's first published work) and *Billy Budd, Sailor* (1891; his final work, unpublished in his lifetime) both foreground themes of crucial relevance to *Suddenly* – cannibalism (*Typee*) and a fascination with blond male beauty (*Billy Budd*) – but are not cited in the play. (Not directly, that is. In terms of the latter, Williams all but references Billy Budd, the blond Handsome Sailor who became a homoerotic icon in the twentieth century when Catharine reports of Sebastian's shifting tastes: "Cousin Sebastian said he was famished for blonds, he was fed up with the dark ones and was famished for blonds."[6])

Set in a "mansion of Victorian Gothic style in the Garden District of New Orleans on a late afternoon," according to the stage directions, the play begins with the conversation between Violet Venable and Doctor Cukrowicz – a young and ambitious surgeon at the Lion's View clinic looking for an endowment from the rich widow.[7] Financially motivated though he is, the doctor is not prepared to accept money if it means he will have to take it as Violet's bribe. Violet wants Cukrowicz to perform a lobotomy on Catharine, who keeps telling the improbable story about the circumstances of her cousin Sebastian's death when the two were summering last year in Cabeza de Lobo (literally, "wolf's head"), Spain. As Catharine recounts in her climactic monologue, the young urchin males that Sebastian sexually preyed on – with her ambivalent help – cornered, attacked, and devoured him as she watched in horror.

Violet figures intertextual desire through her devotion to literary high art, uncertainly embodied by Sebastian, of whose literary legacy she remarks: "D'you know it still shocks me a little?" (to realize that Sebastian Venable the poet is still unknown outside of a small coterie of friends, including his mother, who zealously revises precursor texts).[8] (Writing close to the time that *Suddenly Last Summer* premiered, James R. Hurt treats Sebastian's art, the poem that takes nine months to come to term, witheringly: "A pretentiously amateur poet, he produces an annual 'Poem of Summer': in its difficulty of delivery, an ironically convincing proof of his sterile invention."[9]) Opposed to Catharine though she is, determined to silence her story, Violet is also a woman who witnessed an atrocious event and wishes to exorcise this sight through language.

Violet extends and deepens the world Melville evokes in *The Encantadas* by adding a dimension of horror to its mystical realm. Establishing that Sebastian read her Melville's descriptions of the islands, Violet discusses the voyage she and her son undertook to see the islands themselves:

> we saw something Melville *hadn't* written about. We saw the great sea-turtles crawl up out of the sea for their annual egg-laying … Once a year the female of the sea-turtle crawls up out of the equatorial sea onto the blazing sand-beach … to dig a pit in the sand and deposit her eggs there. It's a long and dreadful thing, the depositing of the eggs in the sand-pits.

The exhausted turtle-mothers, crawling back "half-dead" into the sea, do not ever see their infants hatch; "but we did," Violet adds.[10] Writing in 1960, James R. Hurt finds the reference to *The Encantadas* "startlingly apt," and argues that Violet does indeed underestimate how directly Melville has anticipated her own vision.[11]

The doctor asks if they went back to the islands, and Violet responds yes, they did return to the "Terrible Encantadas," with their "extinct volcanoes," to watch the beach turn "the color of caviar," covered with turtle hatchlings. "But the sky was in motion, too …' – Violet's words elliptically create an ominous scene. This writhing sky, "almost as black as the beach!," teems with "flesh-eating birds and the noise of the birds, the horrible savage cries of the –" The doctor adds, "Carnivorous birds?" The doctor is correct. Violet reaches the pinnacle of her horror show:

> And the sand all alive, all alive, as the hatched sea-turtles made their dash for the sea, while the birds hovered and swooped to attack, and hovered and – swooped to attack! They were diving down on the hatched sea-turtles, turning them over to expose their soft undersides, tearing the undersides open and rending and eating their flesh.[12]

At the end of play, after Catharine has finally told her story, her enemy Violet shrieks to the doctor: *"Lion's View! State asylum, cut this hideous story out of her brain!"*[13] Yet the play commences, more or less, with Violet's own hideous, elaborate narrative of the sea-turtle infants being meticulously devoured by these relentless, ravenous avian predators. The repetition of "hovered and swooped to attack" – especially the dash before "swooped" in the second iteration – models the rapacity of the predatory birds' assault in language; as a result of the dash, the second "swooped" swoops at the sentence and the reader. Implicitly, we are the defenseless newly born turtles, prey to attack from above. Clearly, Violet doesn't see the irony in her position relative to Catharine's – and vice versa, that both have a terrible story to tell of something they witnessed in Sebastian's presence. Nor does she empathize with the pain Catharine feels after having (arguably) beheld a far more incomprehensible and horrifying event. These women have similar experiences across the board, but the parallels do not bring them closer – quite the opposite.

Melville, while certainly capable of conjuring gruesome and horrific tableaux (one thinks of the sharks gobbling up whale carcasses in the 1851 *Moby-Dick*, or the decapitation of Babo in the 1855 "Benito Cereno"), maintains a mystical approach to the near-mythic ancient tortoises in *The Encantadas*. His narrator describes them as apparitions in a dream, phantoms of memory: "I have seemed to see, slowly emerging from those imagined solitudes, and heavily crawling along the floor, the ghost of a gigantic tortoise, with 'Memento * * * *' burning in live letters upon his back."[14] William B. Dillingham argues that the tortoise reminds one of death; a "memento mori" that signifies the "stark remains of exhausted life." Melville's ancient reptile also signals "death in life, which takes two

principal forms: degradation to bestiality and the changeless state of cata-
tonic hopelessness."[15] While Melville's representation of the tortoises oscil-
lates between the mystical and the comic – whatever reverential attitude he
may have toward them, the narrator humorously decides that "their crown-
ing curse is their drudging impulse to straightforwardness in a belittered
world"[16] as he observes their often hopeless negotiation of the objects in
their path; moreover, he and his crewmates happily gorge on three tortoises
brought onboard, using their prodigious shells as soup tureens – the grim-
mer, more ominous resonances in his descriptions inform and galvanize
Violet's much more lurid, visionary meditation on Melvillean themes. She
adds the notes of Darwinian savagery to Melville's mystical–comic reverie,
transforming his idyll into iconic grotesquerie.

This is to say that Violet is a figure of the author, and that her narrative
reflects intertextual desire: it remakes and reimagines the precursor text in
order to express both the inexpressible and the deeply idiosyncratic. The
relevance of these aspects of Williams' play to a study of erotic literature lies
in the similarities between Violet's narrative and Catharine's climactic one.
Both women narrate a story of impossible and/or unfathomable events that
metaphorize the unseen, dead Sebastian's sexuality, which cannot be represented but only inferred. Their narratives also likely metaphorize their own
desires; equally "impossible" because bordering on the incestuous (and certainly on the voyeuristic) and because they verge on making female sexual
desire explicit. (Catharine and her family are not Violet's blood relations;
she takes great pains in telling the doctor that the Holly family, whom she
abhors, belong to her late husband's side of the family.)

While Catharine's monologue models the "memory theatre" famously
thematized in the playwright's works – especially *The Glass Menagerie*
(1945) and *A Streetcar Named Desire* (1947) – Violet's narrative similarly models memory theater. (Indeed, William Mark Poteet argues that
Suddenly is the author's "most realized dramatic examination of the theater
of memory."[17]) Moreover, her narrative focuses on her and her son's *shared*
experience of this violent spectacle – which seems to have had a far greater
emotional impact on her – and can be seen as an anticipatory reordering
of not just Catharine's story but also her particular way of narrating it.
The two female narratives evoke the famous structuralist literary theory of
Russian Formalism and the distinction it drew between story (*fabula*) and
plot (*sjužet*) – *fabula* being the chronological sequence of events in a story,
and *sjužet* the imaginative manner in which the story is told. Sharing the
same *fabula*, despite bitter oppositions, the women share an artistry that
emerges in their bold manipulations of *sjužet*.

One of the most powerful intertexts for *Suddenly* is Melville's *Typee*, a fictionalized version of his experiences as a sailor in the Marquesan islands. Tommo, the first-person narrator, finds himself the captive of the titular natives when he and his friend Toby desert their oppressive ship. The threat of cannibalism looms large here, as his gentle, graceful, but fearsome captors threaten to do unto Tommo what they do unto their enemies, the Happar (Melville pointedly confuses the issue of which tribe actually cannibalizes the other). Melville became instantly famous (a fame that was short-lived) as the "man who lived among the cannibals." As Caleb Crain has shown in his essay "Lovers of Human Flesh: Homosexuality and Cannibalism in Melville's Novels," while homosexuality could not be explicitly represented in nineteenth-century texts, cannibalism could be. Using the French painter Théodore Géricault's 1818–1819 painting *Le Radeau de la Méduse* (*The Raft of the Medusa*) as an example, Crain demonstrates that cannibalism as a subject provided a useful metaphorical register for the articulation of unspeakable acts and desires – the male eating of male flesh; the intimate physicality of male bodies entwined. (Géricault's painting depicts a real-life contemporary event. The artist was inspired by the 1816 wreck of the French Royal Navy frigate *Medusa*, sent off on a mission to colonize Senegal; an account by two survivors documented the event.)

Suddenly extends the conflation of cannibalism and homosexual male desire that Williams daringly established in his short story "Desire and the Black Masseur," first published in 1948.[18] A contemporaneous text does the same, and deserves mentioning. Alfred Hitchcock's controversial film *Rope* (1948) contributes to a queer genealogy of male bodies, racial and sexual panic, and the symbolic *and* literal threat of cannibalism. The gay male couple Brandon and Philip all but serve their murdered friend David Kentley to their dinner guests. The mid-century gay texts extend and deepen Melville's themes while adding troubling and galvanizing provocations of their own.

For James R. Hurt, the other crucial Melville intertext here is *Moby-Dick*. "Ahab, like Sebastian, fancies that he has beheld the face of God. And Ahab's error, like Sebastian's, is that he fails to see that this 'God' (the cruelty of the universe) is uncaring." But, Hurt writes:

> There is an important difference in the visions of Ahab and Sebastian … : Sebastian's vision is glimpsed in a strong context of sex. The destruction of the turtles, it will be remembered, is the result of the annual ritual of egg-laying "on the blazing sand-beach of a volcanic island." Sebastian's wound, too, is not a missing leg, but his homosexuality. If we read Sebastian's characterization in this light, the play may be seen as a struggle for the soul of Catherine between the dead Sebastian and Dr. Cukrowicz.[19]

I concur with Hurt, save for one point: I do not believe that Dr. Cukrowicz is nearly as significant a character as either Sebastian or Violet. If there is a battle for Catharine's soul, it is waged between the dead poet and his mother; or, more properly, between them as figures in Catharine's psychomachia. To elaborate on Hurt's suggestion, homosexuality itself emerges here as an intoxicating vision that threatens to consume the devotee.

Until recent years, reception of the play has tended to view it as homophobic; indicative of Williams' internalized homophobia, to be precise. The same holds true for Joseph L. Mankiewicz's film version *Suddenly, Last Summer* (1959), for which Gore Vidal – a fellow gay artist – co-wrote the screenplay with Williams. Vito Russo denounced the film as homophobic in his book *The Celluloid Closet*, which argued for positive images of homosexuality. (Russo's pioneering work retains a great deal of value, but its relegation of works like this film to the homophobic film canon did a serious disservice. D. A. Miller offers a very distinct queer theory approach to the film, but similarly – and I think misleadingly – treats it as homophobic.) Michael Paller and Michael S. D. Hooper represent a welcome newer approach to Williams. Both critics see the complexity in *Suddenly* and do not view the play, for all of its darkness, as homophobic. "Unless one is looking very hard to find them, there is neither homophobic discourse nor indirect language in [*Suddenly*]," Paller argues. For this critic, the play is not actually "about" homosexuality to begin with. Indeed, *Suddenly* offers "an unusually 'positive' image of a gay man, in that its gay man has a desire to live life at its furthest edge, to engage it at its most sensual extreme, to be himself no matter what anyone else might think or how high the price of such experience may be"; "the play is a full-throated defense of living one's life according to one's own lights."[20]

Hooper directly states that his "approach defends Williams' work from charges of internalized homophobia."[21] Importantly, he notes that "Sebastian lived by his poetry, something of a mask for his homosexual predilections. In this play, the poet is not merely synonymous with the homosexual. Poetry and oral storytelling are variously used as means of covering and uncovering the truth that kills Sebastian." Hooper also reaffirms the centrality of the character: "Though dead, Sebastian's presence is everywhere. He is central to a power struggle in the present between Violet and his cousin, Catharine Holly."[22]

In general agreement with Hooper, I argue that Sebastian's single-minded devotion to his own principles has a distinctly galvanizing effect on the two women in his life. Sebastian, a dead unseen figure only alive through hearsay, functions for both distinctly enterprising women in Lacanian terms as "the Real of desire, the *objet a*: not the desired itself but that which controls and flows from desire: inchoate, unspeakable, horrifying, overwhelming, that which always escapes the ordering of the symbolic, a presence surrounded by mystery."[23] (Henry Krips describes the ghostly titular presence of Toni Morrison's 1987 novel *Beloved* here.) For Violet, Sebastian's vision of the world represents the power of art, before which her son appears to humble and purify himself, evacuating the body. We might add that Sebastian's artistic endeavors reflect a *commitment* to art, rather than art itself, given the strong implication that he is not a terribly good or interesting poet. Sebastian's vision of the world, unsparing and almost nihilistic, speaks to Catharine, in my view, because it represents a break with the normative demands of the social order that she wishes to effect herself. Nevertheless, his pitilessly unsentimental views and determination to accept the world as it is, in all of its brute immediacy, frightens as much as it rivets her. When his companion, Catharine, attempted to safeguard Sebastian from a looming perdition predicted in his philosophy, her role was to save him. "Save him from what?" asks the doctor. "Completing! – a sort of – *image* – he had of himself as a sort of! – *sacrifice* to a! – *terrible* sort of a – ." The doctor completes her sentence: " – God?" Catharine, affirming, responds, "Yes, a – *cruel* one, Doctor!" Again, Williams' language models the subject: Catharine's jagged speech, the words ripped apart by the dashes, the emphases making certain words wounds of intensity, mirrors and anticipates her account of his rending by the ravenous boys.[24]

While the conjoined issues of homosexuality and homophobia have informed criticism of the play, and while both issues are certainly crucial, an equally pressing theme here is the psychoanalytically rich one of desire. Clearly, given the title of one of Williams' greatest works, desire was an important subject for him. I argue that *Suddenly* continues the feminist work of *A Streetcar Named Desire* through its exploration of female desire and the strictures placed on its possibilities in the social order. (Blanche DuBois is another female character haunted by the memory of a gay man who died by violent means – her dead husband, Alan, a gentle soul that Blanche accidentally discovered having sex with another man. Alan committed suicide after Blanche rebuked him, and the memory of Alan, her rebuke, and his death grievously and enduringly haunt her.)

In her study of 1940s women's cinema, *The Desire to Desire*, Mary Ann Doane glosses psychoanalytic theories of female desire. Her feminist lens illuminates the gendered dynamics of *Suddenly Last Summer*:

> subjectivity in its psychoanalytic formation is always a desiring subjectivity.
> Desire is a form of disengagement – from need, from the referent, from the
> object – which is crucial to the assumption of the speaking subject ... It is
> with the Oedipus complex, the intervention of a third term (the father) in the

mother–child relation and the resulting series of displacements which refor-
mulate the relation of the mother as a desire for a perpetually lost object ...
Distance from the "origin" (the maternal) is the prerequisite to desire; and
insofar as desire is defined as the excess of demand over a need aligned with
the maternal figure, the woman is left behind.[25]

While desire in the Lacanian scenario is intricately associated with loss, the
male gender at least wields the right *to* desire, whether this desire is voyeuristic or fetishistic. In contrast, female desire, which Doane describes in terms
of spectatorship, "can only understood as the confounding of desire."[26]
According to classical psychoanalytic theory, the woman does not even have
the ability to desire in the perverse forms of voyeurism and fetishism. We
can add to Doane's gloss that if "distance from the 'origin' (the maternal) is
the prerequisite to desire," the male homosexual does not make this necessary break from the maternal. For Freud, the male homosexual inhabits his
mother's desire, wanting to love another male as she loved him.

The psychoanalytic valences of these dynamics are important to Williams'
play and to the playwright himself, who was heavily in analysis at the time
of the play's composition. Lawrence S. Kubie, the eminent New York City-
based psychiatrist who treated Williams, took the approach of "cutting off
all his addictions: drink, men, travel, and writing. This strategy of depriva-
tion was a classical Freudian maneuver, predicated on the assumption that
Williams' addictions were a form of acting out."[27] It's easy to see *Suddenly*
as an outpouring of sublimated energies (or as an act of desublimation),
as many critics have. But while "Dr. Sugar" (as Violet calls him when she
learns the Polish meaning of his name) is not a terribly distinctive or impres-
sive character, he comes across as a decent and conscientious man, not as
a parodic figure that reflects Williams' mockery of psychoanalysis. Indeed,
his function in the play is to oppose the repressive regime of Violet's obsessive control, to allow Catharine to speak truth to a particularly formidable
female power.

While Sebastian's desire would appear to be foregrounded in the play,
I argue that it is the desire of the women that centrally fascinates Williams
and that remains the play's chief fascination. Parsing Lacan, Bruce Fink discusses the allure of the symbolic phallus, which incites the subject's desire and
has its phantom origins in the maternal phallus, which does not exist in reality but has a powerful hold on unconscious fantasy. The "obsessive" patient
makes these dynamics salient: "The obsessive's objects are able to cause his
desire as long as their association with the mother is not unveiled. Once this
association is unveiled, the contraband object (mistress, "whore") can no
longer be desired but only idealized (madonna) or abandoned."[28] Williams's

work allows us to see that, for all of its brilliant insights, Freudian–Lacanian psychoanalysis fails to account for the intensity and urgency of women's (or gay men's) desire. *Suddenly Last Summer* addresses – redresses – this lack in psychoanalytic thought through its analysis of the stakes involved in the women's appropriation of Sebastian's life, legacy, and body for their own counterpurposes. This is not to suggest that Sebastian has not appropriated them – far from it. Indeed, his desire is the most appropriative of all, connected to his social and sexual tourism, which the play as I see it submits to a class critique. Sebastian is an extremely sympathetic victim of an unimaginable crime, yet we are also invited to maintain a distance from him; to see him as someone who "devours" the economically disenfranchised youths of places like Cabeza de Lobo. His predatory attitude toward them likely reflects his internalized homophobia – but also, inescapably, reflects a sociopathic indifference to others' suffering. This indifference is also embodied by Violet in her utter solipsism and disregard for Catharine's suffering and her fate should Violet's plan succeed.

The procuring theme, which the play makes famous, cries out for a feminist critique. Sebastian's use of the women to attract his sexual quarries evinces the "traffic in women" that sociologists and literary and queer theorists have maintained as the crux of patriarchal relations and theories of sexual difference. Drawing on the work of René Girard and Gayle Rubin, Eve Kosofsky Sedgwick developed a theory of triangulated desire: males express whatever desires they have for one another, including sexual desire if it exists, through the exchange of women.[29] Sebastian exchanges his mother and cousin for sexual goods, turning them into alluring spectacle. Indeed, he deploys the male gaze for his own ends, beaming it onto the women's bodies and inciting male desire while he hides in the shadows – observing, waiting, wanting. That his exploitation of them comes from need having become incessant demand – from reserves, one imagines, of pain and fear and longing – qualifies but does not mitigate its brutality. Having said that, though, it's clear that Violet at least has lived through her son – here, the exploitation seems mutual, made possible by her hysterical fantasy of his chastity. She avers to the doctor: "My son, Sebastian, was chaste. Not c-h-a-s-e-d! Oh, he was chased in that way of spelling it, too, we had to be very fleet-footed I can tell you, with his looks and charm ... I mean he was c-h-a-s-t-e! – Chaste."[30] Williams invites a Lacanian reading through his brilliant exposure of Violet's own conflicted and duplicitous agenda through her use of language. His orthographic rendering of her speech allows us to see how thoroughly language – its manipulations and mutilations – expresses and embodies the subject's desire. But if psychoanalysis maintains that the subject's desire revolves around the impossible goad of the maternal phallus, Williams upends this idea, forcing us – allowing us – to see that Violet (as mother) desires the homosexual phallus, even if both her desire and the specificity of its source are unknowledgeable. No sooner does Violet insist on her son's chaste purity than she establishes that his beauty made him a natural sexual prospect; no sooner does she describe him as an object of sexual fascination than she includes herself in his magnetic sexual appeal: "*we* had to be very fleet-footed I can tell you, with his looks and charm."[31] Indeed, she seems unable to stop herself from revealing the incestuous foundation of her obsession with him: "We were a famous couple. People didn't speak of Sebastian and his mother or Mrs. Venable and her son, they said, 'Sebastian and Violet, Violet and Sebastian are staying at the Lido … have taken a house in Biarritz for the season,' and every appearance, every time we appeared, attention was centered on *us*! – *everyone else! Eclipsed*!"[32] As if responding to the Freudian reading of male homosexual desire as narcissistic and rooted in an identification with the mother's desire, Violet immediately follows up this self-aggrandizing rant with: "Vanity? Ohhhh, no Doctor, you can't call it that," to which the Doctor quietly retorts: "I didn't call it that."[33]

Violet's denial of her son's homosexuality takes the larger form of a denial that he possesses any kind of sexuality at all. It also takes the form of denying any knowledge about her role as sexual procurer for him. (If Catharine's view is accurate, Violet does not know she played this role – a subtle gesture of sympathy on the part of the young woman for her tyrannical oppressor.) Yet Violet's revelry in the incestuous image of them as a glamorous, buzz-generating couple threatens to expose the lie; only Sebastian's lack of sexual interest in women could facilitate this public show, unless the incestuous nature of it took literal form. Moreover, Violet sees in the handsome young doctor a fit match – mate? – for her dead son: "You would have liked my son, he would have been charmed by you. My son, Sebastian, was not a family snob or a money snob … He was a snob about personal charm in people, he insisted upon good looks in people around him."[34]

Suddenly has its basis in Williams's conflicted relationships with his mother Edwina and his sister Rose Isabel Williams. Catharine, locked in mortal combat with Violet, perceives the bond she maintains with her son as something he wanted to break – and indeed did break: "something had broken, that string of pearls that old mothers hold their sons by like a – sort of a – sort of – *umbilical* cord, *long – after*."[35] Williams had an agonized but deeply emotionally connected relationship to both women. He was devastated to learn that his mother agreed to the bilateral prefontal lobotomy that was performed on the mentally ill Rose in 1943.[36] One of the indicators of her mental illness was a tendency to speak in sexually provocative language and to shock others with graphic sexual imagery, according to reports. Fascinatingly, Catharine needs to speak about having witnessed socially forbidden sexual acts, and for this she faces the same invasive procedure that Rose underwent, maternal authority being the decisive factor in both art and life. But Catharine is also the victim of horrific sight; witnessing Sebastian's fate has left her in a traumatic state, possessed by the image of horror. (As Cathy Carruth has theorized in a now-standard study, "to be traumatized is precisely to be possessed by an image or event."[37]).

Anne Meacham, who starred as Catharine in the first, off-Broadway production of the play, reported that Williams "was absolutely terrified of this play."[38] Its themes also touched on the intense relationship he had with his devoted agent, Audrey Wood. He would not allow Wood to come to casting sessions or to rehearsals; he delayed even showing her the play. Donald Spoto reports that Meacham recalled: "Audrey was a mother to him in a way that Edwina never could be, and this may account for a hesitation that would otherwise seem inexplicable. In this play he accused himself of 'devouring' others by buying sex and by paying for counterfeit emotions," modeling Sebastian on himself, Violet on Edwina.[39] Violet, in particular, most likely reflected negative aspects of his relationship with the beloved Audrey Wood, a powerful woman invested in a homosexual author's art. (Williams, in a notorious action, abruptly fired the devoted Wood in the 1970s, when his plays met continuous failure with critics and audiences.)

Catharine's traumatic narrative – which makes her role one of the greatest female roles in American drama – chiefly recounts the scene and the spectacle of Sebastian's murder. While the murder is of deep significance, I argue that her narrative also serves as a defiant expression of her needs and demands; it is her opportunity to express her autonomy as a desiring subject. When the Doctor encourages her to: "Go on with the vision, Miss Catharine," she immediately responds, "*Oh, I'm going on, nothing could stop it now.*"[40] She claims the momentous occasion of her narrative performance for herself, now no longer needing the Doctor's approbation or goad. Given that female sexual desire was submitted to the same regime of silence that engulfed homosexual desire in American culture of the 1950s, Catharine's climactic narrative, while not about her active pursuit of her own desires, nevertheless echoes and extends her earlier declarations of sexual interest and aversive accounts of amorous adventure. Catharine understands herself as a sexual transgressor as well as adventurer, as her pursuit of married men evinces. As we have established, it is precisely her own sexual history and awareness of its implications for both the social order and herself that allows Catharine to understand her role in Sebastian's sexual campaign with such crystal clarity. If not a willing procurer, she is certainly a knowing one. This makes her role as witness – and more precisely, *what* she witnesses – something of a punitive act on the part of the play; she must confront an act of mayhem that shames and terrifies her, even as it renders her powerless to stop it.

Of most significance, Catharine's climactic narrative reflects her own status as intertextual artist. She matches Violet's example and creates horror tableau in her description of the urchins who will devour Sebastian: "they made gobbling noises with their little black mouths, stuffing their little black fists to their mouths and making those gobbling noises, with frightful grins!"[41] Her evocation of Sebastian's horrible fate at the youth's hands is an aesthetic rendering of it, taking this earlier description further:

> Torn or cut parts of him away with their hands or knives or maybe those jagged tin cans they made music with, they had torn bits of him away and stuffed them into those gobbling fierce little empty black mouths of theirs ... Sebastian, what was left of him, that looked like a big white paper-wrapped bunch of red roses had been *torn, thrown, crushed*! – against that blazing white wall.[42]

The contrast between the "black mouths" of the youths and the "red roses" of the murdered poet's remains renders the scene of death a riotous pageant of opposing color imagery. Catharine's apprehension of the dead body seeks and discovers a poetic metaphor for the ravages it has undergone, and memorializes the tenderness and vulnerability of her cousin in life. Again, the language models the action it describes – his body has been *torn, thrown, crushed*, as if Sebastian has been torn down from his throne in order to be crushed. The true horror here is that Sebastian's poetic fantasies of self-immolation have been met with, overtaken by, forces far more rapacious than his own fantasies.

NOTES

1 Williams, *Suddenly Last Summer in Plays*, eds. Gussow and Holdich (New York: Library of America, 2000), 140, capital letters in the original.
2 Williams, *Suddenly*, 141, ellipsis in the original.
3 Chauncey, *Gay New York* (New York: Basic, 1994), 286.
4 Williams, *Suddenly*, 128.
5 "Sadomasochistic desires function like a virus in *Suddenly Last Summer*, infecting the surviving characters with camp potential as they grapple with the repercussions of Sebastian's sexual appetite, which ultimately consumed him," argues Tison Pugh in "Camp Sadomasochism in Tennessee Williams's Plays," *Texas Studies in Literature and Language* 58.1 (2016), 40. While I concur that desire goes viral in this play, and while it's tempting to see an endemic archness in Violet in particular, I do not see this as a camp play at all.
6 Williams, *Suddenly*, 118.
7 Williams, *Suddenly*, 101.

8 Williams, *Suddenly*, 102.

9 Hurt, "Williams and Melville," *Modern Drama* 3.4 (1960), 396.

10 Williams, *Suddenly*, 105.

11 "While she is literally right," Hurt observes about her statement that she and Sebastian "saw something Melville hadn't written about": "Melville's view of the islands was ironically similar to Sebastian's. To him, as to Sebastian, the islands were a place where the masks of civilization fell away and the cruel face of God could be seen" (Hurt, 398).

12 Williams, *Suddenly*, 105.

13 Williams, *Suddenly*, 147, italics in the original.

14 Herman Melville, "The Encantadas," in *The Piazza Tales* (Evanston: Northwestern University Press, 1987), 129.

15 Dillingham, *Melville's Short Fiction* (Athens: University of Georgia Press, 1977), 78–9.

16 Melville, *The Encantadas*, 132.

17 Poteet, *Gay Men in Modern Southern Literature* (New York: Lang, 2006), 82.

18 This story was published in Williams's *One Arm: And Other Stories* (1st ed.) (New York: New Directions, 1948).

19 Hurt, "Williams and Melville," 399.

20 Paller, *Gentlemen Callers* (New York: Palgrave, 2005), 147–8.

21 Hooper, *Sexual Politics in the Work of Tennessee Williams* (New York: Cambridge University Press, 2012), 73.

22 Hooper, *Sexual Politics*, 77.

23 Krips, *Fetish: An Erotics of Culture* (Ithaca: Cornell University Press, 1999), 52.

24 Williams, *Suddenly*, 131.

25 Doane, *Desire to Desire* (Bloomington: Indiana University Press, 1987), 11–12.

26 Doane, *Desire to Desire*, 13.

27 John Lahr, *Tennessee Williams: Mad Pilgrimage of the Flesh* (New York: Norton, 2014), 348.

28 Fink, *Lacan to the Letter* (Minneapolis: University of Minnesota Press, 2004), 34–5.

29 Sedgwick, *Between Men* (New York: Columbia University Press, 1985), 21–8.

30 Williams, *Suddenly*, 110.

31 Williams, *Suddenly*, 110, emphasis added.

32 Williams, *Suddenly*, 111, emphasis in the original.

33 Williams, *Suddenly*, 111.

34 Williams, *Suddenly*, 109.

35 Williams, *Suddenly*, 138, emphasis in the original.

36 Lahr, *Mad Pilgrimage*, 361.

37 Caruth, "Introduction," in *Trauma: Explorations in Memory*, ed. Cathy Caruth (Baltimore: Johns Hopkins University Press, 1995), 5.

38 Donald Spoto, *Kindness to Strangers: the Life of Tennessee Williams* (Boston: Little, Brown, 1985), 221.

39 Spoto, 221.

40 Williams, *Suddenly*, 144, emphasis in the original.

41 Williams, *Suddenly*, 142–3.

42 Williams, *Suddenly*, 147, emphasis in the original.

15

GERT HEKMA

Dutch Gay Novels of the 1950s and 1960s

Introduction

Between the late nineteenth century and the beginning of the Second World War (1889–1940), approximately 22 homosexual novels were written in the Netherlands. Some of these novels arose out of the Modernist movement, while others are strongly based in psychiatric theories of homosexuality, the homosexual rights movement of those years or a mixture of these perspectives. There had been an upsurge of novels with emancipatory and informative aims before 1911, and even more so at the end of the Great War – in which Holland did not participate. In 1911, an anti-homosexual law, article 248bis, was enacted in the Netherlands. This law mandated a different age of consent for heterosexual and homosexual relations between minors and adults; the age remained 16 for the former and was raised to 21 for the latter. The law can be seen as a political response by Christian parties to greater sexual and literary visibility and activism, and was part of a broader set of moral laws on contraception, abortion, pimping, pornography and sex work.[1] This legislation also led to increased levels of activism and visibility, including more gay novels and the start of the first homosexual rights movement: the Dutch chapter of Hirschfeld's *Wissenschaftlich–humanitären Komitee* (NWHK – the Scientific–Humanitarian Committee) in 1912.

After 1945, the Dutch social situation changed. These changes became even more evident after 1960, when the sexual revolution radically transformed Dutch society and its sexual culture through secularization, democratization, individualization, the advent of new political groups such as Provo and the rise of sexual reformist and gay movements. This chapter will discuss the rise of the gay (erotic) novel in that period and the associated changes in contents and contexts. The number of such novels rose dramatically: from 22 before 1940, four in the 1940s and ten in the 1950s to some 36 in the 1960s. This amounts to the same number of books in ten years as in the 72 years prior. The main question is: how did gay novels change during the sexual revolution – or, more broadly, from the end of the Second World War to 1970?

The Social Context Before 1940

At the end of the nineteenth century, the Netherlands witnessed (as did other European countries) new debates about prostitution, sexual laws, erotic literature, medicalization of perversion and the contents, causes and prevention of homosexuality.[2] After a period in which sex work was 'medically controlled' (meaning that police registered prostitutes and doctors checked them for diseases), pimping and bordellos were gradually forbidden, following a long debate on 'legalised lewdness' from the 1860s to the 1890s. New legislation in 1886 raised the age of consent to 16 for all – and, in 1911, to 21 for homosexuals (both male and female) – forbade certain forms of pornography and made abortion and contraception more difficult to obtain, among other issues. Authors of the Modernist movement of the 1880s started to write novels and poetry on sexual issues, taking leads from mainly French examples. Psychiatrists started to discuss sexual psychopathy in line with the work of Karl Heinrich Ulrichs and Richard von Krafft-Ebing, with homosexuality and perversions being viewed as identities with a cause in nature instead of vices resulting from uncontrolled lusts.[3] Liberals lost political prominence and saw the rise of a more conservative Christian sexual agenda.[4]

At the turn of the century, there was a tension between liberal tendencies that had recently developed in arts and in society on the one hand, and the assertiveness of the Protestants and Catholics on the other. The latter began to organise 'pillars': their own communities, which soon would include not only religious institutions like churches and monasteries but also political parties, newspapers, trade unions, schools and universities, sport clubs and other social/cultural services. They even forced liberals and socialists to create their own pillars – although these were not nearly as encompassing. Even economic activities, such as shops and factories, would become the domain of the pillars. The openness of the *fin de siècle* made experiments and new initiatives – such as medical and pseudomedical literature on homo/sexuality and gay themes – possible, but not without objections.

In these years, there was also confusion as to the direction society should take: secular or Christian, liberal or socialist. Alongside feminism, homosexuality was a major issue. Furthermore, although liberals and socialists were seen as more sexually tolerant, they were rarely happy to be aligned with sexual liberalism or homosexual topics.

The First Period of Male–Male Novels[5]

The first gay novels appeared in 1888 and 1891. Five distinctly gay books were published between 1904 and 1909 – including three of the most famous of the pre-1940 era – and another was published in 1911. Between 1916 and 1923, ten rather insignificant homosexual novels were published, representing a high point in this field. Between 1929 and 1935, another five books were released – the last of their kind until after the Second World War.

Critical reception of the Modernist, sensitivist and decadent 'homosexual' novels of Louis Couperus (1891, 1905/6) and Jacob Israël de Haan (1904, 1908) was generally positive regarding literary quality, but negative regarding subject matter. Notably, a word like 'homosexual' was not often mentioned in these books, although they had been influenced by the medical literature (Lucien von Römer in Couperus's case, and Arnold Aletrino in De Haan's). After the new law was introduced in 1911, there was a subsequent increase in novels that emphasized medical theories of an 'inborn' homosexuality. Exemplary of this was Exler's *Levensleed* (*Life's Grief*, 1911), which explained and applied Hirschfeld's theories and contained an introduction by him. Most of these novels sympathised with the suffering of homosexuals. They often portrayed the main characters' misery or death by suicide, and asked for pity for those poor third genders. Often, too, they offered the message that homosexuals are able to live a chaste life and could be healed by hard labour. Most novels cast the homosexuals as youngsters who have recently learned about their homosexuality, live in the city and have artistic professions. Coming out of the closet in that period was unthinkable, and only one novel depicts a homosexual subculture.

Although most theories of the day recognized homosexuality as sexual attraction between opposites (gay feminine with straight masculine; young with old; lower with higher class; sex worker with client; sadist and masochist, and so on), half of the novels show couples who have equal relations – probably because they show ideal love relations that are not overtly sexual – while other novels depicted real, often unequal sexual relations. That was an understandable side of the apologetic literature of the time: it discussed the lives of homosexuals, but rarely their sexuality. Anal sex was often dismissed as highly uncommon – even abject – for homosexuals. The novels of Couperus and De Haan clearly hinted at sex, including anal sex, between unequal partners. The illustrated *Youthful Sinners in Constantinople* by Feenstra Kuiper (1905) offers seductive homosexual texts and images under a veil of moralistic warnings against male prostitutes and bordellos. These three authors also added an intergenerational aspect to their stories, as they had an overt fascination with young men.

These novels form part of a homosexual tradition or 'canon'. They quote certain names like Oscar Wilde, David and Jonathan, Michelangelo and Shakespeare, and doctors von Römer, Aletrino, Krafft-Ebing and Hirschfeld. The titles often refer to gay thematics – grief, masquerade, difference, isolation, etc. – and were not particularly successful in terms of sales. A few homosexual novels in the early 1930s were more influential. One of these authors was Jef Last, first communist and later leftist, and most famous as a guide of André Gide on his travels to the Soviet Union.[6] Last's novels were set among young fishermen on the island of Urk and in Morocco. After 1945, he was active in the gay movement and wrote two more homoerotic novels. Simon Vestdijk became a well-known writer of non-gay books, but did write one homosexual novel in 1935. Most of the authors from this early period, who are now viewed as homosexual (like De Haan and Couperus), were married – including Lucien von Römer. The same was true for Aletrino and Last, who may have been bisexual. In 1939, the lawyer Benno Stokvis published a first Dutch set of autobiographical stories about gays and lesbians. This was quite exceptional, and only repeated in the Netherlands on a smaller scale (three instead of 35 narratives by Riedé in 1970).

The Post-War Period: 1945–1960

The dominant figure in gay literature in the second half of the twentieth century was Gerard van het Reve (1923–2006; later Gerard Reve). He was seen as one of the two principal Dutch novelists of that period – the other being Willem Frederik Hermans. In the mid-1960s, Reve became a leading spokesperson for the sexual revolution. Among his queer stories was a depiction of him having sex with God, who had returned to Earth in the form of a donkey (1965). In 1968, he won a highly publicized court case in which a Christian member of parliament accused him of blasphemy. In the third and final ruling, the Dutch Supreme Court accepted the argument that he had expressed his private beliefs, which included the possibility of having sex with a god who had been reincarnated as an animal. The case was front-page news in Holland and added to Reve's controversial reputation. In 1968, he received the major state prize for literature.[7]

Reve's first novel, *The Evenings* (*De avonden*, 1947), was erotic but not overtly homosexual. At the end of the 1950s, after meeting Angus Wilson and several gay English painters, his work took a sadomasochist and homosexual turn; he used these painters and their friends as characters in his unfinished novel, *The Three Soldiers* (*De drie soldaten*, 1957), which was not very explicit. However, he soon wrote (in English) a highly sadistic gay fantasy, *A Prison Song in Prose*, produced around 1960 and published in

1968, which was accompanied by erotic illustrations of leathermen. From 1963 onward, he started to write unapologetically gay novels that included many 'personal' stories about Catholicism, alcoholism, homosexuality, lovers and sex partners, narratives about torturing young males, friends, literary events and drinking bouts, his daily life and descriptions of seeming nonsense. As mentioned above, the 'donkey' court case made him famous. He moved from communism to Catholicism at a time when most Dutch people were losing faith and many gay men were turning their back on the Church. He was soon living with two friends in an open relationship, and invented a fetish that became known as 'Revism', referring to his preferred sexual triangle of a male adolescent partner who he 'offered' to his beloved for love and torture. Reve went on to make statements against the working classes and ethnic minorities – but, given his ironic tone, it remained unclear whether he was discriminating against these groups. He also spoke out against homosexuals, who he thought were cowardly because, in his view, they never dared to come out or speak out for themselves. In the 1960s, Reve became the embodiment of the modern homosexual: out of the closet, masculine, a man with many male lovers and free of shame.

Reve's reticence in the 1950s was common in the post-war period. The few writers of gay novels in those years had some difficulty dealing with the subject. Progressive tendencies in society flourished immediately after the war, but quickly faded away. Tensions emerged between the pillar system and new existentialist approaches in the arts that stressed the absurd and the senseless. Reve's first book very much fed into these feelings among young people and made him typical of the post-war generation. Social and sexual openings in wider society took longer to come to the forefront, but did so fully in the 1960s. This was the case in Reve's personal life and in the social movement of homosexuals.

The Post-War Gay Novels

Ab Visser's (1945) post-war novel – a historical account of the persecutions of sodomites in the small village of Faan in 1731 – is atypical precisely because it is historical. Partly based on true stories, it focuses on the local judge Rudolf de Mepse (his name, more often written as Mepsche, is the book's title), the clergyman van Byler (author of a classic book on the evil of sodomy, both in the novel and in reality) and the 22 men who received the death penalty for sodomy. In the aftermath of the war, its comparison of the persecution of Jews to that of sodomites is significant. It inverts the roles of the past by presenting earthly and heavenly judges as cruel perpetrators of murder, and the innocent offenders as victims.

The subsequent set of relevant books is again atypical. Johan Alberts's drama about a court case for article 248bis, *Recht* (*Justice*, 1950), depicts the son of the judge being romantically involved with another youngster whose older love, a 'Dutch Plato', is the accused. Blackmail is now used against the father, who acquits the suspect with a glowing speech referencing Plato and Kinsey. In 1952, Alberts also wrote a pamphlet about sexuality and government. Van Andel (1948) published two small volumes of homoerotic poetry and prose for the Dutch gay movement (COC), the latter consisting of three romantic stories. Jac van Hattum was a pre-war author of poetry and short stories with a good reputation who continued to write up until the late 1960s. His collection *Mannen en katten* (*Men and Cats*, 1947) has homoerotic themes; it starts with a story of the same name in which two nude men are hitting each other with cats while salt is smeared in their bloody wounds. The story concludes with the exasperated pair embracing each other just before they die.

Simon Vestdijk's post-war novel *De kellner en de levenden* (*The Kellner and the Living*, 1949) briefly deals with the topic of homosexuality. It is a novel of existentialism and magical realism that includes a homosexual actor, who claims that most inverts are half-homosexuals and are able to have sexual relations with women. Another well-known pre-war author was A.H. Nijhoff, who wrote a very verbose, existentialist novel on the ethical dilemmas of war. A lesbian who had married one of the most renowned Dutch poets, she later had a relationship with the sculptress Marlow Moss. Her novel *De vier doden* (*The Four Dead*, 1950) is about a male protagonist, Evert, who revenges himself against a homophobe; it includes several gay and lesbian narratives and has a message of tolerance and anti-discrimination.[8] Existentialism, with its emphasis on individuality and secularism, was an ideal context within which to consider homosexuality.

Other books would move homosexual literature into the future. In 1954, the novel *Paul's portret* (*Paul's Portrait*) by Frans Berni (pseudonym of Rein Valkhoff, author of children's books) was published. This is an old-fashioned book in keeping with 1920s novels about the difficult destiny of homosexuals. A 20-year-old son of a Catholic family comes out to his father and desires to embrace his sexual identity while keeping his faith, but his father desperately wants him to hide his 'homophilia'[9]: to not speak about, dress or behave like a homosexual. Nature and physical labour are the proposed solutions. In 1956, Winnie Pendèl published her prize-winning novel *Ik ga weg, tot ziens* (*I Am Leaving, Goodbye,*), a relational drama between two students who fall in love. Many of the scenes portray unspoken sexual tension, and as a literary relational drama it is new. Overall, however, it depicts a love that dare not speak its name.

In the course of just three years, the divergence between the narratives of Berni and Blaman could not be greater. The latter was the leading Dutch lesbian author; she wrote a charming story, 'Vader, moeder en zoon' ('Father, Mother and Son') in her collection *Overdag* (*By Day*, 1957). The father in the story becomes estranged from his wife and alienated from his son through the monotonous routine of daily life and work. One day he comes home to find his son in his bedroom, expressively dancing and passionately kissing another young man. When he eventually accepts his son's homosexuality, marital intimacy and domestic harmony are both restored. The story offers a message that could not be more different from Berni's.

The books by Berni and Pendèl portray what became a key theme of gay literature: the existential difficulty of young men living with an 'alternative' sexuality. This theme was already present in Reve, as well as in Kossmann's *De moord op Arend Zwigt* (*The Murder on AZ*, 1951). In the latter, two boys of different socioeconomic classes run away from their homes, taking money from the shop of the poorer boy's family for alcohol and prostitutes. Their daringness develops into a close bond that gradually weakens when confronted with the hardships of their travels. The novel plays out as highly homoerotic, but contains no explicit sexual references.[10]

Cees Nooteboom, a newcomer at the time, is now one of the best-known Dutch travel writers. The themes of mysterious sexuality and leaving home are the starting point of his first novel *Philip and the Others* (1955), in which the main character (Philip) first visits his unmarried homosexual uncle at the age of ten. He discovers his uncle's sexual secrets through the objects in his home and by a neighbour who calls the uncle a 'faggot'. Philip learns much more about him during a second visit at age 16, when he stays for two years in his uncle's house before moving off into the wider world. There is no nuclear family in this book, in which the theme of breaking free from social conventions is inextricable from that of travel.

Bob en Daphne (1955), a series of books by Han B. Aalberse (pseudonym of Johannes van Keulen), discusses the budding eroticism of children and includes scenes of both incest and homosexuality. The main character, Bob, is just 14 years old. The book was initially forbidden, but the ban was lifted in the 1960s. Notably, besides being an editor of sex education booklets, van Keulen was also the publisher of the first Dutch translation of Nabokov's *Lolita*, in 1958.

One of the leading alternative Dutch poets, Simon Vinkenoog, wrote *Zo lang te water. Een alibi* (*That Long Into Water: An alibi*, 1955), which included some probably autobiographical homosexual scenes. In the book, a young man visits an artist and decides to stay for two nights. The young man's father subsequently informs the police and beats his son, which the police also go on to do, but it does not become a criminal case (homosexual sex with minors under 21 years was still a crime in Holland). The young man eventually receives sexual lessons about the 'other' love from a doctor, yet experiments one more time before going back to women – going from male to female love.

In Johan Fabricius's *Jongensspel* (*Youth Game*, 1963), the real 'Baarn murder' that shocked the country is fictionalized. Three adolescents hide a 14-year-old petty criminal from the police; they eventually kill him and throw his body in an empty well. The story received several treatments (three novels, a play and a film); in this early version, the oldest of the three is regularly insulted for his homosexuality. Although the other two boys first attempt to kill the 14-year-old petty criminal, it is the eldest who finally does so, with an axe. The main topic is the murder, but the underlying issues are very much about social class and sexuality.

Jef Last wrote two novels with homosexual topics in the 1930s and another in 1962, the short *De jeugd van Judas* (*The Youth of Judas*) – another story about the sexual confusion of youth. The story focuses on the homosexual Karel and Jewish David from the fishermen's village Katwijk, who enjoy a beautiful summer loving each other. Then, after an anti-Semitic episode, the boys find a complex resolution. The story is remarkable for its portrayal of homosexual love, as well as solidarity between Jews and gays.

In 1960, the publishing house Enclave printed two booklets – *Costa Brava* and *Vervolgde minderheid* (*Persecuted Minority*) – by its owner, Frits Bernard, under the pseudonym Victor Servatius. Both novels are about man–boy relations; the first takes place in the Spanish Civil War and the second in Amsterdam. Enclave was the first paedophile organization in the Netherlands, and marks the beginning of the split between the gay and paedophile movements. The first novella describes a Venezuelan man who saved the 12-year-old son of a murdered right-wing leader by transporting him out of Spain and across the French border, by car and by boat. The man and the boy love each other, but the boy's uncle, who took responsibility for him after his arrival in France, told each that the other was dead. When they met after the Second World War, they realized the deceit and that their love had become impossible – the boy had become a married man. The story in the second novella centres on a high-school student who falls in love with his teacher. After sharing some intimate moments, they are arrested. The elder lover is ruined: he loses his job, house and love. The book includes an afterword that speaks to the prejudices against homosexuality and pedophilia. Interestingly, however, both novels are written from the adults' perspectives, affording little attention to the boys' emotions.

Subtle treatments of the 'other love' were blown away by Gerard Reve, whose work is both homoerotic and violent. His first book of letters, which soon becomes the main form of his literature, is full of information about homosexuality and a mixture of small talk, afterthoughts and stories from his personal life, typically discussing four major themes: religion, alcohol, sex and death. In *Op weg naar het einde* (*On the Road to the End*, 1963), he writes about his visit to a PEN conference in Edinburgh in 1962, where he attacks an Indian writer who wants to keep homosexuality secret. This first book of letters, or confessional literature, is a major success and paves the way for both his later books and all kinds of gay literature to follow. His success in the late 1960s and early 1970s coincides with the sexual revolution, when many Dutch citizens changed their ideas from conservative and religious to liberal and secular.

There were several different schools of gay literature in the 1960s. Modernist writers begin discussing the topic in their novels – sometimes in passing, sometimes with a magical-realist twist. Magical realists included Marc Andries (1963), Ewout Vanvugt (1963, 1964), Enno Develing (1964), Plomp (1968), Venema (1969) and the prolific writer Astère Michel Dhondt (1965, 1966, 1968, 1969). Andries's *Het geduld* (*The Patience*, 1963) starts with the main character abstractly searching for a girlfriend. His search becomes more concrete with a friend from his boarding school, who becomes an object of his obsessive thoughts, as they don't dare to have sex with girls. Vanvugt's novel *Een bijzonder vreemde dief* (*A Very Strange Thief*, 1963) has a looser and more experimental structure. It describes six months in the life of a young man. Most scenes are heterosexual, but others are about male prostitution, queer bashing, homosexuality, masturbation; incest, pedophilia, sadomasochism and a man who feels that he is a woman – the full spectrum of what was considered perverse at the time. In Vanvugt's second book, *Darwin en gezellen* (*Darwin and Company*, 1964), homosexuality is the central theme. He uses different perspectives, the main being that of a 19-year-old father who earns his money by having a love affair with a rich gay man who pays for his house and his multiple travels. The love affair ends in tragedy; a sour ending to a confused novel, but an important representation of a transitional period in queer literature.

Develing's book *Alberto en ik* (*A and I*, 1964) features two main male characters: a stateless Portuguese from Hong Kong and a European official, who are friends and become interchangeable. They drive the same motorcycle, play in the same soccer team, visit the same sex worker and have the same girlfriend. The novel includes many magical stories that show more heterosexuality than homosexuality, but the overall perspective is bleak. *De ondertrouw. Een somber herenboek* (*Notice of Marriage: A Somber*

Gentlemen's Book, 1968) by hippie author Hans Plomp is somewhat similar to Vanvugt's (another hippie author) second book. Here, the girlfriend of a 16-year-old secondary school student gets pregnant while the student starts to live, on and off, with an older wealthy gentleman (based on the rich gay publisher, Johan Polak) whom he exploits and steals from. The young man becomes self-centred, while the gentleman continues to adore him. The novel again displays some magical elements. Adriaan Venema's *Van een bloedrode manchet en een kooikershondje* (*From a Blood-Red Collar and a Decoy-Man's Dog*, 1969) describes the life of a young gay man who becomes an escort. The novel is a mix of realistic and magical stories of gay life in and around Amsterdam. It ends with scenes of ruin and revolt and the flooding of Amsterdam – a loose allegorical reference to the city having become a new Sodom.

A variation in this magical-realist tradition is the very active Flemish author, Astère Michel Dhondt. His work describes a fantasy utopia in which youngsters rule; later considered paedophilic, it includes (apart from novels) poetry, films and pictures of boys. He focuses on kids in satin shorts who subject adults to their wishes as revenge for what they did to them. His various books are variations on a theme, the style and subject matter of which is established in his first, *God in Flanders*. This depicts a dreamy kids' world where magical things happen (people can fly, for instance). In his second novel, he explains that he and his books are opposed to 'mind-killing' sex, sports, history, media, uniforms and masses, to name a few of his least favourite things.

Jac van Hattum wrote gay-tinged stories, such as *Wolfsklauw* (*Wolf's Claw*, 1962), with a literary – and certainly queer – quality. One is about a young man who imitates women so well that no one discovers his play with gender roles. His lover doesn't want him to do so, but forces stronger than himself make him do it, causing him personal grief. Another of van Hattum's stories is about a not-very-strong, half-German boy who would have liked to be a slave in Roman times. As a youngster he loves the brutishness of Calvinist Biblical language, and as a young adult the authority of Nazi speech. In the Second World War he joins the German army, and dies far away on the Eastern Front while his German mother joins the Dutch resistance. In 1965, van Hattum publishes the story of the murder of a young, decadent and well-to-do queer who lives with his aunt, the *Ketchupcancer* (her nickname and the title of the book). Van Hattum's fascination with violence anticipates the later literary fascination with sadomasochism.

Although both Van Hattum and Reve preferred more traditional Biblical language, the ways they presented homosexuality could not have been more different: van Hattum being closeted and Reve being completely 'out' since 1963. They knew each other and shared an interest in sadomasochism, as seen in a poem Reve sent to van Hattum:

> Laatst geseld' ik een mooie jongen,
> die 'k, uitgekleed, met riemen bond,
> Hij heeft voor mij van pijn gezongen
> bij elke zweepslag op zijn kont.
>
> [Lately, I caned a cute guy
> that I, undressed, bound with straps.
> He sang for me out of pain
> with each lash on his ass.]¹¹

In 1959 (when this poem was written), both authors were friendly with each other; however, Reve would later be annoyed by van Hattum for his homosexual self-hate and for being closeted. Reve preferred the courageous author Jaap Harten, a man of a younger generation (1930) who started out as a poet. Harten's first prose work, *Operatie Montycoat* (1964), includes a story of the same name about a young man who hangs out with a Canadian sergeant after the liberation of Holland from Nazi rule, and eventually travels with him to Paris, where they explore the gay scene together. His next gay book (1968) is about the lively Berlin gay subculture of the 1930s, with its transvestites, hustlers, soldiers and noblemen. Homosexuality is shown as something culturally constructed, and the destruction of the gay subculture as the work of the Nazis. The destruction of the gay subculture gives an impression of the Nazis' total ruin in 1945. In 1969, Harten published a book of letters sent to him by other writers, including Reve and Hanlo, in which homosexual themes are specifically addressed.

Other notable authors from the period include Huub Janssen, Steven Membrecht, Wim Heerings, Tiemo Hofman, Max Heymans, Harry Thomas, Robert van Maroey, and Willem de Vuyst. Janssen (1910–84) was from an older generation, and the lover of popular gay comedian Wim Sonneveld. He produced several novels and a collection of stories. In 1966, he published his only explicitly homosexual novel, *Neef Constant is onbereikbaar* (*Nephew Constant is Unreachable*). This is an old-fashioned novel in ceremonious language that relates to past times. Steven Membrecht, the pseudonym of Jochem van Beek, was a prolific author who published many books before and after 1970, several of which can be considered gay. His book of short stories, *27 verhalen uit de homosuele sfeer* (*27 Stories From the Homosexual Sphere*, 1969), is more psychological than sociological; it is about the double identities and self-hate of gays. Wim Heerings was one of the first authors to experiment with pornography, an example of which is his book, *Schandknaap van Napels* (*Hustler of Naples*, 1961), about a poor boy (Marco) who loses his parents and becomes a member of a gang of young criminals. Although the story is polysexual and includes all kinds of perverse scenes, the book itself is illustrated with pictures of a nude straight couple. Heerings also wrote *Begeerde hippie* (*Desired Hippie*) and *Jongensslipjes en slippertjes. De homoliefde van Maurice en Johan* (*Boys' Briefs and Quickies: The Gay Love of Maurice and Johan*).

Another productive author was Tiemo Hofman, alias Paul Monty, who was the only Dutch gay man to receive an indemnification as a homosexual victim of the Second World War. He tried to make money by writing stories about his life as a steward on passenger boats. In *De nichten* and *De nichten* Part II (*The Sissies*, 1965, 1966), he wrote about his many sexual meetings – never in detail – aboard and ashore all over the world. His third book, *Zo waren zij geschapen* (*Thus They Were Made*, 1966), was a novel that featured two farmers' sons, a lesbian sister, their many lovers and a homophobic mother who finally recognizes the error of her ways. More popular than Hofman was Max Heymans, Holland's first fashion designer, whose campy autobiography *Knal* (*Pop*, 1966) features a cover of him in one of his own dresses. He became famous because of his many appearances in the gossip columns of the main Dutch daily. The book tells about his coming out, a visit to a doctor who tells him he is born 'like this' ('*zo zijn*' in Dutch, which he likes better than 'homo' as a term) and that there is nothing wrong with that. The book describes the quickly expanding homosexual subculture of Amsterdam, where he gives shows in dresses,[12] explores his unmasculine characteristics and explains why fashion designers are so often gay. Many people, Heymans states, object to homosexuality because it is about sexuality and boy prostitution – but, he argues, there is nothing wrong with either. Like Reve, he received fan mail from gay men who feel enlightened by his openness and desire for self-determination in gender and sexual issues.

Harry Thomas was the man of the *Partij voor Homofielen* (Party for Homophiles) who started the Dutch struggle for same-sex marriage and became a kind of one-man gay movement working next to the COC.[13] In 1969, he wrote *Herman. De liefde van een homofiel* (*Herman: The Love of a Homophile*), which is full of sad stories of discrimination and misery, suicide and murder, and marriage and prostitution. His second book, *Een homofiel wordt geslagen* (*A Homophile is Beaten*, 1970), starts with paedophiles and sadomasochists and includes highly sexualized depictions of Dutch gay sadomasochist clubs, which show movies and stage sexual bondage and beating shows, as well as providing male sex workers. Thomas more or less advertises such clubs, but at the same time criticizes the Dutch gay movement COC because it promotes promiscuity rather than monogamy within stable friendships. Another important activist was Robert van Maroey, author of *Zij kregen niet eens een nummer. Een schokkend verhaal over homoseksuelen naar waarheid geschreven* (*They Didn't Even Get a Number: A Shocking True Story about Homosexuals*, 1969) – stories about the difficult and alcohol-drenched lives of gay men, largely set in bars and subcultures.

The final book in this set is Willem de Vuyst, *Mijn vrienden. De martelgang van een homofiel* (*My Friends: The Tormented Ways of a Homophile*, 1969) – the autobiography of a working-class Rotterdam man born in 1902, who has some 16 male lovers, the first being the best and the others mainly unhappy and abusive. He is jailed six times, serves close to five years and is nonetheless against the complete abolition of the law that forbids homosexual relations with minors under 21 years (he proposes an age of 18) because young men, not girls, need protection from men like him. He gives a traditional definition of homosexuality, following in the footsteps of the founder of the homosexual movement Karl Heinrich Ulrichs: 'A homosexual is a boy (man) who is born with a normal male body in which since childhood, a female soul developed' (p. 7). To a certain extent, this is probably representative of quite a few unhappy gay lives at that time[14] – the story takes place mostly during the period in which the anti-homosexual law was actively enforced.

Conclusion

A story by lesbian writer Blaman marks a watershed in the history of the gay novel in the Netherlands.[15] Gerard Reve builds on her liberating view. After these two leading authors, the gay literature of the post-war period becomes more positive about homosexuality. It stops seeing the homosexual as an inborn sexual/gender pervert. Homosexuality becomes a culturally constructed role or identity, rather than a natural and innate condition. The idea that the homosexual is a normal, masculine male who comes out of the closet, goes into the streets and has sex with other gay men becomes the predominant narrative.

Gerard Reve provides the best examples of this. In his work (as in that of Vanvugt, Develing and de Vuyst), young heterosexual men and young male queers enaging in prostitution slowly disappear, as does the figure of the unmasculine queer or 'sissy' who goes for tough men (present in the work of Heymans and Mario). Parallel to this is the frequency with which the chaste paedophile is presented in the literature (an exception being in the depictions of Harry Thomas, in which the paedophile is mixed up with the sadist). Next to boy love, cruelty is part of the work of van Hattum and becomes sadomasochist fantasy in the *oeuvre* of Reve and Thomas. Both men were conservative and religious, also in their gay activism, and propose same-sex marriage. It is remarkable that their more conservative approach allowed for sadomasochism and paedophilia, neither of which the mainstream gay movement endorsed. Mainstream activism was in favour of same-sex adults having loving and stable relations with their equals, but not marriage. Other references to 'perversions' appeared in the literature of this period, and every year between 1965 and 1970 a translation of a book by the polysexual Marquis de Sade appeared in large numbers. There is also a strong magical-realist trend in the literature that suggests a distance from gay themes. Authors embrace writing autobiographical literature for the consumption of other gays with different approaches to homosexuality – often sad stories and, in the case of Hofman and Heerings, endless narratives of erotic exploits – but, like the other authors, these rarely become very sexually explicit. The authors often complain about the destructive attitudes of their own kind: alcoholic, cowardly, in the closet – but promiscuous. These characteristics are ascribed to social discrimination rather than innate qualities. Gay men have to deal with the prejudices and negative feelings of family, workplace, neighbours and the general population. Queer bashing happens; gays are insulted. Realism replaces the existentialism of the immediate post-war period. The topic of travel becomes prominent, and the nuclear family disappears. The books are often about sexual initiation, but remarkably their characters rarely venture into queer bars, parks or restrooms. One gets the impression that they meet each other accidentally, in any place – but rarely in the gay world.

The present-day alphabet soup of LGBT (lesbian, gay, bisexual and transgender) is not present in these novels, as such. Bisexuality occurs everywhere in the books, but is mainly a topic of the sexual fluidity of trade and hustlers; Heerings' porn novels are an example. Transsexualism (as it was then known) is present with the theme of gender inversion, but only becomes prominent as a specific theme in the 1970s. One could say that the trans issue comes to the fore at the moment when gay men become masculine and lose their expected effeminacy, offering space for transgender people to rise out of the ashes of sissies (and butches) in the 1990s. Around 1900, there was a tension between homosexuality and the various influences of new Christian politics, Modernist art and the sexual sciences – with conservative outcomes. In the 1960s, secularization combined with individualization and democratization to produce new, more positive sexual sequels – certainly for gay men. In both periods, the social issue was a sexual issue that resulted in opposite consequences: less, rather than more, legislation and control.

The 1960s can be seen as characterized by a lack of clarity about what gay literature and life mean; in this period, 'gay' encompasses a wide range of gender options and sexual interests, including fetishism, pedophilia and sadomasochism – we are far from homonormativity. The homosexual rights movement was on a breaking point: moving to acceptance of sexual difference (whatever this may mean) and abolishing ideas of sin, crime and disease. Homosexuality was culturally constructed and needed no such explanation as 'being inborn'. The Christian parties that had initiated the anti-gay criminal law article were now at the forefront of the parties that wanted to get rid of it, because it was now finally 'proven' that homosexuals did not – and could not – seduce youngsters into homosexuality. Psychiatrists who had claimed homosexuality was a disease now said 'it was simply the same' as being heterosexual.[16] From the 1950s on, and with great energy in the late 1960s, the Amsterdam gay subculture moved overground (or should we say went underground?) – away from its world of parks and urinals, and into bars and clubs.[17] There was also a shift from ideas of identities and relations being based in gender and sexual *opposites* to being based in *equal* relations: the 'gender inverts' adopted a 'normal' gender (gay men becoming masculine, and butches becoming normal feminine lesbians) and preferring 'normal' men and women like them, with no 'sexual inversion'. The sexuality that had been intergender – queer with trade – now became intrasexual – gay with gay. So novels and real life ran parallel to each other; both showed confusions and new horizons.

In the long run, the largely unrealistic dream of sexual equality worked out positively for gays and lesbians (for example, the introduction of same-sex marriage) and negatively for paedophiles, zoophiles, the BDSM community, sex workers and their clients; the relations between the latter groups were seen as unequal and unacceptable, albeit a bit more accepted in the 1960s and 1970s.[18] Ideas about sexuality radically changed in that time for homosexuals, but less so (or in a different direction) for other so-called sexual minorities. The sexual revolution opened a new world for gays in which they were more 'accepted', but other groups have still to wait for their turn.

NOTES

Thanks to the copyeditor and publisher for their support with the text.

1 On the backgrounds and consequences of this law, see Gert Hekma and Theo van der Meer (eds.), *'Bewaar me voor de waazin van het recht.' Homoseksualiteit en strafrecht in Nederland* (Diemen: AMB, 2011).
2 These developments were different in the various European countries: Germany and France created sexology and medicalized perversion (particularly homosexuality and sadism) and France was strong on erotic literature, while England

saw far fewer of these changes. The Netherlands took a middle position; it was the second European country (after Germany) to have a homosexual rights movement. Belgium had little of all of these until the 1950s. See Wannes Dupont, *Free Floating Evils: A Genealogy of Homosexuality in Belgium*, PhD thesis (Antwerp: University of Antwerp, 2015).

3 For the medical invention of homosexuality and other sexual variations, see Julie Mazaleigue-Labaste, *Les déséquilibrés de l'amour. De la genèse du concept de perversion sexuelle, de la Révolution française à Freud* (Paris: Ithaque, 2014); Harry Oosterhuis, *Step-Children of Nature. Krafft-Ebing, Psychiatry and the Making of Sexual Identity* (Chicago, IL: University of Chicago Press, 2000); and Robert Tobin, *Peripheral Desires: The German Discovery of Sex* (Philadelphia, PA: University of Pennsylvania Press, 2015), among others.

4 See Hekma, *Homoseksualiteit, een medische reputatie. De uitdoktering van de homoseksueel in negentiende-eeuws Nederland* (Amsterdam: SUA, 1987).

5 For the gay novels of this period, see Adriaan Venema, *Homoseksualiteit in de Nederlandse literatuur* (Amsterdam–Brussels: Paris-Manteau, 1972); Gerrit Komrijj, Komrij, *Averechts* (Amsterdam: Arbeiderspers, 1980); Hekma, 'De benoeming van het onnoembare. 'Homoseksueel' proza in het eerste kwart van de twintigste eeuw in Nederland', in F.W. Kuyper & B.C. Sliggers (eds.) *Liber amicorum A.G. van der Steur.* (Haarlem: Schuyt, 1988), 35–60; Maurice van Lieshout, 'Dutch and Flemish Literature', in Claude J. Summers (ed.), *The Gay and Lesbian Literary Heritage* (New York: Henry Holt & Company, 1995), 211–16. For a general overview, see Hekma, *Homoseksualiteit in Nederland van 1730 tot de moderne tijd* (Amsterdam: Meulenhoff, 2004).

6 For his friendship with Gide and the voyage to the Soviet-Union, see Last, *Mijn vriend André Gide* (Amsterdam: van Ditmar, 1966). The books by Gide on this voyage led to ferocious criticism of both writers.

7 See Jan Fekkes, *De God van je tante ofwel het Ezel-proces van Gerard Kornelis van het Reve* (Amsterdam: De Arbeiderspers, 1968); David Bos, 'Vooral protestants opgevoede mensen zullen dit moeilijk kunnen verwerken.' Het proces-van het Reve als vertoning van katholieke en homo-emancipatie', in Agnes Andeweg (ed.) *Seks in de nationale verbeelding* (Amsterdam: Amsterdam University Press, 2015), 47–76.

8 There was one more openly gay novel of this period, written in 1952 but not published until 2005: Hans Warren's *Een vriend voor de schemering* (Amsterdam: Balans, 2005). Warren became famous for his 23-volume diary.

9 Homophilia was used by the post-war gay movement, and so by certain novelists, to desexualize homosexuality and stress its loving (philia) sides.

10 In 1962, Kossmann translated two novels by Leopold Sacher-Masoch, including *Venus in Furs.*

11 Quoted in *Album Gerard Reve*, Joop Schafthuizen (ed.) (Amsterdam/Brussels: Elsevier, 1983), opposite p. 29.

12 On this subculture, see my *De roze rand van donker Amsterdam* (Amsterdam: Van Gennep, 1992). I argue that this subculture that moves from the outside (parks, urinals and other public locations) to the inside (bars, dances and hotels), and at the same time from gender and sexual inversion to gender and sexual equality.

13 See David Bos, '"Voor de grote massa". Harry Thomas, de Homofielenpartij en het dito huwelijk, *Tijdschrift voor biografie* 4:3 (2015), 49–58.

14 Pieter Koenders and Tussen Christelijk, *Réveil en seksuele revolutie: Bestrijding van zedeloosheid met de nadruk op repressie van homoseksualiteit* (Amsterdam: IISG, 1996).

15 Half of the novels in these years were published by De Bezige Bij, which started during the war as an illegal enterprise and kept its progressive leftist image after the war.

16 Wijnand Sengers, *Gewoon het zelfde. Een visie op de vragen rond de homofilie* (Bussum: Brand, 1968).

17 See Hekma and van Stolk, *Het verlies van de onschuld. Seks in Nederland* (Groningen: Wolters-Noordhoff, 1990).

18 Sexual equality is unrealistic because desire is always pervaded by differences in cultural, social economic and sexual capital. See Alan Sinfield, *On Sexuality and Power* (New York: Columbia University Press, 2004) and Hekma, 'The Drive for Sexual Equality', *Sexualities* 11:1 (2008), 51–5.

FURTHER READING

Barthes, Roland. *Le plaisir de texte*. Paris: Seuil, 1973.
  Sade, Fourier, Loyola. Paris: Seuil, 1971.
Bataille, Georges. *L'Erotisme*. Paris: Minuit, 1957.
Beccadelli, Antonio. *The Hermaphrodite*. Ed. Holt Parker. Cambridge, MA: Harvard University Press, 2010.
Berlant, Lauren. *Desire/Love*. Brooklyn, NY: Punctum Books, 2012.
Bersani, Leo. *The Culture of Redemption*. Cambridge, MA: Harvard University Press, 1990.
Boucé, Paul-Gabriel. *Sexuality in Eighteenth-Century Britain*. Manchester: Manchester University Press, 1982.
Brewer, John. *The Pleasures of the Imagination: English Culture in the Eighteenth Century*. New York: Farrar, Straus & Giroux, 1997.
Colligan, Colette. *The Traffic in Obscenity from Byron to Beardsley: Sexuality and Exoticism in Nineteenth-Century Print Culture*. London: Palgrave, 2006.
Darnton, Robert. *The Forbidden Best-Sellers of Pre-Revolutionary France*. New York: W. W. Norton, 1996.
Davidson, Arnold. *The Emergence of Sexuality*. Cambridge, MA: Harvard University Press, 2001.
Desmond, Marilyn. *Ovid's Art and the Wife of Bath*. Ithaca, NY: Cornell University Press, 2006.
Elfenbein, Andrew. *Romantic Genius: The Prehistory of a Homosexual Role*. New York: Columbia University Press, 1999.
Evans, Ruth, ed. *A Cultural History of Sexuality in the Middle Ages*. Oxford: Berg, 2010.
Evangelista, Stefano. *British Aestheticism and Ancient Greece: Hellenism, Reception, Gods in Exile*. Basingstoke: Palgrave Macmillan, 2009.
Fiedler, Leslie. *Love and Death in the American Novel*. New York: Stein and Day, 1966.
Foucault, Michel. *Histoire de la sexualité*. Paris: Gallimard, 1976.
Foxon, David. *Libertine Literature in England, 1660–1745*. New York: University Books, 1965.
Greven, David. *The Fragility of Manhood: Hawthorne, Freud, and the Politics of Gender*. Columbus, OH: Ohio State University Press, 2012.
  Gender and Sexuality in Star Trek: Allegories of Desire in the Televisions Series and Films. Jefferson, NC: McFarland, 2009.

Ghost Faces: Hollywood and Post-Millennial Masculinity. Albany, NY: State University of New York Press, 2016.

Hagstrum, Jean. *Eros and Vision: The Restoration to Romanticism*. Evanston, IL: Northwestern University Press, 1989.

Hales, Shelley and Paul, Joanna, eds. *Pompeii in the Public Imagination from its Rediscovery to Today*. Oxford: Oxford University Press, 2011.

Halperin, David. *How to Do the History of Homosexuality*. Chicago, IL: University of Chicago Press, 2004.

One Hundred Years of Homosexuality: And Other Essays on Greek Love. New York: Routledge, 1989.

Hekma, Gert. *ABC of Perversions: The World's Most Erotic Encyclopedia*. Paris: Speakeasy, 2015.

A Cultural History of Sexuality in the Modern Age. London: Bloomsbury, 2014.

Hekma, Gert, and Giami, A., eds. *Sexual Revolutions*. London: Palgrave Macmillan, 2014.

Hekma, Gert, Steakley, James, and Oosterhuis, Harry, eds. *Gay Men and the Sexual History of the Political Left*. New York: Haworth Press, 1995.

Hitchcock, Tim. *English Sexualities, 1700–1800*. New York: St. Martin's, 1997.

Hopkins, Amanda, Rouse, Robert, and James, Cory, eds. *Sexual Culture in the Literature of the Medieval Britain*. Cambridge: Brewer, 2014.

Hunt, Lynn, ed. *The Invention of Pornography: Obscenity and the Origins of Modernity, 1500–1800*. New York: Zone, 1996.

Kendrick, Walter. *The Secret Museum: Pornography in Modern Culture*. New York: Viking, 1987.

Krafft-Ebing, Richard von. *Psychopathia Sexualis*. Philadelphia, PA: F.A. Davis, 1894.

Krips, Henry. *Fetish: An Erotics of Culture*. Ithaca, NY: Cornell University Press, 1999.

Ladenson, Elisabeth. *Dirt for Art's Sake: Books on Trial from Madame Bovary to Lolita*. Ithaca, NY: Cornell University Press, 2007.

Laqueur, Thomas. *Making Sex: Body and Gender from the Greeks to Freud*. Cambridge, MA: Harvard University Press, 1990.

Lipton, Emma. *Affections of the Mind: The Politics of Sacramental Marriage in Late Medieval English Literature*. Notre Dame: University of Notre Dame Press, 2007.

Lochrie, Karma. *Heterosyncracies: Female Sexuality When Normal Wasn't*. Minneapolis, MN: University of Minneapolis Press, 2005.

Lutz, Deborah. *Dangerous Lover: Gothic Villains, Byronism, and the Nineteenth-Century Seduction Narrative*. Columbus, OH: Ohio State University Press, 2006.

Pleasure Bound: Victorian Sex Rebels and the New Eroticism. New York: W. W. Norton, 2011.

Marquis de Sade, Donatien Alphonse François. *The Complete Justine, Philosophy in the Bedroom, and Other Writings*. New York: Grove, 1965.

McCalman, Ian. *Radical Underworld: Prophets, Revolutionaries, and Pornographers in London, 1795–1840*. Cambridge: Cambridge University Press, 1988.

Moulton, Ian. *Before Pornography: Erotic Writing in Early Modern England*. New York: Oxford University Press, 2000.

Mounsey, Chris. *Developments in the Histories of Sexualities*. Lewisburg, PA: Bucknell University Press, 2013.

Mudge, Bradford K. *The Whore's Story: Women, Pornography, and the British Novel, 1684–1830*. New York: Oxford University Press, 2000.

Mudge, Bradford K. *When Flesh Becomes Word: An Introduction to Early Eighteenth-Century Libertine Literature*. New York: Oxford University Press, 2004.

Murray, Jacqueline, and Eisenbichler, Konrad. *Desire and Discipline: Sex and Sexuality in the Premodern West*. Toronto: University of Toronto Press, 1996.

Noble, Marianne. *The Masochistic Pleasures of Sentimental Fiction*. Princeton, NJ: Princeton University Press, 2000.

Orrells, Daniel. *Classical Culture and Modern Masculinity*. Oxford: Oxford University Press, 2011.

Sex: Antiquity and its Legacy. New York: Oxford University Press, 2015.

Pateman, Carole. *The Sexual Contract*. Stanford, CA: Stanford University Press, 1988.

Peakman, Julie. *Mighty Lewd Books*. New York: Palgrave, 2003.

Pettit, Alexander, and Patrick Spedding, eds. *Eighteenth-Century British Erotica*. 5 vols. London: Pickering & Chatto, 2002.

Phillips, Anita. *A Defence of Masochism*. London: Faber & Faber, 1998.

Poteet, William Mark. *Gay Men in Modern Southern Literature*. New York: Peter Lang, 2006.

Réage, Pauline [Anne Desclos]. *Histoire d'O*. Paris: Pauvert, 1954.

Rembar, Charles. *The End of Obscenity: The Trials of Lady Chatterley, Tropic of Cancer, and Fanny Hill*. New York: Random House, 1968.

Robertson, Elizabeth and Rose, Christine. *Representing Rape in Medieval and Early Modern Literature*. London: Palgrave, 2001.

Rolle, Richard. *The Fire of Love*. Trans. Richard Misyn. London: Kegan Paul, 1896.

Rosario, Vernon. *The Erotic Imagination*. New York: Oxford University Press, 1997.

Roudinesco, Elisabeth. *Our Dark Side: A History of Perversion*. Trans. David Macey. Cambridge: Polity Press, 2009.

Salih, Sarah, ed. *A Companion to Middle English Hagiography*. Martlesham: D. S. Brewer, 2006.

Salih, Sarah. *Medieval Virginities*. Cardiff: University of Wales Press, 2003.

Scanlon, Thomas. *Eros and Greek Athletics*. Oxford: Oxford University Press, 2002.

Sedgwick, Eve Kosofsky. *Between Men: English Literature and Male Homosocial Desire*. New York: Columbia University Press, 1985.

Epistemology of the Closet. Berkeley, CA: University of California Press, 2008.

Sha, Richard C. *Perverse Romanticism: Aesthetics and Sexuality in Britain, 1750–1850*. Baltimore, MD: Johns Hopkins University Press, 2009.

Shattuck, Roger. *Forbidden Knowledge: From Prometheus to Pornography*. New York: St. Martin's, 1996.

Sigel, Lisa. *International Exposure: Perspectives on Modern European Pornography, 1800–2000*. New Brunswick: Rutgers University Press, 2005.

Governing Pleasures: Pornography and Social Change in England, 1815-1914. New Brunswick, NJ: Rutgers University Press, 2002.

Sigler, David. *Sexual Enjoyment in British Romanticism: Gender and Psychoanalysis, 1753–1835*. Montreal: McGill-Queen's University Press, 2015.

St. Jorre, John de. *Venus Bound: The Erotic Voyage of the Olympia Press and Its Writers*. New York: Random House, 1996.

Toulalan, Sarah. *Imagining Sex: Pornography and Bodies in Seventeenth-Century England*. Oxford: Oxford University Press, 2007.

Toulalan, Sarah, and Fisher, Kate, eds. *Bodies, Sex, and Desire from the Renaissance to the Present*. London: Palgrave, 2011.

Toulalan, Sarah, and Fisher, Kate. *The Routledge History of Sex and the Body: 1500 to the Present*. London: Routledge, 2016.

Turner, James Grantham. *Libertines and Radicals in Early Modern London: Sexuality, Politics, and Literary Culture, 1630–1685*. Cambridge: Cambridge University Press, 2007.

   One Flesh: Paradisal Marriage and Sexual Relations in the Age of Milton. Oxford: Oxford University Press, 1993.

   Schooling Sex: Libertine Literature and Erotic Education in Italy, France, and England, 1534–1685. Oxford: Oxford University Press, 2003.

Turner, James Grantham, ed. *Sexuality and Gender in Early Modern Europe*. Cambridge: Cambridge University Press, 1993.

Ulmer, William. *Shelleyan Eros: The Rhetoric of Romantic Love*. Princeton, NJ: Princeton University Press, 1990.

Vignali, Antonio. *La Cazzaria: The Book of the Prick*. Ed. Ian Frederick Moulton. New York: Routledge, 2014.

Wagner, Peter. *Eros Revived: Erotica of the Enlightenment in England and America*. London: Secker & Warburg, 1988.

Wyngaard, Amy. *Bad Books: Rétif de la Bretonne, Sexuality, and Pornography*. Newark, NJ: University of Delaware Press, 2013.

INDEX

Cambridge Companions To ...
AUTHORS

TOPICS